A CERTAIN AGE

A JOHN HOPE FRANKLIN
CENTER BOOK

A CERTAIN AGE

COLONIAL JAKARTA
THROUGH THE MEMORIES
OF ITS INTELLECTUALS

RUDOLF MRÁZEK

DUKE UNIVERSITY PRESS
Durham and London
2010

© 2010 DUKE UNIVERSITY PRESS
All rights reserved. Designed by Amy Ruth
Buchanan. Typeset in Monotype Fournier by Tseng
Information Systems, Inc. Library of Congress
Cataloging-in-Publication Data
appear on the last printed page
of this book.

An earlier version of chapter 1
appeared as "Bypasses and Flyovers:
Approaching the Metropolitan History
of Indonesia," *Social History* 29,
no. 4 (2004): 425–43.

For Ben Anderson

CONTENTS

PREFACE: *Promenades* ix

Technical Note xv

ONE. *Bypasses and Flyovers* 1
TWO. *The Walls* 25
THREE. *The Fences* 73
FOUR. *The Classroom* 125
FIVE. *The Window* 187
POSTSCRIPT. *Sometimes Voices* 235

Notes 253
Bibliography 293
Index 303

PREFACE

PROMENADES

> We might ask: who would learn from this? Can someone
> teach me that I see a tree?
> —Ludwig Wittgenstein, *Remarks on Colour*

The people of this book with few exceptions are of a colonial and Indonesian urban elite of the twentieth century, which means a group to a lesser, larger, or overwhelming extent touched by and induced into the Western culture of imperial modernity (predominantly secular, among other things, which explains why so few devout Muslims appear in the book). The group in particular distinguishes itself by its possession of Dutch literacy. It never made up more than about 0.5 percent of the colony's population,[1] which, however, amounts to as many as three hundred thousand men and women, living in towns and cities as a general rule. Since the early twentieth century, through the late colonial era and national revolution and deep into independence after 1945, the *urban intellectuals* became a major irritant and inspiration, injecting their sense of the new, of progress and of freedom, into the colonial and postcolonial society at large.

Between 1990 and 2000, on every university vacation, and once in 1995 on a six-month visit, I interviewed elderly people of Indonesia, mainly in Jakarta (formerly Batavia), the Indonesian metropolis, about their youth and childhood. The old people lived through the colonial period, the Japanese occupation during the Second World War, and the years of independent Indonesia after 1945. I expected that I would be told about the transition to modernity, from colonialism to postcolonialism, and about the failed (or unfinished) Indonesian revolution. I also hoped to learn more about the interview situation, about the relation between written and oral documents and, namely, about how the tone and accent of both interviewer and interviewee might cast the research and its conclusions.

Indeed, it turned out that the most rewarding part has been how the talking went; how we moved and stumbled across a particular landscape that was theirs and, in a revealingly different way, gradually, also mine. As I listen to the tapes now, I have a sort of Le Corbusier feeling: "The coordinated physiological sensations in terms of volume, surface, contour and color," now as then, "afford an intense lyricism."[2]

The image, notion, and sense of *promenade* remained with me throughout the research for, and writing of, this book. As for promenades, nothing seems, of course, more out of place in the hot, muddy, mosquitoey, dusty, and overcrowded Indonesian towns and cities, Jakarta in particular. But exactly because of that, perhaps, the image and the word have stuck with me. Le Corbusier's (again) "promenade architecture" brought the term to me very early on—the high modern and avant-garde city builder's device for making the living space into a passage, to abolish (or at least to soften, to make less noticeable) the walls and all the other barriers and restraints of twentieth-century urban life. Bertolt Brecht, a poet and another big presence as I was writing this book, articulated Le Corbusier's promenades well:

> Cover your tracks ...
> Go into any house when it rains and sit on any chair that's in it
> But don't sit long. And don't forget your hat. ...
> Cover your tracks. ...
> Soon no dirt any more, but
> The hard mortar with which
> Cities are built.[3]

This rang in my ear. *Pictures at an Exhibition*—and I still have that cassette with Modest Mussorgsky's music on the shelf among the other tapes for this book—the theme in particular that recurs and connects the whole piece: it is called "Promenade." As I listen, I feel as if shuffling through an exhibition, stopping now and then, as the music wants it, by this or that picture on the

Preface

wall. I learn that many paintings appeal in their richest, touch me closest, tell me most, when they just flicker in my eye as I walk, in passing.

During the writing, Walter Benjamin was there with me—and I am afraid, never enough—in particular, he at a certain age, as he tries to escape the sinking Europe in 1940, leaving the trunk with his "On the Concept of History" behind.[4] Benjamin's *Passagen* (translated as *The Arcades Project*) is teaching me that a landscape appears truest when glanced over furtively, over one's shoulder, indeed felt as if already almost in the past. This was, too, why Benjamin's essay "Berlin Childhood" was especially important to this project. Not exactly because it smells and sounds so much like my childhood's big, gray, and homey housing block in Prague, but more because it had been written as a glance toward where the writer was not going, from a place of exile, or running, when all the past was already on the brink of being lost—or of becoming history.

I want Benjamin, Brecht, Le Corbusier, and the others who came later to appear in this book like flickers, or like the pictures at the exhibition, like fellow walkers—and like those elderly Indonesians who for some reason decided to talk to me, as if in passing.[5]

✳ ✳ ✳

The first chapter, "Bypasses and Flyovers," finds a city—colonial/postcolonial—sinking in crises and, by the logic of it, increasingly experienced as a web (and I wish the word to sound as postmodern and indeed electronic as it can). Speed and lightness over the mud and dust define the city and this observer of the city as well—my keeping a distance from my subjects, my passing by, the burden of my method. As it was said about another watcher of this kind, "he knew that it was possible for him to make his escape at any moment with a flap of the wings."[6]

Like one of those Brecht wrote about, I got to (almost) any house there was, and I never stayed long. In a fleeting way, and this admission is crucial, I have observed the intimacy of the inside of the homes. This is my chapter two, "The Walls." A distinct sense of childhood was eagerly given to me, and with the same eagerness I accepted it, and as such I try to describe it in this section of the book. Rumbling from the outside, the unsheltered, unbelonging and un-intimate, as we talked was most closely upon us. Were these people self-protective, inventing, censoring? How much did it matter? At no other moment had nostalgia given me such a sharp picture of the city.

Promenades

More than the others, this chapter confirms the surrealist idea that truth can best be found in dreams "as they are slipping away."[7]

In chapter three, "The Fences," the space of intimacy, as recalled, is expanding. The children of the past are running in the chapter (as the elderly people of the present are talking): through gates rarely locked, over fences mostly low and porous—as far as the street. Almost surfing, lightly (progressively, that is), the street becomes a *commonplace*, hominess upgraded. Depressingly, as one thinks about it, edges of the intimate, thresholds, windowsills, crossings in these memories are missing.

Chapter four, "The Classroom," is here to make sense of it all—as all was supposed to be ordered, tabulated, articulated, inside and by the modern and colonial classroom. The classroom was as far as the best and brightest children of the colony were ever to get—through the gates, over the fences, along the street. Measured by time scholastically divided and by the architecture of the classroom (rows of benches, the blackboard, the portrait of the Dutch Queen), the youths of the colony were made to grow. Colony as a big classroom—it may seem an apocalyptic vision. But this is how it was widely, and sort of fondly, recalled to me.

As for myself, I certainly remember that feeling well: the classroom, more than anything, made one wish to look to a window; even a picture on the classroom wall made one wish that the picture were a window, a break in the wall. Chapter five, "The Window," tells about the birth of the window, mainly out of this classroom way of looking. How might one wish this? To (make a) picture (for) oneself, a picture as window? How might one wish to break a wall in the ultimately architectural, best-of-the-bourgeois, colonial space? In chapter five, the main theme of *A Certain Age* hopefully becomes clear—a possibility of freedom.

It may well be that, in the process of writing this book, I became complicit in what is clinically known as the "refusal . . . of children or of the very old . . . to summarize."[8] It may be reluctance, on my part as well as on that of my interviewees, to leave the land of aphasia that gave us so much pleasure and that also gave me the archive for this book. Or it might simply be my desire "to avoid the arrest of the last word."[9]

In any case, I wish the postscript, "Sometimes Voices," to be read as a largo of the book, as my last attempt to capture what I believe is crucial, what motivated this book in the first place, and what, I am afraid, in spite of all my efforts, still remains unconveyed—the true force of this history, or better, the sense of a certain age: "A color, a tone of voice, a tactile choice of word, a simple vibration"; the "unstable, incomplete, unsettled, irreducible to the word."[10]

I am deeply grateful to the University of Michigan, its Department of History, to the university's Institute for the Humanities, and to the Henry Luce Foundation, which supported this project initially and through the many years it took to complete. I also thank the editors of *Social History* at the University of Hull for permission to use in chapter one a version of an article published with them.

It happens that I have friends and colleagues and passersby in Ann Arbor, Ithaca, Leiden, and Jakarta especially, who inspired me, made me happy, and thus made me able to write: collectively they were vital to me. Eri Kusmeri and Arif Budi Santosa earned my gratitude by carefully transcribing hundreds of tapes. The elderly people of Jakarta and beyond, some cited and some not (sadly only a few of them are still alive), received me in their homes, talked to me, and let me talk to them. I love them all, and the book tries to say this and not much more.

TECHNICAL NOTE

I use the old (which is pre-1972 and pre-1947) spelling for the Indonesian words in the text: *wajang*, *krontjong*, or *petjok*, and not *wayang*, *kroncong*, or *pecok*. It was how my interviewees spelled the words throughout their lives and mostly still when I met them. The local names, in contrast (again following my interviewees), I spell in the post-1972 way: *Jakarta* not *Djakarta*, *Bandung* not *Bandoeng*, or *Yogyakarta* not *Djokjakarta*. Personal names, also, I spell depending on how I saw a particular person write his or her name: thus *Soemardjan* (in the old spelling) or *Mangunwijaya* (in the new spelling).

In an interview, all in one language (as a general rule, Indonesian), a word or part of a sentence might suddenly be uttered in another, in most cases in Dutch, often in English, sometimes in Javanese or in other local languages and dialects. There was always a significant reason for this change: the switch or slip always marked some memory of the past, some moment of the present, mostly both. The flavor and the substance of the interviews thus changed. Only most crudely am I able to evoke this difference by using italics for these words and events. (This is why sometimes an English word or sentence in my English text, *strangely*, appears in italics.)

When mentioning or quoting Indonesians, I often use their name that comes first, for instance, "Rosihan" for Rosihan Anwar. It does not signify any particular familiarity between me and the person. It is the way Indonesian names (not the family name following the given name necessarily) are structured and used.

Lastly, I do not introduce and explain my interviewees by giving their bibliographies as they enter. I want these people to appear (like me) carried by the moment of our talking. I believe that all the facts and dates relevant to what they and I wanted to convey are there, in how we talked, at a certain age, in this promenade fashion. A list of the interviewees, with their full names and the dates and the places of the interviews, can be found at the end of the book.

CLASS IN A GRADE SCHOOL PROBABLY IN METRO, LAMPUNG, SOUTH SUMATRA. AROUND 1940. KONINKLIJK INSTITUUT VOOR TAAL-, LAND- EN VOLKENKUNDE, LEIDEN

CHAPTER ONE

BYPASSES AND FLYOVERS

> *Riding, riding, riding,* through the day, through the night, through the day.
> ... And courage is grown so weary, and longing so great. There are no mountains any more, hardly a tree. ... Alien homes crouch thirstily by mired springs. ... And always the same picture. One has two eyes too many.
> —Rainer Maria Rilke,
> *The Lay of the Love and Death of Cornet Christopher Rilke*

ARCHITECTURE, HISTORY, AND THAT WAY OF TALKING

Already in the late colonial era "the road network in Jakarta had been asphalted and many trees cut down to make way for electricity and telephone wires and poles. The effect was to make it much harder on the eye."[1] In the time of independence, after 1945, the Sukarno era, the poor and untidy quarters around the axes of the metropolis were progressively (albeit slowly) cleared, and cleared out.[2] Since the 1970s, in the post-Sukarno years, the tempo quickened. Jakarta has been officially called BMW—*bersih,* "clean," *manusiawi,* "humane," *wibawa,* "ordered."[3] It became a correct feeling (if there is such a thing) that one might ideally comprehend Jakarta in one glimpse: "Jakarta can be immediately seen on the map. The shape or layout of the city is marked by the flyovers and motorways running east, south, and west, cutting through the metropolis and heading out into the countryside."[4] Not yet, but almost, postcolonial (and postrevolutionary) Jakarta has become a postmodern metropolis, like Los Angeles, for instance, "whose mystery is precisely that of no longer being anything but a network of incessant unreal circulation—a city of incredible proportions but without space, without dimension."[5]

The traffic lights of Jakarta throughways and avenues, after the sun sets and the still remaining poor neighborhoods disappear in the dark,[6] offer a perspective that is geometrical and logical. The straight lines, abstract and thus pure, meet at vanishing points. They are like the continuity of a political task, or like the "rails of revolution"[7] that Sukarno, the president and the engineer, talked about: "Do you want to live forever? So pull back to the moment of the Proclamation of our Independence . . . back to the purity of our souls, . . . back, and straight on, to the moment when our Revolution began!"[8]

The rows of lights—of traffic and of revolution—as in Siegfried Kracauer's vision, "create an appearance of a plentitude of figures from zero" as they "progress in one-dimensional time"; this logic, the geometry, and the politics "work hard to reduce everything to the level of the zero out of which [they want] to produce the world."[9] The lights in straight or correctly curved rows, indeed, dazzle the observer and mold his memory as they "emerge from the past without substance, purged of the uncertainty of existence, [and] they have the stability and outline of algebra."[10]

As one walks and drives through the avenues and highways of Jakarta, one can feel that the city and the revolution might have been built in the same way:

> The Indonesian Republic can live 1 year, 2 years, 3 years, 30 years, 300 years, and, straight on, till the end of time. . . .[11]
>
> One year since the Proclamation of our Independence became 2 years, 2 years became 3 years, 3 years became 4 years, 4 years became 5 years, 6 years, 7 years, 8 years, 9 years, 10 years, 11 years . . . and God Willing these 11 years will become 110 years, 1,100 years, maybe 11,000 years![12]
>
> Today we experience the 17th anniversary, *17x17* Augusts of freedom! 2x, today, we experience August 17th, the Proclamation of Independence Day, the reckoning that is great and holy![13]

To move through that kind of space and along those kinds of lights brings, kind of, a sense of liberation. Trying to observe and absorb this post-Palladian, postcolonial, and almost postmodern metropolis, one might almost convince oneself that "the community of human destinies is experienced in the anonymity of non-place, and in solitude."[14] Almost, thus, one might comfort oneself that in a non-place like this, any "spectator," acceptably and correctly, "is a passerby."[15] The omnipresence of the hard surface,

Chapter One

of the asphalt of the roads and of the concrete of the walls, may, almost, bring satisfaction to a scholar.

Not being able to penetrate, not seeing much beyond reflections (the walls are not just of concrete but of glass as well, and the wet asphalt is like a mirror), may cause a pleasing sensation: "There is no sub-text. . . . The enunciative domain is identical with its own surface."[16] By the very contours of the metropolis, the view and the thinking of the passerby is "drawn close to the surface of the architectural frame. . . . This relationship [is] further pressured [by] reducing the foreground elements of architecture while emphasizing the horizon itself as an object, maintaining the spatial hierarchy of perspective by bringing it up to but not over the limit."[17] This kind of architecture, of horizon, and of counting, it has been argued, is built as a "monumentalizing of age." To live and die through this space, as well as merely to pass by this space, it may become (it may be reduced to) "an act of remembrance."[18]

I think of Mrs. Sosro as the most beautiful apparition. She was a woman of a little over ninety when I met her in 1992. She was my first (memorable) interviewee in Jakarta on the metropolis project.[19] She could not easily walk anymore. She received us sitting in her bed, a big brass structure, with a single long, hard pillow and a mosquito net half pushed aside. The gauze of the net softened the light coming from the outside. Thus Mrs. Sosro's face, as well as the whole space around her, was blurred. This was the late colonial beauty of fading photographs that we postcolonial scholars do not wish to admit. It is difficult for us to convince ourselves that, perhaps, "different concepts touch here and coincide over a stretch. But you need not think that all lines are *circles*."[20]

Mrs. Sosro received us in her house "in a native neighborhood" (one would say "native" if it still were the colonial times), a poor area, off the highways and promenades of Jakarta, yet very much in the center of the metropolis. I could easily imagine her, if she were not bedridden, waiting for us looking out of her window with her elbows on the sill. She had a wrinkled voice.

Mrs. SOSRO: I used to sell herb drinks, prohibited herb drinks. Thus they call me *Siti Larang* [Lady Prohibited]. I used to sell them on the street, and I announced my ware by the chimes of a bell. They used to ask me, "Where do you stay?" I used to say, "I don't know." They asked me, "What is the date?" I said, "I don't know." I did not wish to know. I did not wish to know what had been. Have you met Kartodirjo—?

RUDOLF MRÁZEK (RM): Sartono Kartodirjo, the historian?

Mrs. SOSRO: Sartono. He said, "He who does not understand history is like a patient in a mental hospital." I think he is crazy.

Two friends had come with me. One is a colleague, a historian, who came from the West like me. He is interested in herbal medicine. The other one is an incurable political activist. As an Indonesian revolutionary and former leader of the communist youth, he spent thirteen years in the post-Sukarno prisons of General Suharto. It was he who brought me here, because he had concluded that my research was useful and that Mrs. Sosro, a freedom fighter among other things, would be useful to me.

OTHER HISTORIAN: Mrs. Sosro, during the Dutch time [before 1942], you were selling tonic?

Mrs. SOSRO: True.

OTHER HISTORIAN: And you helped other fighters?

Mrs. SOSRO: Yes, if they needed.

OTHER HISTORIAN: You sent food to the Suharto internment camps [after 1965], too.

Mrs. SOSRO: Djoko [a friend] helped me with it, before he died. Then his mother-in-law helped. I thought of her just yesterday.

Talk hopscotched over and between national struggle, prisons, exiles, and herb-drink peddling. We three kept to our way of questioning, and Mrs. Sosro to her way of answering. Only at certain short moments—it was becoming clear to me, the most precious moments—the logic of the interview halted. An answer, and then sometimes also a question, strayed. On these few happy occasions, some of the answers and some of the questions frayed at their edges. We were getting off perspective.

OTHER HISTORIAN: You got the "Golden Pen," didn't you? How did it happen?

Mrs. SOSRO: It is from the Union of Indonesian Journalists. They believe that I am the oldest journalist still alive.

Chapter One

RM: Mrs. Sosro, what kind of school did you go to?
Mrs. SOSRO: No school.
RM: So, you had no school friends?
Mrs. SOSRO: No school friends. Just friends.
RM: How did you get into the nationalist movement?
Mrs. SOSRO: My *vader* [father] was political. Thus I am political.
RM: I see.
OTHER HISTORIAN: I see.

My friend, who had been in prison for so long, became more than a little impatient, and he began to push:

Mr. HARDOYO: Auntie Sosro, Auntie Sosro, Rudolf has written about Tan Malaka. You worked on a journal directed by Tan Malaka?
Mrs. SOSRO: I do not remember.
Mr. HARDOYO: You knew Tan Malaka! Everybody says so.
Mrs. SOSRO: Oh, yeah. When I was in prison, I read his *MADILOG*. When I got out of prison, there was the Proclamation of Independence. And I lost the book. I still can't find it!
OTHER HISTORIAN: Did you meet Tan Malaka in Jakarta or in Bogor?
Mrs. SOSRO: It was a little book. Well, not so very little. Thin, but large. Like this.
Mr. HARDOYO: He came from Banten [West Java], right? What kind of man was he? Tan Malaka.
Mrs. SOSRO: He was short. And funny. So funny, my!
OTHER HISTORIAN: But you have read his books?
RM: *Patjar Merah*?

Patjar Merah (*The Red Darling*), is an Indonesian and revolutionary version of the French and antirevolutionary *Scarlet Pimpernel*. It is supposed to be Tan Malaka's life — *MA*terialistic, *DI*alectic, *LOG*ical (it was his *MADILOG*), a thriller, and a tale of magic — a reading suited for a (victorious Indonesian) freedom movement.[21]

Mrs. SOSRO: *Patjar Merah*, yes.
RM: You've read it?
Mrs. SOSRO: Oh, yes. But Sherlock Holmes was better. In prison I read Sherlock, Sherlock, and Sherlock again.

Bypasses and Flyovers

This marked the moment of my first (memorable) failure on this project. Soon, yet too late, I realized that I should have questioned Mrs. Sosro next about *The Hound of the Baskervilles* and then *A Scandal in Bohemia*. That chance has never returned, of course; she was ninety at the time.

> RM: You read it in the Dutch [colonial] prison?
> Mrs. SOSRO: Of course. In the Japanese time [1942–1945], in prison, we could not read. We had to sew caps and sweep the floor.

Mrs. Sosro was not exactly getting tired. Her delicate body was not exactly failing her. Merely, through her increasingly strident breathing, longer moments of forgetting (or of thinking to herself), through "the rhythmic interruption of the logos,"[22] she was trying to tell us, increasingly—the three of us, so bad at hearing—about a journey, and about a history, for which, as Cornet Rilke knew, "two eyes are too many."[23]

> RM: So, in the Dutch prison, you were allowed to read?
> Mrs. SOSRO: Only when I was sick. And I was sick for a long time. I was brought to the prison hospital, and a plainclothes policeman came. And he asked me: "Can you read, girl?" "Of course she can read," the doctor said, "she is a political." So they put a book under my pillow. You understand: because I was sick and in the hospital.

Whatever is being asked and answered, increasingly, happens as if under a cloud of pain, a hospital, and a cemetery. She talks in *tombeaux*,[24] and, by the power of it, the interview begins to flow in spite of the three of us asking our questions—against the traffic, so to speak. Even more important, in spite of and against my asking, I begin to listen, and thus get closer, perhaps, to a "dialogue, this articulation of speech, or rather this sharing of voices."[25]

> OTHER HISTORIAN: Soesanto Tirtoprodjo?
> Mrs. SOSRO: The one who died? I was sick at the time. I could not do anything for him. I could go to Hatta [former Indonesian vice-president]. I wrote to Hatta, but then he got sick also.
> OTHER HISTORIAN: When Hatta died, did you go to his funeral?
> Mrs. SOSRO: Oh, no, Hatta was buried in . . . .
> OTHER HISTORIAN: Tanah Kusir.
> Mrs. SOSRO: Tanah Kusir. I was sick.

My friend still does not let go. He cares about my research:

> Mr. HARDOYO: Auntie, Auntie, do you still remember Tan Malaka's Fighting Front?
> Mrs. SOSRO: Oh, I remember. I was in Malang [East Java]. Salirah, my sister, came to see me: "Get up! How can you sleep?! Don't you understand? Tan Malaka has been arrested!" I did not understand. I was ill. I couldn't move. I couldn't eat. In the end they wanted to shoot me as well. "Well, you please yourselves!"

It was hard to hear it, and it is much harder to write it down, but Mrs. Sosro was giving us her life not exactly as history—more disturbing still, for a professional, there seemed to be not even a story. Because, I now think, in Mrs. Sosro talking to us, there was nothing of the "frantic passing of the petty present."[26]

> RM: So, you were poor most of your life?
> Mrs. SOSRO: Yes, 200 percent poor. The rich natives were 100 percent poor.
> RM: But, there was a fresh newspaper at home every day?
> Mrs. SOSRO: Oh, yes.
> RM: No radio?
> Mrs. SOSRO: No.
> RM: No *gramophone*?
> Mrs. SOSRO: His Master's Voice? No, just a dog.
> OTHER HISTORIAN: And in the Japanese time?
> Mrs. SOSRO: No change.
> OTHER HISTORIAN: No change!
> Mrs. SOSRO: Well, it was not easy. But it would still get worse: people will become sentimental. They will forget what anger is. Hardoyo, you know Pranoto Reksosamoedro?
> Mr. HARDOYO: He just died, last month.
> Mrs. SOSRO: Oh, he died!
> Mr. HARDOYO: He died.
> Mrs. SOSRO: Well, during the Japanese times people were beaten and others were ordered to watch it. But nobody at that time would come and declare that this or that had to be razed: ordering people that they raze things without even thinking about it. Houses are being razed at

Bypasses and Flyovers

present merely because the people who lived in them have died. Just because of that!

At this point my two friends left for other assignments, and I stayed behind for a few more minutes.

> RM: Do you talk to your grandchildren like you talk to us?
> Mrs. SOSRO: What do you mean, my boy?
> RM: Do you talk to your grandchildren like you talk to those who just pass by? Do you talk to your grandchildren about history?
> Mrs. SOSRO: About history? Yes, sometimes they ask me.
> RM: What do you tell them?
> Mrs. SOSRO: I tell them stories.
> RM: So that they will not forget?
> Mrs. SOSRO: Yes, but I am not happy about it. I am not happy about it at all. I do not enjoy in the least that feeling after I finish a newspaper: "Who was where, what happened, was it in Yogyakarta, was it in Malang, was it Soesanto. . . ."

Mrs. Sosro, it seems, forgot that she had already told me this. Or perhaps she was explaining to me, at last, why someone like Maurice Blanchot might write: "Whence this injunction, do not change your thought, repeat it, if you can."[27] Her last words to me, ever, were about that historian again.

> Mrs. SOSRO: Oh, when I read, "He who does not understand history is—"
> RM: Sartono Kartodirjo?
> Mrs. SOSRO: Yes. "If you do not understand history, it is the same as if you were locked in a madhouse." I have heard this, my! If it were so, I should be locked up. That Sartono, he must be— [end of tape]

MRS. SOSRO'S THEOREM

If it is true that everyone has a past of his or her own, it nonetheless happens that some, those who remember having lived fragments of their past with others, can sense they have shared at least this memory with them. . . . The complicity that emerges from this parallelism—no matter how

capricious and subjective memory may be—sometimes materializes unexpectedly, in a serendipitous meeting or along a detour in conversation.
—Marc Augé, *In the Metro*

There has always been much killing in Jakarta, but there has never been an age of barricades there—omnibuses turned over, "flag fastened to an axle,"[28] paving stones "dragged up to the top floors of the houses and dropped on the heads of the soldiers," "stripped bodies of the gravely wounded thrown contemptuously onto the barricades to make them higher,"[29] signs proudly affixed to barricades like that in Paris of 1871: "Barricade of the Federates, Constructed by Guillard Senior."[30] All the pathways of Jakarta that somehow seem to matter to history are obviously asphalted. Actually, as Brecht wrote,

> What's wrong with asphalt—?
> It's only the bog that denounces its black brother asphalt,
> so patient, clean and useful. . . .
> In the asphalt city I'm at home.[31]

Since the 1950s, the high tide of the Sukarno era, modern Jakarta has been designed, and dreamt out, around the axes of a few black, patient, and useful throughways—General Sudirman Street, Thamrin Street, General Subroto Street—with a linear city of multistoried hotels, department stores, and office buildings along them.[32] The soul of Jakarta has been designed geometrically, and with all the modern respect for geometers: "Geometrical order [is] methodical and faultless . . . geometers and all those who act methodically . . . impose names to things in order to abridge reasoning . . . geometry teaches perfectly. . . . nothing is freer than [geometers'] definitions."[33]

I recall most often the Jakarta as it was at the moment of the riots of 1997 and 1998. The wide and smooth throughways of the city then, at last, began to function as designed. Models came alive. Highways came forth into becoming. They became arteries (and I will come to the blood soon). Never before might a historian have covered the distances of the metropolis as efficiently as during those days. A trip for an interview at another end of the sprawling city—usually one to three hours of speeding, braking, and calling it a victory—could now be made in twenty minutes. Horizons seemed opened. Or, rather, there were no horizons any more; only the open road.

At last, as well, there was an easily, mechanically definable order of things: streets were jammed = there was no riot; streets were empty = there was a riot somewhere. A specially designed FM radio station, Sonora, was always on the air as we were on the road. Its programming was made up of drive-on music and riot forecast only. Rational driving, by the force of the riots, came forth into becoming at last. A few times, of course, one had to swerve, turn around, and, guided by Sonora, take an alternate road.

> *A small group of students appears on the road, about twenty of them in all. A chubby and sulky girl, a few steps ahead of the others, walks slowly with a big wreath. Others carry flowers. Pathetically, they walk against whatever might be on the twelve-lane road. As we come closer to them from behind, my taxi driver slows down and makes an elegant maneuver to pass the group, while I, sitting inside, in the back of the car, safe and from elsewhere, think of making some idiotic gesture, like a thumbs-up, for instance. After another few hundred meters of driving, we can see vendors on the sidewalk gazing back to where we had come from, making sure the group is really as small and as studentish as it appears, still far away, to be. We drive fast again. Looking back, I can still see the students, very small in the distance, and the vendors packing up their shops, just in case. To the north and to the west, there is smoke. We know from Sonora that this is the Senen Market burning. The road is empty again, just one lonely motorcyclist through the whole trip. The armored vehicles, which we had seen in front of Hotel Indonesia on the way there, had disappeared. "Army is afraid," the driver comments. Marines are taking over.*[34]

There were moments when the goods from looted shops—TV sets, refrigerators, electric fans—were heaped in the middle of the road and burned: a specter of a barricade, a specter haunting the metropolis.

> He who offers for sale something unique that no one wants to buy, represents, even against his will, freedom from exchange.[35]

But mostly the looted commodities were taken home.

The roads and highways of the metropolis reflected the mood, led the traffic, and channeled the despair. Yet they themselves were inviolable.[36] They were merely dirtied and trimmed, sometimes sidewalked, by the upheaval:

Chapter One

Glodok erupts after raids on pirated CDs. . . . Along the way they damaged several shops and broke flowerpots.

Commemoration of 1998 shooting marred by clash. . . . The protesting students, who were blocked by troops while attempting to get closer to Suharto's residence, became enraged and burned the Megaria Police post and vandalized many public goods such as flowerpots along the Diponegoro Street.[37]

The Semanggi (Trifoliate) interchange became a place and name possibly most closely identified with the riots. It equaled the events. The demonstrations, and the killings by the army, culminated here, at this foremost flyover of Jakarta, the exact point at which the north-south and east-west axes of the metropolis intersect.[38] Here, the arterial bleeding happened. It could be observed from quite a distance, from the sidewalks, from the slopes of the flyover structure, and from the windows of the skyscrapers around. The people, as they watched, trimmed the highways. A little (collateral) girl of five was among the victims. Her father had raised her on his shoulders to let her see better. An army bullet hit her as it flew over and passed by.

From the window of my hotel, on the fourteenth floor, not far from the Semanggi interchange, I could watch the morning-afters of the bloody days.

November 15, Sunday. In spite of everything (maybe because of everything) that happened yesterday, at 8 a.m. sharp, there is the usual walking, jogging, bicycling, and footballing of the Jakarta middle class in shorts on Thamrin Street, toward the Merdeka [Freedom] Square, and back to Sudirman Street and on to the Semanggi. The two faster lanes in each direction are closed to the traffic as on every Sunday morning. Tens, and at about nine o'clock, hundreds, of people are here to do their sporting on the road. The highway is all white, all green, red and white, green and orange, and all pink, as the workout uniforms go. Jakarta burned yesterday and, if nothing out of the ordinary happens, it will also burn today.[39]

Count Harry Kessler, in 1919, also from a leisure window, watched another metropolis: Berlin, Germany. Sitting in a cabaret near the Potsdamer Platz, the heart of that city at the time, he heard some shots during a dance number. It was an attempt at a German revolution: "Not one paid any attention [amid the] big-city life . . . [amid] the immeasurable depth, chaos, and might of Berlin. . . . This colossal movement [the attempted revolution] only caused slight disturbances in the much more colossal ebb and flow of Berlin."[40] Eighty years later, in Jakarta, in the postcolonial (and postmodern) metropolis, not even the noise of jazz bands, closed doors, and curtained windows was needed. The mere jazziness of the street itself had done the trick.

✴ ✴ ✴

Professor Roosseno Soerjohadikoesoemo, the engineer, was a jazzy man. When I met him in 1995 he was in his eighties, but he still complained that he could not — after an accident, for the time being — motorcycle to downtown Jakarta to hunt for English paperbacks in the secondhand bookshops. He was a jazzy, modern man. As early as 1938, a Javanese magazine thanked him for installing, free of charge, an antenna for the first-ever Indonesian "Union of Eastern Listeners" in Bandung [West Java].[41] With his friend Sukarno, who was eight years older and a graduate of the same elite technical college, Roosseno, still deep in the Dutch colonial era, established an architectural bureau in Bandung. There, he and Sukarno designed a number of houses, two of which, at least, quite nice, still stand.[42]

There are just three or four "native" names to be found in the colony's most prestigious technical journal *De Ingenieur in Ned.-Indië* (*The Engineer in Neth. Indies*). Roosseno's name appeared there repeatedly, and with flair. His articles dealt with the most modern, avant-garde, rational, and calculable way of building — with reinforced concrete. It was a passion and *à jour* of the time. Nina Kandinsky has recalled how, in the 1930s, she and her husband visited one of Le Corbusier's houses in France, and how they found even "bookshelves made of concrete."[43]

I met Mr. Roosseno less than a year before he died.[44] We sat on the porch of his house in South Jakarta. Shrubs with white blossoms separated us from the street. I was a day or so before leaving Indonesia on emergency — I had a bad infection in my only working ear. He was, as I had been warned, indeed deaf as a post. I asked my questions, and he gave his answers. Neither of us, it transpired, understood a word spoken by the other. Yet we were happy, which is clear from the tape — both of us, or rather the three of us, because, as I found out back in the United States, there is also a parrot on the recording, were shouting and uproarious. I listen often to this interview. As André Breton wrote, truly, it appears that "dialectic misunderstanding [is] what is truly alive in the dialogue. 'Misunderstanding' is here another word for the rhythm with which the only true reality forces its way into the conversation. The more effectively a man is able to speak, the more successfully he is misunderstood."[45]

Mr. Roosseno's life was long; this he tells me on the tape, and then he goes on, beginning squarely in the middle. When the Japanese came close to invading Java in 1941 (he was in his thirties at the time), Mr. Roosseno was ordered by the Dutch authorities to destroy bridges. "One hundred and fifty bridges," he says, and I can hear his smile. Half a year later, the Dutch surrendered, and the Japanese occupation authorities ordered Mr. Roosseno to rebuild the bridges. "Expertly," he says; he did it, as well: "One hundred and fifty-plus." In August 1945, the Indonesian revolution made a move as if to begin, and Sukarno, who became the president and top leader, summoned Roosseno, you know why — there were just a handful of Indonesian engineers available to the new nation state. Roosseno (the fighting against the Dutch was in full swing) established and led a "Weapon Laboratory," where he taught the most *à jour*, rational, and calculable methods of how to blow up "bridges in particular."[46]

He remained close and useful to both Sukarno and the revolution, he said, because he was "so good at the calculus": "This was not a way of doing things in some knightly manner. I was a friend of Sukarno, and as his friend I had to help. And there was nobody who could really count. I was regarded as the man who was smartest of all, namely, in calculating the right mix of concrete."[47]

In 1955, with the independent Indonesian state internationally recognized and settling down, Roosseno was sent to Paris on a trip paid for by the Indonesian and French governments to study an even more progressive technology, the method of building with prestressed concrete. In this way, he told me, he confirmed himself and his nation to be "an element of the modern." This also became his, and his nation's, history:

> ERA OF PHILOSOPHERS: . . . Archimedes (287–212 B.C.) discovered the meaning of *Center of Gravity* . . .
> ERA OF GENIUSES, 1450–1590: . . . da Vinci . . . Galileo . . .
> ERA OF MATHEMATICIANS, 1636–1815: . . . Robert Hooke, Johann and Daniel Bernoulli, Euler, and Legrange. . . . In 1660 *Robert Hooke* stated, in Latin: *ut tensio sic vis*, which means in English: *The power of any spring is in the same proportion with the tension thereof.* . . .

ERA OF GREAT ENGINEERS, 1785–1918: . . . Müller Breslau was a giant . . .

PRESENT ERA AND THE FUTURE: . . . In 1930, the technique of construction with prestressed concrete developed, pioneered by Eugène Freyssinet (died in 1962), who was called by the world of technicians the Father of Prestressed Concrete. Freyssinet was a genius, who had worked by intuition. . . . I hope that there is or will be born, here among us, incarnations of Robert Hooke and of Euler. I trust that the intellect of the Indonesian nation is good enough for this.[48]

When I met Mr. Roosseno, he was still consulting and still by far the most respected civil engineer of the nation. Reverently, he was addressed as the "Father of Indonesian Concrete."[49] He in a sense equaled, totaled, Jakarta and thus the revolution. Throughout the Sukarno era, and still after it ended, Roosseno designed and dreamt out the *concrete* face of the metropolis, and of Indonesia as far as it aspired to be modern—read the metropolis's reflection. Roosseno was the brains behind Jakarta's and Indonesia's first five-star (and concrete) Hotel Indonesia at the major city junction of Sudirman and Thamrin Streets; he was the brains behind Mesjid Istiqlal,[50] the concrete and biggest mosque of Southeast Asia, right in the geometric center of Old Jakarta; he was the brains behind the National Monument, a monolith just a few hundred meters from the mosque, the spiritual (at least so designed) focus of the nation.[51] The National Monument bore a special meaning for Roosseno, he told me and many before me, because here he used the technique of prestressed concrete fully for the first time.

Concrete, and prestressed concrete especially, was Roosseno's choice for building bridges, bypasses, flyovers—and a sublime space and time as well: "At the opening of the Jakarta Cengkareng Toll Road and Overpass my heart beat with the greatest joy. You ask why? Because when I took a car, and as we drove through the Cawang-Sudirman Interchange, all that my eyes could take in were the giant letters the length of the speedway and high above the city—making the names of SUKARNO and HATTA."[52]

Like Baron Haussmann, the builder and asphalter of modern Paris, Roosseno allowed for no hurdles and certainly for no barricades—nothing that would stand in the way of the progressive, modern, concrete, fast, and sublime. Like Baron Haussmann he knew that "the perspective of an imagined vantage-point above the city gives a sense of more rational order than existed at ground level."[53]

Chapter One

Four years after Mr. Roosseno's death, I met his oldest daughter, Toeti Heraty, in her Café Cemara (Casuarinas), one of the finest art galleries in the metropolis. She told me about her father's last months. When his wife, her mother, died, she said, not long before I had seen him, Mr. Roosseno fell in love again. To the horror of his five adult children, he decided to set even this matter straight, and he married again. He (still with the motorcycle) moved into his new wife's house.

> Mrs. TOETI: To live in the right with her, he had to change his religion, to leave Islam, and let himself be baptized; the woman was Christian. When he died, very soon afterward, we children visited the woman and asked her if she would let him be buried next to our mother. She had consulted her religious experts. In the end, it was arranged like this: first, the Christian services were held in the woman's house; then to the church, before they brought him here, to Cemara; then we drove him to the mosque, for the prayers, where he was received back into Islam; then across the city again, to the Karet Cemetery, where he was buried next to our mother, his first wife. We made it all in one morning.[54]

Thus Mr. Roosseno's journey was consummated as it had been designed. Across the enormous metropolis, through, or rather above it, in a single morning, thanks to the throughways and bypasses, of course. In his death, after the Christian and the Muslim prayers, in style, Mr. Roosseno has been united with the fourfold—the modern, historical, architectural, avant-garde, metropolitan fourfold—the Aristotle-turned–Le Corbusier fourfold: "(1) highways (earth), (2) railways (fire), (3) waterways (water), and (4) airways (air)."[55]

CLOSING IN ON THE VANISHING POINT

THEOREM: . . . the last line of a proof.
PROOF: . . . a procedure that brings conviction.
—Simon Blackburn, *The Oxford Dictionary of Philosophy*

In the fall of 1998, I was told that the menu of the poorest of Jakarta, a fistful of rice with chili sauce and the smallest piece of fish, came to about 2,500 rupiahs. Thus every beggar on the sidewalk had to beg 4,000 rupiahs a day, a frightening sum, to keep up hope of survival.[56] For the months I stayed in the city (mostly in the better-off parts), I saw four-year-old children in the streets, living there day and night, without any related elder in sight, except us, the more or less sentimental passersby.

Already during the 1950s, President Sukarno had to see this coming. This certainly was why he talked so much, in one breath, and with increasing emotion, about sublime places, architecture, revolution, and stars.

If we are not able to fly, we will crawl.[57]

Don't say that I talk *bombast* or *humbug* when I talk about the spirit of the [large black hawk] *Radjawali*! . . . Let us fly to the skies, and again to the skies! . . . Oh, Lord, although I live on the Earth, the child of the Earth, — I was feathered by the starry sky.[58]

I am not saying that I am like the Prophet, no — I am just an ordinary human being, who, however, as an engineer has been given aspirations by the Almighty God — high aspirations, thanks to the Lord who be praised, not low aspirations. Not aspirations that wallow in the mud, my Brothers and Sisters, but aspirations that — and why not say so — are suspended from high in the sky.[59]

There is something of Sukarno, and Roosseno, and Le Corbusier in each of us — and in a postcolonial metropolis more than elsewhere. I tried to get over the impact of the toddlers on the streets, and so on, and so on, by having, for instance, a cold beer or five at a sixteenth-floor bar on Thamrin Street, close to the stars, in one of the skyscrapers that Roosseno helped to project and that Sukarno dreamt about.[60]

One other place in Jakarta, where it seemed that I might get away for a while, was a little park, a barren space rather, a half-hour walk or five-minute drive from the skyscraper beer place. Here a one-story colonial-style house used to stand before the revolution, belonging to a Dutch official. Then, beginning in 1942, Sukarno lived here. From the porch of this house, on August 17, 1945, at 10 a.m., he proclaimed the independence of Indonesia.

Very few photographs of the house still exist as far as I know.[61] On August 15, 1960, two days before the fifteenth anniversary of the Proclamation of Independence, and at the height of his power, Sukarno ordered the house to be demolished. Henk Ngantung, a close friend of the president, a painter and a high official on the city council at that moment, opposed, so he writes in his memoirs, Sukarno's idea to obliterate the historically significant house. But the president shut him up: "Are you one of those people who want to show off my underpants?" The only thing Henk Ngantung was permitted to do was to "make a two-square-meter replica of the building, showing the same materials and colors as the house." "But I don't know where is the replica now," Henk Ngantung writes.⁶²

Where the now destroyed house used to stand, there is an empty space. As if to enhance the emptiness, at one end of the area (there used to be a garden behind the house, and it is gone as well), two larger-than-life statues were put up—Sukarno reading the proclamation, and Mohammad Hatta, his deputy, standing at his side. At the other end of the expanse, there is the new, early 1960s, six-story Gedung Pola, the so-called Blueprints and Patterns Building, built as a part of the obliteration (of "zero panorama," of "monumental vacancies," of "ruins in reverse"⁶³): Blueprints and Patterns Building because the nationally crucial urban and rural plans and models were to be deposited there, and—on special occasions—exhibited. This was impossible to prove, but maybe Henk Ngantung's "mini" of Sukarno's proclamation house is there as well. Otherwise, the Blueprints and Patterns Building, as I recall it, is a space of echoes and closed doors. On closer inspection, it seemed empty except for the Central Office of the Pioneers of Indonesian Freedom, which was on the second floor.

Roosseno listed the Blueprints and Patterns Building highest among the achievements of Sukarno, the president and "architect of the nation":

> First of all, He gave instructions to architect F. Silahan to design the Blueprints and Patterns Building. It was He who set up the outlines of the Blueprints and Patterns Building function. He decided upon a needle-pin exact point, the lot at the Pegangsaan-East Street No. 56. When I am passing the Pegangsaan East Street today (now called Proclamation Street), I can appreciate how gloriously designed the Blueprints and Patterns Building is. The house where Sukarno himself used to live for several years can be seen no more.⁶⁴

Roosseno's biographical data compiled by his students (this is how the echoes and the designs work) place the Blueprints and Patterns Building—it is built of concrete, of course—at the top of *his* accomplishments.⁶⁵

Next to the Blueprints and Patterns Building, just a fence away from the barren square—and next to the highway, along which Roosseno's coffin sped the day of his funeral—there stands the house of Mrs. Hartini, Sukarno's widow, one of his widows.

Mrs. Hartini Sukarno's is a big mansion. She moved there, or rather, after Sukarno died, she was moved there from the president's summer palace in Bogor, in the hills an hour's drive south of Jakarta.

"She is still beautiful," everybody was telling me. She is. But the minutes of silence in this interview are long beyond bearing. The tape mostly records my loud Indonesian, as I try to keep the talking going. The rest is Mrs. Sukarno nodding. "Happy?" "Happy." "Siblings?" "Siblings."[66] Ultimately, there is no sense in going on. But, as the tape recorder is turned off, she begins herself. Quietly. Asking about my children, and, as she speaks, I realize that rarely I am asked so nicely. Then, just a sentence: She had always to remain a lady, to everybody.

She says that she stayed behind all the time: "There had to be only one captain on the ship." I say that he was a lover too, and the father of her children, and that he might have had a chance to open himself up to her without being afraid that it would be used against him. She says that in politics one does not show weakness. After another sip of tea, and a pause, she adds that she still has a friend. Yes, they are in touch. It takes me a while to realize that she is talking about another widow, Jovanka, that of Marshal Tito of broken (and now extinct) Yugoslavia. Yes, of course, she is still alive, and beautiful. They do write to each other.

Mrs. Sukarno has been to Prague, also, of course, with Sukarno; and her eyes point me to a low shelf under the window. There, indeed, I can see now the visiting-dignitaries Bohemian cut crystal displayed. As I leave, she sends her blessing to my wife, my sons, and my daughters-in-law as well. A guard sits on a folding chair at the open gate and sleeps. "In his dream, nothing but the desire to dream."[67]

State widows' houses, at least in this postcolonial metropolis, are, let's say, like libraries. In the Indonesian National Library in Jakarta, for instance, there is an electric signal gate, plugged in only when schoolchildren arrive on excursion. A teacher demonstrates to the pupils: he takes a book from a shelf, goes through the gate, the alarm sounds, and the children with all of us in the reading room laugh and applaud. Then, the children are gone, the signal gate is unplugged, and everybody can take from the library, again, whatever he or she might wish.

Mrs. Rahmiati Hatta was a widow of the man whose statue is there next to the statue of Sukarno, next to the fence of Mrs. Sukarno's house. In 1998

Chapter One

Mrs. Hatta still lived, and not far from Mrs. Sukarno, in a Dutch-colonial-style house on Diponegoro Street.

> Mrs. RAHMIATI: Thank you, Mr. Rudolf, for coming, even when I do not know yet, in fact, about what this interview is to be. But [as you asked me] I will try to think back in my life. I was born in Bandung, in February of 1926. I had a father, a mother, and a sister four years younger than me. My parents, as was usual in the past, of course, worked with the Dutch, with the Dutch *government*, in the Department of Railways. It was called *Staatsspoorwegen*. Both of my parents worked; it was before the Depression, and, because they were not village people, but educated people, they had good salaries — together, maybe, 400 *guldens*. It was really a lot, so much that the Dutch even suggested that my parents become Dutch. They had become *gelijkgesteld* [assimilated, made alike], so that if something happened to them, in court they would be considered to be Dutch. Thus I was a *privileged person*. I did not live in a village, not knowing whether I would eat the next day, lacking everything. My mother was also a woman of the movement. She was on the board of a *vocational school* for girls. Thus I went to this *vocational school*, and there we learned to cook, sew, keep accounts; learned what was *urgent* and what was not, and, thus, how to lead one's own household — to become women useful to the nation.[68]

When did she meet her husband?

> Mrs. RAHMIATI: During the Japanese occupation. But I knew Sukarno before.
> RM: Do you have your grandchildren here?
> Mrs. RAHMIATI: Yes. A granddaughter.
> RM: Do you tell her about the time when you were a child? Is there that connection between you and the girl?
> Mrs. RAHMIATI: She is still little. But she knows that her grandpa had become Hatta, the freedom fighter, and that he was an *important person*. We can visit him because he has a grave, and because he has a statue. So I can say: "This is the grave of grandpa," and "grandpa was a good man; he is in heaven already. You put your hands like this and pray." But she can't yet understand much. She is a child. Three years old.

Bypasses and Flyovers

Hatta's younger daughter, visiting from New York where she lives, shows me around the house. The whole second floor looks like a nursery for her little daughter, and the girl, indeed, moves fast on all fours, behind and in front of us, as we walk and talk. The largest room on this floor is the celebrated Hatta library, a national monument of sorts too. Hatta is reputed to have carried sixteen (sometimes more, depending on the lore) boxes of these books in Dutch times from one place of exile to another. The bookshelves cover all four walls from floor to ceiling. There are yellow index paper stickers here and there: "Philosophy," "Economy," "Iran," "Goethe." Hatta's daughter tells me the story of the library, and Hatta's granddaughter nods up to her every word: "We hired a librarian when my father was still alive, and he rearranged part of the library into a new system. About half was redone, and about a third was stolen. Then we hired another librarian and after him another. Now we have run out of money. Otherwise, the library is as it was."

There are folders on a long table in the middle of the room. Several of the folders are open; others appear empty. "Some people are interested in publishing Hatta's papers," the daughter is telling me. "Whenever there is a crisis, people return to Hatta."

This is, in Jakarta, in the postcolonial—and postrevolutionary—metropolis, how public-memory persons die. "As something abstractly realized" they "cancel themselves out."[69] The abstractions of theirs fill the space, the houses, the streets, the intersections, and the city where they once lived. For those still living—be they indigenous or visitors—the space so filled is habitable only under certain strict conditions. The space filled with the abstractions, "being wholly mediated, creates a second immediacy, while the man [or the woman] not yet wholly encompassed compromises himself [herself] as unnatural."[70] Those state widows' houses in the (almost postmodern) metropolis are like libraries, and like museums:

> *THE YOUTH-OF-1945 MUSEUM: This is a place where Mrs. Hatta offered to take me after the interview. On a typical day, the only visitors are school groups. I am here on a typical day, and I watch the children as they wander about and then cluster around three veteran cars outside in the museum's courtyard. In the middle, there is "Republic 2" car (used to belong to Hatta), on its left, there is "Republic 1" car (Sukarno's), on the right, a little higher, on a stand, there is a six-cylinder motor (taken out of "Republic 3," the first Indonesian Prime Minister Sjahrir's car).*[71]

✦ ✦ ✦

The "Old Graveyard" in Jakarta, sometimes called the "Old Dutch Graveyard," is half cemetery and half museum. A few years ago, in fact, it was renamed Museum Prasasti, (Museum of Ancient Inscriptions), and one is expected to buy a ticket at the gate, where three ticket masters, every day except Monday, play cards.

As one enters, on the left there is a grave of one F. Darlang, a "captain-flier of the Royal Netherlands Indies Army," who died in 1917 at the age of forty-five. Next to the aviator, there rests what remains of Dr. Willem Frederik Stutterheim (died 1942), a famous archeologist of Java and a companion of Claire Holt, a woman who told me everything about Balinese paintings when I first came to the United States forty years ago. Close to Claire's lover there is the grave of Miss Riboet, "Miss Happy Hubbub," the greatest of the Indonesian roadside-theater superstars, who died, I see here, in 1965. There are about seven hundred graves in the cemetery, and no burials take place here anymore. Glorious, old, and uncared-for trees still vaguely suggest the graveyard's pattern as it had evolved during the past three hundred years (there are some early Dutch governors-general, with their wives and children, buried here as well). Besides this, or rather on this, there is merely the long grass, countless cats (merely visiting, like me), and seven goats, probably property of the men at the gate.[72]

Yet there is some activity going on in the cemetery. Evidently new, shiny metal plaques of a uniform design are being screwed onto the headstones here and there, with inscriptions repeating what is already cut into or engraved on the stones anyway, in a new lettering and a new order: name, birth date, death date, and (these are new categories) number and material (granite, bronze, marble, or sandstone). There is also a newly paved courtyard in a corner of the cemetery, next to the now defunct mortuary. There the ticket men and their families, it seems, spend their nights. The pavement is made of flattened and smoothed (as people walk on them) fragments of gravestones. Some letters, words, and even half sentences can still be read on the crazy-paved surface—"Rest in P[eace]," for instance. As Roland Barthes wrote, "we enter into *flat Death* . . . — As if the horror of Death were not precisely its platitude!"[73]

As I became a cemetery regular, one day one of the guards got up from his cards and went with me from the gate among the graves. There was a secret to be conveyed. After fifty meters or so down the main alley, we came to a wooden shack that I had always passed without noticing. The man undid a deadbolt and let me through a squeaking door. There it was, he pointed — Sukarno's coffin and, next to it, Hatta's coffin. Someone had brought the coffins in, to this half cemetery, half museum, where all these memorable people of the past rested, in secret, from the respective hospitals where these two great men of the country and of the struggle for freedom had died, Sukarno in 1970, Hatta in 1980. Sukarno, of course, is buried in Blitar, East Java, and Hatta's grave is at the other end of Jakarta. But here, next to the center of the metropolis, *and in the center of my writing*, here they were, the two reusable hospital coffins on a sawhorse — sublime, architectural, open, and empty.

In ancient Athens,

> the annual public funeral of the citizens who had fallen in war for the city's sake was one of the most important civic events . . . the conveyance of the bones from the city of the living to the city of the dead . . . [was done in] procession. . . . One empty bier is decorated and carried in the procession: this is for the missing.

In ancient Athens, also,

> the first signs of anarchy occurred at funerals. At the time of plague, for instance, people could not afford to bury their dead anymore, and they would arrive first at a funeral pyre that had been made by others, put their own dead upon it and set it alight; or, finding another pyre burning, they would throw the corpse that they were carrying on top of the other and go away.[74]

There are perfect cemeteries in postcolonial Indonesia, of course — Heroes' Cemeteries. There, all graves are laid in straight rows and perfect rectangles.[75] At least ideally, there are no goats. Each grave is adorned with a helmet of the Indonesian National Army and with the Pioneer of Freedom number. One F. Silahan was the architect who — under the guidance of Roosseno and Sukarno — designed the Central Heroes' Cemetery in Jakarta. He, it may be recalled — with the same people helping — designed the Blueprints and Patterns Building as well. In the Central Heroes' Cemetery, beside the helmet and the number, on some graves, a black cable sticks out from the earth. On select days, bulbs are screwed onto the cables, and power is let in. Then, and through the night, there are hundreds of lights on the graves in perfect rows, like traffic lights, and like souls.

Chapter One

Central Heroes' Cemetery, Jakarta: *Captain Suhadi tells me that there are 4,951 graves of heroes here, as of today. This cemetery's capacity is 15,000. Captain Suhadi is the guard of the cemetery, and he has a gun and a whistle at his belt. On each August 17, the Proclamation of Independence Anniversary, and on each November 10, the Heroes of Revolution Day, the bulbs are lighted. Not this year, alas, for security reasons. There are 482 Heroes' Cemeteries in Indonesia. The Prime Minister Sjahrir's grave, which I came to visit, is no. 89 and has both the helmet and the cable. Still, before I leave, Captain Suhadi tells me that (again) I was cheated. The flowers that I bought at the entrance to lay on Sjahrir's grave are* anggrek biru *[blue orchid], "lovers' flowers," and as for the 4,000 rupiahs, to put it mildly, I was overcharged.*[76]

ROOM IN THE HOTEL DES INDES, BATAVIA-JAKARTA. MID-1930S. KONINKLIJK INSTITUUT VOOR TAAL-, LAND- EN VOLKENKUNDE, LEIDEN

CHAPTER TWO

THE WALLS

> The walls held the room in a close embrace,
> separating it from the rest of the world.
> —Marcel Proust, *The Guermantes Way*

BRICKS, PLASTER, BAMBOO, AND MARBLE

"What then does *ich bin* [I am] mean?" Heidegger asked. "The old word *bauen*, to which the *bin* belongs, answers: *ich bin, du bist* [you are], meaning: I dwell, you dwell."[1] According to Heidegger, "To be a human being means to be on the earth as a mortal. It means to dwell."[2] Which means: "Unless man first establishes himself beforehand in the space proper to his essence and there takes up his dwelling, he will not be capable of anything essential within the destining now holding sway."[3]

There has always been a relationship among dwelling, building, architecture, and language. One can speak about the "language of architecture." There are, in architecture as in language, closures, ornaments, tropes, repetitions, and variations. *Vernacular* is a term used both in language and in architecture. Le Corbusier was said to be under the spell of "the whitewashed vernacular of the Mediterranean";[4] in his Maison Citrohan, he used architecture as a "quasi-vernacular norm."[5]

Architecture and literature became almost interchangeable in modern parlance. "Ceci tuera cela" (This will kill that), the book will kill the cathedral, so the deacon in Victor Hugo's *Notre-Dame de Paris* believed. Karl Friedrich Schinkel, the greatest German architect of the nineteenth century, is said through his buildings "to [have written] an almost philosophical dialogue between connectedness and distance."[6]

There is a television image that remains strongly in my mind, of one of the modern cathedrals crashing, the twin towers of the World Trade Center in New York. High above the world of burning iron and concrete, sheets of office papers are flying, still white, uncharred, and with messages undoubtedly still written on them: *ceci*, the book.

✳ ✳ ✳

The houses I entered in Indonesia were, of course, of a great variety of types and sizes, depending on the island, the level of affluence, or the taste of the builder or the dweller. From the point of view of being, however, and also as I recall them now, they all appear the same.

> Mr. HAMID: Like this house here—in front it was open, in the back it was open, in the middle there were rooms. Like here, on a small scale this is the house. My house back then was about five times as big as this one. But the principle is the same. In the back, there was a garden, here was a porch, very long, like this. In front there was a porch, too, and also a garden, and in between, here, the same, the rooms. Here, there are four rooms, two and two; there we had eight rooms, four and four.

How did a family live in the house?

> Mr. HAMID: Servants [lived] in the back. It was always near the kitchen. Here, there was a kitchen and over there, in the back, there was the servants' place. And then, there were stables, also in the back. Ours was a big house, but not too big; it was a place, actually, *full of small houses*.[7]

Mr. Hardjonegoro was a Chinese Indonesian, but when I asked him about the house of his childhood, he told me about Javanese-style houses:

> Mr. HARDJONEGORO: There are several kinds of Javanese houses. Some we call *kampung* [native-neighborhood] houses, others are *djoglo* types, and there are several types of them, as well. There is a name for each type—[8]

Mrs. Brotodiningrat was a Javanese princess. But she described the palace where she was born not unlike Mr. Hamid, who was an Arab Indonesian, or Mr. Hardjonegoro:

Chapter Two

> Princess BROTODININGRAT: I lived in a palace; I was a daughter of a prince, in the palace of Solo.
> RM: You had a room for yourself?
> Princess BROTODININGRAT: It was very large. There were pavilions; one or several persons lived in one or several pavilions.⁹

Dr. Ong, like Mr. Hardjonegoro, was a Chinese Indonesian, a retired teacher at the Faculty of Literature in Jakarta, a historian, a Yale graduate:

> Dr. ONG: There was a garden, a large garden surrounding the house.
> RM: Between the house and the main street?
> DR. ONG: There was a garden, too, a smaller one, between the house and the street.
> RM: So the life —
> Dr. ONG: It went on on the front porch. Evenings in particular were spent on the front porch; often the other parts of the day also. This was the place for everybody to be.

Mrs. Walandau often slipped into Dutch as we talked, and then she seemed happy to stay in it. When I met her for the first time, she had been for years a sort of first lady in a small Christian Indonesian community in South Jakarta. She smiled when I told her that the very moment I came into her house I knew I had entered a Christian place.

There were well and badly built houses, naturally. There were rich houses, and very poor houses, of course. At the back of all the houses — I never visited really desperately poor people — there was a washroom and a toilet.

> RM: Where was a washroom?
> Mrs. SOELISTINA: Always in the back.¹⁰

Also, the servants, and sometimes poor relations, lived in the back.

> Mrs. MIRIAM: My grandfather was a retired *patih* [vice-regent], and he was also a R.O.N. [Ridder in de Orde van Oranje Nassau, a Knight of the Oranje-Nassau Order]; this, of course, was a very great achievement at the time, and he had a very big house. There my parents stayed, in the back. We lived there with all the [unmarried and widowed] aunts and with all the other people who were living in the back.¹¹

The Walls

The *front*, *back*, and *inside* of a house were a way, as well as a trope, of dwelling and being. Mrs. Gusti Noeroel, the heir of the princely House of Mangkunegaran in Surakarta [Central Java], seventy-eight at the time, on the art deco veranda of her house in Bandung overlooking a green valley and several volcanoes, told me about the inside:

> Princess NOEROEL: My mother was a daughter of the Sultan of Yogyakarta. You should know, Professor, I was born in the Mangkunegaran Palace. I was born there, *in the inside*.[12]

The front, back, and inside defined the space. Never were the front, back, and inside missing, and, as if because of that calm positing, crowdedness, smallness, even oppressiveness — and surely there had been much of it — the memories of them, at least, passed over the space airily.

> RM: It was a small house?
> Mr. HARDJO: The house was small.
> RM: How many rooms were there?
> Mr. HARDJO: Oh, many rooms![13]

> RM: A small house?
> Mr. TIMU: Yes — but much bigger than houses are nowadays. It was an ordinary house. Larger than, how should I put it. . . .[14]

The houses of the past might appear out of focus and blurred in the old people's memories. Yet the image rather, as one listens and looks more closely, is a texture and design made especially of people, staying and moving.

> Mrs. SOELISTINA: I am an old woman by now. When I was little, I lived with my mother. Our house then was big — many rooms: one room three times four meters, a *sitting room* four times five, and then one went into the *dining room*, four times six meters; and we had a kitchen in the back, and there was a place to do laundry, also big.[15]

> Mrs. OEI: There was a well, a place for washing, with banana trees around, and rose-apple and citrus trees, there was one calamondin tree, as well. But inside the house, there was not much room to sit, *no*.[16]

Questions about proximity, even nearness, tend to be answered by the old people by pointing out how the inhabitants — and things — of the house

Chapter Two

of the past were moving all the time, how alive they were, and how large, again, or better, open, the house *therefore* had been.

> RM: People lived close to each other. Were you close to your parents? How intense was it?
>
> Mrs. DAMAIS: I loved my mother. She could not speak Dutch, not at all. She took care of us. The teacher's *salary* of my father, how much do you think it was! Mother provided for *everybody*. She bought a rice field not far from the house, and she bought seed. When the harvest time came, we children were sent there to watch so that people would not steal it. Father protested: why we had to go there, the people would take just a little. We were about eleven or twelve years old, and we had already stayed in the rice fields by ourselves for days and nights. So, *this was the mother*.[17]

There is not much in the memories (or it is glossed over very easily) of what I recall as a dread, in my childhood dwelling in Prague; happiness, sure, but all the time with some dint of claustrophobic awaiting—the dwellers whom Kafka often described in the extreme, and with the utmost precision:

> Some had brought cushions with them, which they put between their heads and the ceiling, to keep their heads from getting bruised.[18]

Neither, I think, did I find in the memories of the old people in Jakarta and beyond the bodyless and wall-less utopias of many of Kafka's European avant-garde contemporaries: "Le Corbusier's houses depend on neither spatial nor plastic articulation: the air passes through them! Air becomes a constitutive factor! What matters, therefore, is neither spatiality per se nor plasticity per se but only relation and interfusion."[19]

The houses of childhood as these people recalled them for me, and certainly not only by reflecting the houses in which we talked, felt physical—frailly rather than robustly, like both old people and children are. We never seemed to be far from a moment at which the old interviewees of mine got tired as they talked, and they often excused themselves in the middle of the talk, to take medicine or to go to the bathroom. The bathroom, actually, never seemed absent from our talk. In that unfocused and frail way—in the back—it often worked as the memories' center.

Mrs. MIRIAM: When we moved to Menado there were four of us—four children. In Menado, although I do not remember the house itself, I remember the *WC*: it was a wooden box set over a ditch, with two openings on the top. It was outside, at some distance from the house. And I remember that the house was near the sea.[20]

Mr. HARDOYO: We had several bathrooms in our house. And we used the water not from a well but from a mountain high above our house. We used bamboo [pipes] to carry the water from the mountain down to our place. There was a large garden in the back of the house. And in front, there was a big yard with a banyan tree.[21]

Father MANGUNWIJAYA: I remember a large yard, big trees, flowers in flowerpots, and a well. This I remember best, because I always took my bath at this well.[22]

Princess MUTER: Some people had a bathroom and some people had to go to the river. For our guests, we had a special bathroom, just for them.[23]

Even in Jakarta, these days, on entering a house for an interview, I will often get a smile of welcome, a towel, and a *sarung*, a sarong. In the house bathroom, in the back, still usually a room that is bare except a big cement water tank in the corner, I then will take off all my clothes. With a dipper (plastic nowadays) I then begin to pour the water from the tank all over my body. Refreshed and clean, I am ready for talking while my clothes, left in the bathroom, are being taken care of by souls invisible.

Mr. HAMID: We had as many bathrooms as we needed; one, two, three bathrooms—I think.
RM: Three bathrooms?
Mr. HAMID: Ordinary ones, with a dipper.[24]

The moments when bathrooms entered the conversation belonged to the intense ones. When I asked Mr. Gesang, for instance, an eighty-year-old songwriter of great fame in Indonesia, about his mother, he pondered for a while, and then he opened his autobiography to a bathroom page and read to me what he wrote: "Each morning we were called together to the well. We were washed there and rubbed really hard so that all the dirt will get away. My dark skin became suddenly as if rays of light were coming from it.... I

Chapter Two

had an opportunity to be with my mother in this life for only five years. . . . In 1922, she was called to face Our Creator."[25]

Memories, and gentle memories especially, have always been suspect, and un-gentle scaffolds were constructed to straighten the memories up, to make remembering reliable.

> Talk of memory as rooms, palaces, or purses, as a bottle or a dictionary, as tape recorder or junk box, incorporates into body and mind ways of keeping items safe, retaining control over fluid memories.[26]

Since René Descartes at least, in the West and then all over the world that wished to be modern, images of the past have been suspect in that they remain just *plis de mémoire*, soft, un-hard "folds of memory,"[27] impermanent. There has been an anxiety through the modern age (which is a machine age, after all) that the gentle memories in particular might become the unfit machine that Ludwig Wittgenstein wrote about, for instance, the machine made of butter.[28]

The old Indonesians of the late modern era talked to me about the stuff of which their houses of the past were made, and, as a rule, they talked gently:

> Mr. ROSIHAN: The next house I can remember a little more clearly was not very far from Payakumbuh near Bukittinggi [West Sumatra]. I was four years old at that time. The house was made of wood, and there was a cement floor. The roof was of zinc as in the ordinary houses built in West Sumatra today, unlike in Java, where they have tiles. Some of the windows had glass.[29]
>
> Mr. SUWARDI: My house had walls made of wooden boards.[30]
>
> Mr. TIMU: At that time, our house still stood on piles. And the roof was of tiger grass.[31]
>
> Mr. HARDJO: The houses, roof and everything, were made of bamboo. All that was above and all that was below was made of bamboo thatching, or of leaves and grass. Yet when it rained the houses did not leak.
> RM: What about the floor?
> Mr. HARDJO: Earth, ordinary, earth.[32]

The Walls

This is called "traditional" in textbooks: "The thatched roof, matting walls, and split bamboo flooring,"[33] almost like in Le Corbusier's architectural avant-garde utopia. Except that, besides "sun, space, and green," or perhaps instead of them, memory was flowing through the house, making it subtle and thus three dimensional.

> Mr. TIMU: Simple, yes. Even if a house were just for sleeping in, it already was a house. If there were just a porch, an open porch as was common at the time, it already was a house. Zinc roofs here were rare then. And there were only a few brick walls, and not so many concrete floors. All this usually did not exist. It was still the Dutch age.[34]
>
> Mr. PAREIRA: My father built this house, and it still stands, on the piles from that time. Later I changed only the roof and propped the walls with some masonry. The frame is still of bamboo.[35]
>
> RM: Do you still remember your childhood house?
> Mrs. POLITON: It still stands. It was built of wood, my father's house, and it is the same age as I am. I was born in this house. It was a wooden house.[36]
>
> RM: Did many people live in the house when you were little?
> Mrs. MASKUN: Yes. The house was large, but it was still of bamboo—the Dutch times, still of bamboo.[37]

The houses of the past, recalled and as if, indeed, built up again in the old people's memories and for my, the interviewer's, sake, stand, sway, and tremble as time blows against them. There clearly is an affinity among the houses, the bodies, hands, faces, and eyes of those who recall them—nostalgia, but also the acts of architecture. Like the bodies, faces, and eyes through time inevitably become stiff, calloused, and hard edged, so do the houses—as if aging into modernity, through the same process as the passing of time.

> Mr. ASRUL: After my father died, my mother had to rent a house so that the family could still stay together. This house had a few brick walls, but the upper parts were still only of bamboo.[38]
>
> Mr. DAPIN: Some people were better [off] people, so their houses were large and not just of plaited bamboo. It had been, so to speak, an attribute of the better [off] people—these houses. This meant that all their flowers were in flowerpots, and that they already had tile floors in

their houses. There also was clean water, sweet and clear, not just the water from some well. Not everything was made of tiles yet, but it was already clean enough.[39]

Everywhere at that time, the "time of progress" flowed through the houses and stiffened them up. In Europe, people felt modern in this way: "In stone we feel the natural spirit of the mass. Iron is, for us, only artificially compressed durability and tenacity."[40] As the First World War approached, reinforced concrete joined iron, proudly and appropriately to the times called *béton armé* or *béton brut* (literally "armed" or "crude" concrete).[41] After the First World War, when most of my interviewees were born, Le Corbusier devised "a new way for constructing exterior walls out of hollow asbestos cement casings, the voids being filled with the rubble from war-damaged buildings."[42]

Compared with Europe, houses in the modern colony might appear softer—might *still* appear softer.[43] Exactly because of that, and fundamentally more than in the West, the modern people in the colony were anxious about leaking.

> RM: What about your childhood do you tell your grandchildren? Do you think that they can learn something from it? Do they like to listen?
>
> Mrs. MASKUN: Yes. I often tell them how much I had to go on foot in those times, all the time. When it was too hot, I had to run, so that my feet would not burn. It was like that in the past; not like the children have it now. Now, children have beautiful houses that do not leak. I tell them that when I was little our house leaked. The whole roof sometimes sank, and the water rushed in. I tell them those stories. They all call me *mammy*, my children and also grandchildren; my whole family calls me *mammy*. I like it; when people call you *mammy*, you are not worried.[44]

✦ ✦ ✦

It is well known, of course, that even many modern buildings leak, and some of the supermodern ones leak a great deal.[45] In the increasingly cultured world of modernity, it is often a sense of leaking that matters as much as the water itself. Many ingenious ways are tried to make the sense of leaking—the danger from the exposure of one's space—go away while keeping the house (one might say) in the stream of time. Thus, in the most celebrated buildings of the modern age, walls are made not of bricks, and only secondarily (in a sense) of concrete and iron, but of glass:

> Glass surfaces are themselves practically dissolved in light. . . . [the] entire space of the room could be dissolved in luster.[46]

FINGER PLAY

We need memory as "a possibility: something can exist in it."[47] In the houses of childhood, as in memory, we can exist with other people, many other people. Only thus a house in Indonesia, it seemed, could be recalled at all:

> RM: The house was just for your family?
> Mrs. MIRIAM: No! We stayed there with an aunt who was a widow, and two other widows were there, I think, at the time. One of them had no children and the other one had four. When we left for Menado, we took one of the children with us, a girl. This was common; when you had a big family and the father died, you divided the children—because it was easier on the widow. When we left for Menado we were three children and the girl in the house.[48]

Numbers, the larger the warmer—of people and of everything—tended to pop up in, and to key, the memory, whenever talking touched on intimacy.

> RM: Parents?
> Mrs. TOLANG: Our parents—how many children, yes, seven: two boys, five girls. Two of them still live.[49]
>
> RM: There were all women in the house?
> Mr. OEI: I am child number nine. Number nine among the girls—correct.[50]

Memories of guests in the house of childhood were introduced, truly injected into the talking almost as a rule, whenever I felt that nearness might be on the verge of being recalled. In those moments, the front porch, typically a guest space, appeared both to accommodate and disperse the nearness—this space, always wide open, was made (as it very much still is) the part of the house most full of life, most fully inhabited, most full and com-

Chapter Two

plete, as well as, and this must be said in the same breath, a place most at the house's edge.

> RM: One just rang the bell, or just called out at the gate: "Is anybody home"?
> Mrs. SOELISTINA: Yes, it was polite to do so. Everything was open, as it is here, you see? Inner rooms were closed and sometimes locked; the dining room was closed. But all the space for the guests was left open.
> RM: All the time?
> Mrs. SOELISTINA: There might be a partition, or a window. But it was open.
> RM: The guests would not usually sit inside the house?
> Mrs. SOELISTINA: No.
> RM: They would remain on the front porch or close to it?
> Mrs. SOELISTINA: Yes.[51]

Each of the old people who talked to me looked and sounded fully immersed in it when recalling how many people, guests, used to fill that house of the past.[52] Truly, as the guests, all the passersby and passers-through, were recalled, one by one and all together, the house became real again—by the numbers and the passing.

> Mr. HAMID: We had so many guests and we had them all the time!
> RM: But most times they merely stopped by, and then they stayed on the front porch?
> Mr. HAMID: Oh yes, of course, mostly they did not come in. But there also were many who stayed. They stayed overnight, and they slept in guest rooms. There were guests who came to stay and there were those—just to talk. We were a family well known for how much we liked to have guests.[53]

✦✦✦

Next to the guests passing by and passing through, the other outsiders, servants, were invariably invoked, and in most cases, again, to convey intimacy. The topography and the meaning of the house were made even more profound by bringing the servants into the memories. Houses, rich as well as not, appeared even truer by simply saying: here were the servants.

The Walls

Professor SOEMARDJAN: We had servants. In their rooms, here. So you could not see them from here. (*The old man points at a sheet of paper, on which he sketches the plan of the house as he speaks.*) You cannot see them. They had servants' quarters, here.[54]

Mr. DAPIN: Our house had one, two, three, four, five rooms, big enough; and a room for servants.[55]

Mr. HARDOYO: Here was the bathroom of my parents. Here a bathroom for children, and here for servants.[56]

Like the guests and more, by being "on the margin" and "just passing through," and more, by moving as if through the cracks, through every part of the house, each hour of day and night, servants are recalled as being a tightness of the house; the bricks, the plaster, the bamboo, that kind of tightness.

RM: You had tap water in your house?

Mr. SUTIKNO: Yes. But before that, we had a filter. We had to pump the water from a well. It took at least ten minutes, and then the water poured through the filter.

RM: Don't you think that these kinds of modern appliances, like tap water in the house, were coming at such a slow pace because there were servants? One did not need to give a servant an electric iron, for instance.

Mr. SUTIKNO: We did not have an electric iron. We used hot coals for the iron.

RM: And the servants were doing the ironing in an annex at the back of the house.

Mr. SUTIKNO: Yes. But my parents, unlike most of the other people — well, of course, we had servants, but we children were not supposed to ask them for frivolous things. Our parents told us, "Of course, they are servants, but they are paid labor."

RM: They are not slaves.

Mr. SUTIKNO: Yes, they are not slaves. We were taught how to wash our underwear, we learned to iron, and we learned to mend a little, because we were told: "Don't ask a servant all the time, try to do it on your own; you should become able to do it on your own."[57]

Again, only when servants — or their very visible absence — enter the picture, the house of the past comes truly to life and becomes wholesome.

Chapter Two

RM: How did you choose them?

Princess MUTER: Some of the servants were related to our family, their families to our family.

RM: So you did not place advertisements in a newspaper, let's say, or do it somehow that way?

Princess MUTER: Oh, no!

RM: What happened when they got old and could not serve you anymore?

Princess MUTER: Almost all went away from the house when they got married.

RM: So you had mostly young servants around you?

Princess MUTER: Mostly unmarried servants. But when we were little, some older servants, too, took care of us.

RM: Do you still remember some of these servants with affection?

Sometimes I hear stories about a servant being like a mother.

Princess MUTER: Yes. The older ones took care of us very well. We liked them, and after they left the house we missed them.

RM: Can you think of someone in particular?

Princess MUTER: Yes, I have a special one.

RM: Do you still remember her name?

Princess MUTER: Nini Tandjen, or something like that.

RM: She was with you from early childhood?

Princess MUTER: Yes.

RM: What happened to her?

Princess MUTER: She got old and went home to her family.[58]

Professor SOEMARDJAN: Our servants were family servants. There was no contract or anything. They just were there, and if the family liked them, they were ours, accepted as servants. Some of them stayed many years. I recall one servant who grew old in our house. She actually became like a member of the family. We treated her as if she were of our family. When the servants addressed us, of course, they expressed themselves in a respectful language.[59] But they even might give orders to us children, when we were still little. They might say: "Don't do this, don't do that! Here now, you eat!" Yes, as I said, we were happy. The servants were like family members. They were free to go in here. (*Professor Soemardjan points, in the sketch he had made for me, to the*

The Walls

house's inner living quarters, the center of the house.) And sometimes, when we were little, we slept with a servant on his or her mat.

RM: So it was possible?

Professor SOEMARDJAN: Oh, yes, yes![60]

✦ ✦ ✦

Guests and servants signify intimacy that equals movement and shifting. A house is remembered as secure by its scattered and reassuring openings. To sleep safely in a house is recalled as a sort of moon walking.

RM: Did you have a bedroom for yourself?

Mr. ROSIHAN: No, I slept with my mother in one bed. But not every night; we children especially used to come and go.[61]

Recalling the night walking, like talking about guests and servants, was often an occasion for the old people to draw a most precise and meaningful plan of the house and of the past.

RM: There were no partitions?

Professor SOEMARDJAN: The house was not *separated* into sections. If there happened to be too many guests or members of the family at one time, we made this here (*showing in the sketch*)—*extra*. If there was not enough room—*extra*! This is called *pondok* [cabin]; and here and here, too—cabins. Besides, there was an open space, toward the backyard. I might have my own place, my own sleeping mat, but, in fact, I always chose whatever mat I wished. There were many sleeping mats, for every family member, and each time we went to sleep, we just took one and spread it out, here or here, or wherever we liked.

RM: As you wished?

Professor SOEMARDJAN: Yes. I might like to sleep with my cousin or brother, or whoever: "Let's go and sleep." And he takes a mat and I take a mat and we go.

RM: So, what some might call privacy—there was none; because you were a family?

Professor SOEMARDJAN: There was no privacy. There was no privacy.

RM: Every night you decided whom you liked best at the moment and which place you liked best, and there you went?

Professor SOEMARDJAN: Yes. There was no privacy.[62]

Chapter Two

Intensely, solidly, the house is remembered as a space to move around in and to move through, or, more precisely, to drift through. This may also be why so often the house of the past is most safely recalled as one room.

> RM: How many rooms were there in the house? Can you still recall?
> Mr. USMAN: In Indonesia at that time, usually each house was like one room. Even if a large family lived in it.
> RM: But there were separate quarters? Bedrooms?
> Mr. USMAN: Yes, old people liked to live more in one space, children in another place — if they wanted.[63]
>
> RM: How many rooms were there in the house?
> Mr. TORAR: Oh, I do not recall, Rudolf. But there was a space for everybody. When people wanted to sleep, they put their sleeping mats where they wished.
> RM: It was very simple.
> Mrs. TORAR: Yes, simple.[64]

To belong to a house is recalled as being able to pass through and, also, to move away.

> RM: How old were you?
> Mr. SUTIKNO: Twelve.
> RM: Twelve! And, suddenly, you were taken from your house!
> Mr. SUTIKNO: Oh, that! We were used to it. When I was even smaller, all the time, this or that uncle, an aunt, or a friend of the family nodded that I go with them. I took my coat and went.[65]

✢ ✢ ✢

One may cause a slight linguistic confusion with the old people in Indonesia when one asks about "a bed."

> Mrs. MASKUN: You must mean iron bed. Yes, when I was a child, there were some people who had an iron bed.[66]
>
> Mr. HARDJONEGORO: Bed? Yes, in Javanese, it is called *kloso*, mat.[67]

(In many cultures, asking about the bed may cause awkwardness, especially if one pushes too eagerly. This passage from Kafka's *The Trial* should,

The Walls

for me, be a warning: "His discomfort was still more intensified when the painter begged him to sit down on the bed . . . and actually pushed the reluctant K. deep down among the bedclothes and pillows."[68]) Beds, whatever their variation, are usually a highly charged space of a house and of a home. In Indonesia, as elsewhere, altars (whatever their variation) for gods and ancestors are often built, more or less explicitly, in the shapes of beds—beds for guests that is, for guests and for their servants:

> Professor SOEMARDJAN: One of the rooms of the house was for receiving Dewi Sri, the rice goddess. She traveled from place to place, from house to house. When she came to my home, I mean my grandfather's house, there also had to be a place for her to rest. A bed was made up in that room, with pillows and everything, so that the guest might help herself to it.
> RM: It was for her?
> Professor SOEMARDJAN: And for her attendants. Whoever had arrived with her could sleep in that room. There were beds made up for them as well; not so luxurious, but there were also good pillows on them. Every Friday eve, prayers were said and flowers were laid on the bed as an invitation to her. And fresh, cold water had to be there, too, for her to drink when she was thirsty.
> RM: To refresh herself after the journey.
> Professor SOEMARDJAN: Yes. And it was the task of us children to take care of this. It happened every Thursday night. At other times that room could be used for family members or other guests to sleep there.[69]

Beds, even the "real" solid beds on legs "with pillows and everything"—like the houses—seem to be recalled as safe when crowded and when a space for drifting:

> Mrs. MASKUN: Yes, we had a bed at home, together with my elder siblings and also with my younger siblings. I was number six.[70]
> Mrs. MIRIAM: They gave us a *combong*, you know, that kind of bed. It was a real world in and of itself. The frame was made of hard wood, and there we slept, all the girls. The boys slept in another big, large bed like this.[71]
> Dr. ONG: We slept, all the children together and with our mother. Our

father had his own bed and mother went there only when he invited her. We were all in the one bed. It was a huge bed. I stayed in that bed often and I played there with my toys. It was like a room, rather.⁷²

(I try to imagine my friend Ong, when he was little, in that big bed, "so imbued with the spirit of play and of earnestness of freedom."⁷³)

The most memorable beds of all might themselves be migrants:

> Mrs. MINARSIH: My grandfather passed away in 1927. At the time, I was three years old. What I clearly remember was that he was carried to the grave — he was to be buried — in a bed. He was lying there, and they carried him not on a hearse, in a coffin, or something like that — he was kept in a bed —
> RM: Not in the bed in which he used to sleep?
> Mrs. MINARSIH: I think that he slept in that bed through all his life. It was made of brass and it had mattresses and everything. He was carried to the grave, and the Boy Scouts and the military were there to see him off. I will never forget that scene. I saw him being carried carefully in the bed to his grave.⁷⁴

Mr. Sutikno left Indonesia when he was in his early twenties. Now, in his late seventies, retired, he lived in a small house in Utrecht, the Netherlands, with his Dutch wife (they had married late, a year or so earlier). It was a Dutch summer noon, and we sat in the bright and cool kitchen on the ground floor. The sun was making the glass of milk on the table truly white, the Delft plate truly blue, and the slices of the Dutch cheese on the plate truly yellow. It was this, perhaps, that made Mr. Sutikno tell me about the "flickering light" that he remembered from the house of his childhood. Electricity, even in the modern colonial city Semarang, in Central Java, when Mr. Sutikno grew up there, was still just "flickering."⁷⁵ This, by the way, Mr. Sutikno said, made a finger play by his father for his son, on their house's wall, next to the child's bed, "the stuff of miracles," possible.⁷⁶

Essentially the same story, only told in a slightly different sense of time — instead of modernity not yet coming, the past still being with us — I heard from a former Indonesian Air Force chief of staff, a suspected coup organizer just recently from prison, Mr. Omar Dhani:

The Walls

> Air Marshal DHANI: I was still little and very happy at the time, and my father, when I was already in bed—we were three children in that bed—played a finger play for us—like *wajang*, do you understand?

Wajang (now spelled *wayang*) is an ancient Javanese shadow-puppet theater, with stories mainly from the Hindu-Javanese mythology.

> Air Marshal DHANI: He used his hands, and he talked like a *dalang* [puppeteer]. In this way, I was being introduced to Javanese culture.[77]

The drifting, the night walking, the moving around, the "lack of privacy," in other words, the energy of the house, logically, naturally, normally, inevitably, happily, and almost invariably with an infectious sensual pleasure was remembered as an absence of full light:

> Professor SOEMARDJAN: There was no privacy, yes, but also, at night, we had no electricity. When a night was still young, we hung oil lamps, but often even the oil lamps were not used. So it was dark. It was normal, and deep in the night it was even more normal. The darkness outside and the darkness inside, it was normal—like twilight, like dawn, and like a day, and the other things around.[78]

This is crucial: the lack of privacy is recalled as making light together.

> Mr. DES ALWI: It was called *stormking* [hurricane lantern], and later *Petromax*. *Stormking* is where you pump it up, like this—(*Mr. Alwi energetically showed me.*). And this was a task for us, the children, to pump it.
> RM: Was one pumping enough for the whole evening?
> Mr. DES ALWI: You had to pump for quite a number of minutes and, yes, it was supposed to last for the whole evening. And when it began to dim, later, the adults would pump it again, I think.[79]

Pumping it up and down, and again, this was how the house and people in it were built. This also might be why the flickering light is so thickly remembered; even the sound of it:

Mr. HARDOYO: There was no electricity, not yet. We used a *Petromax* lamp or *pumping* kerosene lamp. You know what a *pumping* lamp was? It used a pump like that. (*Again, I am shown, and it seems, again, that more force is being put into the demonstration than needs to be. Yes, this is a child pumping recalled!*) Kerosene lamp, *you see*, the whole room was in light. There were lamps that had a pump in the front, and there were others that had their pumps at the back. They were glowing! But you had to pump all the time.[80]

Thus electricity was being announced. We all do know, because we all, of a certain age, still, hopefully, belong to the "primitive cultures," Marc Augé writes about (and Sigmund Freud also knew about) that

a person may be killed if awakened suddenly, as one of these "entities," the double that wanders by night, may not have time to reoccupy the body at the moment of waking.[81]

The old Indonesians I interviewed seemed to be both aware of and spared this horrifying death. [82] They were given the shock in installments.

Mr. SUTIKNO: In Semarang, around 1932 or 1933, I saw the electricity coming. I still remember it, because our house, too, got electricity. We still had a *Petromax* and we had to pump it until a reddish cylinder with a monometer showed up; then it was enough. There were tiny pipes leading to—
RM: It happened when you lived with your parents in Semarang?
Mr. SUTIKNO: Yes, I still remember the sound of the lamp, the light of it, but the sound, as well, and how it smelled—it is a strange thing. At first, the electricity was very expensive. We used only very small bulbs—25 Watt or so.
RM: Could you read by that light at night?
Mr. SUTIKNO: Not really. But we still liked the *Petromax* lamp, or that kerosene lamp on the wall. We were used to it.[83]

As one may expect in a house of children, and in the old people's memories of the childhood house, there is always a gentle and powerful presence of toys—toys carried around, sheltered, missing, and wished for. Those houses rest on toys.

The Walls

Prince PUGER: When we were children, we played *dolanan-dolanan Jawa* [Javanese games]. We sang songs that today have almost all disappeared. The children of today play *video games*, I believe.[84]

Some toys flicker gently in the memory. Some, maybe, only now become distinct, and, in some cases, quite hard on the eye.

Mrs. MIRIAM: I remember there was a store in Menado, quite an expensive one, because it was a Dutch store. Once, we were allowed by our father to choose one toy each from the store. I picked out a doll. She was a very expensive doll, and she was real Dutch.
RM: She was blond?
Mrs. MIRIAM: Oh, yes! The shop was so impressive — [85]

Mr. OEY: The only Japanese I knew before the invasion [in 1942] in Malang, we lived in Malang, was the owner of the Mikado shop. He sold all kinds of things.
RM: So you went there?
Mr. OEY: There were things of all kinds — Japanese goods like ice cream, and what children nowadays call *loli* [popsicle], and there were little toy tin cars.
RM: Japanese worked in the shop?
Mr. OEY: Yes, sales agents and the owner. Only later we learned who he was. Just before the invasion he disappeared, and he came back with the Japanese army as an officer; not an ordinary soldier but an officer.
RM: He had worked in the shop as a spy?
Mr. OEY: Yes! It was all in preparation. It became clear that they had been preparing.[86]

Solidity as well as the airs of a house of the past, seen and recalled through toys (not unlike guests or servants), appear more open to the flow of time — and to history — than in other ways.

Father MANGUNWIJAYA: I tried hard not to be envious. I still remember, as we moved to Magelang, I was still a little boy; every Sunday we went to church for a confession. And on the way back home, with my younger sister, I always made sure that we stopped in front of the house of a Dutch official. He was a captain in the army. The Dutch

> captain had children: little ladies and little gentlemen. When they played outside, they always had something like an *autopad* [toy car racing track] and gorgeous dolls. We always stopped where the road passed the house and watched the Dutch children. We were content only to watch; we did not want to admit a feeling of envy, like "Oh, this is colonial! I am just a pauper!"
>
> RM: Did they watch you?
>
> Father MANGUNWIJAYA: No, we kept under a tree. I think it was a tamarind tree. We would sit there, my younger sister and I, sitting and watching.
>
> RM: Were they like ghosts?
>
> Father MANGUNWIJAYA: Sorry?
>
> RM: The Dutch children.
>
> Father MANGUNWIJAYA: Oh, no! They were like elves; supernatural, maybe, but sweet and happy. It was *gratifying*. Not a feeling of envy. Only: "If I just had an *autopad* like him." But it simply could not be. It was *impossible*, right?[87]

The sense of house and hominess, modern and colonial, was given to me gently, as a matter of toys.

> Mr. SUTIKNO: It was the 1930s; I was in the first grade of school and my father had to pay a lot of debts. We didn't have many of those modern things at home. Whatever we played with, we played as the seasons went — kites, spinning tops, or marbles; rather, nuts or seeds, in fact. I was impressed by what the Dutch boys had, but I don't think that I always knew what it was. And then, Santa Claus —
>
> RM: Bringing presents?
>
> Mr. SUTIKNO: Yes! I asked for building blocks, for a toy car, or a toy train, and, sometimes, I got it. But mostly I was thinking, well, those were Dutch customs, that: "Put your shoe with some grass in it under your bed, because Santa Claus's horse likes the grass."[88]

THE SALON

Charles Baudelaire, as in many other matters, was one of the first to see the connection between toys and the sense of the modern bourgeois home.[89] For the poet, Benjamin wrote, the toyshops in nineteenth-century Paris were a

The Walls

primeval (if not originary) space where the "private individual" made his or her "entry into history." The Paris shops dealing with toys (and the Dutch toyshop in twentieth-century Menado, or the Mikado shop in Malang, in the old people's recollections did not look different) appeared and were recalled "to constitute the interior," "phantasmagorias of interior," "which for the private individual represents the universe."[90]

The modern urban toyshop, with its many nooks of pleasure for a child, who can (or is not allowed) to "pick out something" for himself or herself, this display of a miniature and dreamed-about reality, has often been the first complex out-of-home and wished-for modern urban house, "half-childish trifles, half God in your heart," as Goethe might say.[91] In his writing on Baudelaire and on the Paris of the time, Walter Benjamin, describing the new, bourgeois, private person and the person's new space for living, in fact closely describes a (grown-up) child in a toyshop recalled: "In the interior [the private person] brings together remote locales and memories of the past. . . . [The] collector proves to be the true resident of the interior. . . . To him falls the Sisyphean task of diverting things of their commodity character by taking possession of them. . . . the apartment becomes a sort of cockpit."[92]

Salon—however Baudelairian and Parisian, strange and unfitting the word seemed to me at the start, eventually—and very much because of its strangeness—it turned out to be the best word to name the newly emerging bourgeois urban interior in the twentieth-century colony as well. *Salon*—better than its kin *drawing room, smoking room, billiard room*,[93] *formal room*, or *mooie kamer*, "beautiful room," to use a specifically Dutch example—suggests the categorically sublime, the best room in a house and, at the same time, as the dictionary says, "a hall or place used for the exhibition of works of art."[94]

A salon (like a toyshop for a child) is the architectural and urban best of "the myth that had to be assembled,"[95] the densest of "the homogenous matrix of capitalistic space."[96] With undying freshness, and utmost eagerness, the old people in Indonesia recalled what they called by different names, drawing room, *mooie kamer*, often guest room, sometimes salon: the charmed magical space, dense, crowded with curios, useful for nothing much but to be played in and with, to be allowed in or not to. Magically strange, toylike things—fragile, *à domicile*, "hinge works"[97]—were brought in, inspiring nothing much but a wish to bring in more.[98]

(How much more energy this had to demand in the tropics! The air was heavy, stuffy, damp, and sticky. Mosquitoes loved it too. There was progressively less of space, openings, and natural coolness. But this was modern and inspiring a future even more modern—like the coming of air conditioning, for instance.)

"Wherever the living pursue particularly ambiguous activities, the inanimate may sometimes assume the reflection of their most secret motives."[99] But it can also be another way around. The new space—salon or salonlike, "*intérieur* as étui"[100]—might swallow the toylike things, might keep being filled, and might become heavy with the things, with the "novelties, with the "'theological niceties' of the commodity,"[101] and thus it might become heavy and deeply meaningful as well. The living might assume the reflection of the most secret motives of the inanimate.

> Professor RESINK: About the time I was born, my mother came under the influence of Javanese culture and became quite well known as a collector of Hindu-Javanese *oudheden* [antiquities]—statues, bronzes, stones, and so on, such as those described by Dr. W. F. Stutterheim, who was the head of the Oudheidkundige Dienst [Antiquities Service] in Surakarta [where the family lived]. I have to say that, as a child, I was deeply impressed by all those statues—
> RM: It was in the house?
> Professor RESINK: It was all in the house. Later, in our house, there was even *heilig bed*, a ceremonial bed that my mother bought from an impoverished nobleman from the town of M [*sic*].
> RM: Somebody slept in that bed?
> Professor RESINK: Oh, no, no!
> RM: It was just there?
> Professor RESINK: Just there, *ceremonieel*, exactly as it used to be in the old house of the nobleman who sold it to us. It was not slept in, of course; it was purely *ceremonieel*.

Professor Resink might say: it was ritual in a salon way—that kind of prayer.

> RM: It used to be that nobleman's family heirloom?
> Professor RESINK: Yes, holy heirloom. And mother let it be written even in the purchase contract that on every Friday eve our servants would bring flowers, burn incense at the foot of the bed, and do all

The Walls

the other required things. So, this, for me, was the home I became accustomed to.[102]

Through salon-owning (and no less through salon-desiring), a house in a colony—perhaps more exclusively, and certainly more suddenly than in Baudelaire's Paris—became urban, bourgeois; it appeared newly distinct, newly heavy, and thus also newly colorful and flooded with a new light:

> Mrs. MIRIAM: We had—our father had—a complete set of Rabindranath Tagore, in Dutch, small green and orange books. He had the whole set. And so we grew up among them.[103]

Music was among the first things recalled to me as making the salon emerge in the colony. It did not matter much, but it is important to keep in mind, whether the particular music was that of ancient *gamelan* (the Javanese gong orchestra), a mother singing to her child, the popular songs of the time, or Richard Wagner's overtures adapted for piano. Whatever its birthmarks, and thus it is recalled, the music took its cue, indeed its new origin, from the ways of the salon, and it gave them back to the salon—it made the salon more real than it would be without it, it made it be. Ideally, like the bronze and stone statues of Mrs. Resink, the music was to be stored in the salon.

> RM: Was there singing at home?
> Princess NOEROEL: There used to be much singing in the past. Like there is today on TV. When I was a child, there was already electricity, in 1921. So we could have a radio and gramophone, but no TV. I had, of course, to learn Yogyakarta [Javanese] dancing. I was told to, because my mother was from Yogyakarta and from the palace; and so, whenever we had guests, I had to dance for them.[104]

The music, stored in a salon, became a part of the salon's plasticity—indeed, it made the salon playable. This is from an Indonesian novel recalling the 1930s:

> Alongside the wall, on my right, stood a piano, while in the corner near the door to the front room was a glass china cabinet, inside which a Czechoslovakian tea set could be seen. A Philips radio was in the other corner.[105]

Chapter Two

Progressively, a handle could be attached to the music to crank it up, as well as the salon and all that new kind of life:

> Prince PUGER: Of course, we had a gramophone. It was His Master's Voice at the time. There was a dog facing the funnel.
> RM: What kind of records did you have?
> Prince PUGER: We had a special cabinet for them. We had *krontjong* [now spelled *kroncong*, Indonesian-Malay-Portuguese, Hawaii-like popular music and songs], and we had gamelan.[106]
> Mr. HAMID: We had records of Western, Malay, as well as Indonesian music, and few items of Arab music. But mostly we had records of Western music.[107]

Music from the radio progressively, playfully, magically, and mechanically — "whether because of the structure of the apparatus or because of the structure of memory"[108] — still appears, sounds, as a heavy salon item, most emblematic and even originary.

> Mr. ALI: At the time, radio had mainly been Dutch "small talk" and then music. In fact, almost all was music, nothing much else.
> RM: It was a luxury?
> Mr. ALI: Yes, a diversion.[109]
>
> RM: What do you remember hearing on the radio during the Dutch times?
> Mrs. SOELISTINA: Actually, I do not think I ever heard radio at the time. Of course, I heard about it. It was *interesting*. But it was not like those *Walkmans* are today. It was big, inside a house.[110]
>
> RM: Was there a radio in the palace?
> Princess BROTODININGRAT: Of course there was! There was everything. It was a modern place, my dear! We did not have TV yet, it is true, but there was a radio. When Prince B. died, I remember, I heard it on the radio. Big radio. It was like being in the movies.[111]

Melodiously, mechanically, and weightily, radio fit into the salon, filled and gathered the interior and the dwellers of the colony: not all, admittedly, but the most "progressive" dwellers among them.

The Walls

RM: Did you have a radio?

Mr. JUSUF: At that time? I listened. I had a friend from a *well-to-do* family, and they had a radio. They invited me to their home and I listened. At that time, it was *Erres*; they are not anymore. You could not hear bass. It was still before the *hi-fis*.[112]

And there was a telephone, maybe in the hall, at the edge of the interior, but still in the middle of the modern: soundly salon-wise and very deeply in: "And the voice that slumbered in those instruments was a newborn voice. Each day and every hour, the telephone was my twin brother."[113]

RM: You had a telephone?

Princess BROTODININGRAT: Oh, sure! It was *complete*![114]

Not so mechanical, handle-prone and knob-full, yet instrumental and furniture-like enough, another kind of music, newly fitted in, filled the space and did it still more in the modern salon way. More instruments, some with a handle, knob, pedal, others without, playing and on display, made the house shut, open, sound, and turn around — around the salon.

Mr. ALWIN: Since I was little, still before school, I recall that my mother played the violin, and that my father also played the violin and the guitar.

RM: What kind of music?

Mr. ALWIN: All kinds, all music — I first heard the *Donau Wals* ["Danube Waltz"] from my mother. Classical songs.

RM: Did they also play together?

Mr. ALWIN: Yes. Sometimes we even put together a whole ensemble. For us, a *repertoire* was not just the Western or the traditional: *both of them*. We got our first gramophone in Sigli [North Sumatra], I think. My parents bought it at a *garage sale*; it was called *vendutjes* [auctions] at that time. There was a Dutch man selling things because he was moving. Many records came with it, I still remember. It was also the time when we got a piano in our house.[115]

A salon could hardly exist, even be thought of, if a house was too far (still too far) from the market, from a shop, toyshop, art shop, furniture shop, or

Chapter Two

music shop. Indeed, *salon*, as the dictionary says, also means "a shop, business, or department of a store offering a specific product or service, esp. one catering to a fashionable clientele." [116]

> Mr. SOEDARMONO: My father had to know that I liked music because he saw me play the records all the time. At that time, we had an uncle who helped my father in his medical practice; his name was Saleh, and I think that he is already dead. He could play guitar, and I learned to play from him. Once we went to the town, and I saw a guitar in a Japanese shop. It was a small guitar, just for kids, but I wanted it very badly. It was too expensive, but I wanted it so much.
> RM: How old were you?
> Mr. SOEDARMONO: I think about eleven, and I wanted it so much. I had a terrible fit of temper, and I had never had this before.

To tell me that he had "a terrible fit of temper" because of wanting that guitar so badly, Mr. Soedarmono used an Indonesian word, *berontak*, which is more commonly used to say "to struggle," "to revolt," or "to rebel": a powerful verb that, otherwise, from the old people, I heard quite rarely.

> Mr. SOEDARMONO: In the end, after a month or so, my father came home, and he brought me a real guitar. Not just a toy! He found it at a place on the outskirts of town, near a plantation. There was someone who built guitars — so father bought one for me. After that time, I had a guitar. And then we got a piano, too.
> RM: A piano?
> Mr. SOEDARMONO: We had a piano, a broken one. It could not be repaired anymore. At least, there was nobody who would know how to repair it. It came from one of my father's patients, a Dutch man. He owned an ice factory and also a movie house, and he was ill for years. He could not get better, yet my father managed to cure him a little. He was very grateful: "I have a piano. It is broken, but perhaps your boy might like to have it."
> RM: He was Dutch?
> Mr. SOEDARMONO: Yes, and a very good man. So I had a piano. But it was broken.[117]

✦✦✦

The Walls

The salon, with its spatiality, plasticity, and music, appears to make everything — all the possible reshaping of a house and of a home — very much and exquisitely pleasing. The sublime of the salon — and of the house and the home sucked into it — appears to be able to cut through history: colonial, revolutionary, as well as postcolonial. The postcolonial memories of the colonial salon, or a salon as one wished to have it, whatever might have happened to the people and the homes, appear invariably sweet — or scented.

RM: You like piano?

Mrs. MINARSIH: Oh, yes! That is something that is still with me. I just must have it. My sister Nelly was four years older than I, and she took piano lessons, once she was six, with Miss Dijckerfhoff. That was a Dutch lady who came to the house and taught my sister. I will never forget the way she smelled!

RM: Soir de Paris, perhaps?

Mrs. MINARSIH: Ambra, in a tiny blue bottle. When I became six, my mother did not have enough money anymore to pay for my lessons.

RM: I know the feeling. There was a violin and an older brother in our family.

Mrs. MINARSIH: But my sister played really fantastically. That piano is still there with her. It is a piano that my father gave my mother after they married. It is a *baby grand*. Please take this piece [of cake]. And would you like to have another cup of tea? —

RM: So, you liked music.

Mrs. MINARSIH: Oh, yes! We used to have concerts at home. My mother told me, when she was still with my father, they were having *music soirées*.

RM: Yes.

Mrs. MINARSIH: My mother played the violin, and she could sing very well. Even later, she sang a lot. We sang together, "Ave Maria," for instance. Actually, this is not a song, you know, for —

RM: Muslims?

Mrs. MINARSIH: But we loved "Ave Maria"! We had a gramophone, and I learned it as a child. My mother sang it often. And the other song, which I will never forget, it is a French song, and then, of course, "Versunken," what is it? Schubert?

RM: Schubert.

Chapter Two

Mrs. MINARSIH: Schubert. And then there was yet another, a French song that I remember. My mother taught it to me also. (*Mrs. Minarsih sings for me.*) My mother sang in French, German, and Dutch as well. It was really fantastic, for me to grow up in this. It was so *complete*.[118]

The salon never got a fixed name in Indonesia. It might have been called by its many Dutch, English, German, or French names, but it never got a colonial (nor a postcolonial) name of its own. Maybe because the concept was so expansive and all absorbing. As a modern colonial house desired to be soulful, so it desired to be salonful — fully, not just in part.

By the same essentialism, the salon demanded that the salon stuff, every piece of it, be taken seriously and placed exactly. The comfort zones, and arrows and points of the house, all had to be salon-staked — the stuff, the statues, or the music. The positioning of the things made for fullness or emptiness in homes. It was a salon doing, and one's home now breathed that way.[119]

Fork, knife, or spoon misplaced might mean that one was out, or, at least, not (yet) in. The salon dictated an ideal, which categorically demanded a new way of moving and being in space. "Ours was a modern family," Dr. Ong told me.

> Dr. ONG: We met at each meal: in the morning, at noon, and in the evening seven sharp. Not like the people of old. And the food was warm. Most dishes, that is, were warm. Not like the food in the old style, that sits on the table at all times, and whoever wishes picks up what he or she wants. One does not care to warm it.[120]
>
> Mrs. DAMAIS: For lunch, we used to have rice with vegetables, and, for instance, chicken. But we had to be there *on time*, and *together*.
> RM: So you all met, around the table?
> Mrs. DAMAIS: Yes. We were quite modern.[121]
>
> Mr. HARDJONEGORO: At half past seven, we had *breakfast*. At one o'clock, there was *lunch*. In the evening, we had *dinner*.[122]

In their memories (otherwise told to me in Indonesian), people still used Dutch, English, or French to name the ways, the manners, of family being together and being at home.

The Walls

Princess NOEROEL: When we ate, only our mother and father sat on chairs. We children sat lower than them, still on the floor.

RM: Could you talk?

Princess NOEROEL: Our father talked to us, and we answered. Merely, on *Sundays*, the children, my brothers and sisters, and our parents, we did eat *lunch*. Then, everybody asked questions and everybody answered.[123]

Mr. HAMID: There was a big table, and everybody was invited to eat there. Our family was quite progressive. First, the men came to the table —

RM: Where were the women?

Mr. HAMID: Also at the table, but as long as the men were eating, women did not come. Only after the men finished would the women sit down. So the women ate at the table as well. The table was the same, the food was the same; everything was the same.[124]

Home, family, intimacy, and all the other stuff of the interior had been learned by the force of the salon — significantly, as the table manners, and most properly so. What Nietzsche called "brief habits";[125] no rules cut more deeply — how to put food into one's mouth, how to chew, how to swallow, nothing controls and forms the body more: how to breathe — in the new distinct center of the colony and of the modern, at the table.

Mr. SUTIKNO: *OK*, where to begin? My father was of a staunchly Muslim family, but he was educated in Leiden, and under van Vollenhoven among others.[126] My mother got her education from Catholic nuns in Semarang. I was born in Semarang in 1928 and lived there until 1935. And here is the thing. In Semarang, there was a little European restaurant called Au chien qui fume. The owner was *Monsieur* Lacaille, married to an Austrian, and he had a son, Bernard (Bibi) Lacaille. *Monsieur* Lacaille had a lot of, eh, *flair*. He also had fiery red hair. And so my father decided to make our eating habits more Western, so that we would not eat "with our hands" anymore. We were to learn how to eat with a spoon and a fork and so on. So he took us there regularly, to the Au chien qui fume, and there he had a table laid for us in the Western fashion. And we learned how to sit — like not to eat with our elbows on the table —

Chapter Two

RM: Technology of eating?

Mr. SUTIKNO: Technology of eating. We learned how to eat potatoes in the European manner—not put *sambal* [spices, chili peppers] on it, right? This is one of the things I still remember from my childhood. Our father was telling us, if we wanted freedom, then we have to beat the Dutch with their own tools; it is their *organization* and their *culture*. And, he said, we could do it.[127]

Prince PUGER: The Javanese people, and Indonesian people in general, if it was nine o'clock in the morning, they might even have dinner. But, as I was taught, we had to learn the *etiquette* of eating. Our forebears, they were eating, *ck . . . ck . . . ck*. We could not do it anymore.[128] I learned from Mrs. Resink that when I ate chicken, I could use the tips of my fingers, but I had first to ask for permission. Except for this, I always had to use a knife and fork. There was a whole set of rules about how to eat with a knife and fork—one cut a steak, cut and cut, and then might place the knife on the right side and take a fork and eat with the fork. When it came to *pudding*, one had to ask for a special spoon; what do you call it? (*I do not know.*) This spoon was for soup. This knife was for steak. This knife was for this and that. It was all arranged to the smallest spoon; for dessert, this spoon.

RM: A spoon? Not a fork?

Prince PUGER: Yes, because Mrs. Resink taught us so.[129]

At just about the time of Le Corbusier, the home as a machine for living in arrived also in the colony. The sense of dwelling began handle-prone, convertible, and ticking-timed.

RM: What kind of dishes did Mrs. Resink serve?

Prince PUGER: Every day there were European dishes. But on Sunday and Wednesday we ate rice.

RM: It was so regular?

Prince PUGER: Yes. We were taught how things were to be ordered: "Get up, wash, have breakfast, have lunch!"—like that.[130]

It appeared to Walter Benjamin that, in nineteenth-century Europe, in the Biedermeier sense of dwelling, "there is a preference for carmine, orange, and ultramarine; a brilliant green is also used."[131] In this connection he also noted that "nowhere is sensuous, nostalgia-free contemplation as much at home as in color."[132]

I have also felt, talking to old people in Indonesia, that color, spread on the surface, was often recalled to convey fullness. Such color appeared in the memories at moments when homes of childhood might become more uncertain, unsteady, or blurred. Then, "discourse takes on the color of the walls."[133] The coloring of the childhood house's walls in particular was often recalled so that the home of the past came out more geometric and in planes—as a facade, in fact. Bold and primary colors; and that kind of brightness seemed to work best.

> Mrs. MIRIAM: I recall that we liked it very much. There was a pink room. There was a green room. All rooms were of different colors. At that time it felt very modern.
> RM: What can be modern about colors?
> Mrs. MIRIAM: Oh, yes. My room was green! Emerald green!![134]

There was an assuring power of indexing in the use and recollection of the walls—in the distinct and catalogue-legitimate, shop-legitimate, culture-legitimate, easily recognizable colors and shapes.

> RM: What about your house, when you were a boy?
> Mr. HARDJONEGORO: Half-Javanese, half-European. It was *colonial art deco*. Don't forget, we were raised in European way.[135]

> RM: So the house was—
> Mr. ALI: Modern for that time.
> RM: What was "modern for that time"?
> Mr. ALI: How to put it—a little Western, a little Eastern.[136]

I was most touched by those old people in Indonesia who let me deepest into their homes—not just to the open front porch to sit in rattan chairs and watch the traffic as we talked. The people who invited me deep in, as a rule, appeared to be the most pronouncedly modern, and the most pronouncedly colonial and postcolonial. As we talked, with the noise of the traffic dimmed, and often with the lights dimmed as well—I felt fine, indeed grateful, to get so far:

It took a very long time before he got to the gate. Then, he gave me the most gracious and indeed elaborate welcome.

Slowly, through a small garden behind the side gate, we moved into the house. Through a long and dark corridor, ahead of me, he shuffled past several closed doors.

We came into a grand salon, *so he called it, albeit with a touch of irony or, perhaps, sadness. He wore a light-gray freshly ironed shirt, black trousers, and shiny black shoes—not the tiniest hint of inattention. He was pleasant, with a friendly formality. A large oil painting of a castle ruins hung on the wall; it was very dark and in a heavy frame. The room was overfull with big pieces of carved furniture—like the painting, he told me, brought over from a larger place, where he had lived for several decades and from which he had recently been evicted; I heard the story, someone in the new regime wanted the place. He was "reading blind," he said: he could not write, even read, anymore, "merely poetry." Neither could he play piano anymore, merely listen to recordings. In this dark place ("musty," Benjamin might say), with a glass of tepid water in front of me on a low table, I felt fine, to sit on this sofa with this man—two cockpit people.*[137]

WINDS SWEEPING THROUGH THE HOUSE

Naturally, and not only because the people to whom I was talking were so advanced in age, there was always an overtone of secondhandedness in what they recalled:

> Mrs. MIRIAM: Only Poppy played piano; I was the youngest of the three. Poppy wore glasses and she got a bike. I always inherited things. She got extra lessons in sewing, and then she became *padvinster*, a Girl Scout. I never got that because, by that time, we ran out of money, or something else happened.[138]

The modern houses in which many of the old people to whom I talked lived as children—the more modern the houses were, with the WCs, the salons, the more so—had been leftovers. Literally and historically so—a house into which a modern colonial family newly moved, as often as not, had been left over by a family a step further ahead on its road to modernity, a Dutch family in the most optimistic scenario. Through the leftovers, wis-

The Walls

dom might be learned about the time passing as well as about the future of the colony.

> Mrs. TORAR: It was a very large house. I still remember it. There was a big garden in the back. And we had a *swimming pool*; but there was no water in it, so we just played on the bottom.¹³⁹

Indeed, the salon was the cockpit of the house. The salon was a cockpit and a shelter at the same time. In the colony, more strikingly than elsewhere, it was also the space of the house that was most secondhand, most borrowed, and, with all its heaviness, most exposed and most hanging in the air.

Often, as I was leaving a house, my host would say: "Let's go together, I am on my way anyway." Even when this did not happen, I always had a feeling that the old people, and their houses, too, were somehow permanently "on the way." I might have gotten that feeling, of course, because I myself was incessantly moving. I passed from house to house, and the houses responded in so relaxed a manner to my moving and intruding (imagine the sweating me, the tape recorder, and the questions!) that it often happened that all three of us, the host, me, and the house, seemed to be flying and swirling together.

> *From Yogya to Solo, I called Mr. Hardjonegoro (whom I had never met before and who could hardly have heard about me) to ask for an interview and, if possible, to set a date. "The gate is open, just push a little," he said. "Don't you know that?"*¹⁴⁰

Some people may say this is "traditional" or "Eastern" hospitality, and by this they may think they have said it all. I often, and with embarrassment, felt rather something excessively modern—colonial and postcolonial modern—in the way in which the Indonesian houses opened to me. With all the affection and thankfulness I have for them, houses and people, there remains an overwhelming sense of a shortage of resistance—on their part as well as on mine.

> RM: When the new things were coming, what was the feeling? Surprise? Or it was just coming?
> Mr. SUTIKNO: Yes, just coming. When we still had no electricity at home, I already knew from the friends who already had the experience.

Chapter Two

RM: The Dutch often claimed that they did it for you. Did you feel it like coming from the Dutch? Like, "the Dutch are doing it"?

Mr. SUTIKNO: Well, it was the thing, of course. Who else but the Dutch could bring it at the time—in the colonial Dutch Indies?[141]

The Europeans, and namely the Dutch in the colony, had been pivotal in making the change, and they were exemplary in the new ways of dwelling. Thus, more than anyone, they appeared to be constantly on the move and more, as the most visible visitors—guests in a house of sorts, even in a house of their own. European, and namely Dutch, modern houses in the colony, more exemplary than others, had been conceived and were constantly upgraded on the principle of passing by and passing through. Europeans, and Dutch primarily, in the colony much more than their compatriots back in Europe, dwelt on the merit of being the winds of change or—as one might put it in a context of a house—a draft of modernity:

> Professor WERTHEIM: This was how we, the Dutch, lived in the colony. Especially when we were officials, state employees, let us say teachers in a state college like me. To buy furniture, we simply went to the nearest *vendutje*, auction, of some other Dutch official who was being transferred to another post at the time as we were coming. There, we got everything we needed for the new house. When we were leaving, again, we simply auctioned the stuff in our *vendutje*. Thus we were not tied to the things in the house. They were good for four years, sometimes for five years, sometimes just for half a year. Thus, of course, they were not so very interesting.
>
> RM: Do you think that, back in Holland, there was a greater attachment to the things of home?
>
> Professor WERTHEIM: Oh, yes!
>
> RM: Do you think that, in the colony, there was less of the attachment?
>
> Professor WERTHEIM: Much less, because of that auction system. Of course, some people brought some good pieces for their homes from Europe on the ship with them. They did not then use the auctions so much.[142]

Salons of all kinds, the new interior, core of the house, heavy with meaning, the new recluse, were part of the modern colonial culture of constant shifts, deploying, transfer, and auctions, the easy market, the drafty, indeed

The Walls

nomadic mode. The emblematic things of the emblematic salon—the grand pianos, statues, heavy and ornate ebony and mahogany furniture, silver and china, canvases in gilded frames—most intensely exemplified a quality of letting themselves be gotten and disposed of in the greatest lightness of dwelling, at one or another kind of garage sale. The core of the home, undeniably and ostensibly brought from the outside, from the other home, from Europe, secondhand, appeared as constantly on the way.

This was the state-of-the-art networking of the time. To be modern in the colony, to be really "in," meant to be in *dienst*, in "service," auction-light, serving the project of modernity, the country on the move, to be a part of a smallish but fast-marching group, indeed an avant-garde. Inevitably, the houses most intensely remembered as modern, with the most pronounced salon core interior, are remembered as "service houses."

> Mr. SUTIKNO: It would be impossible for us to have such a house as truly our own. Every few years my father was transferred to another post, and so we moved—but from a good house to a good house. We lived in this or in that house, sometimes smaller, more often bigger.
>
> RM: From furnishing to furnishing?
>
> Mr. SUTIKNO: No, no. We had our own furniture.
>
> RM: You moved your furniture every time? It was not easy?
>
> Mr. SUTIKNO: For us it was how things had to be. You see, when we came to visit some relatives in a village, they still lived in a house on piles, like that—(*I can hear Mr. Sutikno on the tape thumping his fist four times on the table.*)[143]

> Air Marshal DHANI: We lived in a service house, always in a service house. When we moved to Klaten, it was a service house. When we moved to the next station, again. So it used to be in the past, in Dutch times. Before each next move, in the best part of the house, home stuff was displayed. It was called *vendutjes*. Do you know what *vendutjes* were?
>
> RM: Yes, I know.
>
> Air Marshal DHANI: And everything was auctioned. Everything.[144]

My being in Indonesia and the old people talking to me about their childhood colonial homes peaked around 1997, at the moment when the military,

Chapter Two

brutally capitalist regime (one old man said "postmodern" with a sneer), after almost exactly thirty years in power, appeared to crumble. As the Jakarta Post wrote,

> Order is broken. Crowds stop cars on the streets and smash their windows. Yesterday (Saturday), Jakarta military commander Suparman and Governor of Jakarta Sutyoso called on the population not to leave their houses after 10 p.m. for the rest of the weekend. "This is not a curfew," Colonel Suparman explained.[145]

In the middle of an interview, in July 1997, the noise coming from Proclamation Street made me wonder whether the tape would catch anything of Mrs. Miriam's voice, or whether only the shouting, petards, and roaring of armored cars would be on the tape. On some occasions, during moments like that, the Japanese invasion of the colony half a century ago, in 1942, the crashing down of the Dutch colonial regime, was recalled.

> Mr. HARDOYO: Oh my! It was very ugly. First, there were muffled sounds, *Dun-dung-dung.* "What is it? What is it?" People came running out of their houses. "It is somewhere near the market!" Then I saw the Japanese soldiers. They wore their caps like that. (*Mr. Hardoyo shows with the palms of both of his hands to his ears, and straight ahead.*) They were short, ugly, strange. Then an Indonesian gave a speech, this is how I recall it: "These are our elder brothers, they came to help us to move Indonesia forward." "Elder brothers," this is what he said. This is how I remember it. I was still little: "Elder brothers, elder brothers."[146]

The year 1942, I was told in the year 1997, appeared like a doomsday to many. Yet this was a wind that was just growing into a storm. It was the same wind, that of modern times. The homes became even more homes, and shelters, to put it in one possible way, became even more shelters—as modern, as advanced as one was able to afford.

> Mr. DES ALWI: Oh, everybody built shelters as the war approached. We had a shelter under the bed. People were urged by the radio to build shelters. Some people did not, but very many did.
> RM: Inside the house?
> Mr. DES ALWI: In the garden, mostly in the garden. But some would make preparations to hide beneath their bed.[147]

The Walls

Fundamentally the same blowing of history, only more robust, shook the houses and made them resist or fall. The volume of the radio, one case of it, was suddenly and brutally turned up, but it was still—often more acutely than before—the old salon instrument playing.

> Mr. HARDJONEGORO: We did not suffer too much because *my grandfather was rich.*
> RM: You could still make and sell *batik?*
> Mr. HARDJONEGORO: There was less work because we ran out of material.
> RM: Cotton?
> Mr. HARDJONEGORO: And silk. And all the time there were the sirens, *alarms on radio.* We were made to feel that *we were at war.*[148]

People recall the three and a half years of the Japanese occupation as a time when their homes trembled but, at the same time, when more than ever in memory they were being pulled inside, close to the core. The war made it now truly a cockpit time:

> General KEMAL: I was in school in Bandung, but in 1941 they called me home. My father had just been transferred from Makassar to Kupang and from Kupang to Sukabumi. He was afraid, as the Japanese invaded, that we might lose contact. He called me home—that is, to Sukabumi.[149]
>
> Mrs. OEI: My father said: "Close the door, people say that the Japanese look for pretty girls. Come in and close the door!" We rarely went outside afterward. Whenever our father thought we might think about it, he told us this again.[150]

With much of the softness gone, the Indonesians were now being squeezed into a space of the before, the modern interior out of necessity, a space thus felt more deeply and fully (more crowded, too) than ever before.

> Mrs. SOELISTINA: We were all at home after the Japanese came.
> RM: At home?
> Mrs. SOELISTINA: This was the difference.[151]

Many homes, of course, were destroyed.

Chapter Two

RM: Did you keep some contact with Mrs. Resink after the Japanese came in 1942?

Prince PUGER: I heard—I do not know if it is true or not, I did not see it myself—that all the antiquities she had collected in her house were taken away by the Japanese soldiers. I heard that she cried and cried, even after some of the things were later returned. She remained dazed, so they said, and then because of the shock she became very ill, and she died. She is buried in Jetis Cemetery, west from the Tugu Crossing. I will show you her grave if you wish.[152]

The owners of the most exemplary salons of the late colonial era, the Dutch and other Europeans, fled the country or were locked into one of the Japanese internment camps. The pianos, heavy carved-wood furniture, gilt-framed paintings and mirrors, and radios had been left behind in houses vacated in haste. Or the salon stuff was even thrown onto the sidewalk, *displayed*, most easy to be looked at, even to be taken—cheaply or for free—to one's own house, when one happened to be an Indonesian with a house to fill, with one's own interior to build, to upgrade.

The salon, where it already existed or where it was merely being conceived and dreamed about, was being dismantled by the impact of the war and the occupation—recomposed into the most arresting fragments:

Dr. ONG: My mother was ever more often away from the house. She liked to gamble and she started to come home really late. Then also my father became *depressed*. These were the days when our town was invaded. They both, if they talked, talked about the war all the time. (*They might be like the German generation of roughly the same time: "We have sat, an easy generation; in houses held to be indestructible."*[153])

RM: Growing fears?

Dr. ONG: Growing fears, yes. The war was everywhere. You might be shot. There might be a gas attack. You might be evacuated, forced to run any moment. For the first time you realized that you could be separated from your sister, from your parents, from everybody. That you could be alone, tomorrow, on the street.

RM: It was like that you realize that there is a family, when it comes to a possibility that they may disappear.

Dr. ONG: *Yes! Yes!* And then, all the members become very close.

RM: What actually happened?

The Walls

Dr. ONG: We had to go. To Malang [in the interior of Java]. We had lived close to the harbor [in Semarang], and we thought it would be bombed.

RM: Did you run? Like these refugees in Bosnia?

Dr. ONG: Not exactly. We went before the first bomb fell.

RM: Inland.

Dr. ONG: To Malang. We had an aunt in Malang, on my father's side. So we went to her house. It was a big house.

RM: Is it still there?

Dr. ONG: The building is, but we do not own it anymore. It was completely changed, and it is a hotel now. It was a very beautiful house.[154]

This was not Paris and that kind of revolution—furniture thrown from the windows as missiles and used to build the barricades.[155] The colonial salons in ruins and fragments, deserted by their former owners, even displayed on the sidewalks, were perfect *vendutjes*, auctions, in fact. Frequently the interior, disassembled, was loaded on a truck or a horse cart and driven through the city streets and village roads. Even more impressively, truly on the move, the salons were now exposed to the agitated nation.

Father MANGUNWIJAYA: All the furniture of the house, the chairs, the wardrobes, everything, had been put on one big truck. I still remember the truck that took all the furniture, piece by piece. Whenever I recall the truck, it is loaded high with the wardrobes and the chairs upon it. The sensation still comes back easily—everything is being carried out of the house, loaded on the truck, and taken away. Where? Very *interesting*.[156]

The most exemplary interiors were broken down, turned inside out, and moved, but also index-legitimized in the new order of the world.

June 12, 1942: Tomorrow, Saturday, all the radios from the Dutch homes have to be handed over at the city hall. There, the receivers will be disabled. [Short waves on which Allied broadcasts might be received were to be disabled.]

January 10, 1943: All servants in the Dutch houses, in two days, must be released from service.

January 11, 1943: Servants must leave the Dutch homes.

> *November 1, 1943* All gramophone recordings in the Dutch houses should be handed in.[157]

The most close-to-perfect modern interiors in the colony were shattered, and thus essentialized. Nothing of the Dutch-era everyday and of the peaceful progress of the salon could ever achieve this deed—bourgeois hominess became epic. A Dutch woman writer, who had lived in the colony for decades before the invasion, wrote in her war diary in the beginning:

> We sat on a railway platform with our children, our luggage, and a few servants who were allowed to help us, carry our luggage thus far. Still at this moment we could not imagine ourselves without servants. . . . Twenty kilos per person was permitted, with a warning that we might have to carry the luggage, except the mattresses, ourselves.[158]
>
> Women talked about what they had to leave behind—not so much about the houses and gardens, books and photo albums, as about the silver, the crystal glass, or the damask tablecloth. The years of our internment will be filled with mourning over those riches.[159]

And at the end:

> *Camp Makassar, 16 May 1945*: Japanese are in a rage over the mountains of goods—embroidered cloth, damask, and so on, that women still manage to carry from camp to camp. . . . "Twenty kilos and nothing more!" roar guards. . . . All the newly arrived women are herded into barracks and their trunks are left in the open, in the center of the camp, guarded by the *heiho* [militia]. One trunk overflows with soft pillow covers, which some woman evidently carried with her throughout. I can hear several of the women loudly crying.[160]

Robustly, violently, and with an accelerating speed, at least where houses and walls were concerned, things were becoming more of the same. After three and a half years of occupation came the Japanese surrender to the Allies. The Netherlands, one of the victorious powers, began feverish efforts to restore the peace, which in Indonesia meant to restore the Dutch prewar colonial state of affairs. Increasing numbers of Indonesians, emboldened by war, resisted. Four years of violent anticolonial struggle followed, after which a compromise (under pressure from the Allies), in 1949, was

The Walls

reached—independent postcolonial Indonesia was internationally recognized.

> Princess NOEROEL: What did I do in the time of the guerillas?
> RM: Yes.
> Princess NOEROEL: I cooked, I was asked to cook for the guerillas. A little later, the Dutch conquered the town and entered the palace. We were very afraid. Later, the communists tried to take over—

There was a power struggle among the anticolonial Indonesians themselves. In 1948, in the middle of the national revolution, it came to a bloody conflict between the left and the right about the social character of the Indonesian future. The left, for many years and until this day, in fact, was crushed.

> Princess NOEROEL: We had to leave home for a while and hide in Tawangmanggu, in the hills.
> RM: Yes, I know the place.
> Princess NOEROE: For almost a month we stayed in Tawangmanggu. When it was safe, we went back home. So it was, Professor.[161]

> Mrs. SOELISTINA: On August 17, 1945, there came the Proclamation of Independence. People hoisted red-and-white flags and I thought: "What is it? Oh, it is the Proclamation. We are free!" Tomo— (*This is Bung Tomo, who later became Mrs. Soetomo's husband. In August 1945, he was the most recognizable voice of the Indonesian revolution on the radio.*) Tomo went to speak on the radio. And everybody listened. From that moment the spirit of nationalism touched my heart. Until this, I was like a child, *innocent girl*, as far as anything like that was concerned.[162]

> Mrs. OEI: When the revolution came, I was still in Jakarta, and we had a difficult time. Our house in Salatiga [Central Java] was looted. My father with two of his siblings, a sister and a brother, took the train to Solo to catch up with my in-laws. But he could not make it in time. He was already old.
> RM: The house was destroyed?
> Mrs. OEI: The house was not destroyed. But nothing remained in it. It was empty. Cleared out. I thought, is this the way we will live now? This was how it was, just after the Japanese left: "Is this how Indonesia is

Chapter Two

beginning?" People who knew us well did it. They forced us out of our home. "What now?"[163]

There were not many grand pianos "in circulation" at this time. But there were some — and the rarer, the more visible they were. And there were other salon things, everywhere, at the core of the houses under siege, some taken away, and some gotten back. Like radios, for instance:

> Mrs. SOELISTINA: I began to listen to the news all the time. Before, I think, I never heard news on radio. Now, I listened about the negotiations and the fighting as it was reported. Radio became so important during the revolution! If there had been no radios, we would have been crushed by the Dutch. The struggle would be of this or that province by itself, this or that island by itself. It used to be like that because there were no radios. After we got radios, we could hear everything and we could move together. Radios were important also for getting foreign help. Australia helped us. America helped us—[164]
>
> Dr. ONG: I remember, the first news I heard about the independence was when I was sick. I was often sick as a child. This time I was sick, I had a fever, and I had to take pills with sugar. And I heard: "Free Indonesia!" and "The Japanese capitulated!"
>
> RM: It was in August [1945].
>
> Dr. ONG: Yes. "What do they mean, 'freedom, freedom'?" Oddly, as I heard about the freedom, the first thing, I had an image that we would live in our servants' quarters and that servants would move to the front, into the main building. This was my fantasy about freedom. Also, an incident happened during the revolution. In our house, radio was very much at the center, at that time.
>
> RM: During the revolution?
>
> Dr. ONG: Radio had been our only communication with the outside world; and then the guerilla headquarters were asking about radios. They wanted the radio. They said that they needed the radio and they came for it. We tried to keep the radio; we refused to give it up. It was a very beautiful, very good radio, *Philips*, I think, *Faust Super*, yes. It was one good thing that had remained in our house after the war. They came, up as far as our front porch, and one of them was shouting into the house. And then he shot his gun into the air.

RM: To scare you.

Dr. ONG: I don't know, but it was a frightening moment. One of the youth shot his gun into the air. It was the worst thing I have ever experienced in my life, I think.

RM: Did you lose the radio?

Dr. ONG: No.

RM: No?

Dr. ONG: No, we didn't lose the radio. We refused to give it up.[165]

"HERE A CEDAR STYLOBATE..."

The home of the past and of childhood, naturally, was also a place of petty loves and petty animosities, all the petty everyday, and the echoes of it could still be heard:

Princess NOEROEL: It is to me sometimes still hard to believe. As I look back it does not make any sense. All the experience — it is perhaps better not to talk about it. There was pettiness, Professor, much pettiness, and much of the time — perhaps because there were so many men and women living together.[166]

Obviously, however, most of the houses of the old people I visited were getting quieter and emptier with each passing year. Clinging to the frame of their age,[167] these people felt lonely. Many of the friends and family they recalled were either dead or, the younger ones, the children and grandchildren, had gone various ways — further on, and away.

RM: Is the little one like his grandfather?

General KEMAL: He calls me now and then.[168]

It is death, increasingly and often solely, that might still be both recalled and trusted to stick around.

Air Marshal DHANI: *My grandmother from the mother side*, she is also already dead, of course. She loved my mother very much. My mother, when she had a baby, my sister, perhaps because there was such a lack of nutrition and vitamins at the time, became sick and she also died.[169]

Mrs. OEI: I married in 1945. My mother was sick in her lungs.

RM: She died of it?

Mrs. OEI: Then our house burned down. It is already fifty years, so—[170]

As death approaches, the world, now made largely of memories, tends to become sublime, and also the house, walls, guest rooms, bathrooms, the interior of the house, of the memory, becomes "classical"—a "house as the place where death could be sovereign, a place where each human being could die [his or] her death."[171] The house, thus, becomes the ultimate test for those who fought during their lives, as well as for those who mostly feared: "Without such a place where one might face the ultimate questions, there could be no freedom, no autonomy, no responsibility and, therefore, no citizenship."[172]

✦✦✦

In search of modern dwelling some try to break walls down and tear the interior open. In 1830, in Paris, the revolutionaries "piled up various objects: furniture from neighboring houses, crates from the grocer's, and, if need be, a passing omnibus, which they would stop, gallantly helping the ladies to disembark."[173] Others, in the same search for dwelling-as-freedom in the modern world, kept at least thinking about it, or dreaming. Thus, for instance, Honoré de Balzac's house at Les Jardines "was one of the romances on which M. de Balzac worked hardest during his life, but he was never able to finish it. . . . On these patient walls, . . . there were charcoal inscriptions to this effect: 'Here a facing in Parisian marble,' 'Here a cedar stylobate,' 'Here a ceiling painted by Eugène Delacroix,' 'Here a fireplace in cipolin marble.'"[174]

On occasion, in Jakarta, and this is what inspired the present chapter, I was let into houses like Balzac's and, at the same time, almost like that the Parisians of 1830 might think about—in the particular context of the place this book is about, houses modern and yet not colonized. In Mrs. Trimurti's house, for instance, I felt (almost) like that.

Mrs. Trimurti was eighty-four when I met her for the first time. She had been an incorrigible rebel all her life, and I could easily imagine her gallantly helping the Parisian ladies to disembark from their omnibus and then helping the men to turn the vehicle over and onto the barricade. She is one of the two women in a historic photograph, next to Sukarno on August 17,

1945, proclaiming the independence of Indonesia. And, I felt it radiant in her house.

> *Mrs. Trimurti lives in a neighborhood of* Kramat Lontar, *about a hundred meters off Jakarta's eight-lane Salemba Road. This has been her house since 1949, when she moved back from the interior of Java, after the Republican government was recognized and also returned to the capital. When I mentioned some residences where her former comrades lived now, she smiled and said: "But I have an* AC *[air conditioning], too," pointing to an open window, "an* AC *from God." She had also been a journalist, she told me, and did many interviews like this. She went to get her notes, and she gave herself quite some time to do it. This turned out to be the most difficult interview as far back as I could remember. Each question had to be answered "as it was asked"; she rarely slipped "away," into a story. The talking dragged stumblingly on, until I, and she as well, it seemed, got rather sleepy in the heat of the day, close to noon. Like in my mother's room, I thought, during my latest visit to Prague two weeks earlier.*[175]

The day after the interview, I was almost arrested because of Mrs. Trimurti. She invited me at one moment as we talked to "a little chat with friends" that she planned to attend that evening in a hotel nearby: "To talk about the future." For some reason, I did not make it, and the next morning I watched on television that there were people "plotting a coup" in the same hotel. The police interrogated "the usual suspects," as it turned out, General Kemal, one of Sukarno's daughters, and three or four others, including Mrs. Trimurti.

> *The window in the guest room opens into a tiny garden in the front of the house and into a very quiet lane behind it. Inside, the wall to the right of the window and the wall opposite the window are covered with photographs of family, of Sukarno, and with diplomas. The remaining wall is made by a huge, ancient wardrobe that separates the room from the now invisible space behind—her bedroom, she says. She lets me deeper into the house, to a very small kitchen, in part already in the open, under a zinc roof in the back yard. There is a well, which takes a larger part of the tiny yard. On the way back, Mrs. Trimurti shows me the room in the front, behind the wardrobe. There is a bed, and a telephone at the small bookshelf at the bed's head. Next to the telephone, above the bed on the wall made of the wardrobe, there is pinned a long list of telephone numbers in several columns and in very small handwriting. It occurred to me that it might*

be the first time in this country that I was being shown a host's bedroom. Then we go back to the guest room and she shows me some exercise she does: deep breath, head down, almost between her knees. Her head almost touches the couch we are sitting on.[176]

Is she happy?

> Mrs. TRIMURTI: Sort of. I think I have possession of myself — my eyes, my tongue, my two ears, one, two; my mouth. (*She laughs.*)
> RM: You possess an *AC*, sort of.
> Mrs. TRIMURTI: *AC* from the Lord. I can also stretch out, like this (*she shows*) — and pump my blood through my body, as much as I want to. Oxygen flows in. I do not need to buy it.
> RM: Besides your exercise, what about politics?
> Mrs. TRIMURTI: We are free. And we are free to do with it what we want. So far.

This seemed to be a house that opened to the world and not because it had been broken into.

> RM: So you are happy?
> Mrs. TRIMURTI: Sort of.
> RM: If you were to live again?
> Mrs. TRIMURTI: Again?[177]

FENCE OF THE HOUSE OF THE DUTCH *ASSISTENT RESIDENT* IN YOGYAKARTA OPENING TO THE STREET. 1936. KONINKLIJK INSTITUUT VOOR TAAL-, LAND- EN VOLKENKUNDE, LEIDEN

CHAPTER THREE

THE FENCES

Sleep in gentle ease,
little eyes shut please,
hear the raindrops in the dark,
hear the neighbor's doggy bark.
Doggy bit the beggar-man,
tore his coat, away he ran,
to the gate the beggar flees,
sleep in gentle ease.
—Lullaby of Wilhelm Taubert

CRIES OF HAWKERS

Most of the memories and (I guess) dreaming that I have recorded in Indonesia, and especially in Jakarta, happened in places where the noise of traffic deafened much of what was said, remembered, or dreamed. I have witnessed and was part of it as the voices struggled to be heard in that modern space. Inevitably, at least in part, the voices sounded as if aiming for a shelter, to be closer to the house, or inside the house, where it might be easier, perhaps, for them to be understood even without shouting.

Most of the talking thus, or so it seemed, happened in a space in between, where both the noise of the outside and the real or imagined quiet of the inside coexisted to some degree. And there were voices, too, heard from the outside—to complicate the world of the talking and the memories, to blur the line, to make the inside, at least in part, open, and the outside, at least in part, intimate. Most memorable (and much of it again is on my tapes) were the singsongs of street vendors, the cries of hawkers, as they resounded in, out, along, and over a house, as they touted their wares on the streets, through the fences, and into the houses.

> Mrs. SOSRO: I used to sell herb drinks. Prohibited herb drinks. It is why they still call me *Siti Laramng* [Lady Prohibited]. People still remember that I used to sell herb drinks on the street—"Herb Drinks from Lady Prohibited." To attract attention, I shouted and used chimes.[1]

Sitting on a front porch or inside a house—the deeper in the house it was, the fainter it sounded—after some time and training, even I was able to tell which sweets or fruits, what prohibited or legal substance, was passing by and might be ordered in. By the pitch and intonation of a voice, the color and rhythm of chimes, bells, a coconut shell, or of two little sticks of wood beaten against each other, different woods for different goods, by a mood of singsonging, croaking, or rapping, I came to know what smell and what taste would follow.

"This speech comes in response to a waiting rather than to a question."[2] It was all passing by and could be called in—not merely fried bananas, coconuts, noodle soup but also books, textiles, furniture—even baby grands, why not—might be coming the dweller's way and by this way of dwelling. When Roman Jakobson looked back on his life as a linguist and social critic (possibly recalling his Saint Petersburg childhood, too) he noted in his diary with evident regret: "Several works remained unfinished—on rhyme, on the cries of street hawkers (*The greengrocer's come, the greengrocer's driven up, peas, carrots, cucumbers he's grubbed up*)."[3]

As old Indonesians recalled their childhood, they often emphasized that "the front gate was open most of the time." One was expected merely to shout across the fence, for instance, *sepada!*, which in Jakarta language means, "who is there?"[4] Gates and fences between a house and the street are also remembered as being easily penetrated by cries and noise, of course, but also by music: troupes of street musicians, playing and singing Malay-Indonesian-Portuguese-Dutch *krontjong* melodies; peddlers of music were passing by.

> [They] wandered through the streets at night, signing serenades. *Kron[tj]ong* competitions were held in parks and public places. . . . The [songs] circulated among the public because the gramophone was becoming widespread at this time.[5]

Chapter Three

The interior of the house in the colony, including the most salon-like, resonated by, and can properly be recalled through and measured by, the sounds of the street. Modernity, throughout the colony and into the houses (thus it was conveyed to me), had been peddled.

> Mrs. DAMAIS: Bread was not a common thing in those years. But to our house, a baker from the city would bring *bread*. He came in a car, *once a week*.
> RM: So *once a week* you had *bread*?
> Mrs. DAMAIS: Yes. It was bread from the city. But it was not for everyone yet. Bread was something, how to put it, *exclusive*.[6]
>
> Air Marshal DHANI: Until now, I still love bread. Perhaps, because in Klaten, it was a small town at the time, but there was already a bakery there. A Dutchman owned it, and, every other afternoon, they came on a bicycle from the bakery. We gave them a list. "What kind of bread do you want?" It was a *door to door*.[7]

This was a colonial modernity, and many kinds of "door-to-door" cries are remembered. Shouting *pinda, pinda*, "peanuts, peanuts," is rarely forgotten. It sounded, and smelled, of warm pleasure to everyone, especially to the children, of course—house-wise, street-wise, colony-wise, and empire-wise. It became an often repeated historical fact, too—some Dutch and Europeans, mostly children again, would cry *pinda pinda*, "you peanut hawker!" as a slur against native kids when they encountered them on the street.[8] The same cry, the same touting, welcomed those Indonesians who got as far as the real metropolis, to the Netherlands, to study, for instance.[9]

As late as during the Japanese occupation, when colonialism appeared to have been crushed once for all, some Dutch women, men, and children, dwelling now in the Japanese internment camps, are remembered to have held tightly to the cry: "This was an unreal feeling . . . a sort of slowing down of our hearts and the capacity to understand, an impotence to realize what one's situation was . . . to look even at the Japanese as innocent. 'They are just another kind of peanut hawkers,' somebody said."[10]

The gates, and fences between houses and between a house and the street, are most convincingly recalled indeed as a passage—as a space filled with

The Fences

the vibrations of sound, light, or dwellers moving through, reflections (as these are memories) coming alive by indistinctly belonging neither here nor there. In a passage, through the fences and the gates, the life of the period seems even to be most productively put into play.

> RM: The neighbors just came in?
> Mr. EFENDI: Just came in.
> RM: There was no fence?
> Mr. EFENDI: There was a fence, very low.[11]

> Mr. DAPIN: Of course there was a fence.
> RM: What for—for the people not to enter, or to keep animals away?
> Mr. DAPIN: Large animals would not come in. And people could step over. It was to make things clear. One could also enter the house though the front gate. That was also nice. One might have, of course, locked the gate. But why lock it, when people could step over? It was like *attributes*. All of this were *attributes*.
> RM: *Attributes*?
> Mr. DAPIN: Yes, it was modern, and it was to make it clear: here was the street; or, over there, there was someone else's house. There was a fence, so that not just any person would come in. Our fence was about half a meter high. And toward the street we put on some stones. They were so arranged, very pretty. So, by that time, and in our provincial town, we were the middle class.[12]

Stealing fruit from a neighbor's garden appears essential to childhood, and it was recalled for me often by the most respectable people: running with the spoil through the shrubs standing in for fences, jumping over them, back home, away from the neighbor's place—like the wind.[13]

> Professor SOEMARDJAN: Sometimes we played ball. But we didn't have money to buy a real ball, so we stole a *djeruk* [citrus fruit] from the neighbor's and we used it as a ball. At night, we children, boys and girls, got together and we played games and sang, until we felt like going to sleep.[14]

Professor Soemardjan shows it to me on a sketch. We sit on the front porch of his small Jakarta house. As he speaks about shrubs, he points to where

Chapter Three

there are indeed some low bushes—by a very high wall separating his and his neighbor's driveways. (It is how it must be to him now: "The old men they've buried upright in the wall covered with gillyflowers.... The fences are so high that you can only see the treetops moving in the wind. Anyway, there's nothing to see there."[15])

> Professor SOEMARDJAN: We had some trees and shrubs all around, here and here. (*He is showing me on the sketch again.*) Here was somebody else's house. But it did not mean that you could not run in here—for the *djeruk*, and that you could not get through here.[16]

When I asked the old people where the house of their childhood had stood, often they answered, "on a street like this," or "precisely like this." Often, a few steps from the skyscrapers, bypasses, and flyovers of Jakarta, I had a feeling—surreal rather than nostalgic—of being in a place "precisely like this."

> *Kebon Kacang [Nuts Garden] is a neighborhood a few hundred steps from Hotel Indonesia and the high-rise heart of Jakarta. It is Thursday, and screams of goats being butchered for the evening meal are heard everywhere. A man in white, with a towel over his shoulder, steps out of a house, looks around, and then slowly walks, probably to a mosque or a neighbor's house for a chat. The parties' billboards are displayed as this is also a time before the elections.*[17]

Especially during my early visits to Jakarta, in the early 1980s, I would be woken up, several times a night, by monotonous booming sounds, at first from a distance, then getting closer and louder, almost deafening for a while before leaving again. Like the gates and fences, the sounds were there to stake out the space. It was a neighborhood watch, *ronda*, making "rounds"— "precisely like when we were little," the old people might say. Almost precisely. These were the neighbors beating drums, sounding the edges of the familiar, like the children did and do "running around and making a lot of noise";[18] or like the hawkers. Only, since the mid-1960s this making rounds and noise was done—mainly—to scare away the communists "lurking in the dark," or so President General Suharto directed. In fact, of course, virtually all the communists had been killed in massacres by that time.

Especially at the moments at night when the *ronda* did not let me sleep,

The Fences

but also in the mornings, as the songs of the caged birds, the children, and the hawkers woke me up again and again, in postcolonial Jakarta, I, too, felt "precisely like," or "almost precisely like," as if I was back in the Prague of my childhood:

> Houses almost exactly alike . . . most of the windows were occupied, men in shirt-sleeves were leaning there smoking or holding small children cautiously and tenderly on the window ledges. Other windows were piled high with bedding, above which the disheveled head of a woman would appear for a moment. People were shouting to one another across the street; one shout just above K's head caused great laughter. . . . A phonograph, which had seen long service in a better quarter of the town, began stridently to murder a tune.[19]

An Indonesian house might be standing on a city street for a generation or more, and yet it might still be inhabited as if lightly on the spot, a little distant to it and a little near.

> RM: Rice field, you said?
> Mr. SARLI: Yes, we had a rice field.
> RM: But you lived in the city?
> Mr. SARLI: We did. But there were people working in the field. There was still also our old family house. The field brought us some money, and we used it to buy kerosene and things like that.[20]
>
> Mrs. MIRIAM: We had a rice field, too.
> RM: You lived in Jakarta and had the village connection?
> Mrs. MIRIAM: Oh yes.[21]

This is often told, like a homily: the father, deep in modern life and thus with only the modest salary of a colonial servant, official, or teacher, yet the mother — it was most often mother — "remained" as an important, basic source of the urban family livelihood. She, in many cases, kept a rice field in a village that the family might or might not still remember as the place they "came from."[22] The urban dwelling and urban time are often remembered as "waiting for the harvest season. Then the house got stocked up, and it also became really lively."[23]

Chapter Three

It became quite common for the houses of the Indonesians in cities, towns, and large villages, and it was almost inevitable in Chinese Indonesians' houses, to have a shop on the ground floor. Sometimes this was a more formal kind of shop, sometimes less so—but always, like a gate or fence, it worked as a space in between. The flow of people, customers, hawkers, servants, guests, and inhabitants is recalled as passing through, again making for the intimacy of the house.

> Mrs. OEI: Our house had a shop in front. We sold groceries and tea.
> RM: Was there an upper story in the house?
> Mrs. OEI: No, only one story, with a porch in front. We turned the porch into the shop. My parents had a room for themselves inside the house, and in front there was the shop. Next to it, there was another room where my grandma lived, and yet another one for us, the children.[24]
>
> RM: You spent much time at home?
> Mr. OEY: Yes. I had to help my mother take care of the shop.[25]
>
> Mr. USMAN: We were poor, Mr. Rudolf. All the time we got, we had to help with the selling, from our house. Mother cooked, and we were selling it around the town.[26]

Especially the Chinese Indonesians' houses are recalled as indicating the modern times—how lightly the dwellings stood on the modern colony ground, and how easily everything, the passersby, the cries of the hawkers, and the winds of the time, were allowed to pass through them. I saw the lightness still, in its postcolonial version, in 1997, during one of the bad and recurring anti-Chinese pogroms. As the mob of the other Indonesians (with the army-supplied provocateurs mixed in) raged through the Jakarta streets, the city's Chinese Indonesians boarded up in haste their shops on the ground floors and front porches of their houses. The people took flight or moved upstairs. And there was that lightness in the notices they put on their boarded shops on the street level, such as "CLOSED JUST FOR TODAY."

Shops in the front of houses, like the memories of the rice fields "back in the village," even if never really seen, and like the cries of hawkers, are recalled to draw the line between the house and the street, to make the neighborhood and the city passable, or at least to quiver, to get blurred, or, best of all, to be lively as an echo or as in a moment of waiting.

The Fences

RM: In your case there was no shop.

Dr. ONG: There was. On the front porch—next, still closer to the street, there were some trees, and yet another row of some plants in flowerpots.[27]

RM: You sold furniture in your shop?

Mrs. OEI: Not furniture. Boards and planks, wood. There was a sawyer and some other workers. My brothers helped in the shop, and we women did the cooking.[28]

Mr. GESANG: We had a stall at the sidewalk in front of our house; like that one over there.

RM: Your mother worked there?

Mr. GESANG: Oh, we all did.[29]

RM: Was there a sign on your shop—like "MR. MINGGU: TAILOR"?

Mr. MINGGU Sr.: No. There was just me, a tailor in the house. They all could see me.

RM: So the people knew.

Mr. MINGGU Jr.: He was famous.

Mr. MINGGU Sr.: If they had no money, they brought coconuts—ten coconuts sometimes.[30]

There can still be seen in Jakarta today, in some streets and sometimes just off the main roads, tailors (or sometimes dentists or scribes) sitting at the sidewalk on a chair or crouching on the ground, with a sewing machine, for instance, working and talking to the passersby. Very much of the street, they exude a velvet intimacy in the public space (let me recall in this place my mother sitting in our kitchen, darning the heaps of my father's, my brother's, my, and her socks and underwear).

It often seems that only across the low fences and through the intermediary space between the inside of the house and the outside of the street, the smells, touches, and tastes of home might satisfactorily be recalled.

Mrs. OEI: In front, in the shop, for some time, we sold leather and hide, buffalo hide. It first had to be scratched on the inside, then soaked in some solution. We also cut the hide in small pieces and made chips of it. I recall this, cutting the hide and making chips of it. Most of the time, my mother did it and we children helped. We had to help to make

Chapter Three

the chips. The smell of the hide filled everything, especially as it dried in the sun. To this day I cannot eat chips. But the same thing, you see, makes me most often recall my mother.[31]

Often by ancient means, yet progressively without a doubt, softly, often sensually, through sounds, smells, and touch, the modern house, as the colony into which it opened, became ever more an itinerants' place. Doctors are recalled as retailing from house to house.

Mr. EFENDI: My father was a doctor, and we had an office and pharmacy in our house. He examined a visitor in his office in the front part of the house, and then mother wrote a prescription. During the vacations, I also worked in the pharmacy.[32]

Mrs. MIRIAM: Father was constantly on the move, from house to house. Doctor calls, they called it. He was always on the move.[33]

A neighborhood made modern sense, was convincingly and correctly memorable, as a space of peddling.

Mr. OEY: I was born into a *petit bourgeois* family. My father died when I was nine, and I lived only with my mother. She opened a small shop and sold rice, charcoal, and kerosene. It was a small shop. She was a peddler.
RM: What did you do?
Mr. OEY: What I liked best were my trips to my uncle. He lived rather far away from us. Once a week, about, I went there on bicycle.
RM: Not for pleasure?
Mr. OEY: Oh no, it was my work! It was forty kilometers away. I went for material, to make clothes. Textiles were very expensive. And then, my mother sold the fabric in town.[34]

As in so many other matters of dwelling and modernity, the coming of the Japanese in 1942 and the thrashing of Dutch normalcy did not stop, or even slow down, the process. On the contrary, under the impact of the invasion, war, and the almost four years of occupation that followed, the modern (or aspiring-to-be-modern) houses and homes in the colony became almost fully, and in many cases fully indeed, peddlerlike and itinerant—

or "nomadic," as Le Corbusier might say about the inhabitants of his high modern and avant-garde creations.

> RM: Was there poverty in all families during the Japanese occupation?
>
> Mrs. RAHMIATI: I would rather say that everybody had to sell things. At the end of the occupation, everybody was selling all kinds of stuff, all around: some began to make charcoal at home and sell it throughout the city. Others mixed and cooked all kinds of oils and tried to sell this, too; not on the *level* of professional merchants, of course, but everybody did it. The salaried people, even those who still worked in an office and so on, had to *switch*, and to make efforts to survive, to do this.[35]

✦✦✦

Buying, selling, peddling — and the smell, touch, and sound of it — seem a crucial part of how the fences were kept low and how the homes opened. Intimacy had been turned inside out. The centuries-old art and culture of batik, the painting, waxing, selling, storing, and wearing of the cloth — the thing most intimately connected with the land, pliable, fragrant, touching, sensual — became a storming modernity carried on a wave of avant-garde, breaking into all places, across the colony.

> NATIONAL MUSEUM IN JAKARTA: *At the entrance to the main hall, there stands an iron tricycle: "Dutch, 19th century, unbroken." Next to it, in a big glass case, there is an enlarged 1902 photograph of a young woman clothed in Javanese batik, painting another piece of batik. Next to the photograph is another piece of cloth like that in the photograph: "Daughter of Regent, Kartini, batiking, and a piece of batik hand-painted by this fighter for the emancipation of the Indonesian women. The width of the cloth: 106 cm, length 260 cm. On loan to the National Museum from Dr. Rahman Santoso, Mrs. Rukmini's [Kartini's sister] grandson, at Hang Lekir Street I/4, Kebayoran Baru, Jakarta 12120, tel. 710428.*[36]

Whenever batik was mentioned to me, a rich connection emerged between home, childhood, and the innermost core of it. At the same time, the street, the market, and all that of the outside came close to home as batik began to be talked about, until both the inside and the outside, by the force of batik, became virtually one thing:

RM: What did you do when you were home?

Mrs. TRIMURTI: I batiked.

RM: Batiked?

Mrs. TRIMURTI: All girls had to batik. The idea was that, in the ideal case, every piece of cloth you wore would be batiked by yourself. Thus to batik was a duty. When I was not batiking, I was helping in the kitchen; or I went to the market with our servants to do the shopping. Since we were very little, we were taught to do this.

RM: Were you close to your parents?

Mrs. TRIMURTI: I was closer to my mother than to my father. Because, for example, when we batiked, we were together. Speaking to my father I had to use respectful language, to speak up, and to behave that way.[37]

Batik was painted with wax inside the house or in the shade of the house. The cloth was then washed and boiled in color in the yard, and finally dried in the sun. It is recalled as a sound of paddling, water splashing, workers singing, and as the smell of wax that penetrated throughout the house and reached beyond onto the street and in the neighborhood — so widely and intensely as did the housework. Through batik home is often recalled both intimately and as a shop, as a "workplace" or often as a "factory."[38]

Of all the things of home, stamping the batik with wax (more expensive cloth was hand-painted, less expensive batik design was made by big stamps dipped in wax) was recalled most often—

> wax stamping the cloth before it was soaked in colors. This was the part of the work that I liked most — perhaps because it required a sense for art, but especially for the rhythmic sound of the stamping. It was like music. Our hands as we stamped were like parts of a machine. I stamped and I hummed to it.[39]

Mr. GESANG: I helped my parents to make batik until my adult years. I went around to buy fabric for the batiking.

RM: All the batiking was done at home?

Mr. GESANG: Oh sure, at home.

RM: How many people have worked there? Your father, your mother?

Mr. GESANG: Father, mother, my sisters and brothers, other workers; about fifteen people.

RM: It was all at home?

The Fences

Mr. GESANG: Yes, at home, from *morning* to night.

RM: So there were many people around all the time?

Mr. GESANG: Many—adults and children; many children.[40]

There is one of the strongest, most agile, and most sensual ways of intimacy recalled with batik—one's eyes, ears, hands, nose; the whole body was involved. At the same time, and it seems to be at the root of the matter, the intimacy flowed through the house and beyond—it was a streamline intimacy.

RM: It looks like only women lived in your house?

Mrs. MASKUN: Yes, and we batiked all the time. A younger sister of my mother became a widow very early on, and she moved in with us. She took care of us because she did not have children, and she batiked day and night, she *batiiiiiked* all the time.

RM: To make money?

Mrs. MASKUN: Yes, for food. We batiked to sell. When a piece of batik was considered delicate, it might sell for ten rupiahs. In the past, ten rupiahs, it was a jackpot![41]

Batik is often remembered as the sublime of the house. It is still frequently a part of a family heirloom, and it is kept in a closet, in the innermost part of house. It can be remembered, at the same time, by the same people, and at the same depth, as the fastest and most widely ranging commodity; hawkers peddled batik from the street, across the fence, into the homes.

Mr. Hardjonegoro lives on Jalan Kratonan, Court Street, near the Susuhunan's, the local prince's, palace. His family is highly respected, as he shows me in a book, "Prominent Indonesian Chinese."[42] *Sukarno's second wife, Inggit, also came from a good batik family, he tells me, and this is why, even when president, Sukarno liked batik so much. He had often asked him to make batik especially for him. He came to this place; often before sunrise to see it all. Mr. Hardjonegoro takes me around. The house had been built around 1900: plaited bamboo, rather curtains than walls divide the space inside. At one side, there are two monumental carved wardrobes; from the eighteenth century, he says. Plaited bamboo also separates the house from the backyard, in the middle of which there is a large barnlike building also of wood and bamboo; about twenty-five meters long and ten meters wide. As we enter it, about two dozen women and girls sit there on the floor in three rows, singing, laughing, and batiking. The fourfold smell of wood, wax, sun, and work is all around. As we head back to the house, on the left there is a much smaller building; just for him, he says. There, he shows me truly an elegant dagger, a* kris, *which he is now working on.* "For the descendants," *he says.*[43]

✦ ✦ ✦

In the new times as in the old, neighborhoods were made by sounds, cries, and songs as they penetrated the house. A rift between the old and the new, especially the one carried by a sound or a song, could sometimes be striking, and other times almost imperceptible.

> Mrs. MIRIAM: We came back from Holland [Mrs. Miriam's father got one of the few scholarships for Javanese medical students in the 1930s] just when my grandmother died, and we went to attend those *ceremonies*. I did not know what *ritual* we participated in, it sounded to a child merely like *allla ullah mullalah*—(*Mrs. Miriam sings a melody but does not make the words.*) It was so very impressive to me because of course at home I had never heard anything like that.[44]
>
> RM: So, you had piano lessons?
> Professor RESINK: I had lessons in [Javanese] *gamelan*, too. And it was a disaster! It had been too difficult for me to learn these two kinds of music at the same time. But the thing was that I got accustomed to hearing gamelan from afar, from the Javanese quarter of the town. And this is still in me, that indistinct music from afar. (*A clock somewhere deep in Professor Resink's house sounds the hour.*) This was my musical education.[45]

Like batik, *kris* daggers, or gamelan, *wajang*—the shadow puppet theater—not merely survived in the modern times and in the memories but it carried the modern times, fast, forward, and through, like the peddlers' cries.

> RM: Where did you learn to be a puppeteer?
> Mr. NARYO: I watched it and I mimicked it: there is a battle, and here is a warrior, and here, you see, is his jaw, moving, like this—it means that

The Fences

he is a nobleman, he raises his hand, like this; then battle is over and he changes—like this.

Jan, my son, introduced me to Mr. Naryo. Jan had taken lessons with Mr. Naryo for the few preceding months, and Mr. Naryo had served as a proxy father in my absence, a year before, at Jan's wedding.

> JAN: Everybody knew that you would become a puppeteer? Since you were a child? You inherited it?
> Mr. NARYO: I was taught. I was ordered to watch. My father sometimes played in our house—for me to watch.
> RM: When you played with other children, you knew?
> Mr. NARYO: Children knew it. I cut puppets from paper, a whole box of puppets. Every day I played and children watched.
> RM: Did you have a screen?
> Mr. NARYO: Just a little screen. For the paper puppets.
> RM: You did not use music?
> Mr. NARYO: Mouth music. But when I was ten or thirteen, I helped by moving boxes and handing puppets to the puppeteer as he played. Then I played myself. We traveled around in a horse carriage.

We did not think, alas, to ask Mr. Naryo how he touted his wares.

> JAN: How much money did you make?
> Mr. NARYO: A puppeteer used to make sixteen rupiahs, which is as much rice as one got in one harvest from two *patoks* of a rice field. A *patok* is about one-fifth of a hectare. It means two-fifths of a hectare for playing one night.

Shadow-puppet theater was performed on the occasion of a home or neighborhood celebration. The puppeteer, who made the puppets move, and speak, and also conducted the music, who brought the homes and neighborhoods together this way, had the respect—and still has—of a priest.

> Mr. NARYO: People used to come to me for various reasons, like when they were not happy with their naughty children, for instance. Sometimes they might come and ask for help in other matters, and the

Chapter Three

puppeteer made a suggestion. When someone in a family had been ill often, they came to a puppeteer and he might help them out. Yes, when I was thirteen, I was already a puppeteer. And I had to know how to do it.[46]

The shadow-puppet theater is recalled by the old people as an itinerant spectacle and much more—space and time opened by and for the play, moving, "running around, and making a lot of noise," between homes and beyond the home, through the gates and fences: like the shadow finger play by the father on the wall of the childhood house, yet unquestionably of the world:

> RM: Such a little girl, and you could stay outside till the morning?
> Mrs. HARTINI: We did not feel sleepy; it was so full of everything. Our eyes were wide open all the time.
> RM: So you could stay there till the morning?
> Mrs. HARTINI: Of course we could; till the morning, till five or six in the morning.
> RM: It meant that it was safe in the dark for such a little girl?
> Mrs. HARTINI: Yes. It was a safe place. Because everybody was there.[47]

The thing about the shadow puppets, as with batik, ceremonial daggers, or the gongs of gamelan, was that they were recalled for me in the postcolonial Indonesia through the filter (and mist) of the colonial, of war, of the occupation, and of the (failed) revolution. Again, one might call it nostalgia. As I listened, however, it began to sound more like a mechanism for living in and passing through penetrable fences, open gates, and houses still well standing.

> Mr. TIMU: People sang. And when something important happened, our place was overflowing with people.
> RM: It was a good life?
> Mr. TIMU: Now, everything is *progressive*. But as lively as it was, it is not.[48]
>
> Mr. JUSUF: Our house stood close to a mosque. But it was not the worship I am talking about. It was the sleeping there—delicious, in the late afternoon, after all the running around, to sleep under a *bedug*. [*Bedug* is a large drum suspended horizontally at a mosques, to summon

The Fences

> people to prayer.] And we always could sleep in such a place, in the mosque; or we could just lie on our backs and see the sky.
> RM: You were young!

(Again, one flaw in this book appears clearly. Out of excessive politeness, or distance, I did not ask about sex.)

> Mr. JUSUF: There were a lot of youths. But also old people—and they asked to be taken there, also, after they would die. My father was always telling me: "After I die, I want to be buried there." There was a sleeping mat—
> RM: Did it happen?
> Mr. JUSUF: Yes, sadly, when I was still too young. He died but yes he was buried behind that mosque. At the place he chose himself.[49]

SIGNPOSTS

Some places where the living space of the house extended into the outside were to be avoided. Especially to the children of the house, this was told with urgency. Some bodies of water, for example, like ponds and wells, should be touched only at the edge.

> General KEMAL: There was a fishpond very near our house. We played at the pond, my sisters and I; and I fished.
> RM: You fished with a rod?
> General KEMAL: Yes, for carp, and my mother baked them.[50]

A river is the life of every community blessed enough to have it. Indonesia, moreover, is a tropical country: everybody bathed in the river in the heat, played at the river, took water from the river; it was old wisdom, too, in many parts of the country, to test one's physical and spiritual fortitude by the river: one might be advised to stay outside and close to a river through the night to bear it and to meditate.[51] It all was done, but done by *lightly* touching the space beyond the usual. This word returns—lightly.

There was always the possibility of drowning. Regularly, too, in the rainy season, water got bloated—in the memories of the old Indonesians, *bandjir* (now *banjir*), the destructive floods killing people and tearing down houses, are never missing.[52]

Chapter Three

Mr. ROSIHAN: Our house stood near the river. Its name was *Bandar Bakalien*, but everybody called it the *Bandjir Kanaal*, because *bandjir*, the floods, were supposed to be diverted by it.[53]

Father MANGUNWIJAYA: We played at the Bandjir Kanaal. We lived close to it, and the older boys took me there to play. My mother did not like it at all. We stole away, my friends and I, we ran to the water, got out of our clothes. I was always scolded a lot when my mother learned about it.[54]

The allure and danger of the ponds and the rivers, besides the water, were the trees around and along. Children in particular had to be told, and in no uncertain terms, that there really was a danger—like the spirits in the trees:

Mr. DAINO: We bathed in the river; we played with the buffaloes in the water. There was so much *excitement* in this, and there still is, when I think about it. But there were many things that made me afraid. Like the big trees, and we were told that there were *Geister* in them. (*Mr. Daino uses a German term for "spirits" or "souls."*) My grandfather told me a story about a *woman Geist*. Sometimes, he said, she changes herself into a white spider—I have never seen it myself. But one day my brother was dying. It was at night, and I remember the darkness outside the house, and the black big trees. It is still in my mind. And people said that—

RM: —?

Mr. DAINO: —they said that there was a white *spider*! My brother cried, he cried to the very end. He could not speak anymore, only: "*Hhhh*..., *hhh*..., *hhh*...." And what was it? Was he not able to say any more what he had seen? I was afraid of those dark trees. There was not much *electricity* yet, you see? It was pitch-dark outside, and these *Geister*—

RM: But when you left for a city? In Bandung, also—?

Mr. DAINO: No, in Bandung they disappeared.[55]

RM: Your childhood, were there not ghosts also?

Dr. ONG: No. Well, there might have been a few. In the big tree in front of our house, there was one.

RM: A w*aringin* [banyan] tree.

Dr. ONG: *Waringin*. They said that that tree could embrace—you may say

The Fences

89

strangle—a rainbow. It was an enormous tree, several trees had grown into each other. Full of mystery. And there also was *gendruwo*, a spirit in our well. There were a number of *spots* around the house where you had better be on guard.

RM: As you wandered?

Dr. ONG: Yes. There was a place, near the garage—[56]

Roads and streets belonged to the family of ponds, rivers, and trees as one moved out of the house, and again children especially needed to be warned. It was ancient knowledge that Kala, the god of time, "may eat those who wander."[57] The danger belonged to the roads and—naturally and progressively—increasingly so as the traffic increased.

Father MANGUNWIJAYA: We could play only close to the house. Luckily, we lived in a small, villagelike lane. Compared to the street in the city, it was still quiet. It was just big enough to play ball on it; when we were children.[58]

A child could even draw on the asphalt road with chalk or a piece of coal. Asphalt roads especially were "abstract, intact, dazzling."[59]

Dr. ONG: I would have liked to play on the street, but the old people were very protective. I could rarely get to the street alone. Somebody was with me whenever I went, even if it was near the house. They were strict.[60]

Like trees, ghosts, and fences, the roads and streets staked out space, as well as the sense of home, neighborhood, and colony, as they changed:

Mr. DAINO: Purworejo [Central Java], where I grew up, was a military-garrison town. There were troops of the KNIL [Royal Netherlands-Indies Army] stationed there, and so there were many Dutch and [Indonesian] soldiers, from Ambon and Menado.

RM: There were parades?

Mr. DAINO: Sometimes. But all the time the streets were like a frontline. Nobody felt really safe. The main streets especially were like conquered territories. People were afraid, and, believe me, I was afraid. These soldiers, of course, would not shoot at you; it was not what their orders were. They all, those from Menado and Ambon, as well as the Dutch, of course, had discipline.[61]

The roads and streets, like the ghosts, in all their increasingly modern, impressive, and often scary strangeness, complemented the home. They extended only as far as the sense of hominess did, to the edge of it. The people warned their children and themselves out of affection: also this is recalled as the warmth of the home. The ghosts and the rest—stretching, groaning, growing in multitude, and in complexity—staked out intimacy.

> Mrs. BEBSI: *OK*, how should I start? Oh, yes—we should not play on the street. At home, we were taught the *elementary things* like this.[62]

It was in the nature of these border things. Ghostly and frightening, yes—yet they suggested themselves to be handled with ease, touched lightly, bypassed, flown over. Often, in that mood, they are recalled almost as toys.

> RM: When as a child you were sick, did a doctor come to your house?
> Mr. HARDOYO: Yes, we called the doctor from town, nineteen kilometers away. He came in a car. When there was no car, it was during the Japanese occupation, it was even more interesting; he came in a two-wheel carriage, with a horse![63]

The first things of the roads and streets, the machines on wheels, to be remembered are bicycles, those one had or those one desired.[64]

> Mr. NARYO: When I was a boy, only a very few people had a bicycle. In our whole place, there might be two or three bicycles altogether. If you were not a well-to-do person, you would not have a bicycle.[65]

The bicycle was called either by its Dutch name, *fiets*, or in Indonesian, *kereta angin*, "carriage moved by the wind or moving through the wind," another spirit of the brink of home.

> Mr. RUSLI: As far as bicycles were concerned, we had to have lock and key. Otherwise the bicycle might disappear. The houses, however, they still used to be left open. There were almost no cars in the town at that

time, just a few, so the streets were not jammed and we children could play on the street. Not high officials, but schoolteachers, even the Dutch ones, traveled around on bicycles. They rode their bicycles in white jackets, white trousers, and boots. My Dutch teacher, she always rode on bicycle to school. So, in the past, streets were more—how to put it—peaceful. They were peaceful, and they felt pretty.[66]

The things with wheels, on the roads of childhood, at the edge of home, ride in the memories, solid, clicking, handle-prone and knob-full, often named like pets (using trademarks), shiny. The roads populated by those spirits become intimate cum modern in an almost good-interior, indeed, the salon way.

Mrs. TORAR: I had a bicycle, *Fongers*. I still remember it. *Fongers*.
RM: There was not much traffic on the street those days?
Mrs. TORAR: Mostly horses. First, we had a *sado* [two-wheel horse-drawn carriage]; in the *sado* two of us sat, side by side, plus a coachman. Then we got a *délman*, and in the *délman*—here sat two persons and here one person and the coachman. Finally, we got a car, *Oldsmobile*.[67]

I was talking to an old lady in Jakarta while a convoy of heavy trucks was passing on the street. She was telling me how she as a girl rode a bicycle on the street and how pretty it was. She shouted over the trucks:

Mrs. RAHMIATI: And sometimes I roller-skated, too. On the street. It could not be done at home [no asphalt there]. There was a small *plein* [square], and we could go on bicycle or roller skates as far as the *plein*. We had girls' bicycles; priests also used them. Men's bicycles had a bar, so you could not wear a skirt.[68]

The roads and streets of childhood felt new, modern, and, in the new and modern way, intimate. The sense of them, their surface and their perspective, it seems, never disappeared since.

Father MANGUNWIJAYA: I still remember that the road led from our house up to the market. Only after I grew up did I realize that the ascent, in fact, had been very small. In the eyes of a child, the street was steep, as if leading up to a big mountain. The impact was so immense. It can never again be an ordinary road from a house to a town.⁶⁹

Even nostalgia, if it was nostalgia, the longing for the lost home, became a feeling of the road.

> RM: When you grew up, what did you do?
> Mr. BENGGA Sr.: I wandered. (*Mr. Bengga Sr. is an old man who does not care terribly much about anything. He is almost deaf, and his son is eager to help me.*)
> Mr. BENGGA Jr.: What do you say, father?! He asked you, what did you do as you grew up.
> Mr. BENGGA Sr.: I wandered. I tramped. In the past, ah—
> RM: In the past what?
> Mr. BENGGA Jr.: He means that it used to be better in the past.
> RM: Because you were young?
> Mr. BENGGA Sr.: This used to be an ordinary place. You did not have to ask everybody for directions as you moved around. You just went. There was Waru, you knew, the hill over there, and there was that big tall stone in the valley, by the river. Some people lived in one place, and other people lived in another place. Nowadays, it is as if even the Waru Hill was not there truly anymore. Once, as I wandered around, I met a girl. Boy, she was gorgeous! And she never came back.
> RM: Modern life.
> Mr. BENGGA Sr.: You said it.
> Mr. BENGGA Jr.: You said it.⁷⁰

"Violence," as Paul Virilio argues, "can be reduced to nothing but movement."⁷¹ Violence as well as anger, depression, or an effort at a change, in a colony as everywhere in the modern world, could increasingly be sublimated, diffused, made to evaporate, when set on a modern road—reduced to almost nothing but a will to keep on moving along the given path.

"Service cars" were most fondly recalled for me, cars owned by private companies or by the state and provided to select employees for as long as they worked for them. Out of the garages and gates of a modern house (standing lightly on the ground anyway) service cars moved onto the street and road. Almost as a rule, by the way, almost as courtesy, in postcolonial

The Fences

Indonesia, I was led into houses through their fronts, which was through the garage.

Through the service cars, as I often heard from my interviewees, the tricky space between a modern house and the modern beyond could be best negotiated—as a weekday trip to work or, even more memorably for the children and still closer to the dream, as a Sunday outing. All that might have been left behind at home, and of home, could then be seen, from the service car, as moving, sporting away, (as) in a rearview mirror.

Or, the vehicle of the new could "only" or "still" be a dream of a service car, a sporting ghost possibly, even more powerful because it involved longing.

> Mr. SUDARMOTO: My father worked in a hospital in town and he often went to the places, around the whole area, to *ondernemingen*—
> RM: Plantations.
> Mr. SUDARMOTO: Coffee and cocoa plantations. He often went there; in a *dienst* car.
> RM: Service car.
> Mr. SUDARMOTO: Yes, he drove it himself, and sometimes he let me go with him.[72]
>
> Air Marshal DHANI: My father had a service car, and sometimes we could all use it. It was so beautiful. Especially at night, with the *fireflies*.[73]

(Note here, as in so many other instances: something like fireflies, not something like mosquitoes.)

> Air Marshal DHANI: When my father was promoted, he got a car that we called *Jeffrey*. *Jeffrey* was *convertible*. A *cabriolet*. It still used a carbide lamp. It was a big and very high car, made in 1915. Then my father got a new model again, *Dodge*. It was always like a present to all of us.
> RM: Could you go far?
> Air Marshal DHANI: Yes, even for a couple of days. When we got a *flat tire*, early on, we did not have a *spare*. We had to carry everything on the outside of the car. But we could go fast. On some roads, we could make 40 kilometers an hour! We might stop at some place and have a picnic. It was nice. When we had a *flat tire*, we stopped at the side of the road; we always took food with us.

Chapter Three

RM: Your father drove?

Air Marshal DHANI: My father drove. But there was always a man who helped us. He sat behind the backseats: the back of the car could be yanked out, and it made a little place for him to sit in. Sometimes, also, we the small children even could sleep at the side of the road, under a tree, when the car broke down. The servant went for what was needed to repair the car. Then, I remember, we got a *Citröen*, a *1926 Citröen*. One man put it *all together*; the motor, *everything*. He shopped for spare parts *all around*. He said: "Now, we need to put motor in." I watched it all. I was very happy at the time, you know.[74]

Ideally, ultimately, in that service (which meant functional) life nothing was impossible — in driving, entering the wider space of the new.

Mrs. RAHMIATI: We had a *French veranda*, as we called it, in the back of the house. In front on the left as you faced the street, we had a *garden*. There also used to be a small *garden* in front on the right side, but we needed a place for the car. My parents had a car, not a big one, I still remember — a *sports model*, an English car; *cabriolet*. We did not have a *driver*. Father liked to *sport*. He always drove the car himself. There were just my mother, my younger sister, and I in the car.[75]

Mr. HARDJONEGORO: Yes, of course, we had a radio. And we also had a car. My *grandfather* had — a most terrific *Buick*.[76]

A new feeling of space was being produced on the road and on the roadside; the new intensity — or, better, speed — of the feeling increased as the vehicles became more powerful. It was a playful sort of freedom in the colony, "something resembling freedom";[77] to drive or to be driven. Some did it, and everybody watched:

RM: But it was just for the rich — the motorcycles and the cars?

Mr. SUTIKNO: We had our first car already in 1936 or 1937, a secondhand one, of course.

RM: You had a driver?

Mr. SUTIKNO: We had a driver, because my father was not interested in driving. At that time we lived in Kudus [Central Java]. There were only few cars in the town. We had number 53.[78]

The Fences

RM: Before the war, did you often travel outside Surakarta?

Princess BROTODININGRAT: Not often, to Surabaya, Bandung, and Jakarta [all on Java].

RM: By car?

Princess BROTODININGRAT: By train. My father had a train carriage; his own *wagon lit*. *De luxe*. It is still there, in Yogyakarta.

RM: *De luxe*?

Princess BROTODININGRAT: It was a *wagon de luxe*. It belonged to us. Papa owned factories. There used to be cigarettes and tobacco made by Papa's company. He was a rich prince, my dear. That *wagon* is now in Yogyakarta, and I keep telling people: "Bring it back here [to Surakarta], so that everybody can see it."[79]

In the new and expanding traffic-excited and traffic-determined space, whoever did not have a wagon-lit, or a driver, or at least a car, so it seemed, might feel free to ride a bus or, say, a city tram:

Mr. DES ALWI: It was so nice. In Jakarta you might go by tram everywhere! It was quite cheap, too. Even when I had no money I could just jump on and watch for the conductor. When he came close, I jumped off. I remember my first time on the tram. We passed through the *Van Heutsz Boulevard*. *Toot toot*, and you could go as far as the harbor. I loved just to sit there, in the tram, just to sit there.[80]

One was supposed to breathe modern as much as one was able — to get on the road in fact or in a sense, in a machine with wheels.[81] One's land, town, city, and the metropolis were also supposed to breathe that way, be modern-livable, and driving-meaningful:

A landscape cut through by an express train or a car loses the describable details but acquires a dense intimacy. The doors of a train carriage and the windshield of a car have one thing in common: they change the aspects of things.[82]

Seeing the world like that, the new sort-of-wholesome, new "volumetric effect," becomes "most intense for a spectator in motion."[83] One has as many chances to survive as avant-garde as one is able to become: "The beauty is in speed."[84] By the same logic and intensity, in the same perspective, most of the roads of the past newly appear strikingly aimless. This is a new nostalgia — one begins to wonder whether such roads ever existed in the first place.

> Mrs. OEI: We just walked. Adults were watching over us. If a road seemed too long, we just sat down, at the roadside. There was always a canari tree somewhere. We sat and we ate canari nuts. All the children were there. We sat there, and not always to have a rest, but for the sitting. Then we went home.[85]

The beauty, attraction, and meaning of the road and of the land along the road were erased and newly produced by the motion — or, better, by speed. The road thus traveled was able to signify — in "a dense intimacy" and without "the describable details" — everything. This was a land that the modern and aspiring-to-become-modern people of the colony were getting — land, certainly, like the people themselves, in motion or, better, speeding:

> Mr. ROESLAN: My father got into the car, and the driver tried to start the motor. He tried for quite long time, *wrrr wrrr wrrr*. It was a *Fiat*. I was told to sit beside my father in the back of the car. He pointed out things to me as we drove. I was nine, it was in 1923, and there was the big railway strike in Surabaya. The communist and Islamic unions were striking in unity. The workers' housings at that time were in Pacarkeling, near the main railway station, and, as the strike began, the Dutch authorities decided to evict the workers from their homes; in the middle of the night! Their flats were to be auctioned to the wealthy Chinese and Arabs in the city. And we went to see it. We drove slowly by and father pointed out for me: "Look at this. See the harshness of the Dutch. In their own land, the people are being evicted, and Chinese and Arabs can buy their houses cheap."
>
> RM: You saw it from the car?
>
> Mr. ROESLAN: It was raining, everything was fuzzy. But I saw something. Police were taking people from their houses, and there was furniture in the rain. Where were these people supposed to go? That much I could see. Father did not dare to stop, of course. There were only few cars around, only three or four, and there were the police everywhere. We just drove on by.[86]

✦✦✦

The Fences

Maybe André Breton was right: "The street," to a modern human, may become indeed "the only field of experience."[87] A poem by a Chinese Indonesian, about an early colonial modern road, a railway on Java, decades before Breton stated it with an even greater conviction:

> With the train there's nothing to fear,
> No need to accompany the freight.
> The line is straight without deviating,
> With the train there is no worry. It is easy.[88]

Theodor Adorno, with his own experience on the modern roads closer to our own, put it in a slightly more complicated manner, yet his message seems the same: "Perhaps the cult of technical speed . . . conceals an impulse to master the terror of running by deflecting it from one's own body and at the same time effortlessly surpassing it. . . . In the fanatical love of cars the feeling of physical homelessness plays a part."[89]

THE ART OF NOT TOUCHING

RM: Your family—
Mr. ALI: Yes, it is of Arab origin.
RM: Wealthy people?
Mr. ALI: Wealthy.
RM: What did they do?
Mr. ALI: The usual thing. They were Arab Indonesian merchants. My father got it from his grandfather. The grandfather dealt in horses.[90]

Mr. HARDJONEGORO: My great-grandfather got the title from the Dutch colonial government—"the lieutenant of the Chinese." He got a license, too, a monopoly to sell *opium* and *salt*. Naturally. This was the Chinese Indonesian thing.

(Repeatedly, from the Chinese Indonesians, Arab Indonesians, and all the other Indonesians, from the "natives" as well as from the Dutch, one gets that sense of "the natural," which is an order that, except for moments of "irregularities," pogroms, most dramatically, evokes the sense of calm.)

Mr. HARDJONEGORO: You should never forget that in all the towns, like Solo, Yogya, or Cirebon, it was the same map: toward the south, there was a palace, north of the palace, there was the main square, and, next to it, there was a Dutch garrison, the government house, post office, and so on. North of the main square, still further to the north, you see there was a Chinese quarter. Why? So that the Chinese Indonesians do not live with the native Indonesians. If they would, the Chinese would be crushed sooner or later. All the [Chinese] merchants have always lived there. In the middle of town, there was the colonial government. You can still see all this in Yogyakarta; the market ends at the palace — and the same in Cirebon.[91]

Mr. OEY: My connection, of course, was only with the Chinese children; no contact with the Javanese children of our age.

RM: No contact? Even on the street?

Mr. OEY: Some, perhaps. But no, there was no social life in common.

RM: But you lived so close to each other?

Mr. OEY: We did. But these were the circles we moved in. Yes, they were there, of course, we knew about them. But there was no closeness between us. My mother sold candies to the Javanese or Arab children. They came as customers to our shop. But as for contact, there was none.[92]

Mr. ASRUL: Social life was like that: Dutch and Eurasian community, Chinese community, and Arab community; the lowest *stratum* were the *inlanders*, the "natives." In Jakarta, the Dutch community lived in Menteng, between the governor-general's palace and the Tosari Street in the south. Jakarta Chinese lived in Glodok, in the north. Even the "natives" in Jakarta lived according to the region or island from which their families came, even when in these cases the lines were not so sharp. But still, for instance, those from Minangkabau [West Sumatra] usually lived here, in Sawah Besar—

Mr. Asrul, one of the best-known Indonesian writers of the century, also came to Jakarta from Minangkabau as a young man and lived in Sawah Besar.

Mr. ASRUL: —some Minangkabaus also lived in Tanah Tinggi. Most of the houses around the Kebun Jeruk belonged to the Arabs. And also, it was *typical* for the cities that the "natives" lived in the little alleys and

The Fences

rarely on a major street. Like you see, you had to walk quite a distance from the bus stop to my house, right?[93]

So it might have been since premodern times. But as colonial modernity pushed through and excited the separate communities, as it made them increasingly into communities on the move, they moved — parallel, and naturally, at different speeds.

> Mr. NARYO: In the past there had been electricity, for certain people, for certain rich people, for certain rich people in the city. The Chinese [Indonesians] had electricity.[94]

Through the multitudes of separate senses of home and the multitudes of separate modes of moving, the colony came to feel wholesome.

> RM: How did it feel to be a child from Menado [Sulawesi] and live in Batavia?
> Mr. WAWOROENTOE: We kept close to the other people from Menado. We tried to stay together. We said: "When among ourselves, let us not call ourselves Jakarta or Batavia folk." We kept feeling like arrivals. Our parents worked here, in the city, and there were also brothers and sisters, cousins, uncles and aunts; and they also came from over there. Some of them later moved even farther, deeper into Java and to the other places. And there also they found other Menado people. Of course it felt like a patch here and a patch there.[95]

Even when on the move, very much so when on the move, when walking on the street or driving through a city, one was fairly sure where one happened to be at the moment. The very style of houses, the very facades, in a blink of an eye, seemed to tell it all.

> Mrs. BEBSI: We lived in Jakarta, Karet neighborhood, at the time, and so our house was an Arab house — with a little courtyard, you know, a flower pool in the middle and all that.[96]

> RM: Was it a big house?
> Mr. HARDOYO: Actually our house looked strange in that place — it was a little like a Chinese house.[97]

Chapter Three

The ultimate late colonial cityscape met the eye with a multitude of patches—Chinese, Arab, Indonesian, and Dutch facades, homes, and lives, each evident in itself, each luminous and colorful in its own way. Ultimately, as the most various people were being ever more tightly squeezed into the urban space, the patches came to more closely resemble a mosaic, increasingly complex or messy, its outlines and shapes increasingly difficult to make out, with each particular tiny piece competing for one's separate attention, rather gray, in fact, in its overall effect—a sort of a newspaper page.

> Mr. SUTIKNO: Some parts of the city were predominantly Dutch. Others were Dutch with a few Indonesians living here and there. Some quarters were Chinese, and yet others were purely Indonesian. We have lived in Rejosari, on the main street, and there the different groups already lived very close together.
> RM: How close?
> Mr. SUTIKNO: Next door to each other on the main street.[98]
>
> Mr. ROESLAN: My father owned a couple of taxis, and so he was an *entrepreneur*. Some people even looked at him as if he were Chinese. He owned a few cabs and he rented them. You must see the place. The house is still there.
> RM: Good neighbors?
> Mr. ROESLAN: Our neighbors were Eurasians.[99]

The Dutch were exemplary in the colony, in this, too, and leading the way, by being the most separate, in their own distinct color—white, "truly white" faces, all-white, in fact, in how they faced the colony and how they dressed. They were the most offish patch of the patchy togetherness. They were symptomatic of it.

> Mrs. SOERONO: As a child, I never met a Dutch person on our street. In fact, I have never touched a Dutch person in my life.[100]
>
> Mrs. OEI: When I was little, we lived in a small town. Our house was not far from a garrison, and on some evenings we could hear drunk Dutch soldiers on the street.[101] Then, we, the children, were ordered to get in, to go to bed early. Until after independence in 1945, I never had any connection with a Dutch person.[102]

The Fences

Mr. MEWENGKANG: I grew up in a village, and there were no Dutch people. Only, on some Sundays, about once a month, a Dutch priest came.[103]

Mr. ROSIHAN: Oh, no, of course, I knew Dutch people before the war. There was a Dutch *controleur* [financial district official], and he was quite close to our family. It was in Talu, Agam, in West Sumatra.

RM: But it was his choice. He could get close, if he wanted.

Mr. ROSIHAN: He could get close, if he wanted. It depended on the person. This *controleur* even used to come to our house! I remember this: during the Lebaran [the end of the Muslim fasting month], he came to our house. My father put on his official uniform, with the *epaulettes* of his rank and all the rest. The *controleur* came with his wife as my parents would wait on the front porch and offer them the chairs. I was about eleven or twelve years old, and I had been ordered earlier not to come outside while they were there: "You stay in the back!"

RM: You did not show up? You just watched?

Mr. ROSIHAN: Yes, always just watched, of course. We called him "Sir." But this particular *controleur* once came to our house and he asked about me. And, actually, my father called me: "Come out and greet Sir!"[104]

Mr. Oey was not a village or even a small-town boy. He grew up and lived in big cities, Surabaya and Batavia-Jakarta, his whole life.

RM: So you met them on the street?
Mr. OEY: Yes.
RM: But not in the house?
Mr. OEY: No.
RM: Where else, except on the street, could you meet them?
Mr. OEY: I could see them at the swimming pool.
RM: You could go there.
Mr. OEY: Yes! There was a swimming pool, and there were the Dutch.[105]

Nobody I knew among the Dutch persons who used to live in the colony had such a good name of being "pro-Indonesian" as Professor Wertheim:

RM: As Dutch, you had a different feel even for the layout of the city than the Indonesians had?

Professor WERTHEIM: Yes, I think so.

RM: When you said "Batavia," or "Jakarta," you would have certain streets in mind. Indonesians might recall different places, right? It was not the same city for you and for them?

Professor WERTHEIM: Of course, you mean there were native quarters, poor native quarters, sure, there were. I sometimes went to a native quarter. I even had a friend who lived in a native quarter! One of my colleagues teaching at the law school lived there.

RM: You are famous for being an exceptionally progressive Dutch person living in the colony. When I talk with other Dutch of your age, almost all of them say that, until the war broke out, they did not feel anything much that would seem fundamentally wrong in the colony. They had their work, easy or complicated, but otherwise the things of the colony appeared to them to be functioning as they should.

Professor WERTHEIM: Yes, it is true.

RM: Might it be that one lived there without a sense that something was entirely not all right?

Professor WERTHEIM: There were moments, of course. Once our maid who took care of our children came and told us that two of her children had just died. There was no doctor available to her. It was a moment when one suddenly felt that something was entirely wrong in that society. At moments like this something occurred to me. But I have to say that my real interest in politics began, I think, not before 1938, when racism became such an important issue in Europe.[106]

The traffic-wise togetherness seems to explain much of the modern urban skill of not touching.[107] If modern and urban, one was expected to move forward and not bump into another or another's vehicle, as they were similarly moving:

> An intersection without gods, without passions, and without battles these days represents the most advanced stage of society and prefigures the ideal of all democracies.[108]

Among the vehicles of modernity (moving forward), of course, modern houses and neighborhoods, and that sense of dwelling were included. Crises of the modern might happen when someone momentarily lost one's focus; stopped looking ahead. *Accidentally*, Professor Wertheim learned about the death of his maid's children.

The Fences

✦✦✦

Much of my talking with the elderly Indonesians happened at the moment of the fall of a bad regime, but also of anti-Chinese riots—of beating and much worse than that, of that kind of accident, that kind of bumping into each other, that way of touching. Especially at this moment, horrified, scared, and with fervent nostalgia, the old Indonesians recalled not so much the peacefulness of the past but rather a normalcy of separation.

Air Marshal DHANI: Oh, the relations between the Chinese Indonesians and us where I grew up were just fine! There were not these—
RM: Riots?
Air Marshal DHANI: Not at all. Nothing of this madness. Nothing at all![109]

Mrs. OEI: Many of us [Chinese Indonesians] are afraid.
RM: Is this new?
Mrs. OEI: Of course!
RM: But when you were a little girl?
Mrs. OEI: It did not exist.
RM: So you don't have any memory of an anti-Chinese pogrom when you were a child? You have not even heard about it happening in the past?
Mrs. OEI: It did not exist.
RM: You have no recollection of it?
Mrs. OEI: Well, after the war ended, in 1945. But those were not the people who lived in your own neighborhood. Now, they know us and still they drag us out of our homes. This is new.
RM: Why is it so?
Mrs. OEI: Yes, it is true—at one time, my father told us that we had to leave in a hurry. And these were Indonesians who drove us out. Perhaps it has been around for a long time. People were never really nice to us, the Chinese. They never had a real feeling for us. But this time, this is new. They break into everything. Everybody is "anti," this is how they feel now. I am so afraid.[110]

Mr. OEY: They always used to call us not pretty names. But I do not think there was as much of this feeling in this as now. Often it was just as if you were not there.
RM: So you were not so afraid at the time?
Mr. OEY: No, it was not like this.

RM: Perhaps because you were a child?
Mr. OEY: Yes, perhaps.
RM: Chinese shops remained opened?
Mr. OEY: Throughout the time.
RM: Opened, not boarded.
Mr. OEY: No, not closed.[111]

In the case of the Dutch in the colony, the dominant and emblematic case, the modern art of not touching was most closely practiced, watched, and it is most vividly recalled. It most closely approximated the colonial urbanity.

RM: What about racism?
Mr. RUSLI: Not really. We did not hate the Dutch. As long as they did not try to come back after 1945, there was no hate toward the Dutch. We just wanted to be free. In the colony, there were many Dutch people who were good. They lived their own lives, and we, Indonesians, lived our own lives. This is, mostly, how it was.[112]

The Dutch as well as the rest cannot be explained without the Eurasians. The Eurasians, a significant group in the colony, yet another patch, had to be as exemplarily separate as the Dutch; they had to work as a layer, buffer, in between the Dutch and the rest of the colony, modern and patchily united. Born to a European (Dutch mostly) father and a native mother, their way of life, of dwelling, and of moving forward was to work as a kind of fence.

Professor RESINK: My father had a pure—Dutch complexion—try this cookie.
RM: Thank you.
Professor RESINK: So he had no trouble in the colony. He did not finish school, the [colonial officials'] academy in Delft. Yet he made it here, and we moved in the circles of very good society.[113]

The Eurasians, as a fence, had to be visible. Both the Dutch and the Indonesians saw the fence as the space—quite penetrable, attractive, luring, in fact—yet, at the same time, as a possible and dangerous line of too-close a touching. Here was the warm kind of feeling of the other that should be evaded—like an illicit love (there was a pervasive lore of young Eurasian

The Fences

men and women as "perfect concubines"[114]), diluting one's character into the other. It should better flash out and stay on the level, let's say, of children street-fighting.

> Mr. SARLI: Do you know that my father was a descendant of Prince Diponegoro [a nineteenth-century Javanese hero fighting the Dutch]? It tells you everything! Like, when I was little, a Dutch boy hit me. He hit me with a stick.
> RM: Didn't an Indonesian boy ever hit you?
> Mr. SARLI: Never. They did not dare.
> RM: Because you were a descendant of Diponegoro?
> Mr. SARLI: Yes. They did not dare, least of all the boys in the village. But this was a son of a Dutchman who worked on a plantation. He hit me with a stick. I was so angry
> RM: He was a son of a Dutch?
> Mr. SARLI: A Dutch boy. Well, he was Eurasian.
> RM: Not a full-blood Dutch?
> Mr. SARLI: No! A Eurasian.
> RM: Didn't you fight with other Indonesian children?
> Mr. SARLI: Yes, it might happen. But there were these fights between the Indonesian children and the Eurasians. These were the real fights.[115]

It was to be expected, almost inevitable and certainly on everybody's mind, that to move toward modernity meant to move close and often through the fence, this layer in between: the Eurasians. This was when one brushed really close to the fence, one of the crucial moments on the road, and the most prone to an accident. Professor Resink, Dutch but born in Java to a family living in the colony for more than a century, began talking to me by saying, proudly, that there was "Javanese blood" in his ancestors. This should have put him among the Eurasians. Yet in his view of himself and of the Eurasians, Professor Resink was quite categorical, or, rather, delicate:

> RM: How did the neighborhood feel to you as a boy? Like playing games, running around in the street?
> Professor RESINK: No! We were not allowed to play in the street. That was a difference between me and the [other?] Eurasian children. In the afternoon, after lunch, we had to go to bed, and servants made it

Chapter Three

sure that we stayed in our room. We were not allowed to go into the street. Because if we did—for my parents Eurasians were a *cultural phenomenon*—the Eurasians loved *krontjong* [music], the Eurasians spoke *petjok* dialect [today spelled *pecok*], the Eurasians had money [were reckless with their spending], the Eurasian children played in the street.[116]

Krontjong, we might recall, was distinctly a *street* music; *petjok*, similarly, was a *street* argot, a mixture of Dutch and local languages. This was all a modern and urban phenomenon, and it gained strength as the colonial system matured and aged. Professor Resink's parents had been *increasingly* conscious of the Eurasians:

> Professor RESINK: My three older brothers could still speak *petjok*. But my sister and I, it was the 1910s and 1920s, we were already strictly forbidden—[117]

This was a moving and a sensing of the modern as much as of the colonial. As the Japanese came and went, as the Indonesian revolution of 1945 happened and failed to achieve most of its aims, the mode of the traffic and the working of the fences—modern, colonial, postcolonial—progressed, and aged, rather than fundamentally changing.

> Mrs. MUNARDJO: During the Dutch times, I often felt insecure. Because, you see, I am the type: I look like a Eurasian. The Dutch sometimes even thought that I might be Dutch. Actually, when I met a Dutch person, I felt often quite at ease. My Dutch also was quite fluent. Often, I felt more awkward among the Indonesians, because I sensed that I might have looked to them like a Eurasian. During the revolution, I took a job as a secretary in the new Indonesian parliament, and when I first came to the session, Sukarno [the president] raised his eyebrows. He said to Hatta [the vice-president]: "Look at her! What is a Eurasian doing here?" I was then wearing my hair like that—(*Mrs. Munardjo undid her hair [still almost no gray in it], so it fell down over her ears.*)
>
> RM: Sukarno said it?
>
> Mrs. MUNARDJO: Yes, he was chairing the session. I also colored my hair at that time. But Hatta said, "She is not Eurasian, she just looks like

The Fences

that. She is from Sumatra." "How do you know?" asked Sukarno. "Oh, I have a student, he is taking economics with me, and I know about her from him." This was what the vice-president said.[118]

Genealogies, family trees, aristocratic and all the others, were often presented to me during the interviews. Sometimes they were very elaborate, illuminated and calligraphic, at other times they were scribbled on a piece of paper as we talked. All of them—like the plans of the houses and neighborhoods of the past—acquired their attractive and reassuring quality from the memory they carried, of course, but equally so from the webs of lines, the names and dates, on the page. Some of the genealogies might begin with Adam, the first man, Prophet Mohammed, or some ancient king or hero. Yet there were not many that felt, and were supposed to feel, originary. Instead, most of them impressed by being light, flat, and geometrical.

> Mrs. LASMIDJAH: My mother is here. Trenggalek [East Java] was the place where we moved with her, a *minus* neighborhood at the time. There were many poor people in the area. I remember a *hongersnood* [famine]: people were being laid down, face up, by the side of the street. My mother bought cassava in the market, she boiled it and she gave a little to each of us. Here is my grandmother.[119]

One can get—and it seems that one is supposed to get—a certain sense of certitude, even purity, with the genealogies or plans or maps in hand, or as one draws them from memory for a visitor. A host, a visitor, or both together, as they recall the past may make themselves capable of seeing, showing, and believing "at a glance" houses, neighborhoods, the land in the past—and thus in the present, too: the people behind and ahead of us, above and below as a scheme is spread out or drawn. Like on the Gunther Holtorf's digital map of Jakara mentioned in the first chapter—an order at a glance.

> *At the end of the interview, I asked Father Mangunwijaya—a priest and writer who had lived in a particular Yogyakarta neighborhood for four decades at least when I met him—if he could introduce me to some working-class people old enough to remember the Dutch time and willing to talk to me about it. He thought for a while and suggested his friend, Prince Puger, whom, he knew, I would see the next day. The next day, I asked Prince Puger, and he suggested*

Chapter Three

> Mr. Daino: "He moves among these people all the time." Mr. Daino, when I met him, after making a few telephone calls, gave me "five options," all of them were through his young friend Agung of the Brawijaya [East Java] Army Division. Agung's wife, Dr. Herni, was an anthropologist and she did "a project on peasants." Mr. Daino showed me on my map: the peasants I might go to see all lived about two hundred kilometers away.[120]

At the time I was talking to Father Mangunwijaya, Prince Puger, and Mr. Daino, a series of killings had just begun to be reported in the Indonesian press, most of the murders occurring on Java, in villages, in towns, and as close as on the outskirts of Jakarta. Dozens and hundreds of victims—sometimes said to be mentally ill, other times simply strangers, deemed to be (flagrantly, radically) not belonging—were killed. The killings were described in the papers as communal—suggesting that neighborhoods, and their self-definition, were behind it. (The murders were still going on as I was writing this book.)[121]

In Paris in the nineteenth century, the builders of the most exemplary modern metropolis called all those in the city who might cause trouble, a revolution even, an "external population."[122] The killing of the "nomads" in postcolonial Indonesia, in villages as well as in the cities, is a high modern phenomenon, and it has everything to do with the new and ever-new urban way of (not) touching. "The bourgeois," Adorno wrote, "is tolerant. His love of people as they are stems from his hatred of what they might be."[123] To put it another way, the bourgeois (modern urban) dwelling or aspiring to dwell is a self-assured way of clearing the urban space for oneself—it is "tactful": "Tact is a discrimination of difference . . . it fails to engage the individual and finally wrong him. . . . The nominalism of tact helps what is most universal, naked external power, to triumph even in the most intimate constellations."[124]

THE COMMONPLACE

The sound of the telephone, so it is frequently remembered, built up the space inside the newly modern house and neighborhood as well.

> Mr. ROESLAN: My family was *middle class*. My father owned a shop close to the main street, and he had a telephone. At that time, when one wished to call by telephone, one had to ask for an operator; not like it is

The Fences

today. We lived close to the center of town and, when father wished to call north, for instance, he had to ask the operator first for "the north," and then he was connected. Sometime the operator might not be there, and so my father had to wait. Other times, he got the operator, but the number was *busy*. Telephone for us was something exciting. People might talk without seeing each other! Father called *centrale*, he was connected, he told the number to the operator, and he was connected again. When he wished to call south, he called *"south,"* and he was connected.[125]

There were also the calls from a local mosque, regular and more predictable than the ringing of the telephone—five times a day, exactly on the movements of the sun, but equally architectural, neighborhood making, and as time progressed, equally modern and urban. The voice from the mosque mixed with the sound of the telephone. There were also, albeit in most places much less so, bells from Christian churches. There were gongs from Chinese temples, too, forming the neighborhood, or, certainly, what Le Corbusier called the "visual acoustics" of landscape.[126]

Radio was like that and even more so. It could sound bell-like as well as croaking-hawker–like. It also built up a neighborhood from a point resting in a distance that could be only imagined. In contrast to telephone—and gods—one was not supposed to be strong enough to talk back.

> RM: So you went to the other people's house to listen to radio? There were no radios in public places?
> Mr. MULYONO: No. Only later did the Japanese put radios on the street, on high poles in the squares, and on main crossroads. There was one radio in the square, in front of the district office.
> RM: Was there any music?
> Mr. MULYONO: Yes, depending on the program. There was mainly music and news from the government.[127]

Princess Noeroel told me about an experiment known to many in Indonesia, in which she and the space-producing power of radio played roles. She had been in the Netherlands, a few years before the war, with her father and some other royals. For one evening, a program had been arranged for Noeroel, and three other princesses who were also there, to dance in front of the Dutch Queen with a Javanese gamelan playing back in Java, in a studio in Surakarta. Philips Broadcasting transmitted the sound. There was some static, the princess told me, but otherwise all went "without a hitch."[128]

> RM: Before the Japanese occupation, who could own a radio?
> Mr. MULYONO: Around 1936, they opened a shop here that sold radios — directly from Europe. There were two types: *Erres* from England [*sic*] and *Philips* from Holland. But then they had to wait for spare parts for a very long time. Those who owned a radio —
> RM: Who was it?
> Mr. MARDI SUWITO: The wealthy.
> Mr. MULYONO: But ordinary people could already listen; they could hear it, at least. In some houses they brought a radio out, on the porch. Then, ordinary people could hear it, too.
> Mr. MARDI SUWITO: From the street.[129]

✦ ✦ ✦

The space-producing sound (and the machines to produce the sounds) progressively and increasingly came from the outside and, as time passed, from farther away. The modernity in that sense, the colonial modernity in particular, became increasingly *perspectival*. To hear, understand, and enjoy, one should focus on the distant, which seemed to be closer to the source. Increasingly, one would better move, led by the attraction, and further on, off one's house, through the fences, through one's neighborhood, beyond.

> Mr. KARKONO: There was a *sociëteit* [club] in town. Near the Gedung Ombo there was the club.
> RM: But it was Dutch?
> Mr. KARKONO: Yes, it was Dutch. Often there was music.
> RM: Had you ever been inside during the Dutch time?
> Mr. KARKONO: Oh, no!
> RM: No Indonesian was ever inside the club?
> Mr. KARKONO: There was a Javanese musician, and he could go in. He played the violin: Soewandi. He was allowed in, but only to play the violin. When he was not there, it was only European.
> RM: All-white?
> Mr. KARKONO: All-white.[130]

The Fences

Walter Spies played in that particular club. He was of German-Russian origin, a painter, a musician, and, especially, an émigré. During his time in Europe, in the few first years after the First World War, he became friends with some of the well-known avant-garde artists of the continent: the painters Oskar Kokoschka and Otto Dix, the musicians Ferucchio Busoni, Alois Hába, and Paul Hindemith.[131] In 1923, tired of Europe as were many of the avant-garde, but more on the impatient side, Spies left—for the Dutch colony in the East. It possibly seemed to him that by escaping the high modernity of the moment he could not aim for a more remote place.

The first job Spies laid his hands on in the colony was to play piano "in a Chinese cinema" in West Java, in Bandung, and to do a few chamber music concerts and recitals in the same city "with other émigré Russians."[132] It is known that at one of the concerts he played a Rachmaninoff sonata, and the rococo variations by Peter Ilich Tchaikovsky, and another famous Proustian sonata by César Franck. He asked his friends in Europe to send him more music: "Busoni-Bach all that is there; Schönberg, three piano pieces; and six piano pieces by Křenek; some passacaglia or chaconne . . . smaller piano compositions by Hába, Petyrek, Hindemith."[133]

From Bandung, after a short time, Spies moved further east, to the town of Yogyakarta, where he played in De Vereniging, The Association, the club Mr. Karkono was telling me about. As the European sugar, coffee, and cocoa planters drank, smoked, and talked, "the band played light classics with Walter Spies at piano."[134] At the same time Spies had been engaged as "the Master of the Sultan of Yogyakarta's Music," with a salary of 100 gulden a month—a low salary, by the way, for a European in the colony at the time.[135]

Like the telephone, a voice from a mosque, bells from a church, or radio, the music from the European clubs was heard—or sensed. The newly significant music sounded through the houses and through the neighborhood. It filled and resounded in the space yet—this was a colony, mostly of houses and neighborhoods still "undeveloped" or "developing"—the new sounds testing the space often found it inadequate for listening, for getting across the message. With an increasing urgency, a new, truly new, modern, and progressive off-fence space was required, where the new sound and music could be played and listened to in full. However artificial, overtechnologized, foreign, *virtual* the space might be—the more so, in fact, the better—there the modernity should resound naturally. Something like the Dutch club Spies played in. Space like that, only more so.

Chapter Three

Mr. Gesang, in his eighties when I met him, still sang and played for his town neighborhood and, in fact, very much beyond. His was the *krontjong* music — now like back in the 1920s, when he started to play it — an Indonesian, popular, modern, and distinctly street music, as much a part of the street as the cries of hawkers. Of the same space, of the same mood.

> Gesang *means "life" in Javanese. It also sounds quite a bit like* gezang, *"song," in Dutch. Of course this does not make any sense linguistically; it is just the sound of it and the man who is, indeed, "almost nothing but a song." As I was getting closer to Mr. Gesang's house in Surakarta, still not very close, neighbors (in this neighborhood of several tens of thousands) took me in their care and, from one street to the next one, they led me to him.*[136]

Mr. GESANG: First I listened at home. It was a lively place, full of work.
RM: There you learned to sing?
Mr. GESANG: There was no learning. I just did it; by myself.
RM: Then you put together an orchestra?
Mr. GESANG: We got together, a few of us.
RM: And eventually you were asked to play on the radio?
Mr. GESANG: Yes, in the evenings, or late in the afternoon.
RM: A live broadcast?
Mr. GESANG: Live. On Monday, it was in the evening.
RM: Did you get much money for it?
Mr. GESANG: Five or six rupiahs, I think, six *gulden*; one group, one broadcast; one hour; or sometimes two.
RM: It was not much.
Mr. GESANG: My, it was nothing!
RM: How many people in the group?
Mr. GESANG: About thirteen: three singers, ten players; one who arranged the things. I did not use *drums*, I had only maraca, ukulele, cello, guitar, violin, few violinists, three accordionists.
RM: There were other *krontjong* groups in Surakarta?
Mr. GESANG: Many. When I was young, about ten.
RM: But not all of them were on the radio?
Mr. GESANG: Sometimes they were. If you became good you got on the radio. You were tested and found good. So they let you on the radio.
RM: How did the broadcast go?
Mr. GESANG: We might have a horse cart, but only when there was big

The Fences

action. Mostly, we went on bicycles. When there was a big action — one horse, one carriage.

RM: What do you think? Is gamelan a more difficult sort of music than *krontjong*?

Mr. GESANG: It is on a higher level. And it is more difficult to play. *Krontjong* is for ordinary people. We sung in Indonesian.[137]

Mr. Gesang still liked to think of himself as a street musician. The space that he entered, filled, and further built up, keyed with his songs, was street, market, neighborhood, with low fences here and there. However, inevitably, the new thing got into it, and it tuned in best with radio.

Mr. GESANG: First we played on the street and, sometimes when there was a celebration, in people's houses. Then we got bicycles. We rehearsed more, and, in 1937 or 1938, we got on the radio.

RM: Who liked *krontjong* at the time?

Mr. GESANG: Everybody liked it.

RM: Javanese?

Mr. GESANG: Javanese, Chinese.

RM: Arabs?

Mr. GESANG: There were not many Arabs.

RM: Dutch?

Mr. GESANG: Not so many. But one Dutch has played with us.

RM: What was his name?

Mr. GESANG: I forgot. His stage name was *Angin Lalu* [Breeze of the Past?]. He may still be alive. He was from here, but he moved to Jakarta.

RM: So he was Dutch?

Mr. GESANG: Eurasian.

RM: It all changed when the Japanese came?

Mr. GESANG: Radio began to be called Hosoo Kyoku. In Solo it was Solo Hosoo Kyoku; in Yogya, Jogja Hosoo Kyoku; in Semarang, Semarang Hosoo Kyoku. No longer SRV [Solo Radio Vereniging]. . . . And we played there.[138]

✳ ✳ ✳

Whenever a feast is recalled, neighborhood appears most distinctly, festive-distinct.

Chapter Three

Mrs. LASMIDJAH: When I was little, we lived in a small town, a regency town. The regent was like a king. He was close to the Dutch *controleur* and *assistent resident*, and his house was like a palace. In the front of the house there was a large open space, and in the middle of it there grew a *waringin* tree. The big tree was to *indicate* that here was *something special*. During a feast, we used to gather there, and first we paid homage to the regent's house—like that.[139] (*Mrs. Lasmidjah made a* sembah *for me— "respectful greeting made with palms together, fingertips upward and touching the forehead"*[140] *—toward the inside of her house on whose porch we sat.*)

Topography and a sense (or map) of order of a neighborhood is recalled as being defined by the feast.

Air Marshal DHANI: My father was a regent, and he was required to report everything to the Dutch administration. And he reported everything: how the people suffered, what they lacked—so that *the family* that suffered too much would not become disorderly. He tried to do what he could.

RM: So there was no disorder?

Air Marshal DHANI: When there was a big feast, for instance, it was always at my father's place. Everybody came and brought something, a chicken or a coconut, whatever one could. When there was a feast at the regent's place everybody had to bring some food, a dish ready to be shared by all.[141]

Through the feasts—which happened at an exclusive or neutral place, or one belonging to the common—togetherness of neighborhood was articulated, and changed in time:

Mr. Timu, as he recalled his childhood, that being together, had a slip of the tongue—or perhaps switched, or perhaps was naturally speaking about the same thing—calling a big feast of the past once pésta, *a "feast," and other moments* atraksi, *an "attraction." When I asked him about it, he explained that "attractions of the past" or "feast" were increasingly "entertaining," as they contained more and more new and curious things like gramophone music, or puppet theater brought from the far away.*[142]

The Fences

This meant from Java, in this case, as I talked to Mr. Timu at his home in Flores. There was even dancing to music, Mr. Timu said, talking about the 1920s: this could hardly be done anymore in one's own house. On the same occasions even a *corso* was recalled.[143]

The feasts and attractions, happenings of togetherness, festive gatherings, defined a space and required a space. They might sound, smell, and appear in an eternal way, but, in the spirit of the modern and the colonial, new kinds of large, open, and neutral spaces offered themselves to accommodate life also for the time to come.[144]

Most flagrantly, festive "amusement parks" and "variety places" emerged in the colony at the beginning of the twentieth century. They were built on vacant, "undeveloped" spots of towns and cities or, rather, on what, at the moment of building, began to look like a vacant spot.

> Princess BROTODININGRAT: Oh, we could be naughty, and we could make some trouble.
> RM: Naughty, trouble; in what way?
> Princess BROTODININGRAT: I had five brothers, all of them younger than I, and we played soccer in the palace. Have you already been there?
> RM: Yes, I saw it.
> Princess BROTODININGRAT: It was some place at that time already! And there, in front of the main audience hall, we built goals and played soccer. Father got angry: "You will tear down the hall!" and so he founded a park of Sriwedari, in 1914, in an empty area, for all kinds of sports and fun. Now it belongs to the Harto [Suharto] family. They took away everything.[145]

During the 1920s and 1930s, as colonialism and its particular kind of modernity culminated, the birthdays of the then Dutch queen Wilhelmina became the most order-guarding, place-defining, spectacular feats and attractions of all—with the loudest of music, *krontjong* as well as brass, and also chamber music and recitals in special pavilions, the most colorful gatherings through and of the neighborhoods. These were the occasions when hawkers were most acutely present. The largest *selamatans*—ceremonial and festive community meals that hold out the promise to live together in peace and harmony—would take place in the new amusement parks alongside the other attractions.[146]

Chapter Three

Even people of the country, who might never have been to an urban space before, visited the parks. The colony is remembered as gathering around the amusement—"the altogether unprecedented gathering," on a site that promised "peace, love and hope," "unprecedented success," the new "technical-media event" that, like language clichés—trivial, ephemeral, and *commonplace*—had a highly attractive quality "to fold in on self."[147]

The space was opened to everything modern, including of course the Dutch government and all the other corporations, plantations, trade companies, and banks in the colony, to participate in this new get-together—of all races and classes—with their own jubilee feasts, processions, and very often also *selamatans*. This quote is by a Dutch writer and, at that time, a soldier of the Dutch colonial army, Willem Walraven. He writes about the time very early in the century and about a young Javanese woman who later became his wife:

> Itih . . . was born in the village of Tjigugur, close to Tjimahi in Preanger [West Java]. While the exact date of her birth was not certain, it had to be before the turn of the century, because Itih recalled the feasts on the occasion of Queen Wilhelmina's wedding. She remembered the time when she was a little girl of four or five, her childhood, foremost as feasts and catastrophes. She recalled the trains that rushed by her village, and she still liked to watch a passing train.[148]

The new feasts were spectacular, and at night their sites were brightly lit. Gates would be wide open. For a moment, people were free to enter a space filled with amusement. As the feast sites emerged and continued to emerge, transient and exemplary urbanity was being established and fixed—stalls and booths, merry-go-rounds, an architecture of the spectacular, bright, and unquestionably modern. In a roundabout way the space approximated the clubs where the likes of Walter Spies played and into which the likes of Mr. Karkono were not admitted. Except that these particular clubs, the varieties of the late colonial, stood welcomingly open.

> Mr. JUSUF: I used to play saxophone.
> RM: Like Clinton?
> Mr. JUSUF: Like Clinton. I could make some money.
> RM: You played in bars?
> Mr. JUSUF: Oh, no, there were no bars yet. We played wherever there was a feast.

RM: Jazz band?

Mr. JUSUF: Jazz band. I played saxophone, there was a trumpet, and sometimes we used two saxophones or trumpets, trombone, piano, and bass. We already had that. We might get three *guldens* for a night. If we played till the morning.[149]

✧ ✧ ✧

The most characteristic and most often recalled, new, urban, virtual, absorbing, and expanding spaces of modernity-equals-amusement, modernity-equals-commonplace, were, obviously, the movies. In Willem Walraven's early-century recollections again, he wrote: "On the other side of the street stood a gigantic movie tent built of bamboo. These were the earliest times of film. As the new posters were being pasted up, I saw Itih shuffle there on her little feet."[150]

Mr. ROSIHAN: I saw my first movie in about 1930.

RM: Do you still remember how the movie house looked?

Mr. ROSIHAN: It was in Padang [West Sumatra] and there were, at that time, already one, two, three, four movie houses, four cinemas. And three of them were built of stone.

RM: They were built originally as movie houses?

Mr. ROSIHAN: As movie houses. One was made of wood, Cinema Pondok.

Pondok in Indonesian means "cottage, hut, or cabin," but also "Muslim boarding school."

RM: That one was more for the ordinary people?

Mr. ROSIHAN: The wooden one, yes, for the people. There, I saw my first silent movies. And, one night in 1930, my father took me to see my first talking movie; in the Cinema Scala, in Padang. We went in our horse carriage. I was eight years old.

RM: Where did you sit?

Mr. ROSIHAN: In a *loge*. Here, you had *geiteklas* or *klas kambing*, the goat section, the third class; here was the second class; here was the first class, and here, there were the *loges*.

RM: The closer to the screen, the lower the class?

Chapter Three

Mr. ROSIHAN: Yes. I went with my father, and he was in high spirits. There were the *starlets*, so we called them.

RM: Did the people behave?

Mr. ROSIHAN: Oh, yes! There was whistling, and applauding.

RM: Noisy?

Mr. ROSIHAN: Yes, it was noisy. People also stamped their feet. This was the first time I saw a talking movie; in 1930.

RM: There were also some traveling theater troupes at the time.

Mr. ROSIHAN: I liked that, too. There was one small group, Troubadour, coming to Padang. But they gave their performances in the open.

RM: Not in a tent?

Mr. ROSIHAN: No, it was in a square. When you wanted to see it from up close, you had to pay. Otherwise you could see it, but from afar, and you could not hear the dialogue.[151]

"*'Lanterne magique! Pièce curieuse!'* With this cry, a peddler would travel through the streets of Paris in the evening and, at a wave of the hand, step up into dwellings where he operated his lantern."[152] As the magic lantern in the nineteenth-century metropolis of Europe, movies in the colony were the new space—off the street, not really of the house, and, thus virtual, truly virtual, to both.

Mrs. TORAR: We went mostly to Decca Park [in Central Jakarta]. It used to be the place for the movies. There was Palace Cinema, and President, and—I forgot the other one.

RM: It was across from the Gambir Station?

Mrs. TORAR: Yes. Oh, Capitol! This was famous. And Globe, too. It was all still very new at the time.

RM: There were Dutch and Indonesians and all the others going to the movies?

Mrs. TORAR: Yes, all of them—*first class, second class, and* the goat class.[153]

Closed to the outside, to the outside noise and light, open to anybody who could pay, the movie house greatly intensified the new, acute, and memorable sense of modern togetherness. There had also been, very early on, the traveling, "circulating" cinemas in the colony.[154] Neighborhoods reached endlessly far, and it became difficult to stay off the net.

The Fences

Mrs. OEI: My father was active in Javanese culture. He owned two large gongs, and he had rented them to various groups of Javanese dancers and to puppeteers for the shadow theater. I liked to watch, but my elder brother, he was *anti*. He said: "Look, what is that!" There was already a movie house in town, and he said: "Better to go to the movies once a week!"[155]

Mrs. DAMAIS: Oh, yes! At that time *talking films* arrived. We girls jumped on our bikes, and off we went.[156]

Movie houses were on the road—the space to which, as it was becoming clear, modern people were to aim. Being at the movies was being (almost) there.

RM: So you moved to Jakarta. How did you feel the change?
Mrs. MINARSIH: Oh, it was fantastic. After we arrived, the first thing was to go to the movies. In Bukittinggi [West Sumatra], we also had movies. But it was all like one third class! When I came here, to Jakarta, the first thing was to go to the movies. It was in Kramat, near where the Gunung Agung bookstore is today—Metro or Megaria, I forgot the name, but it was *fantastic*. They just played that—
RM:—?
Mrs. MINARSIH:—*cartoons*. I was not yet fifteen, so I sometimes smuggled myself in—to see the movies, not just what was allowed to children.[157]

Most of the people to whom I talked left their home and home neighborhood at the age of puberty at the latest. Perhaps because of this, their memories of the place were finite. Perhaps because of this, there was a striking wholeness of their recollections.

Air Marshal DHANI: Father was very strict with us: "Do not run around, do not shout! Behave!" We could play in front of our house, this we could. And sometimes we went to the fields, and we played with buffalo. There was also a little stream near the house, and there we could swim. Women did their washing there, but we did not feel free with them at all; it was not the custom of that time, especially not in

Chapter Three

Central Java. And when someone died, everybody was sad: "Why did it happen? It cannot be!" One had to report it to the head of the neighborhood: "It happened. Where should we dig the grave?" They came as guests, and they were offered something to drink. All the neighbors already knew, and they only asked: "Where should we dig the grave?" "There." Not everyone could dig the grave; there were experts in the community. People brought what was needed: "Do you need *sugar*, do you need *tea*?" so that the family that suffered would not get distracted. Without delay, the one who had died was buried. And there was that *stream*, about a hundred meters from our house. The water was clean in the small river and there were *fish*, of many kinds. Some people knew all the *fish* names. At night there were *fireflies*.[158]

Almost everything the old people recalled was given to me in this form of wholesomeness. Even the cities, as in this song to Jakarta:

To Cikini Quarter, to Godang Avenue,
I sing a sweet melody, my little one,
and you know why —[159]

Yet the old people could not help but recall themselves as children growing up, men or women maturing, and old folks nearing the grave. This passing made their recollections always profound. But what truly gave me the people as real and epical was how they made themselves appear straight, cultured, and thus, *perspectival*: "Perspectival culture, [is] a culture characterized by a manner of thinking that measures itself according to the idealizing abstractions of an ever-receding horizon. . . . The horizon is understood as the repository of all possible perspectives of an object."[160]

Physical violence is a way of touching. In a modern metropolis, and namely in Jakarta in the period, as I talked to the old people, it often seemed that *all* touching would bring violence. The modern, even postmodern, mode of behaving suggested itself as a way to survive in that given space. The place was felt to be bearable if — in a truly postmodern mode — "all things appeared as solved in accidental moments" and if experience did not appear to be formed "in continuous looking back and forward" but in "sequential jolts."[161]

After colonialism, Japanese occupation, and failed revolution, dwelling

The Fences

appeared to reach its ultimate shape as a passing by or a driving through. This is a poem from the time of the revolution quoted to me by several of the old people:

> I run around with them, what else can I do now—
> Changing my face at the edge of the street, I use their eyes
> and go along to visit the fun houses:
> these are the facts as they know them
> (a new American flick at the Capitol, the new song to which they
>   dance) . . .
> Hanging around at the tram stop, we wait for the Jakarta Chinatown
>   trolley.[162]

Georg Simmel's description of the new urbane is perhaps more valid for this colonial and postcolonial metropolis than for the early twentieth-century cities of Europe, where it all was only suggested: "In the metropolis . . . , in the complexity and confusion of the external image of city life, one grows accustomed to continual abstractions, to indifference towards that which is spatially closest and to an intimate relationship to that which is spatially very far removed."[163] In a fundamentally more abrupt shock than their European counterparts, with much less preparation for it, the elderly Indonesians to whom I talked were attacked and overwhelmed by the newness of the modern urban and the metropolitan—by its "fullness"—even more than the early-century inhabitants of Berlin in Simmel's description: "Here, in buildings and educational institutions, in the wonders and comforts of space-conquering technology, in the formations of community life, and in the visible institutions of the state, is offered such an overwhelming fullness of crystallized and impersonalized spirit that the personality, so to speak, cannot maintain itself under its impact."[164] As if Simmel had (almost) seen one of the early-century colony amusement parks or went to a Jakarta movie. In the radiant "*arena* of metropolitan culture," he wrote, people have "to *exaggerate*" their "personal element" "*in order to remain audible*," "even to themselves."[165]

A modern urban experience comes as a jolt, and it is indeed equal to the memories of the people who lived it all and now carefully look back. Both the city and the memories appear to be "committed to illusionism, with every material assuming, calion-like, the attributes of something not itself— columns dissolving into bars of light, or glass walls becoming opaque and marble ones appearing transparent due to their reflectivity—but even more importantly, with a mysteriousness built into the plan such that the building is constructed without an approachable or knowable center and is in fact experienced as . . . a labyrinth. The resistance to the spectator's grasp."[166] In a *labyrinth* for a *spectator* and for a *passerby*, as in an amusement park, and as a commonplace, more than elsewhere, and perhaps only there, things like "comfort civilization," "social standing," or "civic-mindedness," trivialized enough, may go together.[167] The colony becoming urban, like the memories of it, and like avant-garde and postmodern architecture, may be described as an "abstract sublime."[168]

All the old people to whom I have talked wished to fly. Their cities, with all the black exhaust of their aging buses and cars and motorcycles, and even with the black smoke from the riots, still appeared streamlined—or trendy, or trivial—like Le Corbusier's utopian Maison Citrohan, a house designed in 1920 "to evoke the mass-production norms of a Citroën car,"[169] thus "fast." There was equally much in the old people's postcolony, gasping, aging, and even burning, of the other Le Corbusier–like *sublime* and supermodern designs, like the famous chapel in Rochamp in the Alps, built on a model of a "ship's prow," with some of its segments resembling "a full sail" or even "an airplane wing."[170]

In spite of all the government measures, hawkers can still be seen (and heard, where there is less traffic) touting their wares against the background of Jakarta's big and expanding malls and along the huge "avenues of skyscrapers." Many of the old people to whom I talked in Jakarta still lived in those prewar one-story houses with high Dutch, red-tile roofs under the big trees, with skyscrapers sometimes visible and sometimes not. Virtually all of them were both strikingly and eagerly *nonchalant* about it. The octogenarian Omar Dhani, when he talked to me about his friends and neighbors of the past six decades or so, as we were sitting in the front room of his house, gesticulated toward places where they used to live and some even still did: "The most extreme separation between the places it links together—modern . . . motorways."[171]

I had to visit the friends, Mr. Dhani urged me, each time pointing with his thumb (in the polite Javanese way): they live a stone's throw away, just beyond that little stream, a few minutes' walk—if only it were not for this bypass and that flyover. Instead of a few minutes, an hour of driving around and around, from us to them, was needed (if, of course, they were not already dead).

✦✦✦

The Fences

Le Corbusier called some of his most famous urban projects "synthetic." Maison Citrohan, for instance, was "conceived as synthesizing other type forms drawn from metropolitan culture."[172] To put it another way, through a modern urban space as a machine for living, a new sense of belonging was to be created against and over the other desires, tensions, and especially the sense of social difference, injustice, and class. As Marx might say, *brotherhood* (and sisterhood) were to be created: "The phrase which corresponded to this imagined liquidation of class relations was *fraternité*."[173]

When Mr. Dhani pointed me to his existing or no longer existing friends, as if they were still next door, and as if the bypasses and flyovers — as well as the other things in between him and them — did not exist, I thought his gestures were nonchalant. Georg Simmel would call them "blasé": "No psychic phenomena," he wrote,

> have been so unconditionally reserved to the metropolis as has the blasé attitude.... in fact, every metropolitan child shows [it] when compared with children of quieter and less changeable milieus.... The essence of this blasé attitude consists in the blunting of discrimination. This does not mean that the objects are not perceived, as is the case with the half-wit, but rather that the meaning and differing values of things, and thereby the things themselves, are experienced as insubstantial.... To the blasé person... all things float with equal specific gravity in the constantly moving stream of money. All things lie on the same level and differ from one another only in the size of the area, which they cover.[174]

CHAPTER FOUR

THE CLASSROOM

Wherever I go they ask me: "Spell your name."
—Bertolt Brecht, "Sonnet in Emigration"

THE ROAD TO SCHOOL

School was rarely remembered without recalling distance—even the lowest types of schools and the lowest schools' lowest grades invoked distance:

> Mrs. TRIMURTI: When I was very small, I went first to school close to my house. It was an elementary school. Just opposite the house. As close as that house over there, you see?[1]

There always also seemed to be a dusty, hot, and long road leading to the school. This is often the first, and sometimes ultimate, thing to be recalled: "Yes, that going to school, on foot, the same road every day."[2]

> Mr. SARLI: Six kilometers. Every day. It was far. When it was hot or when it rained, I went to school. When it rained too much, I just hid for a while at the roadside.[3]

Children mostly went in groups, and, sometimes, with their guardians. The most privileged of the children traveled a road to school from a very early age:

> Princess NOEROEL: Nanny went with us. She waited for us and, after school, she took us back.[4]

THE FINAL CLASS OF THE HBS FIVE-YEAR SENIOR HIGH SCHOOL AT A DANCE CELEBRATING GRADUATION, CA. 1938. KONINKLIJK INSTITUUT VOOR TAAL-, LAND- EN VOLKENKUNDE, LEIDEN

Dr. ONG: Even the *kindergarten* as I recall was not very near our house. It was quite a distance to go, especially for a small child.⁵

It had been a journey with a clear aim. There had been a point distinctly at the journey's end — or so it seemed and so it is recalled. The exertion fitted the journey:

Professor SOEMITRO: Sometimes I went to school without breakfast. Just a cup of something to drink. Parents made us even believe that it was better to go without breakfast; that it would make us stronger for school.⁶

The road, of course, was a dangerous place. The danger of and the anxiety about the road to school, however, was particularly that it might be blocked. Moving on the road to school was an adventure, thrilling and scary largely because it might at a moment be taken away. It was the possibility, first of all, that the journey might be cut short before the goal was reached that made the journey anxious.

Mrs. MIRIAM: I never got as far [as my brother did], because at one moment the funds were finished, or something else happened, I do not recall what. I never got there.⁷

Mr. SOEDARPO: My elder brother and sister got to attend ELS [Europeesche Lagere School], European grade school. But then our father died, and Soebadio [the brother], my sister, and I could not go to the Dutch school anymore. So we just went to HIS [Hollandsch-Inlandsche School], the Dutch-native grade school; never to ELS.⁸

Mrs. MUNARDJO: Of course, I liked school. But I did not get further than half of the MULO [Meer Uitgebreid Lager Onderwijs], junior high. We tried to keep paying for the MULO, but after two years we ran out of money — no more school.⁹

Even the lowest school had to be paid for. It was commonly called *sekolah setalén*, "twenty-five-cent school."¹⁰ The next one, the "second-class school," cost twice as much already, and then the fees (on the road up) would rise steeply.

> Princess BROTODININGRAT: It was merely for the haves. You had not, you could not.[11]

As this was a colony, and as most of these journeys were being cut short, the dynamics of the adventure, the anxiety and intensity of the journey, surpassed what might have been experienced elsewhere. The modern passions of education culminated here, in this place and at this time.

> Mr. ALWIN: Only much later did I understand it: what an immense sacrifice it had been for our parents. Their *level of income*, of course, was nothing like that of the Dutch families in the colony, but they still wanted their children to get on the *Dutch track*. When I was about to enter the first grade of school, in 1932, when I was six, my parents moved to a "Western address" of town.[12]

> Mr. MOEDJONO: My grandpa owned a small cigarette factory, and so he could help. This is my history. I went to the Dutch grade school for five years, to an agricultural middle school for three years, and then, it was the end. He died.[13]

> Mrs. SOSRO: I was daughter number three. The other girls went to school, Salirah and Jainah. Myself, I could not go.
> OTHER (Mrs. Sosro's friend): "Don't!" they said.[14]

When it came to the road to school, the old people's memories, as a rule, became especially intense. At these particular moments of recollection, the homes and neighborhoods, villages, towns, cities, parents, grandparents, all that was now gone, became distinctly alive—and, more often than not, distinctly helpless:

> Father MANGUNWIJAYA: No! It was a Dutch-native grade school only. Because my father never attained a level on the basis of which his son might be let in—to be educated at a Dutch school. My father got just below that level. I still remember how angry he was that he could not bring me to the European lower school in town.[15]

> Mrs. POLITON: It was simple: "What is your parents' income? Less than this? You cannot be admitted." One had to have school money. My parents did put it together. They paid out of the money they got from our orchard.

Chapter Four

This interview took place in Mrs. Politon's house on a Menado street named after a private college she and her husband founded in the 1950s. It has now long been inactive.

> Mr. SEKO (Mrs. Politon's husband): My family did not have an orchard.[16]

Making it and getting onto the road to school was experienced, and is recalled, much as a compassion for those who "did not make it," who—in the road language—"were left behind," who did not manage to move as smoothly and as fast. A vision was born on the road to school of the unschooled, not-yet-schooled, or not-yet-enough-schooled: the *common people* (often they were named in English to me), the *volk* (in Dutch), or the *rakjat* (in Indonesian, now *rakyat*)). The vision born on the road, inevitably and so as to function well, was as forward-looking, as "pregnant with future," and as straight or softly curved as the road itself.

> Mrs. POLITON: The common people, if they went to school at all, got only to a kind of basic school, the people's school it was called. Three years only.
> RM: Common people?
> Mrs. POLITON: It was also called *Volksschool*. The third grade was the end. They would not even think they might go to a better or higher school. Just as far as that. Then they worked, in the fields and such.[17]
> Mr. MULYONO: My school was an ordinary-people school. The pupils were mostly from workers' families, peasants. It was on the outskirts of town. The school was called *Volksschool*. It was a school for servants (*This was said bitterly.*)—Just three years.[18]

The road to school cut through an increasingly modern colonial landscape—through homes and neighborhoods. To move on the road, a new compass, new musts and must-nots, were needed, and a new perspective. The road to school, of course, had to begin at home. The homes and neighborhoods were the road's starting points, but the road became the pointer, and soon also the axis of the homes and neighborhoods. Even the homes and the neighborhoods, now, had either to head straight and forward—as the road pointed, where the best possible school was—or to be (seen as) aimless.

The Classroom

>Professor RESINK: I went to the best school in town, the so-called Christelijke Mulo [Christian Junior High] — [19]

>Mrs. RAHMIATI: Mine was the second-best school in town.[20]

As one moved on the road to school, one's home and neighborhood, the walls, the fences, the space, and the sound and feel of it moved, too (moved back); the landscape and the whole land became an attribute of the road, sort of, a roadside land.[21] Moving on the road to school, the feel, touch, smell, and shape of it, explained virtually everything, including, most important, one's belonging to it all.

>RM: You felt exactly like Mr. Purbo?
>
>Mr. ALWIN: Yes, everything was the same, except that I had an advantage, because my elder brother had already been admitted to the school, before me. So that nobody was surprised when I applied. He opened the door.[22]
>
>Mrs. DAMAIS: In the past, the system was like that: the European grade school was for the Dutch and for some Eurasians — and some of the well-off people from other groups could also be admitted. For instance, I was *put in* the Dutch school, because my father was a teacher. And there were some other Indonesian children from families of higher officials as well.[23]

There are not many reports of the frightening ghosts on this road, nor in the trees, streams, and dark spots along it. Not that the specters had disappeared. But now, ahead, in this road space of "the preliminary and provisional,"[24] if one only kept on looking ahead and kept on moving, there was a promise.

>Mr. ALWIN: It was in Brastagi in the hills above Medan [East Sumatra], and only now can I *appreciate* that I was able to enter that European grade school. It is not easy to understand how my parents could achieve it. This was something completely new. It was called "planters' school," and it was for the families of the big planters in the area. I was *extremely* lucky, as I said, that I had such progressive parents. So I got into the "planters school."[25]

The road to school offered a new space of transparency, of straightforward (or soft-curved) correctness, promise of safety, and even power. It was exclusive and inclusive at the same time—this is what progress implied. Ambitions and dreams of advancement and even of freedom were to be given to one in this space as naturally as a bit of (or much) embarrassment.

> RM: Do you mean to tell me that you felt more comfortable in the Dutch school than at home? Was it that skill to switch easily?
>
> Professor KOENTJARANINGRAT: Yes, easily, I think so. But also—and I am a little embarrassed to tell you this: I was from that class where your *chances* were to go to school. My parents were of that class. Otherwise there was a limited admission, sorry to say.²⁶

The road to school is recalled as intimacy, a sense of home and neighborhood corrected and constantly upgraded as one moved on the road, and as the road progressed. The prestige and wealth of home and neighborhood, everything that could be *gathered*, went with the travelers. Siblings and cousins went as if in one boat, in the same direction, as far as possible. Boys and girls from the same place tended to go at least part of the way *together*. The "same place," the home, the starting point, besides, was being progressively redefined, "corrected" by the perspective of the road.

> Air Marshal DHANI: I went to school in Gondang [Central Java], which was five kilometers from Klaten. My cousins lived there, and I went with friends.²⁷
>
> RM: So you were not alone in school?
>
> Mr. WOWOR: I was the only one among my brothers who went there. But many other relatives went. And some more distant relatives lived there. With them I went to school.²⁸
>
> Air Marshal DHANI: Then, I went to AMS [Algemeene Middlebare School, senior high] in Yogyakarta. We had an *extended family system* for this. There was an uncle and I stayed with him, rent and board.
>
> RM: Sort of family?
>
> Air Marshal DHANI: Yes. There was a garden pavilion in the back of his house, with two rooms. I got one room and another relative of my uncle, Haryono, he later became army general, you know the name—
>
> RM: Yes.
>
> Air Marshal DHANI: Haryono lived in the other room. He went to the

The Classroom

AMS A [which was a five-year high school with extended instruction in classical languages and cultures].[29]

Togetherness and intimacy are remembered as being upgraded on the road to school. Never too tight, hominess progressively, gradually, and imperceptibly as one moved, was spreading thin to fit the road. The circles of togetherness are recalled as covering an ever wider territory in the new topography. Increasingly, warmth is most intensely defined by the road:

> Mr. DAINO: My father died when I was still little.
> RM: Very little?
> Mr. DAINO: Second year of grade school. My *uncle* took over, because he had money and he could pay for school.
> RM: You moved to your uncle's house?
> Mr. DAINO: Yes, and my mother, from our town, moved with me.[30]

One almost never hears about some sharp line dividing the intimacy of the home and the road to school. The power of the road seems to blur the line. Enframed by the new horizon, where the road aims, the thin and loose warmth of the road is being recalled as growing inward.

> Mrs. TORAR: When I was a girl, yes! We had forty people in our house at one time.
> RM: It was a big house.
> Mrs. TORAR: It did not matter so much, Mr. Rudolf. My father was a teacher, and he did it for education. Everybody at the time wanted their children to go to a good school, and so they sent their children to my father. There were sixteen children, and my father had children of his own — many children; at that moment seven were still at home. The children of my father's *brothers and sisters* lived in the house, the children of one of my maternal aunts — three had already been married, but six of them were still small; they were in the house as well. My mother told me that there were forty people in the house. And there was no additional income to pay for them. There was little money in the house because my father helped so many children.[31]

However curved a road to school might be, as long as one kept on moving, the new space was meaningfully, that is geometrically, indeed linearly, defined. The one who touched the road became animated by the drive to get to the school at the end of the road, there, where it touched the new horizon. One's life, including one's sense of warmth, security, and shelter, was newly projected—again streamlined. One learned to *dwell* on the road.

> Mr. SUTIKNO: I was in the sixth year of grade school. The school was in Semarang and my parents lived in Kudus.[32]

Progressively, gradually and imperceptibly, dwelling began to appear as safe, and as homey, as close as it happened to be to the road, as much one managed to pack oneself with the road's energy.

> RM: You speak so nicely about that kind of life. But were not all these students just a tiny elite? They did not seem to know very much about ordinary people's lives. They lived—where did these students actually live?
>
> Professor RESINK: Some lived with their relatives if they had any near their school. But as they made it to a higher education and a bigger town, and Jakarta, most of them lived in *pensions* for students and in student dormitories.[33]

The increasing traffic-hominess made the passing feel increasingly natural. One walked, drove, covered distances and territories, and felt, increasingly, as if this were one's *rite de passage*—as if this were the same thing as growing up.

> Mr. ASRUL: My elder brother went to school in Jakarta. He stayed in a kind of *boarding* place, Dutch *internaat*. The name was Jan Pieterszoon Coen [the founder of Batavia in 1619]; today there is a military-police garrison there. It was an *internaat* and it was rather exclusive. Mostly Dutch students lived there, and a very select group of Indonesian students, because it was very expensive.[34]

Of course, these were still children or almost children, and, sometimes, crying is recalled.

> Professor SOEMARDJAN: After I finished my elementary, I got to go to another town, Madiun [East Java], to a *boarding school*. It was a

long journey. One had to go by train, and my mother also went to the station. When the train began to move, she cried. I did not cry.

RM: You could not, because you were a man.

Professor SOEMARDJAN: Yes, I was a man. But the first night at the *boarding school* I cried. I did not confess it to anybody, but I cried, I cried all the time.[35]

The road to school, however, as soon as one got over this (or as much as one dared not to confess it), was judged by its instrumentality: how well it was constructed and paved and curved. There was a road skill to be learned; the road's tricky sections or bumps were there to be negotiated and overcome. Actually, it gave the road its infectious and syncopated (modern, exciting) rhythm.

Mr. ROSIHAN: I went with Usmar Ismail, my classmate from Padang [West Sumatra], who was accepted to the same school in Yogyakarta. First, we traveled to Bandung and stayed at Usmar's uncle's one night. Next morning we took a train across Java to Yogyakarta.

RM: It is a long trip.

Mr. ROSIHAN: We started at about eight or nine in the morning and we arrived at six in the evening. In Yogya, at the station, we were approached by people who were looking for boys like us to board with them. I was in fact to stay in a dormitory, called Boedi Oetomo, but I went instead with a Catholic teacher, one of the people waiting at the station: "Why don't you come to my house? You pay twelve guilders only."

RM: Did not it bother you that he was a Christian?

Mr. ROSIHAN: Oh, no! It did not even enter my mind. I didn't care. So we went, and there were already four boys staying with the priest, two from Medan [North Sumatra] and two from Palembang [South Sumatra].

RM: All Muslims?

Mr. ROSIHAN: All Muslims.

RM: Did not your father tell you what kind of lodging you should choose?

Mr. ROSIHAN: No, no, no.

RM: You were free—?

Mr. ROSIHAN: Free. I was on my own: "You find your way." He gave me money: "You find your way."[36]

Chapter Four

There were to be haltings on such a long and adventurous road, and I could still feel the enormous energy that had been invested to overcome each one of them. The old people who had made it, as well as the dropouts, had invested their lives in the sequence of the stumbles being overcome. They were still, in fact, investing as they recalled it for me. Possibly nowhere could I hear it so naked, so clear, and so eagerly conveyed as in a postcolony. Here the stopover memories and stopover lives, stopover ambitions, affections, and warmth—and even the stopover mothers and the stopover fathers—seemed most at home.

> Mr. ROSIHAN: Doctor Tjan Tjoe Siem was a teacher of Javanese. He studied at the University of Leiden and was known as *Professor* Tjan. He was a friend of several Dutch scholars of the time. And he became my father. He said: "You come to live with me." He was not married. He was still young, about thirty, I think.
>
> RM: Did you say he became your father?
>
> Mr. ROSIHAN: Yes. He was the one who taught me to read, with passion you know. He had a big library, and I read everything that was there. He also taught me Arabic. In the afternoons he taught me Arabic, from Dutch and German textbooks. Each Sunday we went to the movies.
>
> RM: He liked movies?
>
> Mr. ROSIHAN: He liked movies, but only in the daytime. In the evening, you had to study.
>
> RM: How long did you stay with Tjan Tjoe Siem?
>
> Mr. ROSIHAN: Till the end. Till the end of the Dutch era that is. When Japan invaded in 1942, I moved to Jakarta.[37]

Since pre-Dutch and precolonial times, young men in the islands would leave their homes and travel to learn. Religious schools, Islamic and Buddhist especially, had always been on the road. Students moved from teacher to teacher, and often also the words in various Indonesian languages for traveler and student are identical. Since ancient times, the farther the journey, so it was perceived, the sublimer the learning.

One new quality in traveling to the modern school had been the extent to which speed, the surface of the road, and the vehicles used on the road played a part in the sublimity of the adventure—the faster the road, the sublimer the learning. Surface especially still holds the memory.

The Classroom

Mr. HARDOYO: As I advanced to the Dutch-native grade school, I had to travel nineteen kilometers. I used a buggy.[38]

Professor RESINK: I went in a small carriage drawn by a pony.
RM: Who was driving?
Professor RESINK: Our coachman, of course.[39]

The more of preparation, of checking the brakes, the tires (or the horseshoes at a time before tires), the more new space appeared to open ahead and the more a road to school appeared time fitting and soul fulfilling. The more the road appeared to be technologically grounded, the more — measurably more — long distance it seemed destined to be.

Mr. ROSIHAN: First, I went to school in our old buggy, with two horses. First we had two horses, and later just one. I do not know what happened to the horse. Maybe he got old.[40]

Next, a bicycle connected with the road to school, and more correctly than with any other road of the colony. School and bicycle became twins; school made bicycle a serious commonplace.

Mrs. SOELISTINA: When I went to school, I went on bicycle.
RM: Because the school was so far from your home?
Mrs. SOELISTINA: Oh, just a kilometer or so.
RM: But still you went on bicycle?
Mrs. SOELISTINA: Yes, of course.[41]

As the road became a space, covering a territory and networking the colony, increasing numbers of students went to school, farther on, by bus and by train.

Mrs. HARTINI: I went to school in Madiun and I lived in an *uncle's house*. Every *weekend* I went home, when I wanted: there was a bus.[42]

Railway stations, especially, became some of the grandest sites of colonial architecture and of newly created space.[43] The stations, the points of departures and stopovers, the arrows, are recalled best in the mode and spirit of a road to school. They marked, and still do, the journey's progress, bigger

Chapter Four

and grander in memory, modern and ever more modern as the train with the student, from a stop nearest home, puffed through the track landscape, approaching a bigger town, the better school.

> Mr. KARKONO: I was born in the provinces and went to school in town. I took the train *every* day.
> RM: To Surakarta?
> Mr. KARKONO: I lived in the area of Sragen, near Surakarta. I got up at half past four in the morning. I boarded the train at six. I was in Surakarta at seven. The train departed back at two.⁴⁴

Modern affections were being built on the way to school, on the train; often affections for life, and thus it is fondly recalled—togetherness from station to station.

> Mr. SOEDARPO: In Pangkalanbrandan [East Sumatra], it was always *fun*. The train was a daily experience. And it was something new. The nice part of it was, and I recall this very well, how the train would fill up with friends as it got closer to the city. Early in the morning we went to school by the *Medan Trein* [Medan Train]. My mother would prepare fried rice, and we would eat it on board. The train had carriages of three classes; the third class we called "cattle class." Nothing is without a problem, of course. Each class was still separated—a section for women and another one for men. So, our sister, who went to school in Medan too, had to go not with us, but in the women's compartment.⁴⁵

The road to school could be explained and argued geometrically, linearly, in pure reason, arithmetically; even, as common sense, indeed a commonplace, it was progressive. From the road, best of all, and soon only from the road, was one able to explain, and argue for, the way in which life should be lived in the colonial and modern time and space.

> RM: So you went to a Dutch school?
> Colonel SIMBOLON: Yes, but only because my father, who was born in 1885, was so very progressive. So I went to a Dutch school, the Dutch *grade school*.⁴⁶

> Mr. ALWIN: Teachers were so much respected in Kota Gedang! It was said that that place was the most advanced in West Sumatra; that in the whole colony there were few places like that. It was said that there were the most progressive and most courageous people there.⁴⁷

Moving on the road to school, one was empowered by the road to see correctly and safely forward, backward, and all around—to see, among other things, those who were left behind and off the road as *doenia kampoeng*, "the world of simple neighborhoods," of *orang desa*, "the villagers," or, indeed, of *inlanders*, "the natives."⁴⁸ Those appeared as *koeno*, "ancient, dated, old-fashioned," or even more fittingly—in the frequently used term as the culture of the road set in—*bodoh*, "stupid, unschooled." One had to move forward.

> Mr. SEDA: It was as it had to be. My family understood it early on: education was a motor of progress. I was given school as a good inheritance from my father, my uncle, and my whole family. This was the best inheritance that could be—not that stuff stored in a treasure box; not there but in the brain. So I was being pushed, and very much so, to go to school.⁴⁹

CHANGING CLOTHES

School has been recalled as a place, shelter, building, like the German *Bildung*—"*Bildung* has no exact equivalent in English: *Bildung* means picture or image; *bilden* to shape or form, but also to educate; *ungebildet*, uneducated, uncultural"—as a space, where the road to school ended; for a moment.⁵⁰

> Mrs. MIRIAM: It was very safe; the school was very nice. I went back, two years ago, and the school is still there. It is quite run down, but it still functions.
> RM: Still a school?
> Mrs. MIRIAM: Yes, still a school. So, it was nice. It was a European grade school.⁵¹
>
> Mr. ASRUL: For that town at the time it was a very fine building. The building is still there. Next to prison, in fact.⁵²

Chapter Four

These are very physical memories of the school at the end (for a while) of the road. The space of the school is recalled as full and filled, divided into segments and thus defined; made unforgettable by the school benches, the blackboard, the teachers' desk, and, of course, the walls.

> Mrs. MASKUN: The benches were of light brown wood.
> RM: A good school?
> Mrs. MASKUN: Pretty.[53]

> Mr. ROSIHAN: It is still there, still used, but not a senior high anymore. It was built of stone, rectangular, and one floor. In front, three classrooms — second, sixth, and third grade; here there was the first grade, fifth, and fourth grade; here, here, and here there were doors, and we sat in the forms, like that. It was a big building; of stone, did I tell you that? On Tanjung Street.
> RM: And it is still there.
> Mr. ROSIHAN: It is still there. I remember, number 47.[54]

> Mrs. OEI: In the front, there was a map on the left, and the portrait of the [Dutch] Queen on the right.[55]

> Professor SOEMARDJAN: Here — (*He is again drawing a sketch for me.*) Here is the school: classroom, classroom, classroom, classroom, and classroom. Here it is open: this is the first grade, second, third, fourth, fifth, sixth, seventh. We started here and went up to here. You could walk through here, and here were the classrooms. I went to the first grade here, and I finished here. Thus, it was very neatly organized. We all understood the system — you came from this room, and here there was the seventh grade. Here you go, the seventh grade. And there were forms, of course, and two of us in each form.[56]

School is remembered physically and accurately. It is recalled as regular, angular, and — more naturally even than a modern home — in numbers.

> Mr. GESANG: I went to school for five years. It began when I was seven, and I finished it when I was — eight, nine, ten, eleven, twelve — yes, a little over twelve.[57]

> Professor SOEMITRO: I passed my examination for the HBS [Hoogere

Burgerschool, a five-year high school], and I was number two, almost the best.⁵⁸

However curved the road they traveled, and from whatever part of the colony they might come, now, in the school, in the formations of the school benches, they faced forward—a little up, too, toward the teacher, the map, the portrait of the (Dutch) Queen, and the blackboard. The symmetry could not be doubted.

> Mr. ALWIN: In the first grade, there were *four parallel classes — twenty-five* students in *each, one hundred* students total. *However,* as we advanced, not all of us made it. In the second grade, there were only three *parallel classes,* in the third grade only two!⁵⁹

✦ ✦ ✦

The space of school, by the force of its perspective and its forward looking, had the potential to expand endlessly—first into a schoolyard, then, a small step further on, into a sports field.

> Mr. HARDOYO: There were sports! Very fine sports. It was a Dutch school: good, a very good one. And there were very fine sports.⁶⁰

The students could play ball, run, and jump in the expanded school space, moved with and by the force of school and the time of school, according to school rules and schedule.⁶¹ This was a school-sport kind of joy, and it is—it cannot be but—recalled in a proper, neat, accurate, sportily school way, in the language of sport, or, actually, in fragments of it.

> Mr. SUWARDI: Not really sports. Not too much of sports. You mean at home?
> RM: But you played soccer as a boy?
> Mr. SUWARDI: We played, yes, in some vacant place. But there was not any real direction to it.⁶²
>
> Mr. ASRUL: We played soccer in school. Later, in high school, there was a real *soccer craze,* and still later *basketball.* We liked *boxing,* also, but the equipment was too expensive. Girls liked *handball,* for us boys it was *voetbal,* soccer.⁶³

Chapter Four

Mrs. SOELISTINA: There were special courts at school for everything, *volleyball*, *basketball*, there was a *track-and-field* course, an approach for *long jump*, a space for *javelin*, a cage for *discus*. Everything was there.[64]

In the colony, one can see more clearly why some social critics in the West feel so apprehensive about a sports field. Avital Ronell calls the thing "the playing fields," and her allusion to "killing fields" is only thinly veiled.[65] According to Walter Benjamin, similarly, "Kafka's gestures of horror are well served by the glorious *field for play (Spielraum)* of which the catastrophe will know nothing."[66]

Siegfried Kracauer, writing about Germany at the same time as the colonial sporting was happening in Indonesia, noted that "physical training expropriates people's energy."[67] It may be the same thing to say that the young people in the colony (and then the same people, only much older, recalling it) overwhelmingly and eagerly accepted the expropriation as an opening of a new space for them, or — if one were to put it even more darkly — as a way of freedom.

RM: Only two Indonesian students were on the soccer team?

Mr. ALWIN: Only two Indonesians, correct. As you ask about it, in fact, I did not think it as anything strange; it was normal. Maybe, because we felt *accepted*, we felt *accepted* by the school and the team. I played *soccer* all the time and very well, so that even the Dutch boys were eager to play with me. I really liked *sports*, I really liked it. I was on the *gymnastics team* of my high school, HBS, as well.[68]

Professor SOEMITRO: I played *defense*, first in the AMS school and then in Madiun. We called our team SH, Setia Hati [Faithful Heart]. At fourteen I began with tennis, at sixteen or seventeen with *track and field*.

RM: Busy?

Professor SOEMITRO: There was that Dutch girl. She would come to see me!

RM: A Dutch girl?

Professor SOEMITRO: Everybody was making fun of me: "Hey, there she is again, your *fee*." They called her *fee*; it is a Dutch word, you know, for some kind of a lofty spirit, like *elf*; sweet. "She is fated to you." And she heard it, and she laughed.[69]

The Classroom

By the force of the new school's perspective, through the schoolyard and the sports fields, ever wider space seemed to open, equally neat and gridlike, extremely playful — nothing in the whole colony seemed to be able to stand in the way of its expansion.

> Mr. JUSUF: Sometimes, in the afternoon, we played soccer in the town square.
> RM: Just Indonesians?
> Mr. JUSUF: Just Indonesians, But in school it was mixed. And I began to play in a Dutch club, too.
> RM: What was its name?
> Mr. JUSUF: The field is still there, in Jakarta, on Cokroaminoto Street. It was called *VIOS*. V-I-O-S — [Voorwaarts Is Ons Streven (Forward Is Our Zeal)]
> RM: You went on the road with them?
> Mr. JUSUF: Yes, for a *match*. Around Batavia and as far east as Surabaya; also to Bandung.
> RM: But what about your patriotism?
> Mr. JUSUF: It was a part of it! I wanted to be better than them. I wanted most of all to be selected for the A-team. I even dreamed about playing in the *World Cup*. I wanted to be the *Player of the Year*. They were mostly Dutch on the team, of course; one was Chinese, and I was one of three Indonesians![70]

It seems that too much already has been said about sports. However, the elderly Indonesians (and not only men as one might expect) kept coming back to sports, again and again as we talked, and this, I feel, has to be recorded in some proportion.

> Mr. SOEDARPO: When I moved from my junior to senior high, there was an older fellow who began to coach me. Every day after school I had lunch, rested for a while, and did homework, but by four o'clock I went over to the courts. In 1939 I ran the hurdles. As matter of fact, some of my friends called me "Westerner" and names like that. But I just did not want to lose a fight.
> RM: There were competitions?
> Mr. SOEDARPO: There were quarterly races in school towns, in Yogyakarta and Surakarta, for instance. There were *soccer, basketball,*

Chapter Four

and *track-and-field* contests. I was good in the hundred-meter sprint, and I was four times on my school team. In 1939, just when the war in Europe broke out, we were here in Jakarta at the big competition at Gambir Square, during the big annual fair.

RM: Aboe Bakar [Mr. Soedarpo's classmate] told me that you used to have your own system of body control.

Mr. SOEDARPO: Rhythm. It was all a matter of rhythm. You had to get the feeling like *pff, pff, pff*— (*Mr. Soedarpo got up from his desk and he showed me, while his two secretaries across the large office watched.*)

RM: So, how was it? The war was coming, and you were doing sports?

Mr. SOEDARPO: It was not so simple. It was a mixture of several things. In 1936, in Yogyakarta, for instance, we had that Chinese boycott of the Japanese. You see, the Japanese owned one big store in Yogyakarta, Kofuji, and there we bought all the stuff for school, necessities like paper, pens, and all that. It was a good shop. There was also a section in the shop where they restrung our tennis racquets. And it was just the sort of catguts we needed. We thought they were extremely good at it.[71]

Gradually, in some towns and cities, there were separate schools established for different Indonesian ethnic communities — for the Chinese Indonesians most often. And here, in that "multicultural" mode, true colonial modernity seemed to be best at work. As whoever one might have been born back in one's home and neighborhood, in the modern school, one became simply the one in the colony who had gotten so far.

Air Marshal DHANI: In our town, there was an HCS, Hollandsch Chineesche School [Dutch-Chinese school], besides a European grade school, another government Dutch-native grade school, and also one Christian and one private Dutch-native grade school. The Dutch-Chinese grade school was also private.

RM: How was it different?.

Air Marshal DHANI: It was the same, modern; almost the same; no more different than, for instance, the Catholic school.[72]

Mrs. OEI: Because he was of Chinese origin, my husband went to a Dutch-Chinese school. But then he continued to the HBS, the Dutch five-year high school, with mainly Dutch students.[73]

The Classroom

An Indonesian word, *tjampur* (or *campur*, *tjampur baur*), meaning "mixing," "mingling," "blending," (nowadays *campur kode*, "code switching," and also "confusing"), appears frequently in the old people's modern and colonial school recollections. It seems to be a word that often best expresses school togetherness, the sense of beauty (fissures of the world "glossed over by education," as Nietzsche has it[74]), or — darkly put again — that kind of freedom.

> Mr. HAMID: I finished the AMS senior high in 1937.
> RM: Were you already conscious at the time of being Indonesian?
> Mr. HAMID: Sure. When I went to the senior high, among all the mostly Dutch classmates, note this, I felt like someone of Arab origin, like a Muslim, but like an Indonesian as well. As I advanced from grade to grade, I learned ever more that feeling of mixing and blending [*tjampur baur*] in the school. Of course, I was conscious of being Indonesian!
> RM: You also attended a Christian school, right?
> Mr. HAMID: Many Arab Indonesians at that time sent children to Catholic schools, because in Christian schools, especially, there was a separation of boys and girls. There was a Christian HBS senior high in our town, and there was no wrong mixing.[75]

> Mr. JUSUF: My elementary school was purely native. The one just higher up, the Dutch-native grade school was already mixed — Chinese, Eurasians, Dutch, and us, "the natives."[76]

> Professor SOEMITRO: In my class in senior high, there were twenty-two students. Out of the twenty-two, about eight were native. The rest were Eurasians, Chinese, and full-blood Dutch.
> RM: How many of the "full-blood" Dutch?
> Professor SOEMITRO: Very few. Most were of mixed blood. One of them sat with me in the form. We sat in five rows.[77]

There might be only one or two "sons (and daughters) of the land" in a classroom, in a school that stood in that student's land, and yet the space and the bodies in that space, full of the foreign and very much made of the foreign, were built up, educated, formed, to feel mixed — or, put another way, perhaps, neutral.

> Mr. ALI: This was ELS, the European grade school.
> RM: How many students?

Chapter Four

Mr. ALI: I think almost all were Dutch or Eurasians. In the end, in the seventh grade, I remember, there were about twenty-five Dutch pupils, including Eurasians.

RM: How many Indonesians?

Mr. ALI: One or two. No, wait a moment, three. Three *natives* made it to the final grade.[78]

RM: How many *natives*, like you?

Mrs. MIRIAM: I would have to look at the class portrait. I think we were the only Javanese—my brother, my sister, and me. And there were a few children from Menado [Sulawesi].

RM: Did you feel pushed aside?

Mrs. MIRIAM: No, not in class. In school I did not feel it at all.[79]

RM: You did not feel a difference?

Mr. PURBO: No, not at the time in school. It could not be.

RM: You liked to learn.

Mr. PURBO: Yes, I was very happy. I can still draw an exact plan of the school for you. There were just two Javanese in the class and four Chinese Indonesians. The rest were Dutch.[80]

RM: Were there many native students in the class?

Mr. ALWIN: Let me see—in the class of twenty-five, I think, three.

RM: It was a very small group, these Indonesians?

Mr. ALWIN: It was small, but we mixed in.

RM: Mixed in.[81]

These were young people who had already for some time been on the road and were still traveling.

RM: Was there a friendship with the Dutch classmates?

Mr. HAMID: No.

RM: But there was no animosity?

Mr. HAMID: No.

RM: It was a cool relationship?

Mr. HAMID: Normal.[82]

RM: Mostly Dutch students?

Mrs. TORAR: Almost all.

RM: But they behaved well to you?

The Classroom

Mrs. TORAR: Yes, they behaved well. It might be because of the environment.[83]

RM: Was there some connection?
Mr. EFENDI: Yes, *student life*.[84]

Mrs. OEI: I did not feel tension, strangely, not even pressure. Life in school was calm. Calm. Strangely, but I did not feel humiliated there. It was just normal, not much else.[85]

Naturally, one may expect the youth, with their bodies close to, or in the middle of, puberty, to feel their school and to convey their memory of it very much in physical terms. This was a tropical colony, a warm and sensual land, not merely in tourist romantic lore. Also the vast majority of these schools, as a matter of the modern, were coeducational.

RM: Just girls?
Mr. HOUTEIRO: Mixed.[86]

Mrs. MIRIAM: There should be no difference between boys and girls in school.[87]

The old men and women, still amazingly graceful and intensely physical as they talked to me and as they moved their hands and eyes, recalled their youth's school as *cozily* intimate and *prettily* warm.

Mr. HARDOYO: Was it intimate? Nice.[88]

The people who had spent years together in the exclusive and crowded space of school, in school forms, remember themselves as *klasgenoten*, the Dutch word for "classmates." That word, as neutral as it might be, appeared to stay with the people — sort of affectionately — till their old age. Only sometimes (as a purely modern word), it is translated into postcolonial English:

RM: Was he a friend?
Mr. PEREIRA: We went to school together. We were — *classmates*. *Classmates!*[89]

This is not to suggest that physical proximity was not mentioned in school recollections. Dancing — specifically "modern dancing," *twee aan twee*, as it

Chapter Four

is frequently named in Dutch, "as couples"—is very much recalled. That coming together of the two sexes was clearly a lasting experience—with its prescribed steps and moves, and smiles, something absorbing, fulfilling, and fitting into the world of school. Still, in the memories, it could make a school into a place to dance.

> Mr. HAMID: I could not dance because I came from a strict Islamic family. But the others often danced. In the MULO junior high I still did not take part. Only in college did I begin to dance, too.[90]
>
> Mrs. SOELISTINA: School started at seven in the morning, then came language classes, then mathematics, and so on. In the afternoon *gymnastics* or so, and in the end, at six or seven in the evening, there might be a *les* [lesson] that you did not have to take, like dancing.
> RM: What dances?
> Mrs. SOELISTINA: Modern, *waltz*, *tango*, and so on.
> RM: There were Dutch boys, too?
> Mrs. SOELISTINA: There were a few Dutch boys as well. I remember we danced to "The Blue Danube." All the girls did. It was an education of the Dutch time.[91]

As the colonial period was coming to its end, in school and while dancing, the young people progressively and ever more absorbingly became—not exactly close but—"mixed":

> Mrs. MIRIAM: Yes, *twee aan twee*—that dancing was *OK* in school. Dutch boys, however, would rarely dance with us. And the Indonesian boys who were there were shy. They could not truly dance. Often I was sad. It was so difficult to dance with them. Some of them did dance, few of them did, but most of them just stood around.
> RM: Why was that?
> Mrs. MIRIAM: To do school work with us, it was *OK*; and to talk to us and so on. But to dance! Also, to ask a classmate for a date, it was out of the question.[92]

The dancing filled in, staked out, and explained much of the school space. For those who experienced the steps, the moves, and that way of the embrace, it staked out and explained the colony.

The Classroom

Mr. ALWIN: In Aceh [North Sumatra] there was very little dancing because it was a *very traditional society*.

RM: Islam?

Mr. ALWIN: Yes. Only after I got to Medan, big city, it became another matter, in the HBS five-year high school.

RM: There were dances?

Mr. ALWIN: Oh, yes!

RM: With girls?

Mr. ALWIN: Yes.

RM: With the Dutch girls, too?

Mr. ALWIN: Yes. There, suddenly, you did not have that feeling of difference.[93]

RM: What about dancing?

Mr. ROSIHAN: Yes, that's it! We never had it in MULO, the junior high. We didn't have it because it was Padang, West Sumatra; Islam and that sort of thing. In Yogyakarta, however, in senior high, we danced with an encouragement from the school principal.

RM: You danced in the school building?

Mr. ROSIHAN: In the school. Once a month, in the *aula*, where we also did our gymnastics. Once a month, we danced there.

RM: Teachers were present?

Mr. ROSIHAN: Teachers were present.

RM: They were dancing, too?

Mr. ROSIHAN: No. They would look, observe.

RM: Could one dance also with the Dutch?

Mr. ROSIHAN: Dutch, Chinese, all mixed.

RM: So you might dance with Dutch girls?

Mr. ROSIHAN: Oh, yes.

RM: Was there a piano?

Mr. ROSIHAN: We had a gramophone. The thing was, we started at seven, and we finished around ten. The principal announced that we were to go home. And do you know what he did? He called out our names, not the first name but the second name. He called "Anwar!" "Ja, Meneer" (Yes, sir). It meant that I was to accompany one of the girls who happened to live near where I lived. We took our bicycles and went.

RM: Might it be a Dutch girl?

Chapter Four

Mr. ROSIHAN: Javanese. It might have been a Dutch girl, if she were to live close to my place. But they all lived in the Dutch quarter of town.
RM: Did you ever accompany a Dutch girl?
Mr. ROSIHAN: Oh, no. Usually a Javanese girl, but sometimes from a noble family. Those lived around Pakualaman, a palace. The principal saw to it that the girls were properly brought home. You knocked on the door—(*Mr. Rosihan knocked on the wide wooden arm of the sofa we were sitting on.*) and there was a servant: "Thank you." And your girl went inside.[94]

✦ ✦ ✦

To set out on the road, one usually changes clothes. Shoes, first of all, were mentioned by the old Indonesians who talked to me. Putting on shoes was repeatedly recalled as the first move, an initiating gesture, on the road to school:

Mr. SOEDARPO: Our mother took care that we went to school in shoes. There is a Dutch word for that special kind of shoes, *gympies* [sports shoes, sneakers], and we wore those. However, we put them on only when very close to school, and we took them off instantly, after just a kilometer or so, on our way home. Later, sometimes, we wore Dutch leather shoes, if we could afford it.[95]

Mr. SUTIKNO: When I began to go to the ELS grade school, I wore shoes; I always wore shoes—going to school and coming back from school.[96]

Shoes *were* the road to school. Shoes, at the moment one stepped onto the modern road, measured all the significant distances in the colony.

Father MANGUNWIJAYA: We wore shoes to church and to school; not another time. When one was among the people who did not wear many clothes, it was clumsy to wear shoes. One had to wear shoes, of course, but one had to be careful, at the same time, not to distance oneself from the people too much. If one came to a poor quarter of a town or to a village while wearing shoes, people would give a certain look.[97]

Wearing shoes—perhaps because it had so much to do with directly touching the surface of the road and perhaps because it announced cars[98]—

is recalled as a momentous gesture, even more than, albeit of the same category, putting on modern clothes.

> Mr. ROESLAN: For my MULO junior high I dressed the prescribed way—shorts, jacket buttoned up to the neck—but still just sandals, not yet shoes. It was 1920, and I still did not wear shoes. I did not have shoes. Only when I was about to enter the HBS senior high—almost all the students there were full-blood Dutch, not like in MULO, where there were mostly Eurasians—I became nervous. However, when the dancing lessons began at the HBS—my mother had understood what was happening—I was already wearing shoes.[99]

As in the biblical story, with their modern shoes and clothes on, the young people of the colony might look at themselves, and newly see what it means to be naked.

> Mrs. TRIMURTI: When I was little, my father became an assistant district chief, and so we came to live in a village. Then I found out how many of the village children were still running around stark naked. Except when they went to school, that is.[100]

The nakedness, like progress and like fashion—or like the road surface and speed—became a momentous commonplace of modernity.

> Mr. PURBO: My father was a teacher, and he already dressed in the Western way. He was very modern. He dressed like a European.
> RM: What was it, jacket, trousers?
> Mr. PURBO: Jacket, a *petji*—

Petji, or in the new spelling *peci* or *pici*, was a rimless cap usually of black velvet—a modern Islamic, and, by the 1920s, thanks to Sukarno in large part, nationalist mode of head wear. The name was derived from the Dutch *petje*, a diminutive for "cap"—in the Netherlands a cap worn mostly by students.

> Mr. PURBO:—and he wore shoes, the European way.
> RM: Was there a difference between how your father dressed and how, for instance, the Dutch principal did?

Mr. PURBO: Not at all.

RM: The same?

Mr. PURBO: Jacket buttoned up all the way, and tie. Father took real care not to be inferior. Because of my father I could go to school.[101]

Mr. ROSIHAN: At senior high we had to dress *complete*: jacket, tie, and all.

RM: It was expensive?

Mr. ROSIHAN: Expensive! It cost me one *gulden* fifty just for the laundry each month.[102]

RM: And you went to school on bicycle?

Mr. EFENDI: On bicycle, in jacket, even when it rained, and in the heat.[103]

Mr. ASRUL: Especially in college, all students dressed in nearly the same way — jackets, white trousers, shoes, and ties.[104]

Uniform became another commonplace, a catchword, or, better, password. Like the uniform shape of the classrooms, with the benches, blackboard, maps, and portraits, it became the sum of what colonial modernity had so far achieved. Like the benches, the blackboard, and the maps, and portraits on the wall, like the design of the road, the uniform fashion also aimed at the fullness, the abstract, and the pure — categorically so.

In the specially designated colonial space, and on some specially designated occasions, a special kind of school uniform, even, might be worn.[105] In that highly charged space, even the *origin*, to use Henri Lefebvre's words, might "fall to the level of folklore,"[106] to be made into yet another modern colonial commonplace. Good students — to manifest the road to school and to the new, to categorize the road's beginning and everything that had been left behind and off the road — might be "ethnic" and wear "costumes."

Mrs. MASKUN: In the Kartini junior high, we were supposed to wear Javanese dress, sort of — a blouse of batik and a skirt.[107]

Professor SOEMARDJAN: At home we just wore shorts. We ran around half naked. It was normal. Of course, when I went to the Dutch school, I had to wear my *batik* — a *kain* [sarong], *sordjan* [long-sleeved jacket], and *blangkon* [headscarf]. The Javanese things, you know, Yogyakarta style.[108]

✦ ✦ ✦

The Classroom

As one moved toward and through the school, one's body became flagrant by the way it was clothed. It was another feat of the power of the trivial and superficial. Like the wrong dress, trousers, shoes, tie askew, or like an uncomplete uniform, one's body and, of course, one's skin, might become unfitting.

> RM: As a child, could you see any difference between your Dutch and Balinese teachers?
> Princess MUTER: Of course I could. The Dutch were white, and the Balinese were brown.[109]
>
> RM: You made such a face now: like that you definitely did not like it.
> Dr. ONG: I didn't like it. I didn't like it at all. The kids were big and white and—
> RM: They were mostly white kids?
> Dr. ONG: Yes, it was an elite school!
> RM: They did not like you?
> Dr. ONG: I don't know. I don't think so. But I didn't like it. I didn't like especially to go out of the classroom during recesses—into the yard.
> RM: Were you afraid?
> Dr. ONG: I was shy.
> RM: What was so threatening?
> Dr. ONG: I still don't like to think about it very much. I suppose it was the big bodies. And I felt that they all could jump higher and run faster. I was so small and thin.[110]

This was not to be felt. Or, perhaps, this was what the school was about. One was to fight it—to get into a school uniform, for instance, to become schooled so that one's body did not feel so awkwardly, even painfully, naked.

> Mr. ROSIHAN: I remember one of my Dutch teachers, a young lady, when I was in the fourth grade. One morning during recess I was sitting in the schoolyard, and she was looking in my direction as she talked with another teacher. They were both looking at me, and I knew that they were talking about me. My lady teacher pointed to me. She was showing her colleague, also a Dutch woman—my legs. All the time I had been aware that they were talking about me, and I knew what they

> were talking about. I had — you know, here, here, and here — there were sores on my legs, what do you call it? (*Mr. Rosihan pulls up a leg of his trousers and points to a blister on his shin.*)
>
> RM: Oh, *blisters*.
>
> Mr. ROSIHAN: Yes, they talked about it; that I had a kind of skin disease. "You!" (*Mr. Rosihan says this suddenly and quite loudly, pointing his index finger straight at me.*) It meant, "You are a dirty native!" or "You take your bath in the river and you defecate in it too, this is why you got this." I can't forget it; still, to this day. I thought: "God's grace!" You see, I might have been privileged, but still I was an *inlander*, a native. Of course it happened because I took my bath in the river. Thus I contracted this. I had put some cream on it, you know, but the blisters were open. They were in several places, and the teachers discussed it. This I remember.
>
> RM: Does it mean that the Dutch teacher never bathed in the river?
>
> Mr. ROSIHAN: I don't know. Oh, no; of course not.
>
> RM: They had indoor bathrooms, and swimming pools?
>
> Mr. ROSIHAN: Yeah, they had pools.[111]

Much of such memorable humiliation was brought on the small and thin, brown and river-bathing people of the land. Most exemplarily it happened in school, and thus — correctly and in the enlightened way — it was taken as that it had to be overcome, again by further schooling.[112]

> Mrs. SOELISTINA: In the seventh grade I had a Eurasian teacher, and he liked me. When I came to school, for instance, in shoes that were not perfectly polished, he would say: *een mooi vlag op een modderschuit*, which means, "a nice flag on a muddy barge." It was in Dutch.[113]

Professor Selo Soemardjan, in his adult life a private secretary of the Sultan of Yogyakarta, talked to me about *kedjawén*, Javanese philosophy and the art of life, when school entered in his reflections:

> Professor SOEMARDJAN: There is something I should still tell you — one of the small things you said you want to hear. At home, when you were to pay homage to the elder people or to those socially higher up, you had to get down, to bow, to sit, or to crouch, to place your head

lower than theirs, to make yourself as little and insignificant as you could. In school, to pay respect to your teachers, you had to stand up. Once I forgot when a Dutch teacher came in. (*At this moment I managed to spill some of the tea from my cup that I was supposed to balance on my knees.*) Oh, sorry. I still feel the effects of it, and I am eighty-two — it was a lady teacher, white and strong. Her name was Weterling, and she was very big. She told us: "You are not allowed to drink alcohol! Stay away from beer!" We didn't know what alcohol was, at home.[114] And: "Do not smoke!" This we knew. Once, because it was forbidden, I had a cigarette. A classmate saw me and reported it to the teacher. She called me up to the front of the class: "Did you smoke?" I said: "Yes." "Lie down on the desk!" I lay down on her desk on my stomach, and she *pak . . . pak, pak*! Of course it was painful. I still feel it now. But it also helped me avoid smoking. I have never since smoked in my life. And, in fact, I cannot stand beer either. You ask me why? I don't know, perhaps it is something I learned in the past.

RM: They never beat you at home?

Professor SOEMARDJAN: Sometimes. I was sometimes punished by my mother. But she did not do it with a stick.

RM: Aha.

Professor SOEMARDJAN: In this case, I was beaten with a stick. And that was different.[115]

CHANGING SOULS

The road to school began before the school age, before an outset of expectation, at a preschool moment — if there was anything like that still left in the colony.

Prince PUGER: Yes, it was *voorschool* [preschool] — to sing, to make little things, like the simplest embroidery, to put your toys in order, to play like that.[116]

Mr. SUDARMONO: First, I went to a kindergarten; we called it *voorklas* [preclass], in Dutch.[117]

Dr. ONG: It all started in *kindergarten*.[118]

Chapter Four

The essentials of "all this"—the experience of school, and the colonial modernity through the school—were often implanted at the edges of memory.

> RM: It had to be a shock for such a little boy.
> Professor SOEMITRO: For my family, perhaps. But for me? I was no more than five years old.[119]
>
> Mr. PURBO: It seemed no problem, the early grades—as if without knowing it.[120]

The edges of memory, in the colony, might be around the age of four.

> Prince PUGER: This had become customary among the better-off parents in my childhood: when we reached the age of four, we were supposed to move to a Dutch place. It was conceived as a sort of a bridge to the West. I went to the Dtuch Resink family. We had to go when we were four, because at the age of five, we were to enter the preschool.
> RM: Difficult?
> Prince PUGER: Oh, because it happened so early, it did not seem unusual.
> RM: You spoke Javanese, I mean, with the Resinks' servants?
> Prince PUGER: Yes, Javanese.
> RM: With the Resinks it was Dutch?
> Prince PUGER: Yes, and also with my brothers, who were sent there, too. I had to speak Dutch with them. If we slipped into Javanese, Mrs. Resink got angry. Because we were there to learn.
> RM: What might a child feel about it—this moving from language to language?
> Prince PUGER: Not much, because it happened every day and from the age of four. I just might think, "Well, it is Dutch, what we are learning." Mrs. Resink hired a person, a *juffrouw* [miss], to watch over us.
> RM: Did not you whisper in Javanese among the brothers?
> Prince PUGER: Oh, yes! But if she heard us, she would become upset.
> RM: But you whispered.
> Prince PUGER: Yes. At the beginning.
> RM: Aha, so later, also when you whispered, you whispered in Dutch?
> Prince PUGER: Yes.[121]

✳ ✳ ✳

Even in a classroom, in the back of it, one might still imagine some noise, echoes, words or fragments of words from (further) behind, from home, of mother tongues—unless even a mother already spoke Dutch at home.

> Mr. KARTONO: My school was known for excellent teaching of Dutch.
> RM: What did you speak at home?
> Mr. KARTONO: My parents could speak only Javanese.[122]

Like one's upper body, hands and fingers, for table manners, one's vocal cords, mouth, tongue, and teeth were trained to stretch and relax, to construct sentences, to make one thus think and define oneself as becoming human—"thoroughly kneaded and pliant but also *formed*."[123]

> RM: You spoke Dutch to both your Javanese parents? Did not your mother, kindly, let you speak Javanese—to her, at least, once in a while?
> Mr. SUTIKNO: No. I had to speak Dutch with both of them. When I was four, they did not tell me: "You will go to Dutch school, and so you have to speak good Dutch." I did not know at the time that this was a condition and that there were those Dutch admission examinations.
> RM: Don't you think it changed your relation to your father and your mother?
> Mr. SUTIKNO: No, not at all.
> RM: It was like before?
> Mr. SUTIKNO: As before. As far as I remember.
> RM: You called your mother *moeder* [in Dutch]?
> Mr. SUTIKNO: When I was at a loss with my Dutch, I could ask a question in Javanese, and my parents would answer me in Dutch.[124]

There are stories of fathers and mothers in their best clothes but not speaking Dutch, taking their child to the admission test at school and doing everything they could to remain mute, letting their already more advanced offspring speak.[125]

> RM: Your father and your mother, they talked Dutch to each other?
> Mr. PURBO: Dutch. Because it was their strategy to get me to a good

Chapter Four

school. They tried to teach me Dutch as my *mother tongue*, not as a *second language*. When my father brought me to the ELS grade school, the first question we were asked by the principal was: "What is this child's language at home?" My father answered: "Dutch," and the second question was: "What language does the child speak with his mother?" And my father answered: "Dutch." I was accepted.[126]

Mr. SUDARMONO: At home we spoke Dutch, because I was to go to a Dutch school. So we had to speak Dutch at home.
RM: Both your parents could speak Dutch?
Mr. SUDARMONO: My father could. My mother was learning. She could write a little but she could not speak, almost not at all.[127]

Mr. SEKO: My mother could not speak Dutch, almost not at all. She tried to sail around it. She might say "opnein" or something like that that sounded Dutch but did not mean anything. We children sometimes would speak Dutch in front of her—it was like a secret language among us. With father we spoke Dutch.[128]

Only when something clicked really wrong, "between cracks of the modern,"[129] the language of the almost forgotten, the off-school, the almost incomprehensible (what should not be called) mother tongue might resound for a moment:

Mr. ALWIN: My parents *engineered* it so that it would be impossible for me to speak at home anything other than Dutch. Only very rarely, like when my mother got really angry, could I hear her say something in what I knew was Minangkabau [a language of West Sumatra, the mother's birthplace].
RM: And after she calmed down?
Mr. ALWIN: Back to Dutch.[130]

The modern, school language, correct, progressive, an awesome thing, mattered especially, of course, as it attached itself to the other correct, progressive, and awesome things of the colony. Modernity was named, and made really what it was by the naming. Modern people of the colony were named and made really what they now were—candidates, students, degree holders, or dropouts. No name—no proof to the contrary, as they should

The Classroom

157

know: "No proof can possibly exist determining the truth or falsity of the undecidable statement in the language of the system within which the statement was formulated."[131]

In the new language and in its spirit, or grammar, people were entered, first of all, into school books—alphabetically, and, thus, in that new way, they were entered into books of life.

> RM: When were you born?
> Mr. HAMID: In 1910. On the books, however, you will find 1912. If I were born in 1910, I would not be accepted to the Dutch school by the time we could afford it. I would be off beat again. To get me to school, my father said that 1912 was my birth year. So, this is my *curriculum vitae*, and in all my degrees and other documents, it is 1912.[132]

Correctly written in, the people thus entered might indeed feel as if they belonged to an awesomely impressive world or, more exactly, universe.

> RM: So, you did not suffer by that *inlander* feeling?
> Professor KOENTJARANINGRAT: Actually not. I was being educated before I began with anything else—*initially*, in Dutch.[133]

Even the language itself, Dutch, overwhelming the speaking at home, corrected in school, by its mythical origin elsewhere and by its complete spirit (its grammar), appeared universal.

> Mrs. MIRIAM: After Dutch came other languages. Greek was less difficult for me than Latin; would you believe it? Reading Tacitus, especially, it was for me like mathematics. Every word had an exact meaning, and you had to put the only correct Dutch word in place of it. Tacitus especially was a real *torture* for me. And besides, I still had a Javanese accent![134]

There did not seem to be much time or space to think—especially for those who wished to think a lot—about languages or universes perhaps lost.

> Mr. HAMID: In AMS senior high, it was called Western-Classical AMS, we learned Dutch, Latin, English, French, and German.[135]

Chapter Four

Mr. SEDA: In Dutch schools, we had to learn four modern languages: Dutch, English, German, and French.

RM: To read?

Mr. SEDA: In HBS five-year high you had to learn to write it as well, all four of them. Only in Latin I did not make it. I just could not.[136]

There was an ultimate modern, abstract, and suggestively universal quality to the school space, and to school language first of all. There was a fullness and, as in all good technologies, solid backup built into the system—in case a glitch might happen in the main program, or for the use of those in the colony who had been as yet inadequately trained or were otherwise still unfit to join in fully. Supporting, fail-safe auxiliary programs had been developed, through the school space and beyond, and on the school drive. The backup that was most used was a language called Malay.

Dienst Maleis, "service Malay,"[137] it was indeed called, by the same Dutch adjective as the *dienst* (service) houses and the *dienst* (service) cars (or like *dienstmeisjes* and *dienstknechts* for the household servants). It was not a language "awash in 'realities'" more than Dutch; it was not vernacular versus classical.[138] Neither did Malay as it related to Dutch fit the linguistic truism that "all languages are equal." It grew out of a colonial principle that languages (like the students of the various ethnic "mixing" in a classroom) ideally should be not translatable but complementary.[139]

For centuries, Malay had been a language spoken in an area in and around the East Coast ports of Sumatra and the Malay peninsula. As modern commerce grew, and as the colony developed, however, Malay, as a thin veil (a plastic wrapping rather) had been thrown over the other languages and cultures of the Indonesian archipelago. It became all-archipelago—not as an outgrowth of some ancient tree of languages, of something beyond or before, but as something perfectly all-colonial.[140] The essential principle of learning the service language was that students were not supposed to learn it at home but in school—grammarized, dictionarized, ordered—and that by the learning, they were not to become better native speakers but better service people: *taalambtenaren*, as it was called in Dutch, the modern land's "language officials."

RM: There was Javanese around the house and then Dutch in your school. What about Malay?

> Father MANGUNWIJAYA: Malay was coming. In the seventh grade, we got the first opportunity to learn Malay. But it was still merely optional, after all the other classes, at two in the afternoon. I forgot who taught it, because Malay was not very popular among the students. Dutch was.
>
> RM: Even among the Indonesian students?
>
> Father MANGUNWIJAYA: Yes.
>
> RM: Why?
>
> Father MANGUNWIJAYA: Because Malay was the language of the low-level offices and, except that, of the street. The hawkers used it, and other street people. It was inferior.
>
> RM: Do you recall when you heard Malay for the first time?
>
> Father MANGUNWIJAYA: I think I heard it for the first time, really, at two o'clock in the afternoon, during those after-class lessons.
>
> RM: But what about before, in the market?
>
> Father MANGUNWIJAYA: On the street, I spoke mostly Javanese. It was a small town and there were not many strangers. And later, in school, the mood was not very favorable to Malay lessons. At two o'clock in the afternoon we all wanted to play, fly kites, go to the river — and we were supposed to study Malay! I went largely because my father ordered me: "You have to go to the Malay class!"[141]

I may be getting a little ahead of myself, but I think it should be noted here that Father Mangunwijaya after 1945 became one of the most celebrated writers in Indonesian, which is slightly modified — grammarized, dictionarized, ordered, schooled, and nationalized — Malay.

> Air Marshal DHANI: In school, to friends, we talked in Javanese, but as we advanced, it was more and more in Dutch. I did not understand Indonesian language almost at all. Almost not at all. Indonesian language was then called *Maleis*.

Maleis is in Dutch; in Malay or Indonesian it would be *Melajoe* or *Melayu*.

> RM: You could not speak it?
>
> Air Marshal DHANI: No, and I did not understand it. We knew Javanese, low, medium, and high, all that we knew. And then Dutch.[142]

This was changing as the colony moved forward, through, and to its end. The Malay grammars and dictionaries (Malay-Dutch dictionaries almost exclusively) became increasingly available — as schoolbooks.

RM: Teachers taught in Javanese in your school?
Mr. SARLI: Yes, because it was the lowest, people's, three-year school. But there was already a little of Malay.[143]

RM: You were not taught Dutch at all?
Mr. PEREIRA: No, at that low level school. Just a little of Malay.[144]

Mr. GESANG: I was child number five and so I went only to a people's school: three years, no more. We did not learn any language; all was in Javanese.
RM: No Malay?
Mr. GESANG: Yes, in fact, a little. Today it is Indonesian.[145]

In the first years of the twentieth century, "standard Malay" was ushered into the modern colonial official existence. In 1908, a government publishing house was founded with a dual, Dutch-Malay, name and mission — Volkslectuur (People's Reading)-Balai Poestaka (House of Books). Books useful for modern readers were being published from that point and till the end of the colonial era,[146] some explicitly in the form of textbooks, others of a textbook spirit. Libraries in many places through the colony, and also circulating libraries, were established.[147]

Mr. ALI: In our town, we had a *bibliotheek*.
RM: Balai Poestaka?
Mr. ALI: Yes, it was a wonderful library.
RM: Malay books, too?
Mr. ALI: Most of the books were in Dutch. There might have been some books in Malay. I liked Karl May, Winnetou,[148] and Dutch novels, books like that.
RM: Dutch books?
Mr. ALI: There was not much choice. Every week I finished one book.
RM: Everybody could go there?
Mr. ALI: All of my schoolmates, yes.[149]

As colonialism matured and aged, through the 1920s and 1930s, increasingly good care was being taken of service Malay. Even affection and warmth were injected into the working of this language as a part of contemporary life—children's books, calendars, and novels were published in Malay by the Dutch government publishing house, in growing numbers. Much of the care, of course, had to be applied toward making the Malay as dissimilar as possible to how the hawkers cried: impure, messy, not belonging to the classroom, street language dangerous to the colonial modern, foreign to it, what became often to be called "Chinese Malay" to make the point.[150]

> RM: You were born to Sikka [language of Flores]?
> Mrs. HOUTEIRO: Yes.
> RM: Then you had to learn Dutch?
> Mrs. HOUTEIRO: In school, Malay. And after three years of Malay we got Dutch.
> RM: How did you like it?
> Mrs. HOUTEIRO: I was happy. We learned Dutch from Malay. Still today, I sometimes slip from Malay [meaning Indonesian] to Dutch. And then right up I am embarrassed; as if I did not have my own language. When I get excited, I sometimes become embarrassed like that. My friends laugh. But for them it is also like that—except that they think that it is nothing strange, that it is normal.[151]

✦ ✦ ✦

The modern school suggested a wholesome space, a veritable "metaphysical fantasy of completion,"[152] in multiple, complementary languages, and as rich as the immense repertoire of the Western civilization that had been placed at its disposal. The modern and colonial school offered a texture as dense and as complex as any correct textbook could withstand. And this became the quality of the textbooks—like the grids of all modern urban planning and building, the schoolbooks and the power in them could endlessly expand.[153]

> Mrs. MIRIAM: We had also *kunstgeschiedenis*, history of art, and there we learned about various styles—Doric and Ionic in Greece, and all the other styles there were. We had to know all the details about them, and then, of course, we learned about the Gothic period, the Renaissance and so on. Thus I was brought up on those things and, because of it, I

Chapter Four

also became interested in history and, very much, you see, the history of the East. One of my heroes was Alexander the Great, because he had moved on to the East and because he tried to bridge both cultures, Eastern and Western. And also, I became interested in Persia and the Persian people, because I learned about the Persian wars against the Greeks; and the Persians, they were so sophisticated that even Alexander the Great thought of them highly! And later, I became very interested in the American Indians, in Maya culture.[154]

A limitless (and well-networked) universe was being learned in school.

> Mr. SOEDARPO: We knew that, again and again, we would be tested in Dutch. Incessantly. To be good in Dutch, we had to read Dutch. We had to read the Dutch literature. Then we had other, required or optional, languages. Thus you had to read at least a couple of German and French books. For example, I improved my grade in German by reading that book — I cannot recall the name at the moment — but I got an idea of what life in Germany was like at that time. We got that kind of understanding. And we had to read *The Thousand and One Nights*, in Dutch. We had to read it — a part of it. And *Don Quixote* and that stuff. All this was a part of that world, of that *must* reading.[155]

The people in the colony were schooled, like good readers, to be absorbed.

> Mr. SEDA: Since my youth, I liked to read books on philosophy. I liked Kierkegaard.
> RM: Why?
> Mr. SEDA: His heroism. I read Thomas Aquinas as well. I read about *social evolution*, Charles Darwin. I read *detective stories*, like Father Brown. I have read *The Revolt of the Masses* — who wrote it? Ortega, right? At one time I liked Schiller very much, too. Thomas Aquinas we read in Geman.[156]
>
> Professor SOEMITRO: I read Dutch — Roland Holst, the socialist, and Eddy du Perron's *Het Land van Herkomst* [*Country of Origin*]. Through this book I got to read Malraux. I started to read *consciously* when I was about fifteen. I have always been attracted to French literature, *Cyrano de Bergerac*, early on — here is a man who is incorruptible! When I was

The Classroom

in high school I also read Maria Rilke, an Austrian, and Schiller, and some Goethe. It was in 1935 or 1936. You see, I was very continental in my taste. Not so much Anglo-Saxon; rather French-German, that's for sure.[157]

The colony was cultivated, well cultivated, meaning extremely cultivated. The world given to the students in the colony was wholesome, rich, bright, and almost fully imported from the outside.

> RM: You learned about the world.
> Mr. HARDJO: Yes, about Europe: cold countries, snow, and many other things. Like about Wilhelmus van Nassau, and Egmont.[158]

> Mrs. POLITON: I knew much more about the history of the Netherlands than about the history of Indonesia, of course.
> RM: You did not think it bizarre?
> Mrs. POLITON: It seemed normal, because we lived in these circles.[159]

> Mr. SOEMARTONO: Yes, we learned about the tiniest rivers in Holland, they made us memorize them all: in this district, this little river, in that district, that little river.[160]

> Prince PUGER: We learned a lot, like, you had to hear it already, about all the railway stations between Amsterdam and the Hague.
> RM: Did not this feel very strange?
> Prince PUGER: We did not have that *introspection* at the time.[161]

> Mr. OEY: Then, there was *aardrrijkskunde* [geography]. We learned a little about where Jakarta is and where Semarang is: "It is on Java." But as for the Netherlands, we learned everything—there are no mountains like here, so we learned the names of rivers.[162]

Besides, or rather above this, the students learned "patriotic history."

> Father MANGUNWIJAYA: Dutch was subject number one. My father taught geography and history. But it was left to the Dutch teachers always to teach *vaderlandse geschiedenis* [fatherland history]. This was Dutch and Dutch-imperial history, and it was very *interesting*. I loved it. And I loved geography, too, because wherever I might wish to go, my fantasy would take me there.[163]

The magic of the colonial classroom was, as I often heard from the old people, that one might feel safe as long as one got oneself absorbed. There was singing in the schools. *Kun je nog zingen, zing dan mee!* (*Can You Sing, Then Sing with Me!*)—it was the most popular songbook through the late colonial time.[164]

> RM: You still remember?
>
> Mr. USMAN: Of course I do. (*Mr. Usman is singing.*) *Silent Night, Holy Night*, of course, I still remember it. We sang it all the time.[165]
>
> Mrs. DAMAIS: Yes, we sang *Dutch songs* in school. We had the book, *Zing dan mee!* It was large, like that. (*Mrs. Damais shows me.*) When we were in school, we had to sing. I still sometimes do.[166]

It is, of course, difficult to debate singing. One has to listen.

> Mr. SEKO: The teacher played piano and mandolin. He was a Jew.
>
> Mrs. POLITON: German.
>
> Mr. SEKO: Maybe. He was from somewhere close to Holland.[167]
>
> Mrs. TOLANG: We still meet [with classmates]. And we sing the songs. (*Mrs. Tolang sings a Dutch song that I do not know. She points to her heart as she sings and then she laughs.*) It is still there. This was what we did. We learned it in school. It is funny, but the Dutch songs are so full of energy. Just one more? (*Mrs. Tolang sings another Dutch song that I do not know.*) Which one is this? "_____ en de Hollanders, Oranje"?
>
> RM: (*I am lamely pretending.*) Yes, yes.
>
> Mrs. TOLANG: You forgot! Or this: *Na na na na na*—[168]

Like everything in modern school, music that was learned progressed—in its harmonies, with the school syllabus, toward the more accomplished, increasingly convincing.

> Mr. SOEDARMONO: We had a school orchestra.
>
> RM: What kind of?
>
> Mr. SOEDARMONO: Chamber music. We began with Mozart, Tchaikovsky; then Bach, Debussy, and also *pop*—Cole Porter. Each Saturday there were singing lessons, but not from music at first. Later we learned to read music. And then *akkoords* [chords], *quintakkoord*,

The Classroom

> *sextakkoord, septakkoord*, intonation, tempo, and harmony, second voice, third voice — it was a Dutch-native grade school. After this, we got a school choir; we learned it, and it was beautiful. What *trio* was, when you had to go here with your voice and then there; it had to be this note and not that one. I do not know why, but it came completely naturally to me: there was a *tonic* and there was a *dominant*. It was so attractive. I began to play guitar.
>
> RM: And sing to it?
>
> Mr. SOEDARMONO: Yes, sing, too. My older sister was two years ahead of me, and she also played guitar. We went to the same school, and when there was a celebration we played on stage.[169]

It was that same moment of celebration as in every school in the world.

> RM: Dutch songs?
>
> Mr. SOEDARMONO: Yes, of course, Dutch songs.
>
> RM: Javanese songs, too?
>
> Mr. SOEDARMONO: In this school, yes. Because they taught Javanese in that school, too — children's songs.[170]

Through the absorption, and the singing, a dwelling space was being built for the Indonesians, to last for their whole life or, at least, for a generation. Martin Heidegger's contention that "language is the 'house of Being'" certainly found its validation here.[171] Siegfried Kracauer's descriptions of the modern hotel lobby — abstract and universal — also fit quite well the space carved out by the modern school, and especially in the colony: "the perpetually untenable middle ground between the natural and supernatural [or perhaps rather 'surreal']," the ground that "displaces people . . . to a place where they would encounter the void only if they were more than just reference points, the ground, the lobby, the school, powerful and irresistible because it 'does not refer beyond itself.'"[172]

Discipline, in school memories, is a word often repeated, and most often warmly so. Even when it comes to recalling true hardship, discipline is invoked — related to discipline, the hardship becomes a mode of a positive new order still coming.

Mr. SUWARDI: Strong! There used to be discipline in the school of the past, Mr. Rudolf.

RM: There was physical punishment?

Mr. SUWARDI: Oh no, no, no. Not in my case. The most harsh physical punishment was to make you stand in front of the class till the two-o'clock bell, just that. I had high regard for the Dutch discipline because it meant a good education.

RM: So you were never slapped?

Mr. SUWARDI: No, just made to stand there.[173]

RM: What did you think about the Dutch? You knew well the refined Javanese culture. Would not you see the Westerners as — uncouth?

Mr. HARDJONEGORO: I learned to respect the Dutch discipline.

RM: How did you learn it?

Mr. HARDJONEGORO: In school. Their discipline of knowledge.

RM: So it began at school?

Mr. HARDJONEGORO: Yes. But also *later*, my *professors*, like Hans —, Professor Beerling, like Bernard Campers, like Professor — I hold them all in high esteem — because of the discipline of their scholarship, of their looking at things. When you take the batik and the daggers I made, you can see how I looked back when I was working on them. My work is clean and precise. Things like that. Ask where you wish — mine is the cleanest work, and I think this comes from that time.

Out of the discipline grows Mr. Hardjonegoro's — the Rimbaudian, the Sartrean, the Lacanian — "*Je est un autre.*"[174]

RM: But why not Javanese discipline?

Mr. HARDJONEGORO: In some ways why not? But the Javanese are rather about *dreaming*, and there is too much *feeling* in them. I was lucky to come to know Dutch discipline.[175]

Mr. NARYO: Nobody can deny it: in school during the Dutch time there was discipline. Quality was high because the teacher paid attention. No teacher would just leave his classroom during the school hours. If I wanted something, I had to raise my hand. Today, the pupils——

JAN: But even before the Dutch even came, when people learned to be puppeteers, for example, there was also discipline?

Mr. NARYO: Before the Dutch came? What do I know? I know nothing. I began in the Dutch time—and I know that today there is little discipline. In the Dutch time, there was discipline; for a puppeteer and for everybody.[176]

RM: Dutch discipline?

Air Marshal DHANI: Yes. But it was something, if I may say so, like learning to fly. We were disciplined by the Dutch to read. Sometimes, they even ordered us to come back in the evening. There were *lessons*—we could ask, however not yet to seek directly for ourselves. This was what was meant by *discipline*. In junior high it became a little more free, not very free, but a little more free. In the AMS senior high, teachers could already be asked what was going on, for instance on the outside, in the history class: what was the cause of World War I? Things were becoming more alive, they could be analyzed. So when someone says today that the Indonesians were taught only what had been chewed up first by the Dutch, it makes me uncomfortable. In fact, the Dutch taught me how to analyze; it began in senior high.[177]

That school-slash-universal discipline, that learning to fly, progressively, gradually, as the school space and time expanded, was to become a way of being for all.

RM: Your father was?

Mr. DARIF: A small merchant, at the roadside. A little more than a hawker.

RM: Aha, and still he wanted you to go to school?

Mr. DARIF: So that I would become a [real] man.

RM: The school was expensive?

Mr. DARIF: Yes. But my father managed to pay it. So that I would become a [real] man.

RM: You said that there were also "progressive" teachers among the Dutch in your school.

Mr. DARIF: Good and progressive.

RM: How were they progressive and good in class?

Mr. DARIF: They said: "You must study well, so that tomorrow you can become [real] men. This is the way, they said, to become free—to become [real] men."[178]

Chapter Four

✻ ✻ ✻

The act of being in school as an act of being—and the act of keeping oneself in school and in school ways as an act of growing up and of progressing— was a measurable, quantifiable ritual engendered by perpetual testing:

> The very structure of testing tends to overtake the certainty that it establishes.[179]

> The rush for further education surpasses the desire for knowledge ... so the system protects itself against disintegration.[180]

One becomes "prepared for the test, even reduced to the test, to the degree that it is an extension of the cognitive horizon."[181] The time and space of testing becomes the time and space of being.

> Mrs. DAMAIS: Yes, I never remained sitting in one class for more than one year. And each time when I was about to move up, there was *testing*. After seven years, at the end of the seventh grade, to get to a higher school there was *testing*, an *examination*, for either HBS or MULO. And then as you came to HBS, there was an entrance *examination*. In *public school*, in every school. We lived in a small town, and so we had to go to the residency capital for *testing*.[182] You had to have a *certification* from your school—the Indonesians like the Dutch. In this, we were all the same: we had to get a *certificate*. A *full certificate*.[183]

The way of being the best became *curricular*. The higher one might get on the school scale, the *freer* the discipline, the more school-complex the time and space of being became.[184] The more they—the time, space, and being— became able to feed on themselves. Especially in the colony, where schools shone especially bright in the less school, more twilight landscape, *curricular* came close to the absolute—the best of the students might aspire to become teachers.

> Mr. HARDJO: My teacher told me: "You do not need to become a servant. Go to the *kweekschool* [normal school]. Become a teacher!"[185]

School was that kind of progress that found all the necessary qualities of growth contained in itself. One had to labor hard to succeed—to become ever more of a student:

> Mr. DAINO: Actually, in all the excitement, I felt *minder* [inferior]. I felt like that since the grade school—
>
> RM: Because of school?
>
> Mr. DAINO: Yes, because of school. And as I moved up, the feeling developed. It grew.[186]

SCHOOL CLUBS AND PRISON CAMPS

Like the schoolyards and the sports fields, there were debate clubs attached to, and expanding, the school space even more, throughout the whole colony.[187]

> Mrs. MIRIAM: We did not have only dancing. We also had a debate club, and Koko [Mrs. Miriam's brother] was a member.[188]
>
> Mr. SOEDARPO: Batavia-Jakarta at that time was a place where you had things to do. There were new things to learn. We went to debate clubs and we had discussions.[189]

Debate clubs, intramural as well as extramural, were exemplary of school space. They highlighted and purified the school-space values. Discipline and ambition, as well as testing, manners, and a sense of mission, of being on the road, could not be pronounced as well in any other part of the school and, by extension, of the colony. In the purest school sense, there could also be freedom (or liberty).

> Professor SOEMITRO: I went to the Gymnasium Willem III five-year high.
>
> RM: So again, most of your classmates were Dutch?
>
> Professor SOEMITRO: Some Chinese, some Eurasians, and very few Indonesians, yes.
>
> RM: Did you feel—
>
> Professor SOEMITRO: No! Nobody called me *inlander* or anything like that.

At the time, Mr. Soemitro says, came the famous trial of Sukarno, in 1930, after the Dutch authorities arrested the young and increasingly popular nationalist leader for the first time.

Chapter Four

Professor SOEMITRO: "Oh," one Dutch classmate stood up in the club one evening, "he is a rabble-rouser, *opstandig* [rebellious]." And I said: "No, he is not. He is fighting for his people." It was what I said. Sukarno was my first debating theme. "Well," they said, "but most of your leaders support our state, the princes and so on. They are not ungrateful, and certainly they are not rebels." And I said: "You bought them, through your commerce." I had already learned by then about imperialism, as I started reading history in school. So I got them.

RM: The discussion happened in school? Were there Dutch teachers present?

Professor SOEMITRO: In school, in the debate club. And the teachers were there too![190]

Professor Soemitro later, among other things, served on the Indonesian Republic delegation to the United Nations in 1947 and was a minister of trade and the economy several times in the 1950s, during President Sukarno's time. When I spoke to him, he was a top economic advisor to President General Suharto.

Mr. Hamid, of the same age as Professor Soemitro, had been a prominent leader of the nationalist youth before and during the Second World War and later also one of Sukarno's ministers; he represented Arab Indonesians specifically.

RM: So you began with politics at an early age.

Mr. HAMID: Yes, in the *debate club* of my AMS senior high.

RM: What were you debating, do you still remember?

Mr. HAMID: Oh, I remember it very well. I was regarded as an extremist. "Hamid is wild," they said. "During the *meetings*, he really dares the Dutch." Only then, in fact, did I realize that I was like this. When I debated I felt the heat of debating. "Hamid goes too far," they said. And there was a teacher there, his name was _____

RM: He was present at the *debating group?*

Mr. HAMID: He was there, and he let us talk about politics; whatever we wished. He was assigned by the principal to supervise the club. But he was very progressive, and he gave us full freedom.[191]

RM: Did you meet often?

Mr. ALI: Once a month.

The Classroom

RM: And the club was in school?
Mr. ALI: Yes.[192]

Mr. ASRUL: When I was still in grade school, I remember, children sometimes said very extreme things, and the teacher, full-blood Dutch, did not cut them off.[193]

Like an eager and curious student, the debate clubs made the school space glow.

Mr. ROESLAN: It was 1933. There was the Great Depression in Europe and also here, and there was a mutiny of the Dutch and Indonesian sailors on the Dutch war ship, *Zeven Provinciën*. The principal of school, Dr. S⎯⎯ came to our class. We had just had physics. The principal asked the teacher to wait, and he made an announcement: "Students, listen to this: The cruiser has just been bombed near Bengkulu [South Sumatra], and all the mutineers surrendered." One of the Dutch girls, Pauline, I knew her well, she was a sweet child, jumped up: "*Hurrah, hurrah, hurrah,*" she was so happy. The principal, however, became quite angry: "You should not shout hurrah, hurrah! They were not simply mutineers. They were desperate men demanding a better chance to live. Imagine, officers' salaries were cut by 5 percent and sailors' by 25 percent. You must understand, this is not fair!" "It was not simply a mutiny," the principal said. I was startled.[194]

For most — for all, indeed, so well educated the colony wished to be — the idea of politics and power might have arisen at home, but it was articulated, it materialized (this was the dynamics), out of the sublimity of the school. Every idea of change, even the most radical one, if comprehensible, was as if it first were written on the blackboard.

RM: You heard about the Indonesian Youth Oath of 1928?
Mr. THEODORUS: Yes, we had already learned about it in our *volksschool*, but in a secret way. We learned that the youth will make Indonesia free and that the government would pass from the Dutch to them.[195]
RM: The secret was shared among the pupils.
Mr. THEODORUS: Yes, it went from child to child. It was not taught in school in an open way.
RM: Did you know some names of the nationalist leaders?

Chapter Four

Mr. THEODORUS: Just a few. Nothing was clear to us yet. All the names came to us in a secret way. Mostly we overheard our teachers.[196]

Mr. EFENDI: I have a story to tell you. When I entered the TH [Technische Hoogeschool, the Technical Institute in Bandung, West Java, one college, of four existing, in the colony]—Sukarno had already graduated from this school some years earlier, and he became a political *person*. He was giving all those speeches—that Indonesia would become free. And yet, there were still several of his drawings on display on the wall in the *aula* of the school, as examples for us, the other students, of how to draw a machine part, and, I think, a bridge. In 1930 he was put in jail, released, arrested again, and sent to exile, in Banda, was it not?

RM: Flores.

Mr. EFENDI: Yes. In the Technische Hoogeschool, the student senate would talk about it. They knew that Sukarno was in exile and that he was against the government. Yet they did not think it right that the drawings be taken from the wall. He was a rebel, but you could see in his drawings—

RM: That he was *brilliant?*

Mr. EFENDI: —and an *alumnus* of the school.

RM: That tolerance?

Mr. EFENDI: And after 1945, he became our president.[197]

There were so-called Kartini schools in the colony since the 1910s, bearing the name of a young Javanese woman, a daughter of a regent, who died in 1903, a pioneer of indigenous, and especially women's, education. Kartini's birthday, April 21, is still celebrated as a national holiday in Indonesia. On her merits as an educator, she is often seen as the mother of the nation.

RM: There were also Dutch teachers in your Kartini school?

Mrs. SOERONO: The *principal* of the school was a Dutch lady, and there were four other Dutch teachers, I think.

RM: But there were also Indonesian teachers in the school?

Mrs. SOERONO: There were some.[198]

Mrs. MASKUN: I went to a Kartini school.

RM: What did you learn there?

The Classroom

Mrs. MASKUN: Dutch, Indonesian — it was called Malay at the time — Javanese, counting, singing —

RM: Teachers were Javanese?

Mrs. MASKUN: All were Javanese, but the principal of the school was a Dutch lady.

RM: How many years was the Kartini school?

Mrs. MASKUN: I went there for two years. I could not stay longer. My parents asked me to help at home. My mother got sick.[199]

Mrs. HARTINI: In my Kartini school in Madiun all the teachers were Dutch. Well, there were two, I think, or three Indonesian teachers, but they were perfectly fluent in Dutch. All our teachers spoke Dutch, all the time.

RM: Did you hear much about Kartini there?

Mrs. HARTINI: Yes, of course. It was in her spirit that we learned Javanese; and batiking. We also learned Javanese script — *ha na tja ra ka*; and gamelan music and shadow-puppet theater. There were textbooks for all this.

RM: Textbooks?

Mrs. HARTINI: Textbooks.

RM: There were no Dutch students in the Kartini school?

Mrs. HARTINI: Oh, many.

RM: Why would a Dutch girl want to go to a Kartini school?

Mrs. HARTINI: Because Kartini was for *all girls*. It was a girls' school. We were *all girls*. We were all students.

RM: This was that culture?

Mrs. HARTINI: Yes, and we learned Indonesian dances.

RM: Javanese?

Mrs. HARTINI: Javanese.

RM: Not Western dances?

Mrs. HARTINI: Oh no![200]

There were, besides the Kartini schools, Taman Siswa schools, in the same realm of school alternative.

Mr. PURBO: Some of my friends say: "We went to a Taman Siswa school and thus we are truly nationalistic." I can only say to this: "I went to a Dutch school, and I gave proof of my patriotism also."[201]

Taman Siswa, in Javanese (originally Arabic and Sanskrit), means "Garden of Students."[202]

> RM: All teachers in the Taman Siswa school were Indonesians, right? No Dutch.
>
> Mr. KARKONO: They were all Indonesians, mostly Javanese; some were from Sumatra. When I graduated from the school I was sent out, on a *mission* for Taman Siswa.
>
> RM: As a teacher?
>
> Mr. KARKONO: No, I never made it to become a teacher. But they appreciated what I did. On my eightieth birthday I got a present and a letter of acknowledgment that I was a part of Taman Siswa.
>
> RM: What was the school about, when you went there, in Yogyakarta?
>
> Mr. KARKONO: There was especially much about culture in the school.
>
> RM: What culture?
>
> Mr. KARKONO: Javanese culture mostly. There was a large *pendopo* [open audience hall] where there was a gamelan and there we learned dance, drama, music, krontjong, and so on.
>
> RM: Krontjong, too?

(Krontjong, we recall, were popular songs, music of the street, not far off from hawkers' cries.)

> Mr. KARKONO: Krontjong, too. We learned to play krontjong.
>
> RM: Was there a radio?
>
> Mr. KARKONO: No. Or, maybe, Ki Hadjar Dewantoro [the Taman Siswa founder and the principal of the Yogyakarta school] had a radio. Yes, we were all quite happy, playing gamelan and krontjong. Actually, I became a krontjong devotee. I even wrote lyrics for krontjong songs — like "*Swadeshi*."
>
> RM: Do you still remember the words?
>
> Mr. KARKONO: No, it was in 1936. Swadeshi was a Gandhi movement; like *Ahimsa*, and we all knew about it. They wore clothes in India made of stuff that they were supposed to have woven themselves. Not like the *textiles* are nowadays. — Now, I recall the first line: "Properly dressed, I look at you, so beautiful and glowing." It was about a young woman, with her hair let down to her shoulders; she wore batik. She was beautiful and glowing. And so on.

The Classroom

RM: Did you write any other song about politics?

Mr. KARKONO: I wrote a song about Taman Siswa—it was accompanied by gamelan—"Ladrang Taman Siswa." This I wrote for a Taman Siswa reunion, the fiftieth anniversary, in 1972.

RM: In Yogyakarta, you lived in a Taman Siswa dormitory?

Mr. KARKONO: Yes. We, the older students got permission from Ki Hajar Dewantoro to manage our dormitory ourselves—there were twenty-five of us. It was called Asrama Merdeka [Freedom Dormitory]. Younger students mostly lived in the homes of the teachers. Girls lived in the home of the principal. Mrs. Dewantoro, her name was Wisna Rini, took the girls in.[203]

Intensely, and perhaps even more purely and devotedly than in the "non-alternative" modern schools in the colony, everything in Taman Siswa is recalled as moving, maturing—and even dying, if enough time is given—in the school space.

RM: Is there anybody, in politics or in life, of whom you think often as being close to you?

Mr. KARKONO: There was a man, and he was also a man of the movement, who accepted me like a son. He was from Taman Siswa; his name was Ki Soetopo Wonobojo. He was from an aristocratic family, and he joined the [nationalist] movement early on. But *principally* he was of Taman Siswa. I met him in 1932 or 1933. I was about eighteen.

RM: What happened?

Mr. KARKONO: He taught me. In the way of Taman Siswa. He gave me the broad outlines of life, of movement, of nation, of everything. Thus I was allowed to grow up.

RM: How did it happen?

Mr. KARKONO: He liked me. He invited me to his house and we talked. Also, when he died, he was buried at Taman Siswa.

RM: You still feel close to him.

Mr. KARKONO: He left me a dagger, as an heirloom. He did not leave the dagger to his children but to me.

RM: You still have it?

Mr. KARKONO: Once a year I bathe it in a prayer house.

RM: Will you leave it to your children?
Mr. KARKONO: I do not know.

We were having tea now.

Mr. KARKONO: So, you will write about this?
RM: Yes, it will be about modern people living in a colony.
Mr. KARKONO: Yes, but the Taman Siswa people were not modern. They wanted to carry on with the cultural heritage, with what we got from our ancestors. We wished to apply this to the modern world, to cultivate an education that was appropriate to this society. There were Dutch schools. Taman Siswa was—half of it was—like a Dutch school. But it contained the Javanese, Indonesian culture. Our idea was—

Mr. Karkono used two Dutch words to say this.

Mr. KARKONO: —*Nationale Onderwijs* [National Education].[204]

✦✦✦

The people in the modern colony—working, suffering, and dreaming as much as elsewhere in the world—needed leaders. And the modern and colonial schools provided for leaders—for all leaders—and more totally than elsewhere in the world. It seemed to happen lightly. Particles of school energy and learning spilled, scattered through the colony, made for the articulation of, and indeed substituted for, politics and even revolution. The school energy veiled, and meshed with, the struggle for freedom—and made it *learned*.

Mr. MAWENGKANG: As a teacher, I planned to enter politics. When I got a teaching job in Makassar [Sulawesi], my attitude toward teaching—how to put it—loosened. Besides teaching, I began to work at a newspaper. I became a correspondent for a newspaper.
RM: It was a way to politics?
Mr. MAWENGKANG: It just went by itself. At the time the only political party in the place was Sarékat Islam [Islamic Union]. No other organization had gathered enough courage yet. So I joined Sarékat

Islam. Then Sukarno founded PNI [Partai Nasional Indonesia, Indonesian National Party]. So I joined that.

RM: As a member?

Mr. MAWENGKANG: At the moment I joined, I was made a cadre. Because I had been to school and was a teacher, I instantly became a leader. At that time, one did not have to bring anything into the party, but one had to be willing to *learn* what politics was. We took courses. We learned and thus we grew up with politics. Already in 1927 I got close to Sukarno himself. We often had our meals together. He was a technical college graduate, a civil engineer, but he did eat with us.[205]

To enter politics, to move on, and to grow up, if only because the Dutch were too powerful to be challenged any other way, was done by learning.

RM: Do you still recall the moment when you entered the movement?

Mrs. LASMIDJAH: It was like: *everything is going to make me like that.* I read a book by Multatuli.[206] And by Hatta — "we have to become free," it was his thinking.[207] I was still young, with a lot of dreams. And our teachers were not always able to keep up with it. Thus, *in such situation,* I remember, I told myself: "We all have to learn more, we must know how," and it made me say: "Why not?" Some older friends, better educated than I, founded an organization: all members were to teach: "OK, each of us contribute one *gulden*, and we buy pens and notebooks." Then we had a *meeting*. We did not know what a meeting was and what might be the technique of a meeting. Then they said: "You will be the chair person." Perhaps because I was so respectful to them.

RM: What did you do?

Mrs. LASMIDJAH: We founded a school. An evening school. The students came to our houses. There were women, many of them widows. We organized lectures — *to get together!*[208]

In the 1910s and through the 1930s, as the colony's masses increasingly suffered, and the colonial system was increasingly shaky — nationalist, anti-colonial, modern, and increasingly sophisticated political parties emerged in the colony.

RM: Because you were a good student?

Mr. KARKONO: I was one of the good students. And in the best school, it

Chapter Four

is true. At the time, a group called Indonesia Moeda, Young Indonesia, was founded and in 1931 I joined it. I was still in the first year of senior high. Instantly I became the chairman of the city branch.

RM: Then you entered a political party?

Mr. KARKONO: Parindra [Partai Indonesia Raja, Party of Great Indonesia].

RM: Of Dr. Soetomo.

Mr. KARKONO: Yes, Dr. Soetomo. I joined him in 1935, when I was twenty-one. I became a member of the *centrale*.

RM: In some photographs from that time the Parindra youth are raising their right arms. It looks like a Nazi salute.

Mr. KARKONO: These were Dr. Soetomo's youth cadres, Soerja Wirawan [Heroes of the Sun]. They had a salute like this. They were the Parindra youth. They had a *uniform*, as I remember it, green shirts with red and white ties.

RM: Red and white?

Mr. KARKONO: Yes, nationalist colors. Like the Boy Scouts, except they had long trousers. The Boy Scouts wore shorts.

RM: Boys and girls?

Mr. KARKONO: Yes.[209]

There were spaces and spots in the colony as exemplary as schools, sports fields, or clubs, and in the same category. They often represented a space and stage as elevated and pure as the modern and schooled men and women of the colony might ever reach. The next stage. The ultimate stage.

Mr. DES ALWI: One day, I swam in the Banda-Neira lagoon. I liked to swim there. It was February, which is during the western monsoon, and there were big waves, but in the lagoon the sea was calm. All of a sudden, a police officer appeared: "Get out of the water!" A Dutch ship was coming, *Kapal Putih* [White Ship]. We knew the ship; she used to carry internees to and from the Boven Digoel camp. I felt a bit annoyed to be chased away, and so I gathered my clothes but remained in the harbor and watched. I liked ships very much. One day I wanted to become a captain; in a white uniform, you know. The ship landed, several policemen went on board, and they came back with two men really nicely dressed. One of them was wearing glasses, both had white

The Classroom

jackets and white trousers, white shirts but without a tie and with an open collar. There was a hustle in the harbor. The Buginese coolies carried out the two men's luggage. One of the men, the one without glasses, came to me and addressed me in Dutch. I answered: "*Ja meneer*" [Yes, sir]. I knew that they were coming from Boven Digoel, from the camp, because their faces were so pale, from malaria, you know.[210]

This is a story of two prisoners most exemplary of the late colonial times, Mohammad Hatta (with the glasses) and Soetan Sjahrir, the top leaders of the nationalist movement who ten years later, in 1945, would become the first vice-president and the first prime minister of the Indonesian independent state. The moment is described by then a boy who later became an adopted son of Sjahrir. The internment camp on the Upper (*Boven*) Digoel River in New Guinea, where the two just came from, was the most notorious, and *exemplary*, part of the Dutch colonial "Tropical Siberia."[211] Hatta and Sjahrir were being moved to a new place, Banda-Neira, the capital of Banda archipelago, still quite isolated, but halfway closer to the center of modern colonial civilization in Java. After one year at Digoel, the two men were allowed to a softer place of exile, less malaric and less lonesome, because they were "academicians." This was the official explanation: Hatta held a degree of *doctorandus*; he was a PhD candidate from the Rotterdam School of Commerce. Sjahrir, as far as it was known, had enrolled and attended lectures for a year at the venerable University of Leiden.

There is of course nothing new in the connection between modern prisons, internment camps, knowledge, and pedagogy; not just in a colony.[212]

> Mrs. SUKARSIH: Yes, Hatta had a gramophone in the Digoel camp. And yes, we regularly got together in the camp, listening, coming to see Hatta, debating. There were several among us who went to Hatta's place to take lessons. He taught us.[213]

It was the greatness of the camp, truly a myth of the camp, that made the space outside the camp — along the road to the camp, like the space away from school — appear and feel like as yet at large, on the lam, as yet not en-camped. In contrast to not-yet-like-that towns and neighborhoods in the colony, made of "workers, petite bourgeoisie, officials, etc., etc.,"[214] the camp at Boven Digoel was made of "cadres," political activists, who had passed the courses and the tests. (Indeed, a serious attempt was made, in that *select place*, to plant the first seed of a future Indonesian "communist society."[215])

> RM: What was most difficult in Digoel?
> Mrs. SUKARSIH: There was not enough food. There was not enough happiness. Things were lacking.

Mrs. Sukarsih was in her mid eighties when I met her. She went to the Digoel camp accompanying her husband, Mr. Moerwoto, an activist for Sukarno, Hatta, and Sjahrir. After seven years in the camp, husband and wife went different ways. He later married another woman.

> Mrs. SUKARSIH: In the end, I lost everything, everything that makes one happy.
> RM: Tell me more about the camp. How they kept you there?
> Mrs. SUKARSIH: There was a camp for the military guards, and it was surrounded by wire. But there was no wire around our camp. We often had *picnics*, and sometimes went up river, in canoes. We paddled and then we had a lunch up there.

How was it that she joined her husband? Who paid for her trip?

> Mrs. SUKARSIH: The government did.
> RM: It means that the government wished you to go?
> Mrs. SUKARSIH: They asked us: "Do you want to keep the family together? If you do, if you go, the government will pay for the trip."

They met as high school students in Bandung. Moerwoto was in Pergerakan Banteng, the Wild Buffalo Movement, she in Sadar Istri, the Conscious Woman, which agitated against polygamy and organized "alternative schools."

> Mrs. SUKARSIH: From Bandung we were taken by police. By train, we went to Tanjung Priok [Jakarta harbor], and then by ship to Surabaya, Makassar, Ambon, Banda-Neira, and Digoel.
> RM: It was a difficult trip?

Mrs. SUKARSIH: Ordinary. Because we were of the movement, it was relaxed.

RM: When you arrived at Digoel, was there some shelter ready for you?

Mrs. SUKARSIH: There were barracks built of logs. Only Hatta had a house built for him beforehand. Because he was a *doctorandus*.

The other internees had to build their own houses.

Mrs. SUKARSIH: We built a house, for the two of us. We had to get the timber ourselves.

RM: There was a kitchen —

Mrs. SUKARSIH: Yes, there was a kitchen. A simple one, like the village people in Java usually have. Some friends brought their own chairs and tables on the ship, beds, complete, bedding and kitchenware.

The internees were even allowed to have servants.

Mrs. SUKARSIH: Yes, the *Kaja-Kaja* [name given to Papuans, supposedly meaning "friends"]. From the forest. We had to teach them first.

RM: Like how?

Mrs. SUKARSIH: They used not to wear any clothes. Just a strip of something, you know, around here. Fortunately, we had some spare clothing, so we put it on them. And they stank. We had to teach them to wash. We gave them soap and made them put clothes on, trousers, shirts, and skirts. The women had their breasts uncovered.

RM: But they were good people?

Mrs. SUKARSIH: Good, yes, good. When they were good, we were also good. But just the look of them! They were often sick, and they often left — many of them, when they were sick, to die in the forest, we were told.

There was in the camp, and maybe essentially more than in the colony at large, an acute sense of civilization, progress, and especially learning — "sublime and grotesque, atrocious and laughable . . . beyond tragedy."[216]

Mrs. SUKARSIH: There was a band and we would sing. There was some pleasure. It was not so difficult.

RM: You were a young woman.

Chapter Four

Mrs. SUKARSIH: Yes, there were *sports*, tennis, badminton—

RM: Was there some dancing in Digoel?

Mrs. SUKARSIH: Oh, yes! There was a band. Sjahrir especially liked to teach us to dance. Waltzes, foxtrots. There was a concert almost every day.

RM: Krontjong?

Mrs. SUKARSIH: Hawaiian.

RM (*recalling that white ship in Banda-Neira*): Did not you find it strange, maybe even unfair, that Hatta and Sjahrir were allowed to leave Boven Digoel, after just a year or so, for a softer place, while you were made to stay?

Mrs. SUKARSIH: No. It was because they were academicians. It would not be nice to be jealous. And in 1942 [six years later], I was also allowed to go. I returned to Bandung.

RM: Your parents were still alive?

Mrs. SUKARSIH: Yes.

RM: They must have been happy.

Mrs. SUKARSIH: They were happy to see me again, very happy.[217]

It was chilling perhaps, but a language of freedom, with a modern and colonial sense to it, in which Mrs. Sukarsih let me know about Boven Digoel.

Mrs. SUKARSIH: And we also played theater in the camp.

RM: You played?

Mrs. SUKARSIH: I did not play. I just watched. And there was a debate club, too; and gamelan, the Javanese music, and Sumatran music—

This interview more than others was impressive, powerful by being repetitious, repetitious, repetitious like that life.

Mrs. SUKARSIH: The first thing in the morning, I boiled water for drinking. Then Moerwoto went to the garden. I did not. I was afraid. Bad things might happen if we dared too far from our house, to the edge of the camp where there were no guards. Some Kaja-Kaja people might be after us, after our clothes, or our axes. I was afraid. — But we had to have servants.

RM: Kaja-Kaja men? And women, too?

Mrs. SUKARSIH: Men and women, too. Couples.

The Classroom

RM: So it was not so bad if you did not go too far?

Mrs. SUKARSIH: It was *OK*. I had servants, one time a couple, and I taught them to read.

RM: In what language?

Mrs. SUKARSIH: Indonesian, of course. At the beginning, they just watched us: *nyam nyam*, it was their whole language. We taught them Indonesian, and also to boil the water in the morning. They brought it to the house, in front of the door. Like here. (*Mrs. Sukarsih points from where we sit, outside, toward the door.*) They learned. To boil water and to cook a little. They got trousers and shirts. But when they left, they often did not take it with them.

RM: They had children in the camp, as well?

Mrs. SUKARSIH: We took them into our house only when they had no children. When the woman got pregnant, she went away. They called me *mama komunis* [mammy communist], and the men were *papa komunis*. When *mama komunis* was around, they wore trousers. When *mama komunis* was not, they did not.

RM: There were movies, right?

Mrs. SUKARSIH: Oh, yes. There were not yet talkies in the camp. We had only silent movies, and we were not happy about it. The talkies already existed and we still had only silent movies. Oh, yes, and there was also a gramophone.

RM: Yes, you told me.

Mrs. SUKARSIH: Hatta brought one. And also books, he brought sixteen boxes of books. His house was full of them.[218]

Mr. Mawengkang was sent to Boven Digoel in 1936, and stayed there until 1943.

RM: Was there a place to stay ready for you in Boven Digoel?

Mr. MAWENGKANG: When we arrived I moved with friends. Later I built a house for myself. I asked for a plot of land, close to the edge of the camp, so I could have a larger garden. I got metal sheeting for the roof from the government. It was a small house, three by four meters.

RM: One room.

Mr. MAWENGKANG: Bedroom and guest room; the kitchen was outside. Three by four.

RM: Was there a window?

Mr. MAWENGKANG: Yes.

RM: With glass?

Mr. MAWENGKANG: No. We used bark.

RM: Were there lamps?

Mr. MAWENGKANG: If there was money for kerosene; otherwise we used candles. We began with candles.

RM: What about water?

Mr. MAWENGKANG: We tried to build a house close to the river.

But there were crocodiles in the river.

Mr. MAWENGKANG: There were crocodiles. It was risky. Some people did not dare.

RM: Was there anything to read? Books?

Mr. MAWENGKANG: Oh, yes.

RM: Newspapers?

Mr. MAWENGKANG: Newspapers arrived every six weeks.

There were schools in Boven Digoel. More schools per capita than in the colony outside the camp.[219] There were quarters in the camp with names: A, B, C, D, E, and F.

Mr. MAWENGKANG: To go outside was always risky. Mostly we stayed in the camp. When we were inside, we could talk with friends, borrow a book here and there, and study. Several friends went outside and never came back. When this happened, we did not know what to do, and the person was probably already dead anyway. (*Mr. Mawengkang takes some photographs out of his desk drawer.*) Here is a Catholic church. Here is a mosque. This is the doctor's house. These are some Digoel internees who have just arrived.

RM: You never thought about escape?

Mr. MAWENGKANG: We did plan it often, and once I tried. I ran for three days.

RM: Just you?

Mr. MAWENGKANG: There were two friends with me.

RM: Did you have a map?

Mr. MAWENGKANG: No. We tried to keep close to the river.

RM: Did you have any weapons?

Mr. MAWENGKANG: Machetes. We always had machetes when we went to the gardens.

RM: You were in the forest for three days? There was no hope?

Mr. MAWENGKANG: The Kaja-Kaja had bows. They could hit you from afar. We had just machetes. Machetes cannot fly.

RM: After three days you went back to the camp?

Mr. MAWENGKANG: Back.[220]

This was, perhaps, as close as one might get to what I call "promenades": through a test site that might occasionally grow into a wasteland,[221] with all possible unrest "canalized . . . in a manner that leaves untouched the material foundations of society,"[222] with a body "still [perhaps] capable of being sacrificed," that still, perhaps, "retains and persists in making sense";[223] in the world of "anguished liberality," where one is "more or less allowed to run free and expose his wounds."[224] Run fast and, by all means, along

> . . . high-speed roads and railways, interchanges, airports . . . , or the great commercial centers, or the extended transit camps where the planet's refugees are parked.[225]

> . . . toward campsites, youth hostels/barracks; camps everywhere, the great camp of territory.[226]

"The precious lesson of the camps and the gulags," as Paul Virilio wrote, "has not been heeded, because it was erroneously presented not only as an ideological phenomenon, but also as a static one, an enclosure."[227] Through a "postproletarian park" of sorts,[228] through commonplace, before a revolution could ever be attempted, rebels like Mr. Mawengkang struggled without a map (true, some others had a map—the *Bos School Atlas*). Along the avenues, paths, and promenades of the highly modern, and professionally designed cities, landscapes, and camps,[229] Mr. Mawengkang and his generation of magnificents moved.

Chapter Four

CHAPTER FIVE

THE WINDOW

Dream. The O—s showed me their house in the Dutch East Indies. The room I found myself in was paneled in dark wood and gave the impression of affluence. But that was nothing, said my guides. What I must admire was the view from the upper story. I thought it must overlook the expanse of sea that was nearby, and so I climbed the stairs. At the top I stood at a window. I looked down. There before my eyes, was the very same warm, paneled, cozy-looking room I had just left.

—Walter Benjamin, "Thought Figures"

BRINGING THE PICTURE IN

In Indonesia, when a painting on the wall of a colonial house is recalled, a real painting, oil on canvas, in a frame, it is most often to make a point of how rare it was.

> Professor RESINK: Well, my great-grandfather was so famous at the time that a portrait of him was painted, in the middle of the last [the nineteenth] century, and for decades it hung in the hall of the *directie* of the Koninklijk Bataviaasch Genootschap voor Kunsten en Wetenschappen [Royal Batavian Society for Arts and Science]. It was on Koningsplein [King's Square, now Freedom Square, Jakarta].
> RM: In your house, you, too, had paintings?
> Professor RESINK: Yes. But there were no Javanese paintings at the time. We had no painting by a Javanese. But we had painters of the so-called Haagse School [Hague School]. It was all *naturalistic*.

THE BEAUTIFUL INDIES, OIL PAINTING IN A WOODEN FRAME. SAHRI SUMARJONO, DATE UNKNOWN. KONINKLIJK INSTITUUT VOOR DE TROPEN, AMSTERDAM

This was all happening, and hanging on, the walls at home—the images of Dutch cities and landscapes, and of the gray northern sea—before Professor Resink had seen Europe with his own eyes.

> RM: Was not it strange—in Java, the paintings were of Europe?
>
> Professor RESINK: It was *exotic*. There was a painting by a painter named Goedvriend, and it was a view of a fortress; Ehrenbreitstein, on the Rhine. Or there was a framed pencil drawing—of a woman with a white sheep and a *schaapskooi*, a sheep cote. Yes, it was another world. But we also owned some Indische School [Indies school] paintings, one of the [Hindu-Javanese] god Semar, by Antoine Payen, a French painter who visited the Indies. In our sitting room there was an oil portrait of my grandfather with the governor general, and next to it was a portrait of my grandmother in a big hat with ostrich feather; this one was a photograph; my grandfather had all his stars and medals on.[1]

Memories were rekindled through the pictures as they were pointed out to me: some dark, almost black oils, some very yellowed photographs, some very faded drawings—this was how the climate worked on them—some framed, some pinned on the wall. Not rarely, memories were pictured over, substituted by the pictures.

> Professor SOEMARDJAN: Look, here is my grandfather; he lived in the sultan's palace. You know that?
>
> RM: Yes.
>
> Professor SOEMARDJAN: My father died when I was four.
>
> RM: So you don't remember him?
>
> Professor SOEMARDJAN: I don't remember him very well. But I remember his face because I have this photograph.[2]

> Mrs. BEBSI: Whenever I wish, I can look at it. This is *paatje* [daddy], here. And in my brother's house we have his *bust*. Here, do you see, *paatje* looks from the canvas at us?
>
> RM: Yes, I see.
>
> Mrs. BEBSI: It was painted in Bali. *Paatje posed* for it.[3]

The picturesque—which still excites and forms the imagination, memories, and sense of the past in the old people—had arrived from the West, together in a package with the other newness like bricks, electricity, or railways. The urge to recognize the world in the pictures was driven by the same energy as that to dwell modern or to go to school. This is why the heavy oil paintings hanging glumly by themselves, rare and charged, can be pointed out to us and be recalled with the same intensity and with the same significance as — to move on to the most exemplary pictures of a modern colony — newspaper cuttings.[4]

> *Mr. Prinsen led me to his bedroom just behind the front porch. At the head of his bed, or rather cot, that filled more than half of the room, facing me as I entered, was an almost life-size oil portrait of president Sukarno with his third wife, Fatmawati. It seemed to be the largest thing in the room. A bit later, after Mr. Prinsen mentioned so warmly several of Sukarno's nonfriends (to say the least), I asked him why the portrait was here, why so big, and why at the head of his bed. With a soft smile he said that one Mr. Sulistyo gave the painting to his daughter, that they liked the Sulistyos and could not say no. On the other wall, along the length of the bed, there were four little drawings in a row, not framed, just glued (so it seemed) to the wall. The first one on the left, Mr. Prinsen said, was by his father: it was a figure of a worker, a steel-mill worker, it seemed, realistic, social, socialist, to the point, full of that spirit. Next to it, there was a small light watercolor, by his brother, he said, who still lived in Amsterdam — a calm and pleasant Dutch town scene. The last two pictures in the row were reproductions of* van Gogh, *evidently cut from a magazine, of two of the master's early paintings from Borinage, Belgium, where he lived his painter-missionary life among the miners.*[5]

Cuttings from books, magazines, and from newspapers especially, appeared somehow as the most befitting, the closest to "real art," and the most "powerful message," the most striking of all the pictures on the walls of the former colony that I have seen and have been told about. (Paul Virilio speaks about "the cunning chronology the history books used to cut and paste."[6])

> Mr. ROESLAN: There was Soeara Oemoem [The Public Voice] paper owned by Dr. Soetomo and his Great Indonesia Party. Once there was an article in the paper about Mahatma Gandhi — how he challenged the *salt monopoly*. My father read the article to my mother, they talked about it, and I listened. My father then took the newspaper — there was a picture of Mahatma on the page — he cut out the picture, and pinned it on the wall.[7]

Chapter Five

Like the paintings, but more in a flash, and indeed in depth, the daily and weekly newspapers cuttings, sometimes pasted on the wall and sometimes just lying around in the house to be picked up as they struck one's eyes, evoked a world. The more distant the world, the more flashing the image, the flatter the picture, the more profound—blatant, distinct, direct, modern, and temporal, which, of course, mostly meant *passing*.

> Mrs. TOLANG: Here is a photo of my husband and our boy. They both have left already.
> RM: Where?
> Mrs. TOLANG: To the hereafter.
> RM: Both of them?
> Mrs. TOLANG: Oh, no, my husband. Our son defended his *thesis* and he became a doctor. In Java.[8]

It seems that, increasingly, I am meeting people in empty houses. Here in Menado, for instance, all relatives and friends worth talking about are either dead or "in Jakarta." Sometimes there is an ambiguity in their telling me about the absence—is it in Jakarta or is it death? An absent one may be also dead or in Singapore, dead or in America. This is a theme belonging to the chapter on paintings and windows, very much so. Regularly, at moments like those, talking turns toward a picture if there is any. The faces on them are very often serial, as in the Monets, *repeatedly, at all times of day, in changing light, trying to capture on canvas, now the haystack, now the cathedral.*[9]

By pointing at a picture, people appeared to make it, to make their memories efficient, coherent, and, at last, meaningful to me as well as to themselves. In this very direct, physical, and instrumental attachment to the two-dimensional thing, if only by pointing their index finger, or by merely thinking about cutting a picture out of a printed page, these people, their lives, their history, their landscapes, and also their visitors, were, at last, formed. Touch the picture and, for that moment at least, you are in the picture.

> Mr. ROESLAN: I knew the great Dr. Tjipto [famous Indonesian freedom fighter]. When he came back from exile in Banda, I was asked to pick him up in the harbor. Do you want to see his photo?[10]
>
> Mr. DAINO: I knew Sukarno when I was a boy.
> RM: His name?

Mr. DAINO: I knew him. Already in Purworejo I knew him. Already when I was in the grade school.

RM: What did you know about him? That he was an Indonesian hero?

Mr. DAINO: Yes, Indonesian hero. I knew him, his black velvet cap, his photo.[11]

Like the lives and the memories, pictures—and particularly the photographs and pictures cut from the papers—were perishable. But this clearly made them more real. Especially in the tropical and humid colony, where everything was more perishable than elsewhere in the modern world. Paper, canvas, and, most of all, the cheap newspaper stuff did not last long. There have always been paper-devouring and canvas-chewing bugs in multitudes, and, of course, poverty and, of course, recurring waves of other destruction. All this marked this place and its pictures in particular.

Mrs. SOELISTINA: I have no pictures from that time, none at all.

RM: They are gone?

Mrs. SOELISTINA: Gone.[12]

Through the pictures, touchable, touching, and perishable, colonial memories are modern. The pictures materialize memories even in the pictures' absence or loss: they made memories storable, exchangeable, priceable—yes, I too bought some of the touching pictures and took them away with me. Suggesting homeland, the pictures at the same time permit—to use Walter Benjamin's words—the "spectacular," meaning "phantasmagoria of accumulation."[13] This is a type of caption that often repeats in the colonial archive, where there are heaps of pictures, paintings, and drawings like this:

A man is holding a painting that was given to him on the occasion of his retirement after one turn of service; ca 1930.[14]

During the Japanese occupation Sukarno got an opportunity to take paintings from the collection of the [Batavia] Art Circle which was seized by the Japanese.... Almost the entire Art Circle collection was handed over by Japan to Sukarno, and it is for this reason that he owns many paintings by European artists.[15]

Sukarno's collection mentioned here, it should be noted, has become a picture treasure of postcolonial Indonesia, the model of the new nation's imagination. The picturesque and thus material and real, alive and collectible, enabled the modern in the colony—like the collector of the bourgeois salon, the *intérieur* as *étui*[16]—"to gather" the world as one gathers pictures.

> RM: So the boys liked cars?
> Mr. SUTIKNO: And also, there was a fashion among us, from the *lagere* [lower] to the senior high school, and beyond, to collect pictures—picture postcards of film stars—Rin Tin Tin, Bing Crosby, Harold Lloyd, these were most popular. We also collected postcards of Sukarno, like in the cap and jacket.[17]
>
> RM: Did you, boys in the school, collect photos of actresses?
> Mr. ROESLAN: Not yet. But there was one thing—photos of Sukarno. Those we liked to collect; just those.[18]

Albums and boxes full of photographs were often, almost always, shown to me in Indonesia; often even before tea and snacks they were brought in—as a gesture of welcome. They certainly were what Kafka might call "albums for sightseers"[19]—modern houses opened themselves through them and like them; the guest was made welcome in the house as a sightseer. By the same gesture, as pages were turned or photographs taken out from the box and passed around, as the collection was shown, all of the past and the present, the near and the distant, had been gathered and, also, ideally, entered into the collection.

> Mrs. POLITON: My father was Arnold Elias Politon. He was a low-level official during the Dutch time: here, this photo.
> RM: Can I make a copy of it?
> Mr. SEKO: Sure.
> Mrs. POLITON: Actually, he is here. Yes, here is my father as he became a teacher in Central Sulawesi. Later he came back and became a low-level official in Tondano. Have you already been to Tondano?
> RM: Yes. Do you still remember the house?
> Mrs. POLITON: There is a photo of it somewhere.
> Mr. SEKO: Here are her parents.
> Mrs. POLITON: My parents. My father was well respected. This is a photo of him in full uniform. He goes to an audience by the *resident* [top Dutch official] in Menado.[20]

The Window

The albums and the boxes appeared more of one piece than a single photograph ever could—purer and more focused, more natural, more alive, more pertinent. Opening the photo boxes and turning the albums' pages with the photographs loose or glued just so, and the glue aging, with the pictures sometimes falling out and being picked up and put back, mostly at random, as we talked, the past did not so totally look like "collection and recollection" anymore.[21] The world was being gathered as well, perhaps, as this world might ever be.

> RM: So this is your father. Was he strict with you?
> Princess BROTODININGRAT: Oh, boy, we were disciplined! Here is a regent, this is from Holland.
> RM: Where are you? Here?
> Princess BROTODININGRAT: Oh, no, I was not born yet.
> RM: And this?
> Princess BROTODININGRAT: This is the time of the revolution [1945]. Here is my father.
> RM: This is a wedding, right? And this?
> Princess BROTODININGRAT: Here, he became king. It is the inauguration of the king.
> RM: Here, he is with some Dutch—a governor?
> Princess BROTODININGRAT: I was not born yet. If you want it—here I am, see—I can make a copy for you. I can make a color copy for you.
> RM: Yes, please, in color.[22]

There was a sense of liberation that only modernity seemed capable of bringing about. Pictures, especially when in plural, in an album box, or among other modern things, on the wall, appeared self-evident and could be trusted. With the picture thus present, as long, at least, as one was looking, and as long as one looked as a sightseer, one was strong enough to make the world trustworthy. Especially when in plural, the picture had the capacity to gather the world and the sightseer. It empowered trust, recognition, and also self-recognition in that picture way.

> Mr. ROESLAN: This is in my HBS high school, and we are about to play a soccer match. (*Mr. Roeslan hesitated and looked over his shoulder toward his secretary.*) According to Kuiman, here I am.[23]

Chapter Five

There was a modern lightness, and it struck the colony very early on, at the same time as, and sometimes it seems more forcefully than, it struck the West. This is a confession of G. B. Shaw from a letter he wrote to a friend in the fall of 1916 after watching a German zeppelin crash over London and burn along with all the people on board: "I grieve to add that after seeing the Zepp fall like a burning newspaper with its human content roasting for some minutes (it was frightfully slow) I went to bed and was comfortably asleep in ten minutes."[24] The historian Jay Winters, who quoted this, used the phrase "'cinematic' reduction of human suffering."[25] He might also say "picture" or "newspaper" reduction.

✦ ✦ ✦

Like the pictures clipped from newspapers, or looking like the clippings, newspapers with pictures, or with stories as impressive as if they were pictures, filled the modern or wishing-to-be-modern house in the colony, teaching about, and acting as, space.

> Princess BROTODINIGRAT: Newspapers, oh, yes, Locomotief, later P____—lots of them. We could read everything.
> RM: You read papers every day?
> Princess BROTODINIGRAT: Every day.

In the newspapers, as in the early and also very impressive diorama, panorama, or panopticon, "not only does one see everything, but one sees it in all ways."[26] One gets a "heightened expression of the dull perspective."[27]

> RM: You knew about the world?
> Princess BROTODINIGRAT: We knew everything.[28]

Dwelling, the learned-about and acting space, if modern enough, has become a space of picturesque crowdedness recalling a *Schablonstil*, or cliché style, of a newspaper or magazine page[29]:

> Interior of a house of a Dutch family in the Dutch Indies. Probably Batavia 1924.[30]

> It is enough to make one shudder to see a bourgeois family taking its morning coffee without ever noticing the unknowable that shows through the tablecloth's red and white checkered pattern.[31]

The Window

The kind-of Le Corbusier avant-garde houses in the West of the 1920s and 1930s had famously been conceived as "machines for living in."[32] Modern colonial houses of the same time, in an avant-garde and colonial mode, are often recalled as having also been conceived as newspapers for living in. Like a newspaper—where "catchy, familiar phrases anchor[ed] the [life] in the everyday"[33]—these dwellings opened themselves to the world. To dwell and to belong was newly presupposed to be as if of a newspaper. To look newly at the world, and at one's life, if one wished to see fully, one was supposed to look at it as if it were a (picturesque) newspaper story.

This was a situation sort of good for the house. As one read enough newspapers and looked enough at the pictures, in papers, in boxes, on the wall, one also came to realize that "the true city" was "the city indoors":

> What stands within the windowless house is the true. . . . (What is true has no windows; nowhere does the true look out to the universe.)[34]

"Let two mirrors reflect each other" and you get "the perspective on infinity."[35] It may be called, of course, "dumping the exterior space."[36] But it also might seem, particularly in places like a colony, the only way of becoming new and, yet, "looking the everyday in the face."[37] Then, of course, one had to accept that one was leaving only a special trace on the world, like marks on a canvas or on a windowpane (not through the window)—a "touch," in painters' terminology *patte*, literally a "paw mark."[38]

"Das Licht der Öffentlichkeit verdunkelt alles" (The light of publicity dims all), Hannah Arendt says Martin Heidegger said.[39] The closer one dared to get to the world, the more pictures were supposed to be pinned on the wall, and the more newspapers were supposed to be brought in and spread around.

> Mr. HARDOYO: In Dutch times, we subscribed to newspapers from Surabaya. I have forgotten the names, mostly *blad-blad* [papers] in Dutch. My father read Dutch, so when there were papers, they were mostly in Dutch.
> RM: Not all in Dutch?
> Mr. HARDOYO: Many. And there were also some papers left behind by people who passed through. I can't remember it exactly. I only know that I saw a lot of Dutch papers everywhere in the house. Yes, there were also some Indonesian papers. In later years, there was a magazine in Javanese. Mardi Siswi was the name. My father also kept many issues

of Sukarno's newspaper, Pikiran Rakjat [People's Thought] from the time father was in Bandung. It was in the house, as well. Whoever came brought in some newspapers.[40]

RM: You girls read much?
Mrs. RAHMIATI: We did not have many books, but we had all the magazines.[41]

More, it seems, than in the advanced West, in the colony there was a distinct scale in the status of reading and looking at a page. Far from everybody in the house, or neighborhood, or town, or nation, one could read, line by line, column by column, fluently, as the letters went. Much more, just looking at the thing, and the sense of a layout, is recalled—a book, a newspaper, a magazine, a text as a picture.

RM: Does it mean that not all the young people so excited about newspapers, as you say, could read? Dutch, Malay, or Javanese—that not one of these they could well read?
Mr. KARKONO: Mostly they could, sort of.
RM: They knew it well enough to leaf through a newspaper?
Mr. KARKONO: Yes, sort of.[42]

The colonial, and this is one argument of this book, signaled the modern especially clearly and often ahead of the West. What Siegfried Kracauer detected as a new trend in Germany of the 1920s was at the time in full force in the colony: "The penchant for distraction demands and finds an answer in the display of pure externality; hence the irrefutable tendency . . . to turn all forms of entertainment into revues, and parallel with this tendency, the increasing number of illustrations in the daily press and in periodical publications."[43]

Mr. ROESLAN: There was an article, for example, about Aceh [North Sumatra], and about it being secretly supported by the king of Turkey. And there was a portrait of the king, in all his robes and with his wife. We had that portrait in our house—not a portrait, I mean, the picture from the newspaper—of Sultan Hamid of Turkey, and it was there next to Mahatma Gandhi.
RM: Did you have still other pictures?

The Window

Mr. ROESLAN: Of Dr. Soetomo.
RM: Also clipped from a newspaper?
Mr. ROESLAN: And put on the wall as well.
RM: Still more?
Mr. ROESLAN: It had a big influence on me.[44]

The papers lay around, and they filled the space. They were accessible, pliable (also moldy in the humidity), absorbing the place into themselves, offering themselves to be picked up and taken to whatever corner of the place one wished to. They had been one sure way capable of making one — wherever one might actually be in the colony — to be still at home.

Dr. ONG: There was the war. In 1940. I remember the scene in our house.
RM: Was it excitement?
Dr. ONG: Not really.
RM: You knew about the war in Europe, the invasions by Hitler, the war in China!
Dr. ONG: Yes, I mean, I remember my father very seriously reading a newspaper.[45]

Mr. ALI: I was still in school, and my grandfather was already old. He could not read very much anymore, because his eyes were ailing. But he was interested in politics. So I came home from school after two, and at four he called for me to read the newspaper to him. He listened. I was, I think, in the fifth grade, very young. I did not understand much what politics was and what all this was about.[46]

Newspapers newly connecting the house, neighborhood, town, and country through the events in the paper and through the pictures made the communities and the dwellers, fast and irreversibly, ever more paper-thick and picture-dense.

Mr. KARKONO: I loved to learn. And I had the passion, since I was little, to follow the national movement. My father subscribed to newspapers, nationalist newspapers, Malay newspapers at the time, and I took them in stride. Later, my father even forbade me to read newspapers, but I did it anyway.
RM: Why would he want you to not read newspapers?

Chapter Five

> Mr. KARKONO: He was afraid that I might be expelled from school. I went to a good school, for the children of officials and people from the palace; for important people. So he was afraid. And he did not have a good education. Also, I was not getting my education from my father, but I read the newspapers. So I knew about the movement.[47]

✴ ✴ ✴

Like the salon furniture, like the paintings on the wall, the newspapers and the books were newly brought into the house. A house, and all the space in the colony with paintings on the wall, with furniture, books, and newspapers around, stood for communication: it promised to shelter its inhabitants as modern.

> Mr. HARDOYO: Sometimes the friends of my parents or some uncles and aunts came to visit. There was a sort of reading corner in a guest area in the front of the house, with books and magazines—reading for children as well as for adults. It was just behind the front veranda. There was a large mat on the floor, a pretty mat, and a long low table, sort of the Japanese style. People came, they sat around, talked, and read. Many people came to this place, relatives, friends, visitors from out of town.[48]

The pictures, papers, and books made for a landscape, and for a social landscape.

> RM: So you read at home?
> Mr. SUWARDI: It was a matter of economy. It was a matter of being clothed properly, what kind of fashion there might be at the moment—it was very confusing. I thought that only the people truly of the *elite* would go to the public library.[49]

Newspapers, magazines, and books, and the pictures in them, were closely related to furniture and, with the furniture and the rest of the salon things, they heightened ever more the dreaming, the dreamy seeing and sensing of other places—the new awareness of home as identified with other places.

> Professor RESINK: We had at home what I called to myself a "terror Bible." It had a special shelf for itself, in a bookcase among the books

The Window

of my parents, very high for me to reach. And this bookcase was never opened. I thought to myself: "Why?" Do you know why? Because the illustrations in the book were by—Gustave Doré! (*Here, Professor Resink's voice went down [up, on second thought] into quite dramatic a whisper.*) Awesome! *Echt* [genuinely] awesome, truly a Bible! Those pictures, I mean! It had nothing whatsoever to do with the Bible we read at school.[50]

Mr. ISLAM: We were free, we could read anything. It was like this: if I wished for a book, I would tell my father: "Why would you like to read it?" "*OK*!" Then I could take the book and bring it to the table.[51]

Nowhere in the world, when one opened a book, one saw as far as in a colony.

Mrs. OEI: My father had many books, and there were pictures in some of them. I looked at the pictures; it was like a real theater.[52]

Also Goethe, of course, attempted "to understand the Revolution as something like a *coup de théâtre*."[53]

Mrs. BEBSI: There was a man in a picture in one of our books, in a straw hat, in a *garden*, without a *jacket*, sitting in a lounge chair, smoking a cigar. And on the next page, there might be a *Mijnheer* [mister] driving a car. You see? In the books that we used, in school especially, Indonesians were cooks, maids, *et cetera, et cetera*.[54]

Mr. ROESLAN: Sometimes there was a story about an *inlander* [a native], and there was a picture of him: he was stupid, uneducated, *inlander*, dirty. And there was a *Mijnheer* in an armchair. There was a picture of him, and an Indonesian sat on the floor. Then we had large pictures on the walls in the classroom: "Sit straight! Correct!" And there was an Indonesian boy or girl sitting like that. (*Mr. Roeslan shows me— straight up, hands behind his back, looking forward, chin [trembling a little like old people's do] thrust forward and a little up; with that sense of flying, seeing the world as being there, ahead—a little like that.*) I soon began to like history, I was very happy studying history. There were so many wonderful books in our HBS school library. Like ____: there it all was: 1870, *the era of modern imperialism* and what it meant. *Modern*

Chapter Five

> *imperialism*, and *forward movement*, how modern Indonesia was opened up—[55]

Mr. PEREIRA: What do you call it? *Geography*.
RM: Of Indonesia? Flores?
Mr. PEREIRA: Geography of the whole world! We knew it all by heart. We knew all the countries by heart: Germany. Belgium. What is next? Austria. Hungary, at one time it was called Austro-Hungary. Then Czechoslovakia—[56]

BIRTH OF THE WINDOW

> A proposition is a picture of reality. A proposition is a model of reality as we imagine it.
> —Ludwig Wittgenstein, *Tractatus Logico-Philosophicus*

I visited an old observatory above the hill city of Bandung, about a four-hour drive from Jakarta—the famous Rudolf Boscha Observatory built in the 1920s, a jewel of the modern colony. The smog covered the city below and made it impossible at night to see many stars anymore. This I was told by Dr. Bambang, the observatory director. (He also showed me an old Festschrift of the colonial Bandung Technical College, with a list of all the graduates. Sukarno's name was highlighted, probably by the director's hand.)

Almost nothing of the skies, in fact, could be seen anymore for the purpose of a serious astronomy. Yet the observatory remained a lively place, and it was still a jewel. A row of computers, a gift from abroad, had been installed in the building next to where the big, old, beautiful brass telescope was still being dusted every day. Behind the computers, when I was there, there were students from the present Bandung Institute of Technology. They came here regularly "to practice." The picture they could see of the sky was the picture of the screen. Nothing new or special, of course. Arthur Rimbaud, more than a century before this, might have felt like this, and so do I: "I am the scholar in his dark armchair. Branches and rain beat against the library window."[57]

Once I told a friend in Jakarta about my favorite image of a window, in Proust's *In Search of Lost Time*. The boy Marcel is already in bed in his nursery, he listens to his parents and some of their friends talking in the garden. He waits for his mother to come up and give him a kiss good night. Curtains float and wave in the open window (in the tropics, a mosquito net around a child's bed might have made it even more Proustian). Then, my Jakarta friend gave me his story in exchange — of his window as he was waiting as a child for his mother to come. The window was up, he said, very high, on the upper floor of their Chinese Indonesian house — a shop on the ground floor more or less open to the street, with living quarters upstairs, "safely high," like "a tower," just in case.

> RM: Like a celestial mountain?
> Dr. ONG: Maybe. Yes, indeed, you could meditate up there, if you wanted. You might meditate in the tower, if you wanted.[58]

The French surrealist André Breton said: "It is impossible for me to consider a picture as anything but a window."[59] Breton's contemporary, and a contemporary of my interviewees, René Magritte, titled his famous paintings of windows, *The Human Condition*.[60] What the two artists were saying, I believe, was that a window, like a picture, and like a proposition, could rarely be a mere transparency, and rarely a mere opening in the wall.

> RM: Was there glass in the window?
> Mr. DES ALWI: Oh, yes. Lead glass, beautiful design.[61]

As statements, pictures, and propositions of newness, windows matter as a thing (as a machine), by the technics through which they let in the light and color, and the world, by the kind of glass, by their design, by their frames, by the angle at which they face the outdoors or (as in Benjamin's dream) at which they face the indoors. Listening to the old Indonesians, one may recall Benjamin again, his as their acute sense of this modern way of looking, with the windows as propositions, with the (salon) power of it: "Do not touch the items on display."[62]

Thinking of windows, again, colonies indeed seemed to have been modern before the modern of the West truly happened. What the avant-garde architects might have thought of as the state-of-the-art window — in Germany, in the United States, in the glass-and-steel era of the 1920s and 1930s — appeared to be built into the roots-of-roots origins of colonialism.

> In the Tugendhat House, the high-tech frame [is] mechanically equipped so that an entire wall of windows [can] slide down or be pulled up at the push

of a button, just as we operate the window in our cars. . . . This . . . [builds] a challenging ambiguity between inside and outside.[63]

Especially at night, when the gaze can travel through the building undisturbed by reflections on the glass walls, it frames a view . . . like a picture.[64]

If you view nature through the glass walls . . . it gains a more profound significance than if viewed from outside.[65]

It is as if Le Corbusier, designing his "walls of light," has built his windows from the same ambition and anxiety as those of my friend, Dr. Ong, and all the others who talked to me about the colony: "The house is . . . a mechanism of viewing. Shelter separation from the outside is provided by the window's ability to turn the threatening world outside the house into a reassuring picture."[66] This seemed to be the aim: the space to which home opened would be made into "no more than this constructed horizon."[67] Le Corbusier, in fact, "always insisted that the secret of his architecture lay in his painting" and, even, that the houses he built were to be understood (and lived in?) as "three-dimensional equivalents" of his canvases.[68]

An urge to bring a picture in and to hang, pin, or glue it to the wall—the proposition, and the need for windows in the modern colony—might come very close to what Heidegger called "enframing": "The ordering belonging to Enframing sets itself above the thing, leaves it, as the thing, unsafeguarded, truthless. In this way Enframing disguises the nearness of the world that nears in the thing. Enframing disguises even this, its disguising, just as the forgetting of something forgets itself and is drawn away in the wake of forgetful oblivion."[69] And the frame was but an aim; it could never be made into a perfect abstract line. Like the low fences and bamboo walls, the signposts, streets, and bypasses, frames marked the colony. An art critic wrote: "It is perfectly possible to imagine a case where the frame comes first and the painted panel, like so much decorative filler, comes afterwards, tailored to the measure of the more opulent, resplendent frame."[70]

If one believes strongly enough in those windows and those pictures, it appears professional and natural, or at least possible, that everything—in painting and beyond—might be resolved "through the invention of a painterly form."[71] The frame becomes "the threshold of perception"[72]—it means one can of course dare to step out. "But the frame, the limit of visibility," becomes (or seems to become) "what makes conscious objectification possible."[73] In a colony in particular, by the way of the windows, the way they were built, and by the way of the pictures, the way they were painted, hung, and so on, "perception of the world has imploded."[74]

Making a proposition as looking at a picture, putting the picture under the glass, looking out of a window, and framing thus the colony and oneself was a critical act of building the modern and of becoming modern. (There were many possibilities, of course—the already mentioned lead glass, painted and frosted glass, mullions, lattices, wrought-iron work, and, significantly, bars in windows; there was an increasing number of optical gadgets aiding the windows—stereoscopic viewers, kaleidoscopes, and, of course, slide shows and film.) Benedict Anderson's words come to mind: "framed by coloniality."[75]

> Leo Eland working on his panorama at the Colonial Exhibition in Paris 1931.[76]

> Charles Sayers working on a Javanese mural for the Paris Colonial Exhibition of 1931, that later burned down.[77]

Not by accident, panoramas were brought to Europe by Robert Fulton, the American engineer: "Pure realism ought to manage things so that a represented object would seem within reach of your hand."[78] Even "cloudiness and transparency can be *painted*."[79]

Listening to old Indonesians as they recall looking through or at their windows when they were young, one feels that colonial windows, that kind of architectural device, of wall, of optics, were the subtlest and most powerful modern edifice erected. It could make the world into a "pleasure of the eyes," a visual pleasure that "includes street kiosks, automobiles, cinema, and photographs."[80] And all this could thus be handled.

The world could be made to move as if on the screen. The train rushing at them did make the audience run away in panic—just in the first moment of shock.[81] The pictures soon "diffused" the world in picture time,[82] they "juxtaposed" the people "to an environment that is boundless," "collated," and thus made the people feel "connected to the whole world,"[83] meaning "the area of the frame."[84]

Then, as Proust, the expert on windows, knew—sooner than his contemporaries in Europe and as early as the colonial moderns in the faraway East—if it came to some real trouble, one could make it just more of a picture. The view from his apartment, Proust found, could be "placed under glass by the closing of the windows."⁸⁵ Space might be repaired; a multitude of "universal spaces" might be created as "space frames within which anything might be accommodated."⁸⁶

+ + +

School, the emblematic space of the modern colony, has been recalled as a well-designed picture, bright, painted, ideally in bold primary colors, indeed with commercial paints.

> Mr. ASRUL: In grade school I was already writing short stories, and I read a lot. I wanted to become a writer. But it was a puppy love; it came, and then it went. I entered a technical college, and I became so proud of wearing the sky-blue jacket of the school.⁸⁷

Schools and classrooms appeared as modern as they were bright.

> Father MANGUNWIJAYA: Some of the Dutch teachers were so interesting! One, *Broeder* Dujis, taught Dutch in the second grade. He taught by drawing everything on the blackboard, a *pen*, a *man*, all was a picture. It was so very *interesting*. When he taught us about the Netherlands, oh, it was such a pleasure! The Javanese teacher, he did not make it *interesting*.⁸⁸

Schoolbooks were primary-color intensive. The lightness of being at school was made of geometry and of colors. School was a colored picture. And there were colorful, bright, orderly, and instructive pictures on the school and classroom walls. The walls were made into pictures.

> RM: Do you still remember some pictures in school?
> Mr. GESANG: Oh, yes, a *kaart* [map].
> RM: What *kaart*?
> Mr. GESANG: Surakarta, Java, everything.⁸⁹

The modern and colonial way of picturing and looking at the pictures was filled with energy. Some pictures were merely black and white, but they were moving! Even more than the rest of the enframed colony, they were a proposition and at the same time a commonplace. Modern Indonesia, after school, went to the movies to be in the world.

> Mr. SOEDARPO: Twice a week, I went to see the movies. It cost twelve and a half cents: a quarter a week, a guilder a month. Ten cents I paid for a ticket and two and a half cents for sweets or lemonade. It was a *routine*. I wanted to see America, no doubt about it.
> RM: What kind of America? Indians?
> Mr. SOEDARPO: That's it — Indians.
> RM: It was America to you?
> Mr. SOEDARPO: Oh, later, of course, there were the other things, too. When I got to the middle school it was Thomas Edison, or *From the Log Cabin to the White House*. The world of possibilities.[90]

Filmmakers, in the words of a French film inventor, "gave life to images, which henceforth flew like birds."[91]

> Mr. EFENDI: My friend's name was Sam. We were in Dutch-native grade school together, and we went to the movies all the time. Sam would say, "Hey, let's go to the movies, there are cowboys." We went not to the front of the screen but behind it. We could see the film from behind. We learned to read from right to left
> RM: People were shooting with their left hand?
> Mr. EFENDI: Yes, we could see it all.[92]

Like a picture in a book or on a wall, or like a window, the movies convincingly worked like the world, like a moving world, like a world on the move or, at least, like an opening to it.

> Mrs. VIOLETTE: I have seen countless movies. Donald Duck, I still remember.
> RM: The cartoons.
> Mrs. VIOLETTE: And later _____ _____ *Scarlet Letter*, and *Gone with the Wind*.[93]
>
> Mrs. MINARSIH: Martha Eggert, she was a German star. Martha Eggert, and Charles Boyer.
> RM: You saw it in Bukittinggi [West Sumatra]?

Chapter Five

Mrs. MINARSIH: Yes, Charlie Chaplin and Donald Duck, and who was it, the little one?

RM: Shirley Temple?

Mrs. MINARSIH: Yes, Shirley Temple; she was a marvel.[94]

Whatever I was asking, I think I never heard this in so many words:

> Like the young child, the moviegoer suffers from limited corporeal mobility and becomes dependent on hypertrophied visual experience, which produces a superreal sense of reality that cannot be tested.[95]

> Our body itself undergoes a sort of temporary depersonalization which robs it of the sense of its own existence. We are nothing more than two eyes riveted to ten meters of white screen.[96]

> In the movie theater, however far away I am sitting, I press my nose against the screen's mirror.[97]

Film was energy, movement, life (never mind the smell, heat, and all kinds of biting and flying bugs, before air conditioning arrived to the upper-level movie houses and froze the spectators to a happy-land close-to-death state). One can write a full-fledged commonplace history of the modern and the colonial by listening to people talking about watching the screen.

> General KEMAL: My world at that time was a world of film. I was so very happy when I could go to the movies, *I watched film* twice, even three times a week, how to put it — *my favorite stars*. It was my world. Every month I bought the magazine *Picture Play*, to look for the films and film stars. I had an album, and I also made a *songbook*. Every year I made a new *songbook*. All the film songs, I took my wisdom from it. (*Mr. Kemal used* hikmah *for "wisdom."* Hikmah *means wisdom, philosophy, or a lesson drawn from an experience.* Meg(h)ikmati, *a transitive verb from* hikmah, *means to cast a spell on, enchant, or bewitch someone.*) And also my English improved. *It was my hobby.*[98]

Expanding numbers of people, much faster expanding than those in schools, were allowed to see the moving pictures, their eyes riveted to the screen, their noses pressed against the screen's mirror:

The Window

> Mr. ROESLAN: At that time we told a *joke* in school. Simin and Siman went to the movies. In the movie house, in the front, there was a goat [third-class] section. So Simin and Siman went to the movies. At one moment, the Dutch queen Wilhelmina appears on the screen, the Dutch anthem is played, and Simin claps his hands. Siman asks him in surprise: "Why do you clap your hands? They are colonizers." "I do it not to fall asleep," Simin says. It was a *joke*.⁹⁹

✣ ✣ ✣

To dare that pictures and movies were not the world, or at least windows into it, one might be threatened to deal with the possibility that, once a picture was taken down, one may face a blank wall.

> Mr. SUTIKNO: Because of the cowboy films, of course, many of the boys began to look like cowboys. They swaggered like that. They learned those tricks, of the vaudeville. You know, *rodeo shows* passed through here.
>
> RM: Oh, really?
>
> Mr. SUTIKNO: Yes. We could not even think, of course, of having a horse. So some posed on a log, for instance. They got a rope, *lasso*, and they tied the rope like that, as if it were on a saddle, behind their backs.¹⁰⁰

Life, even in a colony, might be made to appear like a movie. In and through the pictures and the movies, the roads of life might be traveled most energetically; horizons constructed in this way seemed within reach of one's hand; newspaper, picture, and cinematic reduction could be applied most *naturally* and *freely*.

> Professor RESINK: And then we went to Europe — this was called a European *verlof* [leave] — for six months or a year. We did the *Grand Tour*,¹⁰¹ for a year — Italy, France, Switzerland, Germany.

"One of the great attractions of the travel scenes in the Imperial Panorama," says Benjamin, "was that it did not matter where you began the cycle."¹⁰²

> RM: It was after the war?
>
> Professor RESINK: It was just after the World War I. In 1922. I was eleven years old.

RM: So you ended in Amsterdam?

Professor RESINK: First, the vastness of space—Colombo, Port Said—

"Gibraltar, Suez, Colombo, Singapore," Clifford Geertz wrote for the generation that traveled in the opposite direction; "names with a romance they now have largely lost."[103]

Professor RESINK: In Port Said we already got the first inkling of the things European. Then—Suez Canal—Crete—the Straits of Messina—from Genoa to the Italian and French rivieras, to Nice and Monaco and Cannes and that famous perfume factory in Grasse—Mont Blanc and the real snow, from Bern and Zurich to Garmisch-Partenkirchen and Oberammergau to see the *Passionsspiel—die Schlösser*, the castles, of *Ludwig der Zweite*, Neuschwanstein *und* Herrenchiemsee, *und* Linderhof. *Und*—Salzburg—Mozart!

RM: But then you arrived in Holland?

Professor RESINK: After all that we went to Frankfurt and I saw my first European nude. In bronze. It was the so-called *Ariadne von Dannecker*— (*Professor Resink slips into German at this moment, and he describes for me with the movements of his hands the marble beauty.*) I have seen many naked women in Indonesia, of course. But here was this nude. I can tell you, the style, according to modern opinions, was not very good. But that beautiful lady, naked, on a *sokkel* [pedestal]. And that *sokkel* slowly turned around! And at regular moments the sun through the glass cupola above the statue cast shadows over the naked woman—like veils. I was so deeply moved![104] And then we went on, along the Rhine river. I still remember this: as we arrived in The Hague, it was September and it was raining. I was lucky that my father was so fond of the arts, and that we spent all that time in the museums.

RM: It was completely new?

Professor RESINK: I knew many of the paintings already. From books.[105]

Most of the people in the colony could only dream of a trip to the world such as young Mr. Resink took—and they dreamed it indeed. But there, there was the horizon—that journey and that, truly moving, picture of the world. Or better still, in painterly terms, there was the climax of the road as Professor Resink made it, safely, well, and deep inside the frame, toward a vanishing point of the picture, of its perspective, where the color was densest and the reflections of the window, opening in the wall, most enchanting, where the ultimate colonial and modern hub found its fulfillment—in curios.

> Professor RESINK: My mother was received in an audience by Queen Wilhelmina. The queen had heard that my mother knew a great deal about Javanese antiques; and in the palace, the queen had the so-called *Indische Zaal*, the Indies Room, with the gifts from all the royalties and dignitaries. The gifts were all over the room, and there was also much that was *wirklich wertlos*, true trash.
> RM: Yes, I can imagine Suharto's room of gifts.
> Professor RESINK: Yes. And the queen asked my mother to clean up the room, *de Indische Zaal*.
> RM: So it was empty in the end?
> Professor RESINK: No, not entirely empty. There were some very good pieces, also. But much space was made for the things yet to come.
> RM: Was your mother impressed by the queen?
> Professor RESINK: By her voice! She heard it first as she waited for her in an anteroom. And then from the queen herself. The only thing I remember was that she was deeply impressed.
> RM: How did she describe it? Why? Was it melodious? Or her Dutch was good?
> Professor RESINK: Oh, it was *Queen's Dutch*, of course.[106]

One learned to measure one's life and to handle one's experience—cinematically, painterly, and touristically reduced.

Like modern citizenry everywhere, and like the proudest of the urban in the West, the colonial landscape (and *landscape* is genuinely a painterly term) was built up this way. Karl Marx wrote about nineteenth-century Paris, the epitome of all this, rising to its age of glory, as of "the vandalism of Haussmann, razing Paris . . . to make place for the Paris of the sightseer."[107] The urban, ideally and when things got really bad, was to get closer to a picture, closer to becoming like a picture. The most progressive planners of the urban and the modern (and the Dutch in the colony as in Europe in the first half of the twentieth century were some of the most progressive) took on this landscaping job most eagerly. In one of the most famous examples of the era,

> in trying to solve the problems of mass housing after the [First World] War, Dutch architects like Jan Bakema, Van den Broek, and Van Eesteren

Chapter Five

planned new urban quarters on a vast and inhuman scale. They used slab blocks and standardized units, often transcribing literally formal solutions from *De Stijl* paintings, like Van der Leek's abstract compositions or Van Doesburg's *Rhythm of a Russian Dance*, into three dimensions on an enormous scale. . . . The city was treated as a huge relief architecture. The pedestrian scale at which the city is experienced by its inhabitants—that of the individual housing unit and its relations to its neighbors—was completely ignored.[108]

✴ ✴ ✴

So, it was a beautiful colony in the beautiful world. "Beautiful Indies," indeed, in Dutch *mooi Indië*, became a style of painting, picturing, and imagining that most memorably facilitated the modern in the colony—the (primary colors) green and yellow rice fields, naked brown boys, black water buffalo, blue mountains, the orange sun and/or white moon. The "beautiful Indies" on canvas or paper, oil, drawings, or (mostly colored) photographs, more often than not gilt-framed, mattered a lot in the colonial. First the Dutch, but, progressively, all the better-off urban and modern eagerly paid for the thing to be put on their walls and, for the Dutch and whoever was getting away, to take it "back" to Europe, after one vacationed or retired from his or her business in the East.

For the Indonesians, too, even those not leaving, for the future, in the "beautiful Indies," there was a souvenir, or call it memory.

> Father MANGUNWIJAYA: In Muntilan—oh, it was a paradise! We played at the river, at the canal, we fished, it was so beautiful. The water in the river was clean, and all this repeated every day. Muntilan was so good for dreaming, too. There were those rice fields, the volcano, and the people with water buffalo, splashing them with water or plowing the fields early in the morning.
> RM: Like *mooi Indië*?
> Father MANGUNWIJAYA: Yes, it was *mooi* Indië. In Muntilan the air was clear like a crystal.
> RM: Did you hear your parents praising it like this, or is this the pleasure of a child?
> Father MANGUNWIJAYA: But yes, the world was pure.
> RM: It meant *mooi Indië* for real?
> Father MANGUNWIJAYA: Yes. For us, yes.

The Window

RM: So when you think about *mooi Indië*—?
Father MANGUNWIJAYA: Oh, for children it was a paradise.
RM: Real?
Father MANGUNWIJAYA: *Real* paradise.[109]

This was a device of modernity that colonialism perfected, "the safety zones of hermeneutic horizons and habitual sunsets,"[110] landscapes that become "a reduplication of a picture which preceded it" and that can only "degenerate into ever more lurid copies."[111] The *mooi Indië* implied an order forever.[112] Here was the most salonlike and comforting "stifled perspective," "plush for the eye."[113] The picturesque, the fervent, and the dreamy were made (painterly) identical.

There is an iconic image of Free Indonesia from the late colonial times (or at least thus it is presented), of Rudolf Supratman, the composer of "Indonesia Raja" ("Great Indonesia"), the song that became the most treasured Indonesian nationalist-struggle song and after 1945 the Indonesian anthem. On the night before "Great Indonesia" was first to be performed, on October 28, 1928, Supratman is described in his room as getting to sleep:

> The sheet with music just finished was put into the desk and the drawer was locked. Very tired, he moved to bed.
>
> In a wink of an eye, he was soundly asleep, and with the sleep came a dream. He saw a ship in Tandjung Priok [Jakarta harbor]. The ship was new, it was ready to sail, and its name was the *Empress of Indonesia*. Now the captain of the ship and several officers approached him, paid their respects, and asked him to join them on this extraordinary ship. The trip was to be a pleasure cruise.
>
> As they all climbed on board, he was amazed by the ship's beauty, greater than that of any palace. He met several world-renowned people on board, all of them friendly, approaching him, engaging him in talk, and introducing him to the others. These were personages from political movements, the world of science, diplomats, and so on.
>
> "We hope that you, sir, will join us on the cruise on the *Empress*; it is ready to sail," the captain of the ship respectfully told him, "we will travel around the world in several hours." "Around the world in several hours? What is the speed of this ship?" Supratman asked with surprise. "You will see! This is why we ask you, sir, to accompany us on the cruise!"
>
> So he agreed to go *around the world*. And, like a fish, the ship swam

Chapter Five

through the waters. In a moment they were in Ceylon, in another moment in Manila and then in Tokyo, Shanghai, Bombay, Port Said, Genoa, Rome, Marseilles, Washington, etc., etc. At last, the ship turned around, stopped back in the Geneva harbor, and the tourists were asked to come ashore and visit the building of the *Volkenbond* [League of Nations]. They toured the site where so many important events had taken place, and then they were taken to the Alps Mountains. They taught Supratman how to use *ski*, long and narrow wooden shoes, to climb the Alps Mountains.

In spite of the fact that never in his life he did it — how strange! — he felt as if it was very easy on *ski* to get up the mountain peaks. He was on top sooner than all the others. In the end, he ran on *ski*[s] fast to the highest peak of all![114]

MAKING A PICTURE (FOR) ONESELF

> The story comes from China, and tells of an old painter who invited friends to see his newest picture. This picture showed a park and a narrow footpath that ran along a stream and through a grove of trees, culminating at the door of a little cottage in the background. When the painter's friends, however, looked around for the painter, they saw that he had left them — that he was in the picture. There, he followed the little path that led to the door, paused before it quite still, turned, smiled, and disappeared through the narrow opening.
>
> —Walter Benjamin, "Berlin Childhood"

If anyone is capable of resisting the enframing, one might think, it should be the painters themselves. That kind of praxis, perhaps, may imply a will and power to make a painting out of oneself, textured and composed for oneself, of one's own seeing, in one's own perspective — a courageous, penetrating picture, an open window to the world.

The painter may paint to resist the frame through his or her own rhythm;[115] the inversion of near and far might be attempted"[116] — or what Nietzsche believed he accomplished in his depiction of the world late in his life: "Now I know how, have the know-how to *reverse perspectives*."[117] A painter, perhaps, might try to see the world "in negligée or from a backstage"; like an "ephemeral billboard," like "graffiti or a comic strip";[118] like a "readymade," in "an assertive debunking of the ideas of technical skill, virtuoso technique, and the expression of individual subjectivity," professing "insistent roughness," "rough edges," "aesthetic impurity,"[119] even "by drawing with his eyes entirely closed."[120] This, one may expect, may be attempted as a praxis directed toward freedom.

There are, in the modern history of Indonesia, well-known, celebrated, and frequently quoted images, graffiti, and comic strips with perspective smashed, on the walls, doors, gates, and fences of Jakarta and other cities, and on the cities' moving objects, tram cars, trains, buses—in the fall of 1945: "Freedom or Death," "Watch for the Spies." Pictures like those, or maybe merely of the same painterly techniques, (re)emerged in 1997, as Suharto, the aging military dictator, was to abdicate, as masses went into the streets, and as many, the Chinese Indonesians especially, as usual, feared for their lives.

At that time, taking a week off, on the slopes of the magnificent Kelud Volcano in Central Java, on a pillar of one of the ceremonial welcoming arches (which commonly mark an entrance to a temple, a town street in a feast, or a plantation), I saw, in big red letters, scribbled, in English, and with a crudely drawn shadow-theater puppet silhouette next to it: FUCK YOU.[121] It might be only in the eye of this beholder, but at the moment, not far enough from the burning Jakarta, I thought that I had gotten as close to a daring and avant-garde painting in the postcolony as I could.

There were teachers for all this in the colony. There were, specifically, in the modern colony, good and bad, more, less, or not at all exciting teachers of the arts, drawing, painting, and imagining.

> Mr. HAMID: In the MULO junior high, already all the teachers were Dutch except for the arts teacher. Oh, I am sorry, he was Dutch, too.[122]

There were teachers, half forgotten, who appeared as we talked.

> Professor KOENTJARANINGRAT: I was learning Javanese dance and I also painted. Later I even became a dance teacher. But as for painting or drawing, nobody told me how to do it. I had no teacher.
> RM: What was your painting like? Was it Javanese, like the dance? Or kind of like van Gogh or Rembrandt? You saw much of that, I am sure, in books.
> Professor KOENTJARANINGRAT: Now, as you ask me about van Gogh, yes, I had a teacher. A Dutch man who lived in Indonesia—I might

Chapter Five

still recall his name. He was the only teacher I ever had. Except him, no one would tell me: "do this," "do this if you want to picture that!"
RM: So you drew and painted since your were little.
Professor KOENTJARANINGRAT: Since junior high.[123]

There was a long history of painting in the colony. "Naturally!" It was a Dutch colony.

> Cornelia (1652–1678), a daughter of Rembrandt and Hendrikje Stoffels, lived in Batavia and is buried there. In the spring of 1670, several months after her father's death, Cornelia van Rijn married a painter, Cornelis Suythof (1646–1691), and half a year later they left for Batavia where they arrived on March 23, 1671, never to come back. None of Cornelia van Rijn's three sons, one of them called Rembrandt, ever returned. They all died young. Suythof, Cornelia's husband, is listed in the records as a warden of the Batavia city prison; there is no record of him painting any more.
>
> Also three grandsons of Frans Hals lived in Batavia, Jan Frans, Jan, and Jacob. The first two are mentioned as painters, but there are no more details or paintings.
>
> In a testament from 1709, one painting by Rembrandt is mentioned— "an old man in an armchair."[124]

Modern paintings, inevitably, appeared in the colony, too, imported, as if on a visit or a grand tour moving the opposite way. During the last decades of the Dutch colonial era, several exhibitions of some really important paintings of modern art, Western, of course, and mainly European, were organized in the colony.

> The Laren collector Regnault, the owner of dockyards in India, helped by an art dealer in Amsterdam and painters themselves, made a number of paintings available to the Arts Circle in Batavia. In addition, five times, between 1934 and 1939, Regnault sent selections from his own collection. Thus, the people in the Indies for the first time could see works by painters like Marc Chagall, Kees van Dongen, Paul Gauguin, Gust de Smet, Vincent van Gogh, Pablo Picasso, and others.[125]

There were debates in the colony at the same time, as the era was moving to its end, increasingly animated, heated, even hateful exchanges between different cliques and schools of art, sounding very much like the avant-garde debates and battles of the arts in Europe before Hitler: "He [Piet Ouborg]

The Window

paints his sick masks with extremely distorted features. His violent nature cuts him away from the Indies. His atelier looks like a slaughterhouse."[126]

There were occasionally images made in the colony that looked as if someone might be laughing at the whole thing. On one of the Balinese temples, for instance, on a relief newly made around 1920, one Mr. Niewenkamp, a well-known Dutch Indies painter of the time, is pictured on his bicycle, going out to paint, looking professorial—except for the fact that the axis of his bicycle's front wheel is a big Balinese flower and the gear on the rear wheel, drawn and sculpted with an engineer's precision, has its gear teeth turned in reverse. One more push on the pedal and the painter with all his painter's stuff is down.[127]

There is another image made by a colonial subject, "painting" that appeals to me as close to carrying resistance in itself, containing a force capable even of breaking through the wall and raising beyond the frame. It even almost makes it close to breaking, so it seems to me, the perspective of the dominant. However, this is a "painting," an image of exile, and by an exile leaving one place of banishment for another, and yet for another, in an endless row:

> Slowly we left the city of Amsterdam behind until all we could see were indistinct little groups of houses in the mist. Amsterdam is a large city, about a million inhabitants, but at heart it is only a small town. Scattered here and there are small factories that make jam, sweets, chocolate, bread, and biscuits. The city is full of *winkels*—little stores that are very neat and well stocked, but small for a metropolitan port. The Dutch admire the *Beurs* [Bourse] building as a symbol of modernism in architecture. But it is not a skyscraper—a symbol of the spirit and activity of a young country with a will of steel. The Beurs is a nest of brokers—termites and bedbugs busy bargaining away stocks of other nations ... a synthesis, or, more correctly, an architectural jumble, filled with the spirit of colonials and *kruideniers* [grocers] that we have already known so well. ... Everything is small, moderate, gradual.[128]

✷ ✷ ✷

Mr. Soerono was born in 1914, and he was seventy-eight when I met him for the first time.[129] He lived at the moment, as he did most of his life, in Yogyakarta in a house in a side alley, typical of the place. Inside the house it looked, at first, sort of large but, after a while, empty.

Chapter Five

Mr. Soerono was a painter, a famous Javanese painter, famous for one thing most of all: at the height of the National Revolution, in 1947, at the time when the Indonesian government retreated from Jakarta under Dutch control, into the interior of Java, and when Yogyakarta, in the interior, became the capital of the republic, one night two men came to Mr. Soerono's house. They took the painter to a place near the sultan's palace, where the government resided. That night, Mr. Soerono was ordered to design the first Indonesian revolutionary banknotes, the 25, 100, and 250 rupiah bills.

>Mrs. SOERONO: He lived in Bali a long time.
>RM: When was that?
>Mr. SOERONO: Between 1971 and 1980. Nine years.
>RM: Nine years. You liked that?
>Mr. SOERONO: Have you been to Bali?
>RM: Who is this? (*We were sitting on a sofa and looking through photographs.*)
>Mr. SOERONO: This is the governor of Bali.
>RM: And this?
>Mr. SOERONO: I, maybe.
>RM: Can we talk now?
>Mr. SOERONO: A little.
>RM: A little, because of the *stroke*?
>Mr. SOERONO: Brain. But it is a long time ago.

And so we start. The usual thing.

>RM: What family are you from? Who was your father?
>Mr. SOERONO: Doctor.
>RM: *Dokter Jawa* [medical practitioner trained by the Dutch for the colony only]?
>Mr. SOERONO: Yes.
>RM: Where?
>Mr. SOERONO: In Solo, in the palace.
>RM: You were born in Solo?
>Mr. SOERONO: No, in Cilacap [Central Java, like Solo]. And we moved a lot.
>RM: Everybody says, Soerono, the painter of the first monies of the Republic of Indonesia.
>Mr. SOERONO: I did billboards, too.

The Window

RM: What kind of billboards?
Mr. SOERONO: Cars.

We might have begun to touch on what Marx called the "'theological niceties' of the commodity."[130]

RM: What else?
Mr. SOERONO: I worked for van Dorp and for the printers at Kolff publishers in Jakarta; all Dutch.
RM: And the painters who worked there?
Mr. SOERONO: One was Dutch; there was an Ambonese and a few Javanese; various.
Mrs. SOERONO: He did billboards of Greta Garbo.

Through a side door Mr. Soerono took me to what might be a garage, an atelier, or both. Indeed, a car in the middle took most of the space. It was the thing one had to notice. It was a bright thing, painted all over, like an exotic bird. Clearly, it had not been driven for a very long time, and it looked like it would never run again. Mr. Soerono deftly — as much as his stricken body let him — got into the car. From behind the wheel he nodded at me, winked, smiled, and pushed a tender button. The car screeched indeed like an exotic bird. A fellow painter and also a contemporary of Mr. Soerono (too bad they never met), the German dadaist Kurt Schwitters, would certainly agree that this was also his art:

> I am building a composition without boundaries, each individual part is at the same time a frame for the neighboring parts, all parts are mutually independent. . . . I only know how I make it, I know only my medium, of which I partake, to what end I do not know.[131]

Or otherwise, as Don Quixote's housemaid might say seeing this: "No, it's through the door of his madness that he's bursting."[132]

Mr. Soerono disappeared for a moment under the dashboard. He must have changed some register because the car now roared like a lion; then another trick, a wink, a smile, and there was buffalo bellowing, and cuckoo cuckooing, and next, if my notes have it correct, elephant trumpeting.

RM: Some painter's car!
Mr. SOERONO: Fiat 1956. Old.

Chapter Five

"Critical theory," Benjamin wrote, "cannot fail to recognize how deeply certain powers of intoxication [*Rausch*] are bound to reason and to its struggle for liberation."[133]

RM: You drove it through town?
Mr. SOERONO: Yes.
RM: What did people say?
Mr. SOERONO: Some laughed.

As I looked again, this place indeed had to be something of an atelier as well. Some paintings were still there, on the floor, with their painted sides against the wall. This made me realize that I had not seen any paintings in the room where we sat before and, in fact, anywhere in the painter's house as far as he had shown me around. We started to turn the garage paintings around.

RM: Is this Affandi?
Mr. SOERONO: Yes.

Affandi is now considered the greatest painter of the Indonesian revolution. He had died here in Yogyakarta a few years earlier. His paintings were fetching hundreds of thousands of dollars at Singapore auctions. This particular painting we turned around to look at was an oil half portrait of Soerono by Affandi. They were friends.

Mr. SOERONO: Before I forget, I should tell you that my paintings got lost.
RM: Lost?
Mr. SOERONO: This is my Kodak. (*Mr. Soerono takes a picture of me with the Affandi painting and the Fiat behind as we are talking.*) He asked me if I wanted money and I said yes. I have all the paintings' photographs in an album. He was French, his name was Paul, and he said he would put an exhibition in Jakarta for me. He packed the paintings and took them away. I got 40, 000 rupiah and the paintings got lost. All, all of them.
RM: A foreigner?
Mr. SOERONO: But his wife was Sumatran. This is him. (*Mr. Soerono picked up another painting and turned it for me to see. And another one.*) This was painted a long time ago.

The Window

RM: Who is that?

Mr. SOERONO: Some hero, from the past. (*We are already back in the room with the sofa, and Mr. Soerono places another album on my knees.*) My father had sixteen children. And five of them became painters.

RM: Why?

Mr. SOERONO: I don't know.

RM: You learned it in school?

Mr. SOERONO: I took a course in Batavia.

RM: With a Dutch teacher?

Mr. SOERONO: Yes, and I went directly to work for Kolff. There must still be some of my work there— (*He pointed up, as to the stars, meaning some building in Jakarta where his work might still survive on the facade.*)

RM: Was your father angry?

Mr. SOERONO: No, he was not angry. It could not be otherwise. Done deal. Then my younger sister began to paint. Sapto Hoedoyo. She is rich.

RM: Was the Dutch teacher good?

Mr. SOERONO: His name was Frederickson. But he was too refined. I was not happy with it. So I moved on.

We came, as we had to, to the story about Soerono and the revolution.

RM: Were you interested in politics, in the Dutch time?

Mr. SOERONO: Oh, no. But I was called by Sukarno. Ordered to do the bills. It was dangerous.

RM: You were scared?

Mr. SOERONO: If the Dutch knew, they might shoot me. They would have to shoot me.

RM: Sukarno's soldiers came?

Mr. SOERONO: No, not in uniforms. They said, "Sukarno calls you." I did not know why, but I had to go to see him: "You will design money bills: 25, 100, and 250 rupiah," three bills. I asked: "What pictures?" "I will show you some photographs. You can pick the good ones. Wait a moment, I'll bring them."

RM: Sukarno said it?

All the photographs were of Sukarno. The heads of state seem to do it: Louis XVI was "recognized on the flight to Varennes by a patriot who knew his engraved portrait on paper currency."[134]

Chapter Five

Mr. SOERONO: Yes, he said it. They took me to a place where I could work on it. They locked the room. Even when I wanted to use the WC, I had to ask.
RM: So you did what you learned at Kolff?
Mr. SOERONO: Yes. But for Kolff I used to do _____, _____. Sukarno wanted a dagger or a buffalo.

We went back to the Fiat once again, and then through much of the house; we had a good meal and then got to talking again about what "real painters do."

RM: So you did advertisements for cars? What did you paint when you did not work for Kolff?
Mr. SOERONO: Villages, animals, houses, people around them, horse carts, landscapes.
RM: What the Dutch called *mooi Indië*?
Mr. SOERONO: No. I did not know why they were doing it. Indonesia is beautiful, but I am an Indonesian myself: ordinary.

What Mr. Soerono might have meant, perhaps, was that beautiful was, to use Stendhal's words, *une promesse de bonheur*, "a promise of happiness," that "the beautiful promises happiness," and, thus, that "the beautiful arouses the will."[135]

Mr. SOERONO: I was happy in Bali. They do not always wear sarongs anymore. But I always did. I always wore a Balinese sarong. And I liked all the goings-on around; the Balinese funerals. I also very much liked to do paintings of skulls.

As we honked, talked, and walked through the house, more paintings appeared—in a corner where I had not noticed them before, or pulled out from under a bed; and sometimes as if they stepped forth against us here and there out of the wall.

Mr. SOERONO: I still work all the time. I learn, I have no time for anything else. That Paul was a bad man. But when I paint, or have guests, I am still happy. I dream: "One day, you will sell a painting and you will buy a new house." I am old, but I would still like to leave some

The Window

paintings to my grandchildren. And I would like to see Mona Lisa, Picasso, and van Gogh. I want to see *Nacht Wacht* [*The Night Watch*]. I have a book about van Gogh and Rembrandt, but it is not originals. Have you seen it?

Mr. Soerono, in fact, asked me this question first: "Are you happy?" and I tried to turn it gently back on him.

> Mr. SOERONO: I am happy that the Dutch are gone. I thought, first, that the Japanese would be still worse, but they were clever. The ones I met, they understood art, they understood Rembrandt, van Gogh, because in Japan they had heard very much about Rembrandt and van Gogh since they were children in school. They understood it.
> RM: Have you ever heard about Fujita?[136]
> Mr. SOERONO: Yes. Tsuguharu Fujita. He was an army painter. Propaganda.
> Mrs. SOERONO: He worked in Sendenbu, the [Japanese] Propaganda Corps.
> RM: You worked for Sendenbu, too?
> Mr. SOERONO: I did billboards.
> RM: Cars?
> Mr. SOERONO Posters. What the Japanese told me to do. "The Three A." (*"Japan Light of Asia, Japan Liberator of Asia, Japan Future of Asia."*)
> RM: Was it like Greta Garbo for Kolff?
> Mr. SOERONO: Yes.
> Mrs. SOERONO: It used to be Sendenbu. Today it is the Ministry of Information.

The painter Wahdi lived across the island, in Bandung, West Java, a city in many ways very close to Jakarta, on the map as well as by its distinct style of city-life. Many thought and think of Bandung as even more *à jour* than the metropolis. During Dutch times it was called "Paris of the East."

Mr. Wahdi's house stood at a busy road, almost a highway, almost out of town already. Evidently, the house had in the past served also as a roadside shop, and already then, I think, paintings were sold there among other things.[137] Those days, so it seemed, were now over. Only friends, Mr. Wahdi told me, came, to sit in front of the house and talk.[138] My coming to see him, at the outset at least, sounds (neo)colonial on the tape.

> Mr. WAHDI: I do not feel like anyone special; just an ordinary person. But yesterday they told me that a gentleman is looking for me. I got a telephone call that Professor Rudolf would like to see me in my house. And now you are here. What's up?
> RM: An ordinary person? You are a painter!
> Mr. WAHDI: So you think — that I have a school and a special school, perhaps; some arts academy. I just have a Dutch-native grade school diploma, that's it.
> RM: In Bandung?
> Mr. WAHDI: Yes, in Bandung. I was born in Bandung, October 13, 1917. So I am seventy-five, almost exactly.
> RM: Born here, school here?
> Mr. WAHDI: School in Bandung. I have never left Bandung since I was born. I only moved from neighborhood to neighborhood, in Bandung.
> RM: In what neighborhood were you born?
> Mr. WAHDI: Behind the Savoy Homan Hotel [in the city center].
> RM: You painted already in school?
> Mr. WAHDI: I began in the sixth grade. Because the school needed it. They wanted wall pictures. For us pupils.
> RM: So there *was* a teacher?
> Mr. WAHDI: Not an arts teacher. But there was a teacher who taught me about painting: how to use perspective — for instance, there are telegraph poles, and the farther it is, the smaller it should be in the picture; and how things are to be seen from below, such as this matchbox, or this book; and how they should look from above. See?
> RM: What kind of paintings were you doing? Still life?
> Mr. WAHDI: No, just for the school — like maps, I drew and colored maps; a map of Holland with all the provinces, each in a different color —

"How wonderful a good map is," Samuel van Hoostraaten wrote, "in which one views the world as from another world thanks to drawing."[139]

> RM: A map to be hung on the wall? Was it interesting?
> Mr. WAHDI: It was. Even today I still remember these maps. And I still

like maps very much. If there is news about Azerbaijan—"Where is it? Oh, here!"—I look at a map: "Where is it?" I am happy when I find the place. Or, these days—Iran? Iraq? I like to be with whatever is going on.

RM: You like to travel?

Mr. WAHDI: Yes, I am very happy when I do.

This sounded to me like a painter. And like the promenades.

RM: Around Bandung?

Mr. WAHDI: Around Bandung. Everywhere. To Bali.

RM: To paint?

Mr. WAHDI: Also to paint.

RM: So no higher school?

Mr. WAHDI: There was no money. Father was a small shopkeeper. I went as far as I could, and then I dropped out.

RM: What did you do then?

Mr. WAHDI: I painted, to make a living.

RM: Maps?

Mr. WAHDI: No, landscapes. Like this. (*He points to the wall behind me.*)

RM: Who bought your pictures?

Mr. WAHDI: I don't know. A friend took the paintings from me, on commission. If he thought they might sell, he bought them from me.

RM: He was an Indonesian?

Mr. WAHDI: Yes, a neighbor. But I think he sold them mostly to the Dutch.

So much for the market and so much for money.

RM: Did you know some other painters in town? Did you have some painter friends?

Mr. WAHDI: We were friends with Affandi, Hendra, [Soe]Darso; with Barli; we were very close since we were young. We met and talked about how to paint this and that. We criticized each other. We were not the same; I liked to do landscapes, then another did people, and yet another still life. We criticized each other out of feeling, not science. Just feeling: "You say you are angry, but this is weak. Here is too little light." Like that. So, we became painters together: Affandi, Darso,

Chapter Five

Hendra, Barli, and I. Five of us until now, until our hair turned gray. There was no organization.[140]

There had been a Kunstkring, "Arts Circle," in Bandung, of Dutch and other European artists and "art lovers" living in the colony. The best known of all the arts circles in the land. It did not seem to figure in Mr. Wahdi's recollections.

RM: Did you have any exhibition during the Dutch times?
Mr. WAHDI: Yes, in 1936, In the courtyard of the Provincial House.
RM: Indonesian painters?
Mr. WAHDI: Indonesian. Abdoellah, Soekardji was there, I was there; about eight people altogether.
RM: How many paintings?
Mr. WAHDI: Many. I had one.
RM: What was it?
Mr. WAHDI: A landscape. A mountain and a rice field.
RM: People in the fields?
Mr. WAHDI: No. I am not good at painting figures.
RM: It is difficult — or why?
Mr. WAHDI: I never learned it. I had to have a manikin. If there was no manikin, I could not do it. I never learned to draw from models.
RM: There was much politics in Bandung at the time. Sukarno and the others?
Mr. WAHDI: I was completely blind.
RM: You, a painter?
Mr. WAHDI: I was blind, at least until the war.
RM: What does that mean, blind?
Mr. WAHDI: It means pitch-black.

We sat on chairs at a little spot in front of the house, which was below the level of the road. Traffic was busy and noisy. To sit there, it really felt like sitting in front of a roadside shop. From time to time a passerby nodded to Mr. Wahdi and me. Some stopped and talked to us for a while.

RM: So, here is your atelier?
Mr. WAHDI: It is my son's. He studies architecture.

RM: But the paintings are yours?

Mr. WAHDI: Yes.

RM: All of them?

Mr. WAHDI: These ones, yes. This is Padang, this is Lombok, this is South Banten, and this is a landscape between Garut and Tasikmalaya.

RM: "Fight without end!" here — what does it mean?

Mr. WAHDI: It means "don't despair!"

RM: Why is it here on the wall?

Mr. WAHDI: It is by my son. (*We get up and go into the house.*)

RM: These are your paintings, too?

Mr. WAHDI: Yes.

RM: Are there any of your early paintings here? From the Dutch time?

Mr. WAHDI: Oh, no. None at all.

RM: Do you have any? In a storage?

Mr. WAHDI: I still have some, but only from after the war, after 1945.

In truth, here on the roadside, there was nothing provincial in Mr. Wahdi. He liked his country as a part of the world.

RM: Do you often travel abroad?

Mr. WAHDI: Once.

RM: Where to?

Mr. WAHDI: I had a friend, and he worked as a diplomat at the Indonesian office in Geneva. And he invited me.

RM: Also beyond Switzerland?

Mr. WAHDI: Yes, from Geneva he took me to Paris.

RM: To the Louvre?

Mr. WAHDI: Yes. It was extraordinary!

RM: What did you especially like?

Mr. WAHDI: I thought, "This was around 1700, and how they painted! We got electricity by 1920; but they, what they already were doing!" These paintings by Rembrandt! It was like being struck by lightning.

RM: You had seen Rembrandt before?

Mr. WAHDI: But these were originals. I saw them live. I stood before them and I could not even think! I was numb. My brain was too small for it, and my heart could not even feel it — there it was, and I tried to measure it, to seize it.

Chapter Five

This seemed to be the right moment to ask, as right as any:

> RM: Why do you paint? For whom? For the people, for the public, or for yourself, to feel happy?
>
> Mr. WAHDI: I used to paint to show it to friends, for money, and for myself, to feel good. Now, when I paint, I think: "Is it worth it?" These days, I paint really for myself. When people are happy about it, I am glad.
>
> RM: Have you done many political paintings, revolutionary ones?
>
> Mr. WAHDI: Not many.
>
> RM: Why? You have not felt like it?
>
> Mr. WAHDI: You have to draw figures to do it, and I cannot draw figures. Especially in movement. When you do a landscape, how do you make it so that it contains a revolution? It is difficult.

As we walk through the house, we pass a small portrait on the wall of a man's head.

> Mr. WAHDI: This is by my son. You asked me what did it mean, in the front, "Do not despair!" This is the man.
>
> RM: He suffered?
>
> Mr. WAHDI: See, there were five of us, I told you: Affandi, Hendra, Barli, as long as he was here, I, and Darso. Friends. In 1975 we had a reunion.
>
> RM: All were there?
>
> Mr. WAHDI: Yes, only Hendra was not, of course. It was in 1975. Until 1978 he was in political detention. So he could not come; he was still in prison. The rest of us met in Jakarta.
>
> RM: And this is after?
>
> Mr. WAHDI: Yes, when he got out.
>
> RM: How long?
>
> Mr. WAHDI: Thirteen years.
>
> RM: Where? In the Buru camp?
>
> Mr. WAHDI: No, in Sukamiskin prison, here in Bandung. He was lucky that they did not take him to those faraway places.
>
> RM: He has already died.
>
> Mr. WAHDI: Yes, two of us have already died; so one, two, three are still here.

RM: He suffered? He did not despair?

Mr. WAHDI: His hair turned gray. He does not suffer anymore.

On some occasions Marx might get it wrong. So, at least I hope it was when he wrote, "The victories of art seem bought by the loss of character."[141]

RM: Did Hendra talk about the prison? Could he paint in prison?

Mr. WAHDI: Yes, he never stopped.

RM: Just with a pencil?

Mr. WAHDI: On canvas, with oil. He made the prison guards very rich. No painting could get out except through the guards, so the guards got rich.

RM: So there are paintings by him from that time?

Mr. WAHDI: I have one.

RM: Did he sit for your son when he did this portrait?

Mr. WAHDI: No, it is from a photograph.[142]

✢ ✢ ✢

Unlike Mr. Soerono and Mr. Wahdi, the painter Srihadi was as much a metropolitan man as one could be. Exhibitions of his paintings and drawings never happened on the fringes.[143] He had a studio and lived much of his time in Jakarta, as well as in his beautiful modern villa in Bandung, where I met him. The villa stood in the upscale part of this strikingly modern city. We sat on the house's large terrace high above one of the deep valleys of Bandung, with green, yellow, and silvery rice fields below, with the white, red, and black spots of houses on the opposite slopes. There were blue, and gray volcanoes framing the view. Mrs. Srihadi, who came to sit with us for a moment, complained about the nouveaux riches who planned to build their villas down in the valley and thus do away with the rice fields and the view.

Inside the house, below the terrace in a large studio that also opened to the valley through a wall of glass, Mr. Srihadi began to talk about his life.

Mr. SRIHADI: Just this last month I was promoted to full professor of arts here in the Bandung Institute of Technology. I have been at the institute since the beginning, as a student, then as an assistant. In 1952 I started as a *freshman*.[144]

Chapter Five

This is the college that Sukarno attended in the 1920s and where his technical drawings stayed on exhibit in spite of the fact that he was sent into exile by the Dutch authorities.

RM: But you were born in Surakarta?

Mr. SRIHADI: On December 4, 1931, still during the Dutch time, the colonial period. And I liked to draw since I was little. And I liked to look at pictures; there were Dutch magazines, one of them was called *De Orient.* There were expressionist pictures there, and also European impressionism at the time.

RM: Was there a teacher?

Mr. SRIHADI: No, just the magazines. There was naturalism, too, and many landscapes. (*Mr. Srihadi, as he talks, picks up an art magazine [a current glossy thing] from a pile on the low table and plays with it, turning the bright pages, but mostly looking at me.*)

RM: Did your family have something to do with the arts?

Mr. SRIHADI: Not with the arts really, but my grandfather made daggers.

RM: A smith?

Mr. SRIHADI: What is the word? *Sungging*.

Sungging, the Javanese word, means "painting" as well as "decoration."

RM: In Surakarta?

Mr. SRIHADI: In Surakarta. In the palace of the prince. He was well known. They called him Éyang Hariyo Curigo — *curigo* means dagger in old Javanese.

RM: You remember him?

Mr. SRIHADI: He was still alive when I was little. In fact, he gave me ideas about how to make things of art. He gave me a set of shadow-theater puppets, carved [in leather]. When I was older, he taught me how to play.

RM: So you could play?

Mr. SRIHADI: At that time I could. I tell you this merely as an example. I learned the stories from Mahabharata and Ramayana. But in 1939, grandpa left for Mecca. And that was the end of it.

RM: For the hajj?

Mr. SRIHADI: Hajj. He died there. He left when I was only eight. My

The Window

father was still alive. He made batik, a *home industry*; in the Dutch time and in the Japanese time. I still had my father. But my grandfather was no more.

When the Japanese invaded the colony, in 1942, Mr. Srihadi was eleven years old.

> Mr. SRIHADI: *De Orient* and all the other Dutch magazines that we used to get from Jakarta stopped coming. But new magazines appeared. Like *Jawa Baroe* [New Java]. And there were *pen drawings* and caricatures and pictures of people at work there. Again, I clipped and kept them all. There were sketches of Japanese soldiers as well, in attack, for instance, and all this was so very interesting. And the Japanese made posters — war posters, how Japan came, and trucks full of soldiers and weapons. There were big letters painted over the posters, like "*Alhamdullilah!* Asia Back to Asian Peoples."
>
> RM: This was art?
>
> Mr. SRIHADI: Yes. There were new colors. Some of the pictures were *pastels* and *water colors*. Or *gouaches*. These were *poster colors*. Some were made in oil, smooth and elegant. Now, I wanted very much to paint like that: "How is this done? This surely is done by a Japanese artist!" How fine these posters were! At the time, I only wished to paint in oil or in *water colors*. It was all so beautiful.

Paul Klee, the European painter who painted so much of what I try to say in this Indonesian history book, is said to spend "considerable time working on studies from nature" yet "it seemed to him that 'focusing his attention on the contents of his paint-box' was of *even more* importance." "One day," he wrote, "I must be able to improvise freely on the keyboard of colors."[145]

> RM: Did you know the name Fujita?
>
> Mr. SRIHADI: Yes, we knew about him, he now lives in America. But there was another painter who came with the Japanese army. His name was Saseho Ono. He did drawings of the landings of the Japanese troops. The Japanese came, and there were suddenly so many pictures. In *Jawa Baroe*. Caricatures. I was so impressed by them that I waited for each issue. I collected them. I studied them, especially the drawings by Saseho Ono.

Chapter Five

RM: Saseho Ono.

Mr. SRIHADI: So, I knew *De Orient* magazine. I had the shadow-theater imagination, but these pictures were new. We were used to those landscapes—

RM: With the sun rising?

Mr. SRIHADI: Yes. And here, this was about people, fighting, working in the fields. That was still Indonesia, but it was not that pretty *cliché*—

(Andrey Tarkovsky might put it as "clichés and commonplaces."[146])

Mr. SRIHADI: —not the *mooi Indië* anymore. These were new themes— brought by the Japanese. The climate of war, the people in action. This was *action*. Not those beautiful rice fields, but marches, for instance— the theme of marches, and of everyday life. The Japanese encouraged Indonesians to do art exhibitions in Jakarta, and then to travel with them through the country. They also came to Surakarta.

RM: Propaganda?

Mr. SRIHADI: Yes, war. Exhibitions with those themes, as I told you. To raise up a new spirit. The spirit in the actual time. Not the *mooi Indië*, but a spirit in the climate of war. And there were exhibitions of photographs as well.

RM: That was very important to you?

Mr. SRIHADI: It was. Because I always liked to leaf through the magazines, to clip pictures and to make pictures myself. *Jawa Baroe* had photographs of airplanes, and of warships as they sailed— beautiful photographs. The magazine was full of them.

RM: Airlanes and ships?

Mr. SRIHADI: Or factories. The themes from life in the factory. I remember a textile factory. Brigades at work. Children marching, war games. All this was in the pictures. And the discipline of it!

This part of Mr. Srihadi's recollections sounds crucial. The world appears to open as he speaks. Everything appears possible—in the new themes, new colors, new perspective, and a new frame.

Mr. SRIHADI: And there were tanks, destroyed, Dutch and British tanks.

RM: Did you try such pictures yourself?

Mr. SRIHADI: I still keep some of them. Later I made them into *postcards* and I sent them. Sometimes I still send them.

RM: Can I see them?

Mr. SRIHADI: I still have some. It was the theme. And then it came to a confrontation between the Japanese and us, the Indonesians.

RM: Revolution?

Mr. SRIHADI: Yes, the revolution. And then against the Dutch as they tried to come back. I helped with making posters: *Down with NICA* [Netherlands Indies Civil Administration], or *Down with Dutch Colonialism*. We painted on the asphalt, on the walls, with big letters, in Dutch, English, and Indonesian.

RM: And posters?

Mr. SRIHADI: *Freedom or Death*. The whole city was painted. Sometimes we painted on the trains; we painted on the carriages. And these trains traveled as far as Cirebon and Semarang [important railway junctions in West and Central Java respectively].

RM: You did it in Surakarta?

Mr. SRIHADI: Yes. I was fourteen or fifteen at the time. They took me in a group of revolutionary painters. It was called Balai Penerangan [Office of Information], and it was a part of Badan Keamanan Rakjat, BKR [People's Security], which later became TNI, the Indonesian National Army.

I asked whether Mr. Srihadi knew at the time about the Bolsheviks, Marc Chagall or Vladimir Mayakovski, about Okna Rosta, (Windows of the Russian Press Agency), and that kind of drawing and painting on walls and trains—during the other great revolution.

Mr. SRIHADI: No, I did not. It was all spontaneous—*Down with NICA* or *Freedom or Death*. I can see today that it often was coarse: *Dogs of NICA*, for instance. But the time was like that. They were dogs, *honden*.

Honden means "dogs" in Dutch. We are sitting in Mr. Srihadi's atelier. To our right, there is a wall of glass facing the Bandung valley and the mountains. On the brick wall in front of us there are four square, equal-sized, wall-to-wall, floor-to-ceiling canvases. Mr. Srihadi points to them. They, he explains, are enlarged copies of four little sketches he had done during the revolution, in 1947.

There is an image of the same plane in all four of the paintings. I know what plane it is—the only plane the Indonesian Republic had in 1947. It was shot down on its mission close to the Maguwo airport of Yogyakarta, near where Mr. Srihadi was at the time. The canvases had just arrived back from the Association of Southeast Asian Nations' annual exhibition in Singapore. It was for this purpose, actually, that they had been painted. And, indeed, as Mr. Srihadi tells me, they won a prize.

> Mr. SRIHADI: I put it together from the sketches and little drawings I had made back at the time. I made a piece of art of it. There was spirit in the sketches: it was a documentation of war. It was a VT-CLA plane, that was its name. It flew to India, loaded *medicines*, and, as it was returning, it was shot down, above Yogya. It is done in acrylics. Back at that time, there were no acrylics, merely pencils, water colors, rarely oils and canvas. It was 1947. So now I did it large. Here, you see, there are the *medicines*. All fell on the ground.
> RM: I see.[147]

The broken piece of the plane on the canvas appeared calm, as if in good order, as if not destabilized really, in the painting. I was even tempted to say stupidly: "The goddamn thing wouldn't work!"[148]

> Mr. SRIHADI: There was a terrible smell at the scene. All the *spirits*, the smell of pharmacy, it was all there, and cotton dressings all around. Here, you see, a box was broken in two as the plane crashed on the ground. Here you can see the inside. It was all done as documentation in 1947. But as documentation with a spirit. And I was trying to get it back. So I did it, from the sketch.
> RM: And it is that new theme.
> Mr. SRIHADI: The new theme. Before, there was a *still life*. One drew it as a study, arranged it for the painting, as a *still life*—there was to be, here a flower, and here a vase.[149]

The Window

THE FACULTY AT THE OPENING OF THE LAW COLLEGE IN BATAVIA-JAKARTA, 1924. THE LECTURER IN WHITE, BACK ON THE RIGHT, DR. JACOB KATS, TAUGHT JAVANESE TO THE JAVANESE. KONINKLIJK INSTITUUT VOOR TAAL-, LAND- EN VOLKENKUNDE, LEIDEN

POSTSCRIPT

SOMETIMES VOICES

> Hearing . . . implies an opening toward a sense which is undecidable,
> precarious, elusive, and which sticks to the voice.
> —Mladen Dolar, *A Voice and Nothing More*

HEARING IMPLIES AN OPENING

Already a long time ago now, when I worked, for instance, on the history of the Indonesian military, on Indonesian technical thinking, or on a biography of the first prime minister of independent Indonesia, the documents I read, statistics as much as diaries, sometimes shifted as if uncomfortable and occasionally giggled as I tried to make some sense of them. The idea to interview elderly Indonesians about their early years came to me legitimately; I believed that the people would tell me about Dutch late colonialism as they remembered it amid their postrevolutionary and postcolonial present. A premonition of a giggle might have been hidden in the idea already. Otherwise this would be again a search merely for words—words, words, words.

Noise hit me unexpectedly. Very often I could get no words at all. "Sometimes a thousand twanging instruments will hum about mine ears; and [only] sometimes voices."[1]

It was a tropical noise, first of all, of course. There is a good deal of man-made shade and darkness when it comes to intimacy in Jakarta, but doors and windows are rarely closed. Most of life takes place on the street, on the outside, in a space that is open, like on the porches, where also most of my interviews took place. There is shouting and cries of the people all over my tapes, of children especially, the chirping of birds, from the sharp and aggressive to the most sublime of the caged songbirds put out high on the poles every morning, above the street in front of the house. And, of course, the wailing and sirens of the mosquitoes as the sun went down. Even the palm-tree leaves rattled surprisingly dry, loud, as I tried to listen — to words.

There was, I found out soon, an equally strong postcolonial noise. The drone of traffic, close to the house, almost with us when we sat on the front porch, often deafened everything. The noise of military vehicles seemed most insistent, as these were the last years of a very bad and persistent Indonesian *military* regime. On several of my tapes from 1997 and 1998, the noise of riots can be heard. There are shouts of crowds on the tapes, the thumping of bare feet and of heavy boots on the pavement, the tinkle of broken glass, and again the drone of the military cars. This, too — or so it seemed to me for a long time — made the tapes, as a source for history writing, incomprehensible.

There is an ancient Greek story: "A man plucked a nightingale and, finding but little to eat, said: 'You are just a voice and nothing more.'"[2] My initial feelings as a historian were certainly not how tiny a voice might be. There was no escaping it: the noise was as insistent as the word. My "nightingale" was roaring.

There was, moreover, no word without a noise. The noise, I soon realized, had been inside each word and, only thus, as a part of the noise, the voice (and the words) might really be heard.[3] Voices were made both powerful and weak by the noise they contained.

I met Professor Resink not long before he died. He was in his early eighties at the time. He was born in Java of Dutch parents, but with much Javanese blood in his veins, as he proudly said. His ancestors had lived in Java for two centuries. Professor Resink was legally blind; it was dark in the room where we talked, so that I could barely see the old man's face and hands. I just could hear his voice. There was no noise except a little buzz of a single fly, or so it seemed.

Sociophonetics calls it the "Lombard effect" when, in a voice speaking under and against a background of noise, diction gets excessively distinct.[4] The voice is bent by the noise, and the way it bends echoes the ways of the noise. The voices that struggle the most under and against the noise might be the most appealing.

Postscript

Actually, there was a noise in Professor Resink's room. The voice of the man bent against the noise—toward a fear of accent among other things. Han Resink (he permitted me to call him Han late that afternoon) told me about his childhood in Yogyakarta, the seat of one of the few surviving princely courts in Java. It was very early in the twentieth century, still decades before the end of the Dutch rule over the colony. Han's mother was a well-known collector of Javanese antiques. Javanese and Dutch teachers were paid to give him and his little older sister lessons in Javanese gamelan, as well as in piano. Special care was taken (and here the emphasis came) that he and his sister were not let out to play on the street. Not because of the Dutch or the Javanese children, but because of the *Indos*, the Eurasians (like Han Resink in a way) of mixed Dutch and Indonesian parentage.

It was not one language standing against the other that was the issue, not Javanese against Dutch, but the chattering, the noise in between the languages, the argot, the impurity of words and the accents, often coming from both and many other languages and dialects that might leak into how the Resinks' children spoke.

Professor Resink's father was a middle-rank colonial official, and, as was the custom, at one point of his service, as mentioned above, he was paid an extended several-month leave to Europe. It was in 1922, and Mr. Resink Sr. took his children with him. Did Han have big problems, suddenly, for the first time, coming to Europe, from the heart of Java? Not at all, he told me with a smile. The only awkward thing really happened—he was about twelve at the time—when he somehow got onto a street in Amsterdam, near where they were staying, where he met some lower-class Dutch children. "Pfee, the way those children spoke!" And here the emphasis, the noise and the bending come: "We were taught to speak Dutch Dutch," Han Resink tells me, raising a voice as if he had to—in that quiet room—against the noise, in the most careful, distinct, and flawless Indonesian Indonesian.

Professor Resink had studied at the only college law school in the Dutch colony. He had a successful career, and, after 1945, when it came to the open anticolonial struggle, he was one of the very few Dutch who chose to stay with the Indonesian Republic. He applied for Indonesian citizenship and taught in Jakarta until his retirement.

He recalled to me how he and his Javanese schoolmates at the colonial law school took their Javanese lessons from one Dr. Kats.[5] "Was not it awkward?" I asked, "a Dutchman teaching the Javanese their own language?"

Sometimes Voices

"Why should it be awkward?" Han Resink replied; "Dr. Kats knew so much about the Javanese culture. And he was such a good man."

Sociophonetics also distinguishes a "motherese" way of speaking, or IDS, infant deficiency speech.[6] A mother, or another "good person of authority," in an effort to communicate with the infant in her or his care, and to keep (what the authority understands as) chaos away, speaks with a hyperclear, artful, and artificially exaggerated pronunciation even in the case when the words thus pronounced might appear senseless to a non-IDS language listener (and to the infant, too)—not as words at all. Like the Javanese of Dr. Kats to his Javanese students, motherese, naturally and soundly, always has to be victorious. There is always enough will to teach, to learn, and to grow up—enough for victory.

As I listened to Han Resink later on the tape—talking to me about his life, about music, poetry, history, and most emphatically about his staying with the revolution, with the Indonesians—in the grammar and vocabulary, but most clearly of all in his voice, its timbre, the audible fantasy of accentlessness in it, the ultraclarity and ex cathedra spectacularity—I could hear Dr. Kats distinctly, in a fetal position, close to Han Resink's heart and his vocal cords. Here, there he still was, forty years after colonialism, the good and knowledgeable Dr. Kats, the source and the fruit of the graceful and courageous old Professor Resink's coming out of silence.

The power, the noise, and the voice of Dr. Kats might in fact be more securely there, deep in Professor Resink and in many like him, because Dr. Kats's physical being was gone. In the "quiet" room in the center of the postcolonial metropolis, in the old man's manner of speaking, his breathing, coughing, and pausing, there it was, Dr. Kats's "acousmatic" (that "which we hear without seeing what is causing it"[7])—something much more difficult to grasp, file, and dispel than a speaker carnate. Like many of the old people whom I interviewed in Indonesia, Han Resink, when speaking and pausing, struggled intensely and valiantly against the noise of the colonial and the postcolonial. At the same time and through the same struggle, he was producing and reproducing what Adorno (too easily) has called the "jargon of identity": "The jargon channels engagement into firm institutions and, furthermore, strengthens the most subaltern speakers in their self-esteem; they are already something because someone speaks from within them, even when that someone is not at all."[8]

✦ ✦ ✦

Some of my most lasting experiences came at moments of a voice's or a noise's interruptions.

One of the most memorable and most quoted instances of the interruption of speech in Western history is the hiccups Aristophanes was suddenly "seized by" when it was his turn among philosophers to speak in praise of love. I have a case comparable to this symposium event on my tapes. One day in Jakarta I talked to a young Indonesian woman, a daughter of Sutan Sjahrir, the first Indonesian prime minister. Her father fell out of favor in the early 1960s and was put in prison by President Sukarno. After Sjahrir suffered a stroke in prison, Sukarno allowed him to go into exile in Switzerland.

Sjahrir was still alive, in the last month of his life, in Zurich, when Sukarno was overthrown at the turn of 1965 and 1966, and there is an ongoing debate in Indonesia about what Sjahrir might have thought about it all. It is a debate fueled and indeed made into a political force by the fact that Sjahrir, after yet another stroke, could not speak anymore. His daughter conveyed the power to me. She was five years old at the time: she stayed with her father, and she used to tell him fairy tales. She said that he liked them. "How come," I asked, "he could not speak anymore?" "But he could cry," she explained.[9]

We should take the child as seriously as we should the hiccups, the babblings, and the cries. Let me quote this from Jean-Luc Nancy once more:

> When a voice, or music, is suddenly interrupted, one hears . . . the voice or the music of its own interruption.[10]

When speech interrupts itself, it may happen that "myth stops playing," and we get a rare chance to hear the voice and the community, too, "in a certain way": "When myth stops playing, the community that resists completion and fusion . . . makes itself heard in a certain way."[11]

The loudest interruption of speech I have heard in Indonesia came when the talking got close to the people missing after September 1965. The people arrested or killed, in the bloodiest massacres in modern Indonesian history, as suspected left-wing opponents of the regime—even those who were released after years but still under control, or had resigned, or had been destroyed—they were to be avoided. They had belonged to the brightest and most exciting people of modern Indonesia, and many of them had been the best friends of the people I was now talking to. Often, they reveal themselves (and history "in a certain way") in a ghostly way, through a click and then a white noise on my tape.

Merely to listen to the old people, and then to the tapes, the poetics of the sound was good enough. I would find it justifiable to convey just this experience. Yet what is the poetics beyond the pleasure of just being there and listening? Aren't the voices and the noise just self-evident, like the colors?

> We might ask: who would learn from this? Can someone teach me that I see a tree?[12]

In the perhaps most famous *scream* of the modern West, in Edward Munch's painting from 1893, there might be an opening to an Indonesian answer. There is, in the painting, a human, almost human, head with a mouth gaping: in a scream. The scream, clearly, is coming out of the screaming, tortured body. But there is something more in the painting, and in its *sound*: "Many interpreters (including Munch himself) have seen the distorted landscape in the background as the effect of the scream spreading through nature."[13]

This is a powerful idea in this painting and beyond it: a scream (or hiccup, babble, cry, or breathing), a voice, or noise can produce landscape, and they do so by expanding intimacy. There is a poetic, real, and never to be doubted sense of intimacy, and thus of the local, in a voice. Voices are produced in bodies that resonate—"it is precisely the voice that holds bodies and languages together."[14] Voices, as rarely anything else, are truly intimate and "extimate." Being emitted, voices also hold bodies and the social together—"this resolutely and irreducibly singular (mortal) voice, *in common*."[15]

There was another moment in my interview with Professor Resink that remains with me especially strongly. He was still telling me about the extended leave of his father when he as a boy traveled with him. They passed the Suez Canal, and "the East" (the all-white flannels of the colonial officials, those kinds of skies, of smells, of birds, he explained) still stuck with them. But it slowly fell away from them. On the second night after the Suez, as their ship sailed in the Mediterranean, the captain invited his father and him on *de brug*, the bridge of the ship. It was dark, deep in the night, only the stars and far to the north, lower on the horizon, a few tiny lights flickered. "All of a sudden," Professor Resink told me, "my father said, looking to the little lights: 'This is Europe, my boy!'"

It is still there, in my memory as much as on my tape, the trembling voice, and indeed the tears, the father, who is long not anywhere anymore except in that voice, and, yes, the *historical* landscape. The Resinks' family history in Indonesia reached back to the eighteenth century; rather few of Han Resink's ancestors had ever actually seen Europe, yet Europe in the colony of theirs was present—the longing, the drifting, throughout and hugely, the moisture getting into everything, the salty moisture of the sea around the ship, the tears in Professor Resink's voice, his voice most inexhaustibly, as he was telling me about that close-to-midnight south-of-Messina.

Listening to Professor Resink's voice (and the breathing and coughing that went with it) one knows, at least for the moment, that "people are silhouettes that are both imprecise and singularized, faint outlines of voices."[16] The social, then, also appears not merely to be signified but, indeed, produced by a voice as it is placed into or against the noise. Origins and, therefore, communities are built like that, around the voice, and in the manner of the voice: "He speaks of an origin . . . it is we who stand at the furthermost extreme and who barely hear him from this limit. Everything is a matter of one's practical, ethical, political—and why not add spiritual?—positioning around this singular eruption of voice."[17]

Hearing the old people in Indonesia, at the end of the military regime and long after the failed revolution, at the end of their own lives, trying to place their voices into and against the noise, I knew that, through their speaking, coughing, breathing, falling silent, they were gathering the world—in postcolonial Jakarta as in Nancy's *Inoperative Community*, as in Walter Benjamin's storyteller,[18] and indeed as in the precolonial *hikayat*, histories, lore of voice that many of the people I had talked to knew well:

> And the ruler came and sat down on the doorstep, pages paid homage to him. And also Hang Jebat came in and paid homage, and the ruler ordered him to read a tale because Jebat knew how to present a variety of voices, moreover those voices were very good. And Hang Jebat presented a tale, loud was his voice, and melodious too. And all the girl attendants and ladies in waiting and concubines of the ruler, they all sat down, and behind the screens they peeped at Hang Jebat. . . . Everybody who heard (Hang Jebat's voice) felt love. And the ruler slumbered on the lap of Hang Jebat.[19]

When I asked Mrs. Sosro, over ninety when I met her in 1992, why she had been talking to me so warmly, why she told me so many intimate and beautiful details about her life and about everything, she said that only rarely did anyone come to listen anymore. Her children and grandchildren were gone and almost all of her friends were dead: that was why I got so close to the center of her space, because it had shrunk. This was why I was privileged to hear her less faintly and, as a special bonus, to learn more about a historian's place in all this.

Sitor Situmorang is a poet who spent many years in the prisons of the military regime after the tragic events of 1965. He was released and went into many more years of exile. In the summer of 1997, in the trendy postcolonial Jakarta Café Cemara, I witnessed, *heard*, his homecoming. All chairs and tables in the café had been moved to the walls for the occasion, and we — quite a fashionable crowd — were sitting on the floor, squeezed against each other. Poets, like painters, seem to know best about space as well as voice. We expected a poem. Sitor stood up in the middle of the crowd and, after waiting for a while, said: "Revolution," in an ordinary, flat, everyday voice. Then, he said "No!" a little bit more loudly, and then again and again, "No!", and "NO!!!" and "NO!!!!!!" in an increasing volume, until he shrieked, red in face with the veins in his throat swelling. People were taken aback, straightened up, as if leaning a little away from him. There was a silence, awkward, dead, long, and increasingly senseless. We lost him. Then, in a whisper, tiredly, almost inaudibly (did he still want us to hear?), he said: "yes."[20]

Because voice is intimate and extimate, corporeal and incorporeal, making the body and the social by making them resonate, as much as anything, the voice can tell us how the body and the social *in common* are political.

I have not seen the particular performance by a new-generation Indonesian artist, painter, dancer, and political activist, Ms. Arahmaiani, but my son has, and he told me about it. It took place in the main auditorium of the National Gallery in Singapore, late in 2004. It was Sunday, and people came in from the street to visit the gallery as a part of their Sunday routine. In the colonial grand hall, on the stage made of benches arranged around her in a square, Arahmaiani began by handing out copies of the previous day's Singapore newspapers and by asking the people to choose at random and to read aloud a headline or a line from a column, an advertisement, a market report, a political news bit, or a sports score. The Sunday crowd felt ill at ease, at first, then a few of them mumbled something. Only slowly, and not altogether amicably, they read, and louder, until a few, and then most, and all of them really shouted. In the noise, trying to place her body into it, Arahmaiani danced.

Arahmaiani dancing into the noise struggles to make a space ("practical, ethical, political—and why not add spiritual?") for herself and for an Indonesia of hers, depressed after a series of revolutions that somehow never seem to do. What she achieves: her voice space is cracked, shrill, and threadbare at the edges. It also happened in Singapore, amid the Sunday crowd, in a sort of exile.

One could hear another voice in what Arahmaiani was doing. Two eras before her, Sukarno, the first president of the independent Indonesia, the "Great Leader of the Revolution," had been injecting his voice into the noise of the crowd—also to build a space for his nation. But while Arahmaiani's voice, when it can be heard at all, is wrinkled all over, Sukarno's voice—we can still listen to many tapes of it—sounds smooth like the skin of a newborn baby. While Arahmaiani's voice is working from the edges, Sukarno's voice sounds as if it still is coming from the acoustical—practical, ethical, political, spiritual—center. Arahmaiani makes the world resound by the risqué exposure of her body. But no one was supposed to touch Sukarno's—his mouth, his tongue, and, least of all, his microphone. Sukarno's was a historical era of trust in tools and mechanics that could be tested. In his toolbox, Sukarno trusted his tongue, and he would very much agree with the ancients, what they said about the "little member," able to "boast mightily": "Behold, how small a fire—how great a forest kindled."[21] As for the microphone, Sukarno breathed on the microphone, and concentrated and ever-widening radio waves—an extension of the tongue and microphone—mightily worked to establish a (fundamentally acoustic) nation.

> The whole world today . . . turns its ears to Jakarta. . . . Here, here is the Indonesian Nation. . . . Fifty, sixty million Indonesians now turn their ears to hear what I say! . . . they gather around their radios . . . they tune their sets in . . . they swarm over the radio. . . . [Even the rebels in the jungle listen] Simbolon, Zulkifli Lubis, Hussein . . . I say to them: "My misled brothers! . . . My brothers!"[22]
>
> The whole world today can taste the deliciousness of our revolution. . . . It is her *Universal Voice*.[23]
>
> I am *the extension of the people's tongue*; I am the voice of the people's aspirations.[24]

Voices and noises like Hang Jebat's, Sitor's, Arahmaiani's, or Sukarno's produce a *historical* space. As such, to a listening historian, they can significantly complicate the comfortable, linear, cumulative, capitalist, progressive, and proudly Western notion of time.

When Professor Resink said: "This is Europe, my boy!" his ancestors', theirs, his (and very much my, as well) time was there, present, together, *in unison*, by the very force of Professor Resink's own intellective and affective action, by the rhythm of his breathing.[25] As the voice of Professor Resink became extimate to the other voices and noises, the instant when he said it, it became a noncontinuous event and an indivisible instant,[26] extimate to the others' moments in the past when the glimmers of Europe had appeared, or had seemed to appear.

An alternative periodization of Indonesian history may be suggested by the voices and the noise—by Sukarno's moment and in what pitch he says "tongue" or "revolution," by Professor Resink's moment and with what accent he says "Europe" or "boy." Around these moments—the signs and the building blocks of the past and of the now—moments "brilliantly present" and "totally here,"[27] the logic of history may be assumed to be turning.

WRITING IT DOWN

In ancient Greece young people and freemen were forbidden to play the flute. A reason given was that "one cannot utter words while playing the flute."[28] One might expose oneself to the sound of music, and one might "melt and liquefy," "till he completely dissolves away his spirit, cuts out as it were the very sinews of his soul and makes of himself a 'feeble warrior.'"[29] Many of the old people I interviewed took my breath away. That is to say that often I was on the way to "dissolving" in the old people's voices or, as the Greeks might say, to becoming a "feeble warrior." Yet I was there to write it down!

Their very appeal makes the voices and the noise most difficult to be "read" as documents, which they surely are. The very power a listener might try to apply in an effort to understand might cripple them beyond recognition. Documents, as Michel Foucault has pointed out, have been "always [or too often] treated as the language of a voice since reduced to silence."[30] Literature, scholarly and all the other, or so it appears, on principle and the more so the closer it comes to hearing—to be writeable—tends to invalidate a voice, a noise, and their interruptions. An author, it seems, by the very fact of being an author, does everything not to melt and liquefy: "Under an assumed silence, there is someone standing apart who indeed ought to

Postscript

answer for it. —Then why does he not speak directly? —Because, I imagine, he cannot: in literature there is no direct speech."[31]

✦ ✦ ✦

Mr. Poncke Prinsen, another old person I met in Jakarta, became unforgettable to me by his belonging to a gray zone among noise, voice, and word, and among speaking, listening, and writing. He seemed to be of that zone fully, and the more so, the more he struggled to get out of it.

I met Mr. Prinsen in the middle of 2000.[32] We sat on the front porch of his small house at the outer edge of Jakarta that was already almost countryside. Or, more precisely, I sat: he reclined on a folding bed, which I had helped his wife carry out of the house, because he had wished it so. Here are my notes written the same evening:

> On 16 May I was seeing Poncke Prinsen. I wonder how much I can keep from this amazing interview, a meeting rather. His voice was extremely weak.

(Mr. Prinsen had recently suffered his fourth stroke.)

> The first remarkable thing that comes to my mind now is how stubbornly he insisted on writing everything down as he spoke and, then, how his hand with the pencil trembled—"like his voice," I thought. His way of life has been—and his way of talking clearly remains—that of a man of written words. Books, newspapers, loose sheets of paper were everywhere, much of it written by himself, and he was constantly demanding this or that to be brought to him, to show me; or, at least, he pointed as he spoke, even in the case when the item happened to be inside the house, where we could not see it. Evidently, he was happy on the porch, which was like most of the other porches in Jakarta I knew—a few meters from the traffic, in this case on a little neighborhood alley but also extremely busy. Clearly, too, he was fully at ease with the traffic, the scooters and children most of all, and he did not stop talking even when next to nothing of what he said could be heard amidst the noise. His wife held one or, at moments, both of his hands as we spoke, and a few times he put his hand on mine. He really had very great difficulty producing words, and often rather noises were coming out of his mouth, sometimes like a quiet snorting, other times like little cries, almost a weeping. Yet it all made a perfect sense to me (and to him) as we sat there: his message was genuine and, in this way, unquestionably coherent.[33]

The next morning, Mr. Prinsen sent his daughter to my hotel with an addition, she said, to what he had told me. What she brought was one rather crumpled and little smeared piece of paper. Much of his longhand on it I could decipher only with great difficulty, and some of it not at all. I believe that, where I succeeded, it was only because I was still re*calling* the fullness of the previous day. The scribbling of Mr. Prinsen's hand was like the noises he made.

Listening to the old people's stories—and they always speak in stories, of course—can also help a historian dispel the charm and curse of a narrative. The voices and noises, "brilliantly present" and "totally here," their eruptions underneath and above the stories, and through the stories, may lead a historian closer to what Proust might have really meant by "the search of lost time"—at least Milan Kundera translated it like that: "The search of present time."³⁴

A NOTE ON TECHNOLOGY

Mr. Prinsen came from solid Dutch stock: he was born in The Hague "to socialist parents" (so he put it), was close to the labor movement all his life, took part in the Dutch anti-Nazi resistance as a teenager during the German occupation of the Netherlands, and spent some time in a Nazi concentration camp. In 1947, he was drafted into the Dutch army and sent to the (former) colony to fight the new Indonesian republic. Several weeks after arriving in Java, Mr. Prinsen deserted from the Dutch army, one of only a handful of men who did so, and joined the other side. At the International Institute for Social History in Amsterdam, possibly the largest collection of socialist movement documents in the world, a curator told me that only two archives they kept under lock and key all the time—the Karl Marx papers (the astonishing bequest by Karl Kautsky), because, of course, they were so unique and precious, and those of Poncke Prinsen—because he, the deserter from the Dutch cause, was still so hated in the Netherlands and there was still a credible threat that the institute might be broken into and the Prinsen papers destroyed.

The lock on Mr. Prinsen's papers in the Amsterdam archives, like the tapes of my talking with him that sit here on my shelf, makes me think about the death of the voice. Mr. Prinsen passed away in 2002, but, as I listen to his voice, now, on my tape, it is at times even more moving than when he had actually spoken. His trembling is beamed into my ear through the outlet of the machine. Mr. Prinsen's voice is touching, as if he were on radio or television:

> These means—especially radio and television—reach the people at large in such a way that they notice none of the innumerable technical intermediations; the voice of the announcer resounds in the home, as though he were present and knew each individual. The announcers' technically and psychologically created artificial language—the model of which is the repellently confidential "Till we meet again"—is of the same stripe as the jargon of authenticity.[35]

There is nothing new in this authentic power of technology, and certainly nothing new in the (former) colony. I am touched by Mr. Prinsen's voice on the tape like the Dutch in the colony used to be touched by the broadcast on their early radios—hooked to the network, *touched away* from the place where they actually were, away from the voices and noises of the colony that they might otherwise actually hear—becoming authentic in that other way.

One elderly Indonesian to whom I talked was a man of radio—he had been the director of the revolutionary Republican Radio in 1945.[36] We talked at the time of riots, in November 1998, in Jakarta, and at one moment the voices of the crowd and the noise of the breaking glass came close indeed to the front porch where we sat. We tried to go on for a few minutes as if nothing was happening, but, at last, with a forced smile the old man motioned toward my tape recorder on the table between us and said: "Station break!" We both, in that little joke, were seduced into believing at that moment, maybe, that the riots and all that had turned sour in life and revolution, by the touch of the button, will be touched away.

There is an extensive collection, hundreds of tapes in Jakarta, in the Indonesian National Archives. Some of the interviews had been done with the same people to whom I talked, here collectively described as "the Pioneers of the Indonesian freedom." The audio archive was put together at the moment at which the military regime was at its peak. As the philosophy of the archives put it, the interviews were to be done so that "not only you, who conducted the interview, experienced the atmosphere of the interview directly and base your knowledge on that experience, can understand the interview." The interviews were to be "preserved for history" and be "useful to everybody." Therefore, in the ways in which questions were to be asked and answers recorded, there was to be "uniformity or, at least an effort at uniformity if total uniformity cannot be achieved."[37]

There are rows of cassettes without end in the archives (interviewers were paid by the cassette). There were prescribed questions, disciplined answers, and the ideal has almost been achieved. Usable to all, to use Adorno's description of the jargon of authenticity again, there are on the tapes, "words that are sacred without sacred content . . . frozen emanations . . . products of the disintegration of the aura."[38] Chairil Anwar, the great poet of the Indonesian revolution, and a contemporary of the people in this book except that he died young, might have been, in 1943, prophesying the tapes:

Death.
Maybe it's like this: silent, stiff, that's all,
One day your voice may be compressed into this.[39]

And yet, as Adorno writes, "products of the disintegration of the aura" — this, at least as related to the tapes in the Jakarta archives, allows for some optimism. There are undertones or noises on the tapes.[40] The death, luckily, never fully happened. The badly paid people doing the oral history project in Jakarta did not seem to be able to make the voices into the thing as prescribed. Throughout, and especially at the moments at which a question went astray or the interviewee became tired, or impatient — traces of the present were left on the tape, like a voice underground, or rather a noise.

THE ZONE

> People have often asked me what the Zone is, and what it symbolizes, and have put forward wild conjectures on the subject. . . . The Zone doesn't symbolize anything . . . the zone is a zone, it's life, and as he makes his way across it a man may break down or he may come through. Whether he comes through or not depends on his own self-respect, and his capacity to distinguish between what matters and what is merely passing.
> —Andrey Tarkovsky, *Sculpting in Time*, on his film *Stalker*

On some tapes, I might sound like what Sigmund Freud introduced to our age as a "powerful silent listener." On most other occasions there is not much subtlety either, if only because of my croaking-voice Indonesian or Dutch with a heavy Czech accent. Moreover, out of clumsiness, anxiety, or perhaps arrogance, I seemed always to place my tape recorder (not a very sensitive machine either) close to my chest and mouth. As I listen now to the tapes, my voice, embarrassingly, is booming, and theirs, the old people's, is weak in the background.

This is an admission I have to make for this book to come to some closure. Only occasionally did I get close to what Nancy defines as a dialogue: "Dialogue," he says, "this articulation of speech, *or rather* this sharing of voices."[41]

Very late into the work, I learned about four Indonesians, writers, at least two generations younger than any one of the old people to whom I talked; even a few years younger than Ms. Arahmaiani, who led me to them. I never met them in person; I have only read a little book they wrote in 2004 about a theater performance they decided to do: *Waktu Batu: Teater garasi; Laboratorium penciptaan teater* (The Stone Age: Garage Theater; A Laboratory to Make Theater).

Latif, Andri Nur, Gunawan Maruanto, and Ugoran Prasad, the four, I think, have been trying something very close to my project. First, they make it clear in the book that they are only authors of sorts: the story they put to paper "was written in the stone age." Of course, there was not much writing at that time—mostly or only voices and the noise. The only way to write it down, they found, was to write and keep talking about the writing, to stick to the work as if it were a voice (one never gives one's voice away really); like breath. Here are some of their notes:

> Writer, who writes, who puts his writing to the paper, puts himself there with it and remains there, with the writing. At some distance, but he is still there. Now he has to admit the distance, and it is best done by reading aloud what has been written: thus writing is made and made not different from reading. Then, the writer has to give his text to the actors so that the distance may increase yet a step further. The actors as they act the text are quite at a distance from the text already, and yet they still, and with the author, remain fully in the text.[42]

What Latif, Nur, Maruanto, and Prasad accomplished through this neverending, hesitant and against-themselves process of giving and not giving their text away—to their own voices, to the voices of actors, and finally to the voices and noise of the stage and of the audience—was to stay present and to be writers at the same time. Here are more of their notes (and, yes, they clearly knew about Lacan):

> We tried to force all the abstract concepts we might be supplied with, down and deep, close to, and into the matter that one can see, hear, and touch. What we ended up with, perhaps inevitably, was a sort of *schizophrenia* . . . not of the clinical-psychology type, but a disposition that exists among the sick as well as the healthy, a sense one may get in a space like hallways or waiting-rooms of hospitals. . . . Hospital, in fact, seemed to be all upon us as we worked our way through and as we talked [*tafsir*] above the text of our "Stone Age Version One."[43]

(*Tafsir* is commonly understood in Indonesia to mean "exegesis," "commentary," or, more specifically, "explanation of passages of Koran by supplying additional information."[44])

> As the days of the work passed one after the other, the feeling of a waiting room affected almost all the members of the artistic team. We decided to intensify the feeling even more, and a long scene had been inserted into the play, which actually was to take place in a kind of a hospital waiting room.

To keep truthful to their idea of work, this was not a stone-age–hospital waiting room, but a modern Indonesian urban establishment.

> Time, in which we found ourselves, moved to a collision with itself [*wajah waktu yang bertabrakan*] and yet we were able to feel this as a *fashion*, or, to put it another way, as a bad dream. . . . The world of the waiting room . . . engulfed the team . . . and we were almost there, we almost entered into the fullness of the text. We began to feel a possibility to articulate the story in a subtle way naturally and as an event.[45]

The spoken word can never be frozen. Even if it seems to be caught on tape, it can be heard, really, only as long as the breath of the speaker and of that who hears pull and push, as the mouths, so to speak, can be open. Flow is in the nature of both equally, speaking and hearing. Being a historian and being struck by hearing, to be within earshot, one just is not allowed to become "curious":

> Curiosity has nothing to do with observing entities and with marveling at them. To be amazed to the point of not understanding is something in which

[curiosity] has no interest. Rather it concerns itself with a kind of knowing, but just in order to have known.[46]

The trust in the importance of voice and noise as a source for writing history can be fruitful only if "understood *as a possibility*" and if it is "cultivated *as a possibility*." We must not do anything but to "comport ourselves towards it."[47]

Talking with my interviewees has mostly been flowing, continuous, as long as the tape ran and batteries lasted. Of course, there were the trips the old people took to the bathroom, to take medicine, or, in some cases, to take a nap. But some ruptures in the flow were like when the door in a hospital waiting room opens. There were moments when all might be lost, but they also might be the openings. This was the scary part about the zone — its limits.[48] These might be moments of crashing as well as the moments, at last, to write it down.

✶ ✶ ✶

The Garage Theater was explicitly a history project. History was described — the "Stone Age," the time before the Dutch, the time after the Dutch, the unfinished revolution, the colonialism that seemed to be staying forever:

> It happens here, at the foot of the hills, and nobody is powerful enough to take away the magic . . . the silence. It happens here: the body of a boy is about to be . . . turned in stone. It happens here: the fairy tales of childhood. . . . the boy is about to go to sleep. His mother sings a lullaby, which came from . . . the other side of the ocean: *Slaap, kindje, slaap*.[49]

"Slaap, kindje, slaap," "Sleep, baby, sleep," is, of course, in Dutch. The boy to be turned into stone is Kala, the Javanese god of time.

It is so very difficult to anchor anything as long as one tries to listen and even more so as one tries to write it down. Moreover, the Garage Theater people are Indonesians, they deeply care, but again and again they emphasize that none of them is from Central Java, "where it all happened," and that they "knew nothing" about that, certainly not, when they began to write. They had no choice but with the greatest affection (and here again is a lesson I had to take most seriously) to stick to their foreignness. They make sure that the gods and the people know:

KALA: I am afraid, Mama! I am afraid I will become a stone.
— *Slaap, kindje, slaap* . . .

KALA: Mama! I hear the Garage Theater is giving a play about us. How could they? They are not from here.[50]

✶ ✶ ✶

As I sit back at home with the tapes, and as I listen, even with the buttons to stop the tape and to listen again, even with transcripts of the tapes next to the tape recorder, it still is a sort of waiting-room or schizophrenia adventure, or, at least, a dual hearing—of the sounds on the tape and in memory. The tapes now and the sounds then are paired, like a miracle and the miracle's celebration—or, at least, not "opposed as truth and falsity."[51]

The part of my writing that I want to matter most was done in panic. These were the moments at which I had just finished an interview and walked out of the house, happy that I had done it, that I had it on my tape—and fearful of how much I had missed and was still missing with every moment that passed: "Weren't the batteries dead again?" "Didn't I cover the microphone with my hand again?" "How long will my memory last to keep all the details," each of which, I knew, might be important: her eyes shifting; his eyes getting moist; the door to the back room opening a little, closing again?

In a taxi or a *bajaj* pedicab, if I was lucky to get one quickly, and often still on the sidewalk, in the heat—and the noise was particularly overwhelming at these moments—I scribbled as fast as I could, with the voices still in my ear, having no time to care about grammar, punctuation, capital letters, even letters, scribbling (like Mr. Prinsen mumbled), as fast, as soft, as strong, hopefully, as they had been talking to me a minute earlier, still in and already away, in the zone, still listening—out of breath.

Postscript

NOTES

PREFACE: PROMENADES

1. Of the colony's population of 60 million in 1930, almost completely native, "at best 0.5 percent understood the colonial language." Anderson, *Under Three Flags*, 87n50.

2. Le Corbusier in 1929, quoted in Frampton, *Le Corbusier*, 23.

3. "Ten Poems from a Reader for Those Who Live in Cities," in Brecht, *Poems 1913–1956*, 133–38.

4. Benjamin, *Selected Writings*, 4:389–400, 444.

5. Walter Benjamin, Bertold Brecht, or Franz Kafka, Jean-Luc Nancy, Marc Augé, or Avital Ronell, or Le Corbusier, Theodor Adorno, and some others appear on the pages of this book so pervasively not because they are more profound, articulate, impressive, or, yes, closer to my Western ear than the Indonesians like Sosro, Soemardjan, Soemitro, or Trimurti. The Westerners were not invited to "speak for the silent"; they fell in (and sometimes with a thump), and they remained in the book by the force of their fragility, their will or inability to resist their temptation to join in, their affliction with the modern, and the constant fear of homelessness in their own metropolises, just a step aside, behind, or ahead of that in the colony. They are here as *the other urban intellectuals* of this book.

6. Sartre, *Baudelaire*, 148.

7. "On Surrealism in Its Living Works," 1953, in Breton, *Manifestoes of Surrealism*, 298.

8. Krauss, *Originality of the Avant-Garde*, 253.

9. Blanchot, "Absence of the Book," 326.

10. "The Sharing of Speech," in Irigaray, *Way of Love*, 16, 28. It is a problem of language. Even the kindest editor (and I met the kindest ones at Duke University Press) would not allow me to keep in the book what the Indonesians said in Indonesian, the Dutch in Dutch, the French in French, the Germans in German, and I in Czech. The effect of having all the quotations in English only was to flatten them into a weird kind of contemporaneity: Franz Kafka chatting with Marc Augé, Marcel Proust with Ong

Hok Ham. In some ways I did not mind so much because this might actually suggest a significant sameness in the postmodern and postcolonial world in which we now live. In other ways, however, I minded very much. In fact, increasingly, I despaired. Out of this desperation, in large part, in the end, in the last chapter, I turned to the voices — and to the noise.

BYPASSES AND FLYOVERS

1. Abeyasekere, *Jakarta*, 90–91. Several among the prominent Dutch architects and urban planners in the late colonial era "lamented the disappearance of plants and vegetation, which for years had given character to the 'tropical town.' [At the same time they] noticed an unprecedented tendency in the colony, that is, in the appearance of order or ordering (*ordening*) in the urban environment." Abidin Kusno, "The Significance of Appearance," 5, 17.

2. Peter J. M. Nas and Manasse Malo, "View from the Top," in Grijns and Nas, *Jakarta-Batavia*, 239.

3. Ibid., 241.

4. Kees Grijns, "JABOTABEK Place Names," ibid., 211–28. See also "Pembuat peta Gunther Holtorf memasuki abad digital," in Marco Kusumawijaya, *Jakarta*, 39–46, on a new edition of Gunther Holtorf's digital map of Jakarta. "With reference to the transformation of the city: 'Nothing less than a compass is required, if you are to find your way.'" Jacques Fabien (1863), quoted in Benjamin, *Arcades Project*, 136.

5. Baudrillard, *Simulacra and Simulation*, 13. Friedrich Engels wrote that on boulevards the metropolitan (Parisian) life (in 1848) "'circulates with the greatest intensity.'" Quoted in Virilio, *Speed and Politics*, 3.

6. "The expansion of the city of Jakarta by the Dutch can be described as 'embracing' of the existing native neighborhoods. These were first surrounded by urban roads. Then they became pockets in the expanding city, and much of it still persists today." "Jakarta: kampung besar atau metropolis," in Marco Kusumawijaya, *Jakarta*, n.p.

7. For example, Rél Revolusi [Railway tracks of revolution] in "Speech of August 17, 1960," in Sukarno, *Dari Proklamasi sampai Takari* 444. True distance is suggested here: "No distance was more distant than the one in which its [the train's] rails converged in the mist." "Berlin Childhood," 1934, in Benjamin, *Selected Writings*, 3:387. This was a distance measured in height as much as in length: "The rail becomes the first prefabricated iron component, the precursor of the girder." "Paris, the Capital of the Nineteenth Century," 1935, in Benjamin, *Selected Writings*, 3:33. The girder, of course, has become the crucial element of high modern skyscrapers.

8. "Speech of August 17, 1957," in Sukarno, *Dari Proklamasi sampai Takari*, 344.

9. "The Hotel Lobby," in Kracauer, *Mass Ornament*, 18.

10. Barthes, *Writing Degree Zero*, 31.

11. "Speech of August 17, 1946," in Sukarno, *Dari Proklamasi sampai Takari*, 22.

12. "Speech of August 17, 1956," ibid., 292.

13. "Speech of August 17, 1961," ibid., 481.

14. Augé, *Non-places*, 120.

15. Augé, *In the Metro*, 62. See also: "Anthropology, or anyway social or cultural anthropology, is in fact rather more something one picks up as one goes." Geertz, *After the Fact*, 97.

16. Foucault, *Archeology of Knowledge*, 119.

17. Dan Hoffman, "The Receding Horizon of Mies: Work of the Cranbrook Architecture Studio," in Mertins, *Presence of Mies*, 105–6.

18. Ibid.

19. Interview, Jakarta, July 28, 1992.

20. Wittgenstein, *Philosophical Investigations*, 2:164.

21. Tan Malaka, born in 1897 in West Sumatra, became the chairman of the Indies (Indonesian) Communist Party in 1921. He was exiled in 1922 and lived outside the country until about 1942, when he returned to Java. After 1945 Tan Malaka led the so-called 100 Percent–Freedom Indonesian radicals, and he was executed (as too radical, it seems) by a local commander of the Indonesian republican army in 1949. *Patjar* (*pacar* in the new spelling) has two meanings, at least, in Indonesian—*Lawsonia inermis*, "red henna," and "fiancée, boyfriend/girlfriend, darling." Both of the meanings are used in the *Patjar Merah*'s many stories—the hero leaves behind a *patjar* blossom whenever he just-in-time escapes the police; and beyond any doubt he is a a darling.

22. "Dialogue is the rhythmic interruption of the logos, the space between the replies, each reply apart from itself retaining for itself an access to sense that is only its own, an access of sense that is only itself." Nancy, *Sense of the World*, 165.

23. The translation of Rilke's epigraph to this chapter is by M. D. Herter Norton, except for "mountains," which I have substituted for his "hills," and my "dwellings" instead of his "huts." Rilke, let me note, embarked on his riding expedition from Prague too.

24. "The *tombeau* is a literary and musical commemorative genre dating to the seventeenth century. The historiographical narrative also belongs to this genre. See "The Historiographical Operation," in Certeau, *Writing of History*, 113n116.

25. Nancy, *Inoperative Community*, 77.

26. Segalen, *Essay on Exoticism*, 15–16.

27. Blanchot, *Writing of the Disaster*, 4.

28. Benjamin, *Arcades Project*, 124.

29. Ibid., 138.

30. Ibid.

31. Brecht, *Poems, 1913–1956*, 539n109, 107.

32. Nas and Malo, "View from the Top," 235, and "Gedung jangkung di poros Jakarta," in Marco Kusumawijaya, *Jakarta*, 17–22.

33. "On The Geometrical Mind and the Art of Persuasion," 1657–1658, in Pascal, *Selections*, 173, 176–77.

34. Notebook, fall 1998, no.3.

35. Adorno, *Minima Moralia*, 68.

36. Where I talk about inviolable highways, Siegel talks about the absence of ghosts. There is in Jakarta, he argues, "no room for contesting interpretations," and no room for "survivors of massacres to tell their own stories." This, he says, makes for "communicability." Siegel, *New Criminal Type in Jakarta*, 9, 117–19. Indeed, the power of the postcolonial traffic rests very much on the absence of the ghosts of the likes of Mrs. Sosro, let's say, crossing on red, and telling the stories of the massacred.

37. *Jakarta Post*, May 13 and 14, 2000.

38. "Poros sejarah dan identitas Jakarta," in Marco Kusumawijaya, *Jakarta*, 25–31.

39. Notebook, fall 1998, no. 3.

40. Ladd, *Ghosts of Berlin*, 118.

41. *Berita-V.O.R.L. Madjallah dari Vereeniging voor Oostersche Radio Luisteraars* (Bandoeng), vol. IV, no. 7 (1938): 18.

42. See, for instance, Akihary, *Architectuur en stedebouw in Indonesië*, 119.

43. Kandinsky, *Kandinsky und ich*, 146; also from that time are "the concrete 'trees' created by the Martel brothers for the 1925 Paris Exposition des Arts Décoratifs." Stephen Krog, "Whither the Garden?" in Wrede and Adams, *Denatured Visions*, 95.

44. Interview, Jakarta, August 25, 1995.

45. Quoted in "Dream Kitsch: Gloss on Surrealism," in Benjamin, *Selected Writings*, 1:4.

46. Brotokusumo, "Pasukan trek bom," an illustration of the time and its mood, is a typewritten entry for the competition on the thirtieth anniversary of the Indonesian Proclamation of Independence, 1945; *Arsip Joang '45*, no. 479/xxiv, stored in the Youth-of-1945 Museum in Jakarta.

47. Interview, Jakarta, August 25, 1995. See also "Roosseno tentang Roosseno," in *Roosseno*, 901.

48. Roosseno, "Pidato penerimaan gelar," February 25, 1957, ibid., 756–61.

49. Ir. Wiratman Wangsadinata, quoted in "Pidato penerimaan gelar," 893, and in "Roosseno tentang Roosseno," 897.

50. "Preparations for the construction of Istiqlal Mosque and Hotel Indonesia were started under Sudiro (the mayor of Jakarta, 1953–1960) by the eviction and resettlement of the people living in the areas chosen for the erection of these monumental works. Nas and Malo, "View from the Top," 234.

51. "Politik Ibukota: Antara polisi dan negara," in Marco Kusumawijaya, *Jakarta*, 179; "Ruang arsitektur Lapangan Merdeka: Fragmentasi dan sentralitas," ibid., 125. "The first plan was to make a simple monument, created and constructed by Indonesians. President Sukarno supported the idea. In the end, however, he amended it. The monument was topped with a flame of real gold and constructed by Japanese." Nas and Malo, "View from the Top," 233–34.

52. Roosseno, "Jakarta menghadapi tahun 2000," July 27, 1985, in *Roosseno*, 799.

53. Jordan, *Transforming Paris*, 26.

54. Interview, Jakarta, December 28, 2000.

55. This is Le Corbusier's upgrading of Aristotle's "Four Routes," in Le Corbusier's *Les trois établissements humains* (1945), quoted in Frampton, *Le Corbusier*, 147.

56. Notebook, fall 1998, no. 3.

57. "Speech of August 17, 1947," in Sukarno, *Dari Proklamasi sampai Takari*, 39.

58. "Speech of August 17, 1957," ibid., 351–52.

59. Sukarno, "Speech of April 5, 1965," and "Speech of July 18, 1966," in McIntyre, "Sukarno as Artist-Politician," 193.

60. This beer drinking is historically typical. According to a depressing remark by Michel de Certeau, historians' "discourse is located outside of the experience that gives it credibility . . . [it is] oblivious to the flow of everyday labor . . . [and, by the force of it] . . . allows a classification by periods, [and] a new 'vector space.'" Certeau, "Historiographical Operation," 88, 90.

61. See, for example, the introduction to Sukarno, *Dari Proklamasi sampai Takari*, 6.

62. Henk Ngantung memoirs, quoted in Ida Indawati Khouw, "Real Story behind Demolition of Historical Sites Is Vague," *Jakarta Post*, August 14, 1999.

63. These three terms are Robert Smithson's from his "A Tour of the Monuments of Passaic," in Holt, *Writing of Robert Smithson*, 52–57. Smithson was a major U.S. landscape architect of the late 1960s and the 1970s and most famously the author of *Spiral Jetty* in the Great Salt Lake, Utah. Ideally, in Jakarta, too, it might be like that: after a failed revolution, an avant-garde landscaping.

64. Roosseno, "Pidato selaku Promotor," in *Roosseno*, 742. According to Rosalind Krauss, "the logic of the monument, entering the space," "could be called its [space's] negative condition — a kind of sitelessness, or homelessness, an absolute loss of place." Krauss, *Originality of the Avant-Garde*, 280.

65. "Biodata," in *Roosseno*, vii.

66. Interview, Jakarta, August 23, 1997.

67. Blanchot, *Writing of the Disaster*, 44.

68. Interview, Jakarta, August 18, 1997.

69. Adorno. *Minima Moralia*, 150.

70. Ibid., 216.

71. Notebook, summer 1999, no. 1.

72. Notebook, summer 1994, no.2.

73. Barthes, *Camera Lucida*, 92. To get more of the Barthes's sense here, one should remember that French for "flat" is *plat*.

74. Thucydides, quoted in Pelt and Westfall, *Architectural Principles*, 184, 174.

75. "We must rediscover man. We must rediscover the straight line wedding the axis of fundamental laws: biology, nature, cosmos. Inflexible straight line like the horizon of the sea." Le Corbusier, quoted in Caroline Constant, "From the Vergilian Dream to Chandigarh: Le Corbusier and the Modern Landscape," in Wrede and Adams, *Denatured Visions*, 81.

76. November 10, 1998, was the first time ever, because of the riots, that there were no lights on the central heroes' graves. Notebook, fall 1998, no. 3.

THE WALLS

1. "Building Dwelling Thinking," 1951, in Heidegger, *Poetry, Language, Thought*, 147.
2. Ibid.
3. "The Turning," 1950, in Heigegger, *Question Concerning Technology*, 39–40. Walter Benjamin might be referring to a similar thing, writing at the same time as Heidegger. One should hear "to dwell" as a "transitive verb," Benjamin wrote. Benjamin, *Arcades Project*, 221.
4. Frampton, *Le Corbusier*, 171.
5. Ibid., 36.
6. Mies van der Rohe, quoted in Fritz Neumeyer, "A World in Itself: Architecture and Technology," in Mertins, *Presence of Mies*, 79–80.
7. Interview, Jakarta, July 30, 1996.
8. Interview, Surakarta, August 6, 1995.
9. Interview, Surakarta, August 9, 1995.
10. Interview, Jakarta, August 18, 1993.
11. Interview, Jakarta, July 14, 1997.
12. Interview, Bandung, August 26, 1999.
13. Interview, Blitar, August 13, 1997.
14. Interview, Nita, May 10, 2000.
15. Interview, Jakarta, August 18, 1993.
16. Interview, Jakarta, August 8, 1999.
17. Interview, Jakarta, August 20, 1995.
18. Kafka, *Trial*, 39.
19. Benjamin, *Arcades Project*, 423. On Le Corbusier's famous "utopian urban proposals of *soleil, espace, verdure*," see, for example, Caroline Constant, "From the Vergilian Dream to Chandigarh: Le Corbusier and the Modern Landscape," in Wrede and Adams, *Denatured Visions*, 80.
20. Interview, Jakarta, July 14, 1997.
21. Interview, Jakarta, August 16, 1995.
22. Interview, Yogyakarta, August 3, 1997.
23. Interview, Jakarta, July 28, 1996.
24. Interview, Jakarta, July 30, 1996.
25. Moenzir, *Gesang*, 6–7.
26. Sutton, *Philosophy and Memory Traces*, 13.
27. Descartes, quoted ibid., 64–65.
28. Wittgenstein, *Last Writings*, 1:112–13.
29. Interview, Jakarta, July 19, 1995.
30. Interview, Bandung, July 14, 1995.
31. Interview, Nita, May 20, 2000.
32. Interview, Blitar, August 13, 1997.

33. Reid, *Southeast Asia in the Age of Commerce*, 62.
34. Interview, Nita, May 20, 2000.
35. Interview, Sikka, May 22, 2000.
36. Interview, Menado, July 27, 2000.
37. Interview, Jakarta, July 26, 1994.
38. Interview, Jakarta, July 25, 1997.
39. Interview, Yogyakarta, August 4, 1995.

40. A. G. Meyer, *Eisenbauten* (1907), quoted in Benjamin, *Arcades Project*, 156. But see also Theodor Adorno: "I would question whether cast iron really is the first artificial building material (bricks!)." "Exchange with Theodor W. Adorno on the Essay 'Paris, the Capital of the Nineteenth Century,'" in Benjamin, *Selected Writings*, 3:58.

41. Frampton, *Le Corbusier*, 9, 129. "Iron construction was succeeded by reinforced concrete. This was the nadir for architecture, one which coincided with the deepest political depression." Benjamin, *Arcades Project*, 548.

42. Frampton, *Le Corbusier*, 24, 66.

43. This is about the *modern* colony. Yet in many stories of the archipelago, there are some solid and premodern bronze and iron buildings described or, at least, sung about. For instance: "Thus it was, my dear young ones, / How strong it was in Batu Kumbang. / Bronze walls rammed up to the firmament, / Iron walls concealed the clouds. / Ui, the wind against them could not get through, / Ants walking on them slipped down sideways." Collins, *Guritan of Radin Suane*, second night, canto 221, 248.

44. Interview, Jakarta, July 26, 1994.

45. Beatriz Colomina, "Mies Not," in Mertins, *Presence of Mies*, 211.

46. A. G. Meyer *Eisenbauten* (1907), quoted in Benjamin, *Arcades Project*, 541. The twentieth-century avant-garde has made what might appear as (again) the final step. The movement around van der Rohe especially "was interested in exploring the reflective qualities of glass, hence the prismatic and curved forms. . . . [Buildings were to become] light-reflecting transparent shafts, the interior structure variably perceptible behind the glass skin. . . . [This] use of transparency and counter-transparency [was supposed to] creat[e] the paradox of a perpetual display of everything and nothing . . . [as] ambiguous oscillation of transparency and reflectivity." Phyllis Lambert, "Punching through the Clouds: Notes on the Place of the Toronto Dominion Center in the North America *Oeuvre* of Mies," in Mertins, *Presence of Mies*, 37,42; and Brian Boigon, "What's So Funny: Modern Jokes and Modern Architecture," ibid., 229. Simulacra got closer to be created through architectural means: "Belief, faith in information attach themselves to this tautological proof that the system gives of itself by doubling the signs of an unlocatable reality" Baudrillard, *Simulacra and Simulation*, 81.

47. "In geometry and logic alike a place is a possibility: something can exist in it." Wittgenstein, *Tractatus Logico-Philosophicus*, § 3.411, 18.

48. Interview, Jakarta, July 14, 1997.
49. Interview, Menado, May 29, 2000.
50. Interview, Jakarta, August 8, 1999.

51. Interview, Jakarta, August 18, 1993. It still feels so, let me say natural or even inevitable, to become a guest in a Jakarta house. I know it from my experience, and this is from a well-known author of my interviewees' generation: "Without him realizing it, his feet have brought him to Mardi's house. For a long time he can't answer the questions that are hurled at him. Instead, he rolls his weak and weary body down onto Mardi's mat, and tries to sleep." "Miscarriage of a Would-Be Playwright," in Pramoedya, *Tales from Djakarta*, 96.

52. This is not to say that there cannot be an unwelcome presence in an Indonesian house. The architecture itself can well articulate such a situation; it sometimes actually moans. Snouck Hurgronje, one of the most prominent colonial scholars and an adviser to the Dutch governor general around 1900, helping the Dutch conquest of Aceh in North Sumatra, warned against the Acehnese houses, built so as to, he wrote, alert the inhabitants—by squeaking and sighing when an intruder merely touches them or steps onto their porch. Similarly, Indonesian lore has it that "The great bamboo stairway thundered, / His advance made the corners chatter. / The floorboards shuddered; / Alarmed at his steps people started to rise." Collins, *Guritan of Radin Suane*, first night, canto 37, 86.

53. Interview, Jakarta, July 30, 1996.

54. Interview, Jakarta, July 23, 1997.

55. Interview, Yogyakarta, August 4, 1995.

56. Interview, Jakarta, August 16, 1995.

57. Interview, Utrecht, July 6, 1998.

58. Interview, Jakarta, July 28, 1996.

59. On the status levels in Javanese, see Anderson, "Language of Indonesian Politics"; and Siegel, *Solo in the New Order*.

60. Interview, Jakarta, July 23, 1997.

61. Interview, Jakarta, July 19, 1995.

62. Interview, Jakarta, July 23, 1997.

63. Interview, Bandung, July 14, 1995.

64. Interview, Surabaya, July 24, 1992.

65. Interview, Utrecht, July 6, 1998.

66. Interview, Jakarta, July 26, 1994.

67. Interview, Surakarta, August 6, 1995.

68. Kafka, *Trial*, 149.

69. Interview, Jakarta, July 23, 1997.

70. Interview, Jakarta, July 26, 1994.

71. Interview, Jakarta, July 14, 1997.

72. Interview, Jakarta, August 24, 1999.

73. Harriet Janis and Sydney Janis, "Marcel Duchamp, Anti-artist," in Masheck, *Marcel Duchamp*, 31.

74. Interview, Jakarta, July, 19, 1995.

75. "Heavy shadows against light shadows, a shadowy abyss beyond?" A hearth in

a house, Henri Lefebvre says, has been the "last relic of the shadowy abyss." Lefebvre, *Production of Space*, 248.

76. Interview, Utrech, July 6, 1998. Another shadow play of the kind is described by Mr. Sutikno's contemporary, the novelist Kartamihardja: "I was also frequently told stories about heaven and hell. Mother usually told them to me in bed before I fell asleep. She lay by me, cuddling me. Spellbound, my gaze remained rooted on the top of the mosquito net as though looking at a movie screen. In my imagination the picture of events in hell was displayed on the screen. 'A naughty child who does not pray will go to hell,' mother always said. 'In hell, naughty children will be boiled in a cauldron of bubbling lead. Nobody, not even their fathers and mothers, will be able to help them.'" Mihardja (thus this author's name is spelled in the particular edition of the book by the publisher), *Atheis*, 10.

77. Interview, Jakarta, August 20, 1999.
78. Interview, Jakarta, July 23, 1997.
79. Interview, Jakarta, June 20, 1992.
80. Interview, Jakarta, August 16, 1995.
81. Marc Augé on Akan, West Africa, in Augé, *Non-places*, 61.
82. Like many of the things described in this book, this is not just a matter of the past: still in the early 1950s, "all areas in Jakarta in turn were having their electricity cut off every three days." The new mayor of the city "planned to decrease this to once every six days by building an electricity plant at Ancol [the outskirts of Jakarta]." Peter J. M. Nas and Manasse Malo, "View from the Top: Accounts of the Mayors and Governors of Jakarta," in Grijns and Nas, *Jakarta-Batavia*, 231.
83. Interview, Utrecht, July 6, 1998.
84. Interview, Yogyakarta, August 5, 1997.
85. Interview, Jakarta, July 14, 1997.
86. Interview, Jakarta, August 18, 1999.
87. Interview, Yogyakarta, August 3, 1997.
88. Interview, Utrecht, July 6, 1998.
89. Baudelaire, "Philosophy of Toys," 78.
90. "Paris, Capital of the Nineteenth Century, Exposé," 1939, in Benjamin, *Arcades Project*, 19–20; Adorno, "Exchange with Theodor W. Adorno on the Essay 'Paris, the Capital of the Nineteenth Century,'" in Benjamin, *Selected Writings*, 3:60.
91. Goethe's *Faust*, quoted in Nietzsche, "On the Genealogy of Morals," in *Basic Writings of Nietzsche*, 452.
92. "Paris, Capital of the Nineteenth Century, Exposé," 19–20. According to Adorno, there is a motivation in a collector to "free things from the curse of being useful." "Exchange with Theodor W. Adorno," 3:56. Benjamin speaks more carefully about the "use value" of things as receding "into the background" and into "only connoisseur value." Benjamin, "Paris, the Capital of the Nineteenth Century," 1935, in Benjamin, *Selected Writings*, 3:37, 39. For more recent thoughts about the cockpit phenomenon, see Augé: "The windows of the [Paris] apartment buildings on the third and

fourth floors are often closed and the curtains drawn, as if the happy inhabitants of these places were obliged to 'play subway' at home." Augé, *In the Metro*, 54.

93. A modern hero in one of Joseph Roth's Austrian-German novels perceives "the changes taking place in society" as "the insecurity of the old established classes and their new members, the fluidity of social values and of *the terminal perplexity of modern houses which are built with 'reception rooms.'*" Roth, *Right and Left*, 141; emphasis mine.

94. *Random House Dictionary*, 2nd edn., 1987, s.v. "salon."

95. Koolhaas, *Conversations with Students*, 20.

96. Lefebvre, *Production of Space*, 227.

97. Dickerman, *Dada*, 352, 369.

98. Here is a description of a bourgeois salon in the postcolonial Jakarta of the 1950s: "The dresser, the *zitje* [two or three chairs and a coffee table], the grandfather clock, the dining-room table, the Philips drawing-room radio and pick-up, the desks, the cabinets, the earthenware and porcelain vases from Italy and Czechoslovakia, the curtains from the textile mills of Egypt, the leather benches from Morocco, the Japanese hanging scrolls, and the Chinese embroideries." "Mrs. Veterinary Doctor Suharko," in Pramoedya, *Tales from Djakarta*, 132.

99. Aragon, *Paris Peasant*, 13.

100. Adorno, "Exchange with Theodor W. Adorno," 3:61.

101. Karl Marx, quoted in "Paris, Capital of the Nineteenth Century, Exposé," 18. Also: "The furniture, which is almost as heavy as the buildings themselves, continues to have façades; mirrored wardrobes, sideboards and chests still face out onto the sphere of private life, and so help dominate it." Lefebvre, *Production of Space*, 363.

102. Interview, Jakarta, July 17, 1997.

103. Interview, Jakarta, July 14, 1997.

104. Interview, Bandung, August 26, 1999.

105. Mihardja, *Atheis*, 66.

106. Interview, Yogyakarta, August 5, 1997.

107. Interview, Jakarta, July 30, 1996.

108. "Berlin Childhood," in Benjamin, *Selected Writings*, 3:349.

109. Interview, Surabaya, July 23, 1992.

110. Interview, Jakarta, August 18, 1993.

111. Interview, Surakarta, August 9, 1995.

112. Interview, Jakarta, November 25, 1998.

113. "Berlin Childhood," 3:349.

114. Interview, Surakarta, August 9, 1995.

115. Interview, Jakarta, August 30, 1999.

116. *Random House Dictionary*, 2nd edn., 1987, s.v. "salon," meaning 4.

117. Interview, Jakarta, December 3, 1998.

118. Interview, Jakarta, July, 19, 1995.

119. The hero of the Kafka's *The Trial*, at the opposite end of the world from the colony but "produced" very much by the same urban space, finds out in an instant from shifts of things in his house—a pincushion, a matchbox being misplaced—that the whole world is crashing around him. Kafka, *Trial*, 10.

120. Interview, Jakarta, August 24, 1999.

121. Interview, Jakarta, August 20, 1995.

122. Interview, Surakarta, August 6, 1995.

123. Interview, Bandung, August 26, 1999.

124. Interview, Jakarta, July 30, 1996.

125. "I love brief habits. . . . brief habits, too, have this faith of passion, this faith in eternity . . . deep contentment . . . without having any need for comparisons, contempt, of hatred. . . . That is what happens to me with dishes, ideas, human beings, cities, poems, music, doctrines, ways of arranging the day, and life styles . . . the passage inventories. . . . Enduring habits I hate . . . a permanent domicile, or unique good health." Friedrich Nietzsche, *The Gay Science*, quoted in Ronell, *Test Drive*, 193, 195.

126. Cornelis van Vollenhoven (1874–1933) was a Dutch lawyer and the author of the three-volume *Het adatrecht van Nederlandsch Indië* (1918–1933), the most authoritative "customary law" colonial codex for the Dutch colony. He was equally famous for being and is remembered as a highly ethically minded professor at the University of Leiden, a mentor to many Indonesian students who, during the late colonial period, managed to get as far as a European university.

127. Interview, Utrecht, July 6, 1998. Again, this was a matter of modernity, and in particular, as a child could see itself and the people around him growing into it: "And as I gazed at the long, long rows of coffee spoons and knife rests, fruit knives and oyster forks, my pleasure in this abundance was tinged with anxiety, lest the guests we had invited would turn out to be identical to one another, like our cutlery." "Berlin Childhood," 3:403–4.

128. This is a pertinent comment pointing to how uneasy the progress was: "With the replacement of Dutch rulers by educated Indonesians, Javaneese 'feudalism,' with its complicated forms of etiquette, was disowned." Siegel, *Naming the Witch*, 208.

129. Interview, Yogyakarta, August 5, 1997.

130. Ibid.

131. "Old Forgotten Children's Book," 1924, in Benjamin, *Selected Writings*, 1:409–10.

132. Ibid.

133. This is Michel de Certeau writing on the "colonized university," but it is also applicable, I believe, to other colonial walls, shelters, and discourses: "Discourse takes on the color of the walls; it is 'neutral.'" "The Historiographical Operation," in Certeau, *Writing of History*, 62.

134. Interview, Jakarta, July 14, 1997.

135. Interview, Surakarta, August 6, 1995.

Notes to Chapter Two

136. Interview, Suarabaya, July 23, 1992.
137. Notebook, summer 1997, no. 4.
138. Interview, Jakarta, July 14, 1997.
139. Interview, Surabaya, July 24, 1992.
140. Notebook, summer 1997, no. 4.
141. Interview, Utrecht, July 6, 1998.
142. Interview, Wageningen, July 4, 1998. James Rush describes such auctions at the turn of the century: "The higher the position of the departing official, the larger and more dignified the crowd and the more grandiose the bids. Because of this the auctions of departing residents were carnival affairs . . ." Rush, *Opium to Java*, 132.
143. Interview, Utrecht, July 6, 1998.
144. Interview, Jakarta, August 20, 1999.
145. *Jakarta Post*, November 15, 1998; Notebook, fall 1998, no. 3.
146. Interview, Jakarta, August 16, 1995.
147. Interview, Jakarta, June 20, 1992. This proves also that the "part played by war and armies as productive forces in their own rights" must not be underestimated; definitely not the war's and armies' role in producing space. See Lefebvre, *Production of Space*, 277.
148. Interview, Surakarta, August 6, 1995.
149. Interview, Jakarta, July 15, 1997.
150. Interview, Jakarta, August 8, 1999.
151. Interview, Jakarta, August 18, 1993.
152. Interview, Yogyakarta, August 5, 1997.
153. Brecht, *Poems, 1913–1956*, 108.
154. Interview, Jakarta, August 24, 1999.
155. "Engravings from 1830 show how the insurgents threw all sorts of furniture down on the troops out of the windows." Benjamin, *Arcades Project*, 137.
156. Interview, Yogyakarta, August 3, 1997.
157. This is from the 1942 diary of Mrs. J. J. Husseen, a former teacher at the senior high school in Semarang. "Dagboek 89a (DB 045 en 046)," in Rijksinstituut voor Oorlogdocumentatie Archief, Amsterdam.
158. Vuyk, *Kampdagboeken*, 9.
159. Ibid., 10.
160. Ibid., 75.
161. Interview, Bandung, August 26, 1999.
162. Interview, Jakarta, August 18, 1993.
163. Interview, Jakarta, August 8, 1999.
164. Interview, Jakarta, August 18, 1993.
165. Interview, Jakarta, August 24, 1999.
166. Interview, Bandung, August 26, 1999.
167. This is one of the most profound comments on "a certain age": "We live bizarrely clinging to the level of our age, often with a vast repression of what has pre-

ceded us: we almost always take ourselves for the person we are at the moment we are at in our lives." Cixous, *Three Steps on the Ladder of Writing*, 66.

168. Interview, Jakarta, July 15, 1997.

169. Interview, Jakarta, August 20, 1999.

170. Interview, Jakarta, August 8, 1999.

171. Pelt and Westfall, *Architectural Principles*, 179–80.

172. Ibid.

173. Lucien Dubech and Pierre d'Espezel, *Histoire de Paris* (1926), quoted in Benjamin, *Arcades Project*, 131.

174. Alfred Nettement, *Histoire de la Littérature Française*, 1859, quoted ibid., 224.

175. Notebook, summer 1997, no. 4.

176. Notebook, fall 1998, no. 3.

177. Interview, Jakarta, July 6, 1997.

THE FENCES

1. Interview, Jakarta, July 19, 1992.

2. Nancy, *Inoperative Community*, 48, on Homer's *muthos*. "Such speech . . . as Thales is supposed to have said. . . . [is] a way of binding the world." Ibid., 49.

3. Jakobson, *My Futurist Years*, 68. Jakobson was a member of the Prague Circle of Linguistics and he spent more than a decade in Prague managing Czech so well indeed that he was regularly asked by the best of the avant-garde Czech poets to correct their language. When he regrets not being able to write about the cries of hawkers, he might thus be also recalling the Prague Malá Strana and Staré Město streets of the 1930s.

4. Pramoedya, *Larasati*, 75–76.

5. Salmon, *Literature in Malay*, 42–43. An old songwriter and street singer, Gesang, ends his memoirs with a portrait of a fellow *tukang*, "skilled laborer or craftsman"— *tukang es*, "someone who makes ice cream," and with a note on his cries. Gesang, in fact, could easily call himself *tukang krontjong*, a "music artisan." See Moenzir, *Gesang*, 264.

6. Interview, Jakarta, August 20, 1995.

7. Interview, Jakarta, August 20, 1999.

8. A variation on this is recalled by the son of an Indonesian communist leader in exile, Alam Darsono, from his childhood in Berlin in the 1930s: "Die chinees [Chinese] . . . Neger! Nikker! [Negro, Nigger] . . . bruintje [brownie!]." Darsono, *Kinderogen*, 118–19. *Een bruine jood*, "a brown Jew," would come in Amsterdam a little later. Ibid., 108.

9. Mrázek, *Sjahrir*, 58.

10. Vuyk, *Kampdagboeken*, 11.

11. Interview, Bandung, August 21, 1993.

12. Interview, Yogyakarta, August 4, 1995.

13. It was Mr. Selo Soemardjan, in fact, who later told George McT. Kahin, an Ameri-

can scholar and a friend of his, how he used to climb over the wall of the sultan's palace in Yogyakarta during the Indonesian revolution in 1947 or 1948 — not to steal fruits this time, but to smuggle messages between the agencies of the Indonesian underground government in the city occupied by the Dutch army. George Kahin, personal communication, 1995.

14. Interview, Jakarta, July 23, 1997.
15. "Illuminations," in Rimbaud, *Complete Works*, 217.
16. Interview, Jakarta, July 23, 1997.
17. Notebook, summer 1997, no. 4.
18. RM: "Did you play with neighbors' children, even when your family might be of a higher status?"

Mrs. HARTINI: "Oh, yes, children played together."

RM: "What kind of games?"

Mrs. HARTINI: "Running around, yes, and making a lot of noise."

Interview, Jakarta, August 23, 1997.

19. Kafka, *Trial*, 34.
20. Interview, Jakarta, November 14, 1998.
21. Interview, Jakarta, July, 19, 1995.
22. The place running with springs, "the Land of Valleys and Mountains, where at any moment you can hear the sound of a *ketjapi* harp blowing in the humid wind, where at any moment you can doze off peacefully because the soil always bestows its grace upon the crops." "Ketjapi," in Pramoedya, *Tales from Djakarta*, 128. Or, further back in time: "But morning has not yet fully arrived. / The time is called the 'day's breast scarf.' / At that time the day is already up. / Sunlight strikes one's forehead, / Just a bit topping the mountains. / The bamboo roof tiles curl and shift, / People move about humming and stretching, / The ring-necked cock crows." Collins, *Guritan of Radin Suane*, second night, canto 177, 215.
23. Interview with Mrs. Damais, Jakarta, August 20, 1995.
24. Interview, Jakarta, August 8, 1999.
25. Interview, Jakarta, August 18, 1999.
26. Interview, Bandung, July 14, 1995.
27. Interview, Jakarta, August 24, 1999.
28. Interview, Jakarta, August 8, 1999.
29. Interview, Surakarta, August 8, 1996.
30. Interview, Ende, May 24, 2000.
31. Interview, Jakarta, August 8, 1999.
32. Interview, Bandung, August 21, 1993.
33. Interview, Jakarta, July 14, 1997.
34. Interview, Jakarta, August 18, 1999.
35. Interview, Jakarta, August 18, 1997.
36. Notebook, summer 1994, no. 7.

37. Interview, Jakarta, July 6, 1997.
38. Moenzir, *Gesang*, 7, 27.
39. Ibid., 15.
40. Interview, Surakarta, August 8, 1996.
41. Interview, Jakarta, July 26, 1994.
42. Suryadinata, *Prominent Indonesian Chinese*, 34–35.
43. Notebook, summer 1995, no. 5.
44. Interview, Jakarta, July 14, 1997.
45. Interview, Jakarta, July 17, 1997.
46. Interview, Kartasura, August 14, 1997. Before meeting Mr. Naryo, I had never known anybody who related himself to puppets so powerfully and movingly. Except, perhaps, Don Quixote: "As Don Quixote watches the performance and listens to [his guide's] commentary, which he interrupts from time to time, he grows more and more excited, for it is all very real to him. Finally, as a cavalcade of Moors sets out in pursuit of the 'Christian lovers' [the play is about fair Melisenda and brave Don Gaiferos], he can stand it no longer and leaping to his feet, he draws his sword and slashes the stage and puppets to bits. The audience is thrown into confusion, Master Pedro bewails the loss of his stock in trade, and the ape flees in terror." Cervantes, "Ingenious Gentleman Don Quixote," 520.
47. Interview, Jakarta, August 23, 1997.
48. Interview, Nita, May 20, 2000.
49. Interview, Jakarta, November 25, 1998.
50. Interview, Jakarta, July 15, 1997.
51. For example, "Sitting in the river at night is a Javanese mystical practice." Siegel, *Naming the Witch*, 117.
52. "There is a big destructive flood in Jakarta every five years on average, but there is some flooding every year." Marco Kusumawijaya, *Jakarta*, iv. "When the rains came, water that overflowed from higher ground spilled down into the house. And because the back wall of the house was actually part of a small hill that had been cut open, and because the side of this small hill formed a big drain, the back wall of the house automatically became a nesting-place for field-mice. And when it rained heavily, mud flowed through the holes made by these mice." "Ketjapi," in Pramoedya, *Tales from Djakarta*, 138.
53. Interview, Jakarta, July 19, 1995.
54. Interview, Yogyakarta, August 3, 1997.
55. Interview, Jakarta, August 22, 1999. Among other recollections like these see, for example, "Since he was little, Sumitro [Soemitro in old spelling] showed the courage and spirit of a rebel. In spite that he was repeatedly warned against it, he sat under a big, old and haunted *waringin* tree during the sunset. Together with his brother, he sat directly under that tree." Sumitro Djojohadikusumo, *Jejak Perlawanan*, 7.
56. Interview, Jakarta, August 24, 1999.
57. The anger of Durga, the mother of Kala, the god of time, overflows from time

to time, and then she "attacks roads and burns down markets." "Lampiran-lampiran: Murwakala," in Latif et al., *Waktu Batu*, 86.

58. Interview, Yogyakarta, August 3, 1997.
59. Duras, *Sea Wall*, 261.
60. Interview, Jakarta, August 24, 1999.
61. Interview, Jakarta, August 22, 1999.
62. Interview, Jakarta, August 27, 1999.
63. Interview, Jakarta, August 16, 1995.

64. In 1937, according to the official count, there was one bicycle for every eight residents of the colony. Abeyasekere, *Jakarta*, 91. The bicycle clearly, in the modern world, has been both early and lasting, "a machine loved for its qualities of fate." "Genie," in Rimbaud, *Complete Works*, 255.

65. Interview, Kartasura, August 14, 1997.
66. Interview, Yogyakarta, August 2, 1996.
67. Interview, Surabaya, July 24, 1992.
68. Interview, Jakarta, August 18, 1997.
69. Interview, Yogyakarta, August 3, 1997.
70. Interview, Ende, May 24, 2000.
71. Virilio, *Speed and Politics*, 38.
72. Interview, Jakarta, December 3, 1998.

73. This is something that can be fully experienced only in a tropical place—the "countless fireflies scattered on the bushes . . . like stars, as though the sky had been transplanted onto the earth." Mihardja, *Atheis*, 116.

74. Interview, Jakarta, August 22, 1999.
75. Interview, Jakarta, August 18, 1997.
76. Interview, Surakarta, August 6, 1995.
77. Augé, *Non-places*, 116.
78. Interview, Utrecht, July 6, 1998.
79. Interview, Surakarta, August 9, 1995.
80. Interview, Jakarta, June 20, 1992.

81. This, again, was a global modern romance and a universal Virilio moment—like in the case of this couple in Germany, at the same time: "They drove at 70 kilometers per hour, a speed which is recommended for such a situations by modern authors who have studied the connections between the human heart and the internal combustion engine." Roth, *Right and Left*, 205.

82. Moos, *Fernand Léger*, 61.

83. Detlef Mertins, "Mies's Skyscraper 'Project': Towards the Redemption of Technical Structure," in Mertins, *Presence of Mies*, 59.

84. Filippo Tommaso Marinetti's futurist manifesto of 1909, quoted in Moos, *Fernand Léger*, 63.

85. Interview, Jakarta, August 8, 1999.
86. Interview, Jakarta, July 24, 1997.

87. André Breton, quoted in "Marseilles," 1929, in Benjamin, *Selected Writings*, 2:232.

88. Salmon, "Batavian Eastern Railway," 60.

89. Adorno, *Minima Moralia*, 162, 139.

90. Interview, Surabaya, July 23, 1992.

91. Interview, Surakarta, August 6, 1995.

92. Interview, Jakarta, August 18, 1999.

93. Interview, Jakarta, July 25, 1997.

94. Interview, Kartasura, August 4, 1997.

95. Interview, Menado, May 28, 2000.

96. Interview, Jakarta, August 27, 1999.

97. Interview, Jakarta, August 16, 1995.

98. Interview, Utrecht, July 6, 1998.

99. Interview, Jakarta, July 24, 1997.

100. Interview, Yogyakarta, July 17, 1992.

101. This, or something very close to it, I heard often repeated—ghostly images like that, for instance: "Their hair on fire, their eyes blue" (*rambutnya terbakar dan matanya biru*). "Lampiran-lampiran: Murwakala," in Latif et al., *Waktu Batu*, 63.

102. Interview, Jakarta, August 8, 1999.

103. Interview, Jakarta, July 27, 1992.

104. Interview, Jakarta, July 19, 1995.

105. Interview, Jakarta, August 18, 1999.

106. Interview, Wageningen, July 4, 1998. See also Wertheim and Wertheim-Gijse Weenink, *Vier Wendingen*, 201: "For me," Wim Wertheim wrote, "serving on the city watch [at the time of the Japanese invasion early in 1942] was an opportunity, *for the first time in the ten years I spent in Batavia*, to see the city poor native quarters that were just next to the city center"; empasis mine.

107. Compare Friedrich Engels: "There is something distasteful about the very bustle of the streets, something that is abhorrent to human nature itself. Hundreds of thousands of people of all classes and ranks of society jostle past one another. Are they not all human beings with the same characteristics and potentials, equally interested in the pursuit of happiness? . . . And yet they rush past one another as if they had nothing in common or were in no way associated with one another. Their only agreement is a tacit one: that everyone should keep to the right of the pavement, so as not to impede the stream of the people moving in the opposite direction. No one even bothers to spare a glance for the other. The greater the number of people that are packed into a tiny space, the more repulsive and offensive becomes the brutal indifference, the unfeeling concentration of each person on his personal affairs." Engels's *The Conditions of the Working Class in England*, 1844, quoted—so others also think of Engels as relevant to Jakarta!—in "Jalan, kaki-lima, mall," in Marco Kusumawijaya. *Jakarta*, 67–68. See also Virilio: "Since the dawn of the bourgeois revolution, the political discourse has been . . . confusing social order with the control of traffic (of people, of goods)

and revolution, revolt, with traffic jams, illegal parking, multiple crashes, collisions." Virilio, *Speed and Politics*, 14.

108. Augé, *In the Metro*, 66.
109. Interview, Jakarta, August 20, 1999.
110. Interview, Jakarta, August 8, 1999.
111. Interview, Jakarta, August 18, 1999.
112. Interview, Yogyakarta, August 2, 1996.
113. Interview, Jakarta, July 25, 1997.
114. *Indos* (common name for Eurasians) and prostitution were a theme constantly talked or whispered about in the colony, and thus it is sometimes still recalled. See, for example, this recollection of the first days of the Japanese occupation of Yogyakarta by an Indonesian then living in the city: "During the first days after the Japanese arrived, the high Dutch officials were forced to work as traffic police and they wore a large piece of white cloth pinned to their sleeves as a sign of surrender. . . . Eurasian girls and young women who usually talked and thought of themselves as if they were Dutch persons, were moved to a brothel to serve the Japanese army." Soemardjan, *Biografi*, 98.
115. Interview, Jakarta, November 14, 1998.
116. Interview, Jakarta, July 19, 1995.
117. Ibid.
118. Interview, Jakarta, November 20, 1998.
119. Interview, Jakarta, August 22, 1995.
120. Notebook, summer 1997, no. 4.
121. Notebook, fall 1998, no. 3. Sometimes "the mob had worn masks and its members were therefore referred to as [the Japanese TV cartoon characters] 'Ninja'; they spoke Indonesian rather than Javanese." Siegel, *Naming the Witch*, 144. Notebook, fall 1998, no. 3: "The comments on the murders are flatly one-sided and the murders, with all the blood and other horrors, appear cartoonlike and one-dimensional. The killed are just described as 'mentally ill.' One also hears about the murders in the same vein as about the 'lynching of the ninjas.'"
122. François Guizot, 1830, quoted in Benjamin, *Arcades Project*, 141. See also Baron Haussmann's memo, dated 1864, speaking about "floating mass of workers who have come to the city, ready to leave tomorrow, of families whose members are dispersed throughout the city by their diverse places of work, of nomad renters who are incessantly moving from quarter to quarter, without knowing a fixed residence or a patrimonial place." Quoted in Jordan, *Transforming Paris*, 217.
123. Adorno, *Minima Moralia*, 25.
124. Ibid., 35–37.
125. Interview, Jakarta, July 24, 1997.
126. With all the power of the bourgeois modernity behind him, Le Corbusier built his masterpiece, the chapel of Notre Dame de la Rochelle, on a hill overlooking border-

lands between France and Germany, the site of big battles during the First World War. There, he also used "electronic music, especially composed by Olivier Messiaen for broadcasting throughout the terrain from loudspeakers mounted in an adjacent steel-framed carillon." Frampton, *Le Corbusier*, 168.

127. Interview, Surakarta, July 20, 1992.

128. Notebook, summer 1999, no. 1, and interview with Gusti Noeroel, Bandung August 26, 1999.

129. Interview, Surakarta, July 20, 1992.

130. Interview, Jakarta, August 5, 1997.

131. Rhodius and Darling, *Walter Spies*, 33.

132. Ibid., 19.

133. Ibid., 193.

134. Ibid., 21.

135. Ibid.

136. Notebook, summer 1996, no. 5.

137. Interview, Surakarta, August 8, 1996.

138. Ibid. On colonial radio broadcasts in the Dutch Indies, see also Mrázek, *Engineers of Happy Land*, 161–91.

139. Interview, Jakarta, August 22, 1995.

140. Echols, Shadily, and Wolff, *Kamus Indonesia Inggris*.

141. Interview, Jakarta, August 20, 1999.

142. Notebook, spring 2000, no. 6.

143. Ibid. *Corso* (It. "course"), originally a street in an Italian town in which races and festivals were held; a procession of carriages, or a promenade. See the *Oxford English Dictionary*, 2nd edn., 1989, s.v. "corso." *Corso* might have gotten to the Indonesian island of Flores, where we talked, and into Mr. Timu's vocabulary, I speculate, through the strong cultural Portuguese influence in the region dating back long before the Dutch appeared and lasting into the twentieth century. The clublike and feastlike new space of this modernity was grimly called by Henri Lefebvre a "space of leisure . . . as prodigal of monstrosities as of promises (that it cannot keep)." Lefebvre, *Production of Space*, 385. The new-place connection with freedom (or liberty) might also be noted: the "red-light districts" in the big cities, East or West, had often been called a "tolerant neighborhood." See Virilio, *Landscape of Events*, 4.

144. There were modern and significant connections between amusement parks built on the "empty" lots, the "spontaneous urbanism of the masses," and the progressive architecture and urbanism of the time. See, for instance, the architect Rem Koolhaas's comments on New York Coney Island's "continuing fertility as a breeding ground for revolutionary architectural prototypes." Koolhaas, *Delirious New York*, 70–71. (I would say "avant-garde" rather than "revolutionary.")

145. Interview, Surakarta, August 9, 1995.

146. Clifford Geertz in his *The Religion of Java* called *selamatan* "the core ritual."

Siegel wrote: "*selamatan*, or common feast[s] . . . are found throughout Java, but they are local in the first place because the spirits that are referred to in the rites are local in their habitat." Siegel, *Naming the Witch*, 139–40.

147. This happened in a colony and it was colonial, as, at the same time, it was modern and akin to the new kind of festivals around the globe and far beyond colonialism. The words I used in the text above to describe the colonial, in fact, are the "fest" words Avital Ronell used in writing about the mid-twentieth-century Woodstock and late nineteenth-century Bayreuth of Richard Wagner. See Ronell, *Test Drive*, 294–300.

148. Walraven, "De Clan," 702–3.

149. Interview, Jakarta, November 25, 1998.

150. Walraven, "De Clan," 703.

151. Interview, Jakarta, July 19, 1995.

152. The quote is from Benjamin, *Arcades Project*, 531.

153. Interview, Surabaya, July 24, 1992.

154. Masak, "Le cinéma indonésien," 50. A rapid expansion of this particular form came with the beginning of the Japanese occupation in 1942.

155. Interview, Jakarta, August 8, 1999.

156. Interview, Jakarta, August 20, 1995.

157. Interview, Jakarta, July, 19, 1995.

158. Interview, Jakarta, August 20, 1999.

159. One of the krontjong Gesang's lyrics quoted in Moenzir, *Gesang*, 23.

160. Dan Hoffman, "The Receding Horizon of Mies: Work of the Cranbrook Architecture Studio," in Mertins, *Presence of Mies*, 99–100.

161. Meyer Shapiro, 1936, quoted in Moos, *Fernand Léger*, 32, 33.

162. "I Run around with Them," 1949, in Chairil Anwar, *Voice of the Night*, 140–41. This, again, is planetary, and it often seems to rise to its most intense at moments of failed revolutions. See this quote from Siegfried Kracauer on Germany in the 1930s: "In the evening one saunters through the streets, replete with an unfulfilment from which a fulness could sprout. Illuminated words glide by on the rooftops, and already one is banished from one's own emptiness into the alien *advertisement*. One's body takes root in the asphalt, and together with the enlightening revelation of the illuminations, one's spirit—which is no longer one's own—roams ceaselessly out of the night and into the night." "Boredom," in Kracauer, *Mass Ornament*, 32.

163. "The Sociology of Space," in Simmel, *Simmel on Culture*, 153.

164. "The Metropolis and Mental Life," ibid., 184.

165. Ibid., my emphasis.

166. Rosalind Krauss, "The Grid, the /Cloud/, and the Detail," in Mertins, *Presence of Mies*, 134.

167. These are terms Virilio used to describe the modern and the postmodern "dissolution of the city in its own outskirts." Virilio, *Speed and Politics*, 110–11, 121.

168. Krauss, "The Grid, the /Cloud/, and the Detail," 138.

169. Frampton, *Le Corbusier*, 35.

170. Ibid., 173.

171. Lefebvre, *Production of Space*, 38.

172. Frampton, *Le Corbusier*, 35.

173. Marx's *Class Struggles in France*, 1895, quoted in Benjamin, *Arcades Project*, 123.

174. "Metropolis and Mental Life," in Simmel, *Simmel on Culture*, 178.

THE CLASSROOM

1. Interview, Jakarta, July 6, 1997.
2. Interview, Mrs. Muter, Jakarta, July 28, 1996.
3. Interview, Jakarta, November 14, 1997.
4. Interview, Bandung, August 26, 1999.
5. Interview, Jakarta, August 24, 1999.
6. Interview, Jakarta, August 19, 1997.
7. Interview, Jakarta, July 14, 1997.
8. Interview, Jakarta, July 21, 1995.
9. Interview, Jakarta, November 20, 1997. It is almost always correct to connect the school adventure with ambition, and often hardship is the signal word: "Why was the mortality rate in London so much higher in the new working-class districts than in the slums? — Because people went hungry so that they could afford the high rents." Friedrich Engels, 1872, quoted in Benjamin, *Arcades Project*, 145.
10. Soesilo, *Perjalanan Hidup*, 16. This, too, goes beyond the colonial period. "The local government . . . made elementary schooling in Jakarta free of charge in 1957. This lasted only one year, after which the state decided to rescind the decision." Peter J. M. Nas and Manasse Malo, "View from the Top," in Grijns and Nas, *Jakarta-Batavia*, 233.
11. Interview, Surakarta, August 9, 1995.
12. Interview, Jakarta, August 30, 1999.
13. Interview, Blitar, August 13, 1997.
14. Interview, Jakarta, July 28, 1992.
15. Interview, Yogyakarta, August 3, 1997.
16. Interview, Menado, May 27, 2000.
17. Ibid.
18. Interview, Surakarta, July 20, 1992.
19. Interview, Jakarta, July 17, 1997.
20. Interview, Jakarta, August 18, 1997.
21. Avital Ronell writes about the "experience of enlightenment [as] triumphal narratives of self-gathering, or . . . the bloated accomplishments of successive sieges of alien territory." Ronell, *Test Drive*, 121. There was a large expanse of really strange land to be experienced along the road to school. A study of city-employed coolies in Batavia-Jakarta in 1937, for instance, has shown that "the best housing [the workers] could afford was generally a *pondok* [shack] with an earthen floor, a privy shared by

ten to thirty families, and drainage through open sewers. A *kampung* [urban quarters] study of Batavia in the same period found that most Indonesians were living in impermanent dwellings of the *petak* (one-room apartments giving onto a shared verandah) or *pondok* types." As for the infant mortality among Indonesians [in Batavia-Jakarta] in 1935–1936, "30 per cent of Indonesian and 15 per cent of Chinese [Indonesian] infants were estimated to have died (compared with less than 6 per cent for Europeans), which gave Batavia a worse record than any other Asian city except Hong Kong." Abeyasekere, *Jakarta*, 94. During the same period, "leaving subsistence farming aside, in 1939, assessed per-capita income in the European community in Indonesia was more than one hundred times that in the Indonesian community." Kahin, *Nationalism and Revolution in Indonesia*, 36.

22. Interview, Jakarta, August 30, 1999.
23. Interview, Jakarta, August 20, 1995.
24. Benjamin at the same time wrote about the German students' shelters and stopovers on their way to education: "All these institutions are nothing but a marketplace for the preliminary and provisional." "The Life of Students," 1914–1915, in Benjamin, *Selected Writings*, 1:46.
25. Interview, Jakarta, August 30, 1999.
26. Interview, Jakarta, November 23, 1998.
27. Interview, Jakarta, August 20, 1999.
28. Interview, Menado, May 28, 2000.
29. Interview, Jakarta, August 20, 1999.
30. Interview, Jakarta, August 22, 1999.
31. Interview, Surabaya, July 24, 1992.
32. Interview, Utrecht, July 6, 1998.
33. Interview, Jakarta, July 25, 1997.
34. Interview, Jakarta, July 25, 1997.
35. Interview, Jakarta, July 23, 1997.
36. Interview, Jakarta, July 19, 1995.
37. Ibid.
38. Interview, Jakarta, August 16, 1995.
39. Interview, Jakarta, August 17, 1997.
40. Interview, Jakarta, July 19, 1995.
41. Interview, Jakarta, August 18, 1993.
42. Interview, Jakarta, August 23, 1997.
43. "In larger places the railway stations were the most memorable buildings, made of robust stone, grandly conceived and in often a rich mixture of styles, most frequently neo-classic, neo-gothic, and neo-renaissance with application of Indonesian ornaments of all kinds.... [They were] comparable to the early neo-classical stations in the Netherlands, namely in Haarlem and Amsterdam-Willemspoort dating from 1841–1842.... The larger [colonial] stations were most ostentatious, with luxurious first- and second-class waiting-rooms. They were to recall the Dutch villa- and chalet-

styles with Indies overtones.... The stations, like in Ambarawa, Djati and Poerwasari [all on Java] had a large and very-high-arching iron construction reminiscent of the platform of Haarlem, Hengelo and The Hague." Ballegoijen, *Spoorwegstations op Java*, 22, 28.

44. Interview, Yogyakarta, August 5, 1997.
45. Interview, Jakarta, July 21, 1995.
46. Interview, Jakarta, December 3, 1998.
47. Interview, Jakarta, August 30, 1999.
48. Roeslan Abdulgani, interview, Jakarta, July 24, 1997.
49. Interview, Jakarta, June 3, 2000.
50. A note by Walter Kaufmann to Nietzsche's "Ecce Homo," in *Basic Writings of Nietzsche*, 732n2.
51. Interview, Jakarta, July 14, 1997.
52. Interview, Jakarta, July 25, 1997.
53. Interview, Jakarta, July 26, 1994.
54. Interview, Jakarta, July 19, 1995.
55. Interview, Jakarta, August 18, 1999.
56. Interview, Jakarta, July 23, 1997.
57. Interview, Surakarta, August 8, 1996.
58. Interview, Jakarta, August 19, 1997.
59. Interview, Jakarta, August 30, 1999.
60. Interview, Jakarta, August 16, 1995.
61. Georges Demenÿ's *L'évolution de l'éducation physique* (1889), was the most respected text on modern (and patriotic) sports long into the twentieth century. It suggested a "body in motion, harmonious and curved," and laid all the emphasis on "movement and élan." Quoted in Dagognet, *Étienne-Jules Marey*, 168–73.
62. Interview, Bandung, July 14, 1995.
63. Interview, Jakarta, July 25, 1997.
64. Interview, Jakarta, August 18, 1993.
65. Ronell, *Test Drive*, 324.
66. "Letter to Gershom Scholem on Franz Kafka," 1938, in Benjamin, *Selected Writings*, 3:326.
67. Kracauer, *Mass Ornament*, 85.
68. Interview, Jakarta, August 30, 1999.
69. Interview, Jakarta, July 19, 1997.
70. Interview, Jakarta, December 1, 1998.
71. Interview, Jakarta, July 21, 1995.
72. Interview, Jakarta, August 20, 1999.
73. Interview, Jakarta, July 8, 1999.
74. "Ecce Homo," 1888, in Nietzsche, *Basic Writings*, 689.
75. Interview, Jakarta, July 30, 1996.
76. Interview, Jakarta, November 25, 1998.

77. Interview, Jakarta, August 19, 1997.
78. Interview, Surabaya, July 23, 1992.
79. Interview, Jakarta, July 14, 1997.
80. Interview, Jakarta, August 30, 1999.
81. Ibid.
82. Interview, Jakarta, July 30, 1996.
83. Interview, Surabaya, July 24, 1992.
84. Interview, Bandung, August 21, 1993.
85. Interview, Jakarta, August 8, 1999.
86. Interview, Ende, May 24, 2000.
87. Interview, Jakarta, July 14, 1997.
88. Interview, Jakarta, August 16, 1995.
89. Interview, Sikka, May 22, 2000.
90. Interview, Jakarta, July 30, 1996.
91. Interview, Jakarta, July 19, 1995.
92. Interview, Jakarta, July 14, 1997.
93. Interview, Jakarta, August 30, 1999.
94. Interview, Jakarta, July 19, 1995.
95. Interview, Jakarta, July 21, 1995.
96. Interview, Utrecht, July 6, 1998.
97. Interview, Yogyakarta, August 3, 1997.
98. This is related to the road, to school and to the correct way of walking in more than one way. See, for instance, "The problem of shoes had been posed to civilian industry by the mass armies before that of cars." Virilio, *Speed and Politics*, 28.
99. Interview, Jakarta, July 24, 1997.
100. Interview, Jakarta, July 6, 1997.
101. Interview, Jakarta, August 30, 1999.
102. Interview, Jakarta, July 19, 1995.
103. Interview, Bandung, August 21, 1993.
104. Interview, Jakarta, July 25, 1997.
105. Thinking of the power the costumes have over an urban person, I am reminded of Rilke: "It was then that I first learned to know the influence that can emanate directly from a particular costume itself. Hardly had I donned one of these suits, when I had to admit that it got me in its power; that it prescribed my movements, my facial expression, yes, even my ideas. . . . now mirror was the stronger, and I was the mirror." Rilke, *Notebooks of Malte Laurids Brigge*, 91–92, 95.
106. Lefebvre, *Production of Space*, 53. Lefebvre writes: "When an institution loses its birthplace, its original space, and feels threatened, it tends to describe itself as 'organic.'" Ibid., 274. Brecht, I think, pointed out the same thing: "The People" has "no wish to be Folk." Quotation from John Willett's introduction to Brecht, *Poems, 1913–1956*, xiv–xv. A high-level culture official of the postcolonial Indonesian state is

quoted by Philip Yampolsky as expressing a happy-engineering view that seems still well alive: "Tradition is something that is broken and has to be fixed before it can be used." Yampolsky, "Forces for Change," 711n. In Clifford Geertz's words, also referring to Indonesia: "Peoples . . . 'archaic,' 'tribal,' 'simple,' 'subject,' 'folk,' or 'primitive' became, quite suddenly, 'emergent.'" Geertz, *After the Fact*, 138.

107. Interview, Jakarta, July 26, 1994.
108. Interview, Jakarta, July 23, 1997.
109. Interview, Jakarta, July 28, 1996.
110. Interview, Jakarta, August 24, 1999.
111. Interview, Jakarta, July 19, 1995. There is a variation on the theme in a short story from the late colonial Batavia-Jakarta. Two teenage Eurasian siblings, a houseboy and a maid, are plotting to climb the ladder and get into the better and "truly white" part of society—she as a prostitute, he as a gigolo: "'But your skin is so blotchy and pocked from scabies. You wouldn't be embarrassed, *kak?*' asked his little sister. Sobi giggled. 'When someone becomes Dutch,' he said, full of self-confidence, 'those scars and blotches disappear automatically! When did you ever see a Dutch person with blotches? Only Indonesians get scabies. People like us, Nah.'" "Houseboy + Maid," in Pramoedya, *Tales from Djakarta*, 22.
112. "The pedagogy of Enlightenment stages stupidity, repeatedly casting brutality, prejudice, superstition, and violence as so many manifestations of the eclipse of reason." Ronell, *Stupidity*, 44.
113. Interview, Jakarta, August 18, 1993.
114. "In Kafka's world the Furies descend before instead of after the deed. They even drive the criminal to the crime, to 'catch-up with his own retribution.' . . . Kafka declared: 'it is an essential part of the justice dispensed here that you should be condemned not only in innocence but also in ignorance.'" Pelt and Westfall. *Architectural Principles*, 372.
115. Interview, Jakarta, July 23 1997.
116. Interview, Yogyakarta, August 5, 1997.
117. Interview, Jakarta, December 3, 1998.
118. Interview, Jakarta, August 24, 1999.
119. Interview, Jakarta, July 19, 1997.
120. Interview, Jakarta, August 30, 1999.
121. Interview, Yogyakarta, August 5, 1997.
122. Interview, Yogyakarta, July 19, 1992.
123. "On the Genealogy of Morals," 1887, in Nietzsche, *Basic Writings of Nietzsche*, 522. Jean-François Lyotard speaks of "'absolute wrong' done to the one who is exploited and who does not even have the language to express the wrong done to him." Quoted in Nancy, *Inoperative Community*, 35–36.
124. Interview, Utrecht, July 6, 1998.
125. Soesilo, *Perjalanan Hidup*, 14–15.

126. Interview, Jakarta, August 30, 1999.

127. Interview, Jakarta, December 3, 1998.

128. Interview, Menado, May 27, 1997.

129. "Epistemic interruptions" may be another term for this; see Ronell, *Test Drive*, 81.

130. Interview, Jakarta, August 30, 1999.

131. Kurt Gödel, 1931, quoted in Ronell, *Test Drive*, 57.

132. Interview, Jakarta, July 30, 1996. Again, this is what one can hear often: one was (or was not) born on a correct date. See, for example, Soesilo, *Perjalanan Hidup*, 13–14.

133. Interview, Jakarta, November 23, 1998.

134. Interview, Jakarta, July 14, 1997.

135. Interview, Jakarta, July 30, 1996.

136. Interview, Jakarta, June 3, 2000.

137. One can point again to a German equivalent of it, the *Amtsprache*, officialese. Adolf Eichmann, to mention a beyond-the-pale case, admitted during his trial in Jerusalem that *Amtsprache* had actually become his only language. See Arendt, *Eichmann and the Holocaust*, 19.

138. This may compare with an earlier European situation, of German versus Latin: "Leibniz encourages philosophers to abandon late-born languages that flow out of classical Latin and immerse themselves in those languages, like German, which are awash in 'realities (*realibus*).'" Fenves, *Arresting Language*, 27.

139. In early Malay literature, into the mid-twentieth century, translations from European languages and especially from Dutch were very often not signaled as translations at all. They seemed to be understood as appropriations of something that was still missing for the country to become real and wholesome. If a Malay equivalent could not be easily found, a word or whole phrase would simply be left as it was (real and wholesome?) in the Dutch original.

140. There were other languages in the colony, as ready-mades for the same kind of service, to back up where Dutch (or Malay) might still encounter a problem—there was being developed and taught service Javanese, service Balinese, service Minangkabau, service Sundanese, and so forth. These service languages were more local, less all-colonial and all-Indonesian, more "awash in realities," and also potentially more nostalgic and thus, from the point of view of the colony as a whole and real, not so strongly perspectival (and less dependable).

141. Interview, Yogyakarta, August 3, 1997.

142. Interview, Jakarta, August 20, 1999.

143. Interview, Jakarta, November 14, 1998.

144. Interview, Sikka, May 22, 2000.

145. Interview, Surakarta, August 8, 1996.

146. Balai Pustaka still exists as *the* government publishing house in Indonesia today.

147. Dédé Oetomo, "The Chinese of Indonesia and the Development of the Indonesian Language," in Wolff, *Role of Modern Indonesian Chinese*, 56.

148. I have been repeatedly amazed at how little the people in Anglo-Saxon countries know about the German writer Karl May (1842–1912). May's stories of the "Red Indians" accompanied my childhood as much as that of German, Dutch, and, as I found out, very much also Indonesian children. Winnetou, the Apache chief, and his white brother Old Shatterhand, were the greatest of my, as well as the old Indonesians' and my interviewees', early heroes.

149. Interview, Surabaya, July 23, 1992.

150. Oetomo, "Chinese of Indonesia," 64; also Leonard Blussé, "The Role of Indonesian Chinese in Shaping Modern Indonesian Life: A Conference in Retrospect," in Wolff, *Role of Modern Indonesian Chinese*, 10.

151. Interview, Ende, May 24, 2000.

152. Ronell, *Test Drive*, 183, on computing tests.

153. Foucault called something like this a "fiction of a universal geometry." Foucault, "Nietzsche, Genealogy, History," 158.

154. Interview, Jakarta, July 14, 1997.

155. Interview, Jakarta, July 21, 1995.

156. Interview, Jakarta, June 3, 2000.

157. Interview, Jakarta, August 19, 1997.

158. Interview, Blitar, August 13, 1997.

159. Interview, Menado, May 27, 2000.

160. Interview, Jakarta, July 16, 1992.

161. Interview, Yogyakarta, August 5, 1997.

162. Interview, Jakarta, August 18, 1999.

163. Interview, Yogyakarta, August 3, 1997.

164. The last colonial edition of the songbook, as far as I know, was Stassen et al., *Kun je nog zingen, zing dan mee!*, in 1939.

165. Interview, Bandung, July 14, 1995.

166. Interview, Jakarta, August 20, 1995.

167. Interview, Menado, May 27, 2000.

168. Interview, Menado, May 29, 2000.

169. Interview, Jakarta, December 3, 1998.

170. Ibid.

171. Quoted in Jay, *Downcast Eyes*, 324.

172. "The Hotel Lobby," in Kracauer, *Mass Ornament*, 175–77.

173. Interview, Bandung, July 14, 1995.

174. On Sartre's and Lacan's working with and around Rimbaud's "I is the other," see Jay, *Downcast Eyes*, 347.

175. Interview, Surakarta, August 6, 1995.

176. Interview, Kartasura, August 14, 1997.

177. Interview, Jakarta, August 20, 1999.

178. Interview, Surabaya, July 23, 1992.

179. Ronell, *Test Drive*, 5. "Thus an elliptical circuit has been established between testing and the real: a circuit as radically installed—it is irreversible—cancels the essential difference between test and what was assumed to be real." Ibid., 163–64.

180. Kracauer, *Salaried Masses*, 34, 35.

181. Ronell, *Test Drive*, 166.

182. The *residency* was the next largest administrative unit in the Dutch East Indies below the *province*.

183. Interview, Jakarta, August 20, 1995. Kracauer calls enlightened capitalism "the certification system." See Kracauer, *Salaried Masses*, 34.

184. "It is fair to say that there are no results, just an interminable trial, a series of deferrals." Ronell, *Test Drive*, 13, on Kafka's "Before the Law." Benjamin calls this a "bourgeois education": "Proletarian education needs first and foremost a framework, an objective space *within* which education can be located. The bourgeoisie, in contrast, requires an idea *toward* which education leads." "Program for a Proletarian Children's Theater," 1929, in Benjamin, *Selected Writings*, 2:202.

185. Interview, Blitar, August 13, 1997.

186. Interview, Jakarta, August 22, 1999.

187. Kusno Abidin, referring to James Scott's *Seeing Like a State*, wrote about the making of the Dutch colony into a pedagogical space: "By the 1930s, the urban space had become a pedagogical apparatus or a heuristic device, which, through its organization of space, attempted to create an obedient 'public.'" Abidin Kusno, "Significance of Appearance," 7–8.

188. Interview, Jakarta, July 14, 1997.

189. Interview, Jakarta, July 21, 1995.

190. Interview, Jakarta, August 13, 1997.

191. Interview, Jakarta, July 30, 1996.

192. Interview, Surabaya, July 23, 1992.

193. Interview, Jakarta, July 15, 1997.

194. Interview, Jakarta, July 24, 1997.

195. This was a meeting in Jakarta where young Indonesians promised to give their lives for "One Nation, One Motherland, One Language" — according to the dominant view, the high point of the modern Indonesian nationalist movement in the late colonial era.

196. Interview, Maumere, May 22, 2000.

197. Interview, Bandung, August 21, 1993. See also: "Sukarno was a talented student. His works were displayed in the aula of the Technical College. If only he would not waste so much time of his student days on politics! This is what we heard from our teachers who had known him well." Manusama, *Eigenlijk moest ik niet veel hebben van de politiek*, 33.

198. Interview, Yogyakarta, July 17, 1992.

199. Interview, Jakarta, July 26, 1994. See similarly: "I remember that in the first grade of the HBS senior high I began to read a book by R. A. Kartini in Dutch . . . I got the book from a Dutch who knew my father." Indraningsih Wibowo, in *Jembatan Antar-Generasi*, 190.

200. Interview, Jakarta, August 23, 1997.

201. Interview, Jakarta, August 30, 1999.

202. See Tsuchiya Kenji, *Democracy and Leadership*.

203. Interview, Yogyakarta, August 5, 1997.

204. Ibid.

205. Interview, Jakarta, July 7, 1992.

206. Eduard Douwes Dekker, pen name Multatuli, published his immensely influential *Max Havelaar, of de koffij-veilingen der Nederlandsche Handel-Maatschappij* (Max Havelaar: Or the Coffee Auctions of the Dutch Trading Company) in 1860. It was a Dutch liberal critique of the "unnecessary crudeness" of some nineteenth-century colonial practices. Like the letters by Kartini, Multatuli became required reading in the colonial schools of the 1930s.

207. What Mrs. Lasmidjah Hardi most probably meant was Mohammad Hatta's defense speech from his trial in 1927, a speech instantly published and then republished many times as "Indonesië vrij," "Free Indonesia." For the last complete edition see Hatta, *Verspreide Geschriften*, 210–308.

208. Interview, Jakarta, August 22, 1995.

209. Interview, Yogyakarta, August 5, 1997.

210. Interview, Jakarta, June 20, 1992.

211. This is the title of the chapter on Dapitan, the place of José Rizal's exile, in Anderson, *Under Three Flags*, 138.

212. Much has been written, of course, "on the play of the penal and pedagogical meaning of 'discipline.'" Geertz, *After the Fact*, 182n. And sure, Geertz (with not too hearty an approval) quotes in this passage first of all Foucault's *Discipline and Punish*.

213. Interview, Jakarta, December 1, 1998.

214. View of the Indonesian radicals in Shiraishi, *Age in Motion*, 314.

215. Marco Kartodikromo, *Pergaulan orang buangan di Boven-Digoel*, 30–35.

216. Nancy, *Sense of the World*, 24, 148.

217. Interview, Jakarta, December 1, 1998; also interview with Mrs. Sukarsih, Jakarta, July 20, 1992.

218. Interview, Jakarta, December 1, 1998. This is an important legend told often and with a different number of boxes.

219. There were private schools, organized by the internees themselves, schools for the children of the internees, for the adult internees, as well as thematic lecture series and specialized courses. Among the Boven Digoel surviving papers, under no. 314, for instance, there is a letter by the internee Marsoedi, dated May 5, 1932, informing the camp authorities that a "school of journalism is to be opened"; under no. 315, in the

archives, there is another letter by an internee, one of quite a number of letters of the kind, this one asking the authorities for permission to begin with "Dutch language courses." Boven-Digoel Archief, Indonesian National Archives, Jakarta.

220. Interview, Jakarta, November 16, 1997.

221. Writing about Nietzsche, Ronell notes: "He sensed the test sites would make the wasteland grow and foresaw the concentration camp as the most unrestricted experimental laboratory in modern history, a part of the will to scientific knowledge." Ronell, *Test Drive*, 6–7, 327n.

222. Hannah Arendt, and before her Franz Neumann's *Behemoth* (1944), quoted in Heilbut, *Exiled in Paradise*, 413–14.

223. Ronell, *Stupidity*, 188. As for the death camps: "Of poverty, hunger, deportation, torture, deprivation, ugliness, horror: 'Such are the sacrificed bodies, but sacrificed to nothing.'" Jean-Luc Nancy, quoted in Ronell, *Stupidity*, 189.

224. Ibid., 200.

225. Augé, *Non-places*, 34.

226. Virilio, *Speed and Politics*, 29.

227. Ibid., 77.

228. Koolhaas, *Delirious New York*, 45; Koolhaas also speaks of New York's Coney Island and of Manhattan as the Dreamlands of the modern and the postmodern.

229. Architects "had a unique responsibility in the creation and the perfection of the camps and the death camps as well; professional architects designed the camps, the barracks and the crematoria. . . . not only were the men who designed Auschwitz fully qualified architects, but at least one of them, Fritz Ertl, was even a Bauhaus graduate." Pelt and Westfall, *Architectural Principles*, 120.

THE WINDOW

1. Interview, Jakarta, July 17, 1997.
2. Interview, Jakarta, July 23, 1997.
3. Interview, Jakarta, August 27, 1999.

4. A colony—also in this—might be ahead of the West, namely, in that there in principle and in building up a modern society soon and robustly, the "visual medium has been prints rather than drawing or painting," and that there "prints have been far more influential as a vehicle for the transmission of information." "The Artist," in Fryberger, *Changing Garden*, 2.

5. Notebook, summer 2000, no. 6. It was "Van Gogh, who declared that 'duty is something absolute'; who admitted 'no acclaim could please me more than to have *ordinary working people* wanting to hang my lithographs in their rooms or their workshops.'" Tarkovsky, *Sculpting in Time*, 182.

6. Virilio, *Landscape of Events*, 24. The Indonesian writer so frequently cited already, Pramoedya Ananta Toer, here again conveys a sharp sense of a (post)colonial Indonesian house, in this case with a newspaper as the *punctum*: "When he was home

he always did the same thing; read the newspaper and nothing but the newspaper. Before he finished reading it no one else was allowed to touch it." "The Mastermind," in Pramoedya, *Tales from Djakarta*, 122.

7. Interview, Jakarta, July 24, 1997.

8. Interview, Menado, May 29, 2000.

9. Notebook, summer 2000, no. 6.

10. Interview, Jakarta, July 24, 1997.

11. Interview, Jakarta, August 22, 1999.

12. Interview, Jakarta, August 18, 1993.

13. Benjamin, *Arcades Project*, 10–14.

14. Dossier 88/71, Het Tropenmuseum, Amsterdam; also in Koos van Brakel, "'Immers,' Indië is nu eenmaal geen Land van Kunst," in Brakel et al., *Indië omlijst*, 113.

15. The painter Basuki Resobowo, quoted in McIntyre, "Sukarno as Artist-Politician," 166–67. There is a broad social implication of it: for example, "On August 20, 1979, an exhibition of paintings (among other artifacts) from the Sukarno Collection was opened in [Jakarta]. In 15 days it was visited by 147,713 visitors." Labrousse, "Le deuxième vie de Bung Karno," 189.

16. Theodor Adorno, in "Exchange with Theodor W. Adorno on the Essay 'Paris, the Capital of the Nineteenth Century,'" in Benjamin, *Selected Writings*, 3:61. See also: "The interior is the asylum of art. The collector is the true resident of the interior." Benjamin, "Paris, the Capital of the Nineteenth Century," 1935, in Benjamin, *Selected Writings*, 3:39.

17. Interview, Utrecht, July 6, 1998.

18. Interview, Jakarta, July 24, 1997.

19. Kafka, *Trial*, 199. See also Pierre Bourdieu's comment, quoted in Le Goff, *History and Memory*: "The family album expresses the truth of social remembrance. Nothing is less like the artistic search for lost time than the showing of these family pictures, accompanied by commentaries—an initiation rite families impose on all their new members. . . . there is nothing more decent, more reassuring, or more edifying than a family album: all the particular adventures that enclose individual remembrance in the particularity of a secret are excluded from it, and the common past, or if one prefers, the lowest common denominator of the past, has the almost coquettish neatness of a frequently visited funeral monument" (89).

20. Interview, Menado, May 27, 2000.

21. On history representing "society as a collection and recollection of its entire developments," see "The Historiographical Operation," in Certeau, *Writing of History*, 83.

22. Interview, Surakarta, August 9, 1995.

23. Interview, Jakarta, July 24, 1997.

24. A letter by G. B. Shaw and Shaw's *Heartbreak House* quoted in Winter, *Sites of Memory, Sites of Mourning*, 193.

25. Ibid.

26. "There is an abundant literature whose stylistic character forms an exact counterpart to the diorama, panorama, and so forth. I refer to the feuilletonistic miscellanies and series of sketches from mid-century.... To the plastically worked, more or less detailed foreground of the diorama corresponds the sharply profiled feuilletonistic gesturing of the social study ... [in] panopticon: not only does one see everything, but one sees it in all ways." Benjamin, *Arcades Project*, 531.

27. "The heightened expression of the dull perspective is what you get in panoramas." Ibid., 124.

28. Interview, Surakarta, August 9, 1995.

29. "An old expression for journalese, *Schablonstil* [cliché style], comes to mind here; it might be worth tracing its origin." Adorno, in "Exchange with Theodor W. Adorno on the Essay 'Paris, the Capital of the Nineteenth Century,'" 3:58.

30. This is from the archives of the Royal Tropical Institute in Amsterdam, Album 502/16A, and also Brakel, "'Immers,'" 103.

31. Aragon, *Paris Peasant*, 177.

32. Le Corbusier, *Towards a New Architecture*, 4.

33. Dickerman, *Dada*, 160.

34. Benjamin, *Arcades Project*, 532. This reflects Leibniz's "monads and ideas: windowless and untouchable." Quoted in Fenves, *Arresting Language*, 11.

35. Benjamin, *Arcades Project*, 538.

36. Ibid., 539.

37. Ibid.

38. Dickerman, *Dada*, 281. "The painter's own body, whose restoration we will see demanded by Merleu-Ponty and other(s) ... was effectively banished [as a consequence of] the differentiation of the idealized gaze from the corporeal glance and the monocular spectator from the scene he observed on the other side of the window." Jay, *Downcast Eyes*, 55–57.

39. See George Baird, "Looking for 'The Public' in Mies van der Rohe's Concept for the Toronto Dominion Centre," in Mertins, *Presence of Mies*, 160.

40. Interview, Jakarta, August 16, 1995.

41. Interview, Jakarta, August 18, 1997.

42. Interview, Yogyakarta, July 19, 1992.

43. "Cult of Distraction," in Kracauer, *Mass Ornament*, 326.

44. Interview, Jakarta, July 24, 1997.

45. Interview, Jakarta, August 24, 1999.

46. Interview, Suarabaya, July 23, 1992.

47. Interview, Yogyakarta, July 19, 1992.

48. Interview, Jakarta, August 16, 1995.

49. Interview, Bandung, July 14, 1995.

50. Interview, Jakarta, July 17, 1997.

51. Interview, Jakarta, August 21, 1999.

52. Interview, Jakarta, August 8, 1999.

53. Peter D. Fenves referring to Goethe's *Der Groß-Cophta*, 1791, in Fenves, *Arresting Language*, 307n9.

54. Interview, Jakarta, August 27, 1999.

55. Interview, Jakarta, July 24, 1997.

56. Interview, Sikka, May 22, 2000.

57. "Illuminations," in Rimbaud, *Complete Works*, 219.

58. Interview, Jakarta, August 24, 1999. "From the plane there is no pleasure, but a concentrated, mournful meditation." Le Corbusier. *Aircraft*, 123. Similarly, "in most high-rise buildings the lower parts are full of the enormous inheritance of everything that comes from above. In this building, the construction system allowed the bottom to have the same freedom found at the top." Koolhaas, *Conversations with Students*, 28.

59. Breton, *Manifestoes of Surrealism*, 21.

60. "Describing *The Human Condition* painting, Magritte wrote: 'I placed in front of the window, seen from inside a room, a painting representing exactly that part of the landscape which was hidden from view by the painting. Therefore, the tree represented the real tree situated behind it, outside the room. It existed for the spectator, as it were, simultaneously in his mind, as both inside the room in the painting, and outside in the real landscape." Quoted in Jay, *Downcast Eyes*, 245–46n131.

61. Interview, Jakarta, June 20, 1992.

62. Exhibitions best express this working of the window. "They are a school [school indeed!] in which the masses, forcibly excluded from consumption, are imbued with the exchange value of commodities to the point of identifying with it: 'Do not touch the items on display.'" Walter Benjamin "Paris, Capital of the Nineteenth Century, Exposé," 1939, in Benjamin, *Arcades Project*, 18.

63. Fritz Neumeyer, "A World in Itself: Architecture and Technology," in Mertins, *Presence of Mies*, 81.

64. Ibid., 82.

65. Mies van der Rohe, quoted ibid., 82.

66. Beatriz Colomina, "Mies Not," in Mertins, *Presence of Mies*, 214.

67. Ibid., 217.

68. Frampton, *Le Corbusier*, 213, 37.

69. "The Turning," in Heidegger, *Question Concerning Technology*, 46–47.

70. Krauss, *Originality of the Avant-Garde*, 191.

71. Koolhaas, *Conversations with Students*, 24.

72. Dagognet, *Étienne-Jules Marey*, 41. "The frame of structure, its self-contained boundary, has a very similar significance for the social group as for a work of art. It performs two functions for the latter, which are really only two sides of a single function: closing the work of art off against the surrounding world and holding it together. The frame proclaims that a world is located inside of it which is subject only to its own laws, not drawn into the determinations and changes of the surrounding world. In so far as it symbolizes the self-contented unity of the work of art, the frame at the same

time strengthens its reality and its impression." "The Sociology of Space," in Simmel, *Simmel on Culture*, 141.

73. Virilio, *Landscape of Events*, 38.

74. "The words of Guy Debord . . . that the *Big Night so long awaited* has arrived, if only because our perception of the world has imploded." Quoted ibid., 7.

75. Anderson, *Under Three Flags*, 14.

76. Brakel, "'Immers,'" 122.

77. The photograph is ibid., 126.

78. Antoine-Joseph Wiertz, 1870, quoted in Benjamin, *Arcades Project*, 529. "Panoramas [were] originally designed to be viewed from the center of a rotunda. They were introduced in France in 1799 by the American engineer Robert Fulton." "Paris, the Capital of the Nineteenth Century," 1935, 3:45n11.

79. Wittgenstein, *Remarks on Colour*, sec. III § 70, 26.

80. Pierre Naville, 1925, quoted in Krauss, *Originality of the Avant-Garde*, 99.

81. "*L'Arrivée d'un train en Gare de La Ciotat*. . . . As the train approached panic started in the theatre: people junmped up and ran away. That was the moment when cinema was born. . . . But immediately afterwards cinema turned aside from art, forced down the path that was safest from the point of view of philistine interest and profit. In the course of the following two decades almost the whole of world literature was screened, together with a huge number of theatrical plots. . . . Film took a wrong turn." Tarkovsky, *Sculpting in Time*, 62–63.

82. "Cinema is capable of operating with any fact diffused in time." Ibid., 65.

83. Ibid., 66.

84. Ibid., 73. Throughout, filmmakers like Tarkovsky tried to make their films "to continue beyond the edges of the screen." Ibid., 114, 118. This is how Tarkovsky put it: "I resist structuralist attempts to look at a frame as sign of something else, the meaning of which is summed up in the shot." Ibid., 177.

85. Proust, *In Search of Lost Time*, 785.

86. "Modern architects', like Mies van der Rohe's, 'universal spaces' articulate no function whatever. They are space frames within which anything might be accommodated." Krauss, *Originality of the Avant-Garde*, 236.

87. Interview, Jakarta, July 25, 1997.

88. Interview, Yogyakarta, August 3, 1997.

89. Interview, Surakarta, August 8, 1996.

90. Interview, Jakarta, July 21, 1995.

91. Dagognet, *Étienne-Jules Marey*, 12.

92. Interview, Bandung, August 21, 1993.

93. Interview, Yogyakarta, July 18, 1992.

94. Interview, Jakarta, July 19, 1995.

95. Jean-Louis Baudry, 1970, quoted in Jay, *Downcast Eyes*, 475.

96. Jean Goudal, 1925, quoted ibid., 255.

97. Roland Barthes, "Leaving the Movie Theater" (from his *Rustle of Language*), quoted ibid., 457.

98. Interview, Jakarta, November 25, 1998.

99. Interview, Jakarta, July 24, 1997.

100. Interview, Utrecht, July 6, 1998.

101. This is a tradition reaching as far back as the sixteenth century and since—like modernity (of Europe and beyond)—powerfully expanding. See, for instance: "From the late sixteenth century a large number of foreign travelers visited Italy on the Grand Tour, and the major gardens inevitably were included on their itinerary of sites to see." Claudia Lazzaro, "Representing the Social and Cultural Experiences of Italian Gardens in Prints," in Fryberger, *Changing Garden*, 32.

102. "Berlin Childhood," 1934, in Benjamin, *Selected Writings*, 3:34.

103. Geertz, *After the Fact*, 3.

104. There is a power in "pedestal," and there is a recurring resistance to it. Some sculptors felt that "like a picture frame, the pedestal closes off the virtual field of representation from the actual space around it." Krauss, *Originality of the Avant-Garde*, 74. Some other artists even "expanded sculpture by taking the object off the pedestal." Neal Benezra, "Sculpture and Paradox," in Benezra et al., *Juan Muñoz*, 35.

105. Interview, Jakarta, July 25, 1997.

106. Ibid.

107. Karl Marx, *The Civil War in France*, 1871, quoted in Jordan, *Transforming Paris*, 345.

108. Overy, *De Stijl*, 143–44.

109. Interview, Yogyakarta, August 3, 1997.

110. An affinity between the colonial *mooi Indië* and both the capitalist-realist and the Calvinist (and Dutch) worldview is hard to disregard. Looking at these colonial images, one is almost tempted to exclaim: "The[se] safety zones of hermeneutic horizons and habitual sunsets belong to the Christian solvents." Ronell, *Test Drive*, 207.

111. Krauss, *Originality of the Avant-Garde*, 162–63, 170.

112. *Mooi Indië*, like so many other things of the colony marching forward, tasted of what Jean Baudrillard would later call simulacra: "Belief, faith in information attach themselves to this tautological proof that the system gives of itself by doubling the signs of an unlocatable reality." Baudrillard, *Simulacra and Simulation*, 81.

113. Benjamin, *Arcades Project*, 121.

114. Matu Mona, *Sedjarah penghidupan komponis W. R. Supratman*, 62.

115. "Staccato of the painting can resist perspective.... Jazz [for instance] became a means for the painters close at hand." Moos, *Fernand Léger*, 10.

116. This was the time of cubism, among other things of course, when painters became famous for their inversion of near and far.

117. "Ecce Homo," in *Basic Writings of Nietzsche*, 679.

118. Moos, *Fernand Léger*, 12, 55.

119. Dickerman, *Dada*, 7, 8, 38.

120. Victor Brauner, quoted in Jay, *Downcast Eyes*, 248.

121. Notebook, summer 1997, no. 5. "Pastoral warning sign," Ian Hamilton Finlay might call it. "An Illustrated Dictionary of the Little Spartan War," in Abrioux, *Ian Hamilton Finlay*, 32.

122. Interview, Jakarta, July 30, 1996.

123. Interview, Jakarta, November 23, 1998.

124. Marie-Odette Scalliet, "Twee eeuwen Verenigde Oost-Indische Compagnie, Europese schilders in Oost-Indië in de zeventiende en achttiende eeuw," in Brakel et al., *Indië omlijst*, 16.

125. Brakel, "'Immers,'" 105. See also "*The Fifth Regnault and the Circle Collection of the Dutch-French Avant-Garde*: A New Exhibition by Modern Painters in the Building of the Batavia Arts Circle on the Van Heutsz-Boulevard—van Gogh, Kandinsky, Utrillo and others," *Kritiek en Opbouw* (Bandung), vol. 2, no. 19 (1939): 320–21.

126. On a painting called *Two Masks* (1935) by Pieter Ouborg, see Brakel, "'Immers,'" 125–27.

127. Ibid., 131.

128. Tan Malaka's autobiography *From Prison to Prison*, 1948, quoted in Abidin Kusno, "From City to City," 335–36.

129. Interview, Yogyakarta, July 17, 1992.

130. Karl Marx, quoted in Benjamin, "Paris, the Capital of the Nineteenth Century," 1935, 3:37.

131. Quoted in Dickerman, *Dada*, 177.

132. Cervantes, "Ingenious Gentleman Don Quixote," 428.

133. Benjamin, *Selected Writings*, 3:442.

134. Jay, *Downcast Eyes*, 94.

135. Friedrich Nietzsche on Stendhal in "On the Genealogy of Morals," in *Basic Writings of Nietzsche*, 540–41.

136. On Tsuguharu Fujita and his life and work among the Paris avant-garde around First World War, see Rivera, *My Art, My Life*, 59–61.

137. Mr. Asrul: "Later, after my parents moved from Sumatra to Bandung, we lived in a street near a prison. Next to the prison, there was the house of Wahdi, the painter. I remember only his paintings of landscapes around the Mount Merapi and Bukittinggi [both in West Sumatra] from that time. Always, his scenes were set as if in the morning and always the colors were bright, from orange to red. His skies were *flamboyant*." Interview, Jakarta, July 25, 1997.

138. Interview, Bandung, July 13, 1992.

139. Quoted in Dickerman, *Dada*, 165.

140. Interview, Bandung, July 13, 1992.

141. Karl Marx, quoted in Benjamin, *Arcades Project*, 554.

142. Interview, Bandung, July 13, 1992.

143. Interview, Bandung, July 13, 1992.

144. See also Asikin Hasan, quoted in *Srihadi dan Paradigma*, 45.

145. Düchting, *Paul Klee*, 17; emphasis mine.

146. Tarkovsky, *Sculpting in Time*, 24.

147. Interview, Bandung, July 13, 1992. See also "Sketsa I: Pesawat Dakota VT-CLA yang ditembak oleh dua pesawat pemburu P40 Kitty Hawk." in *Srihadi dan Paradigma*, 2; also ibid., 5, 41.

148. There is a story about a Dada artist's relative, a manufacturer in his "real life," invited to a Dada exhibition and, in front of a "painting of a machine," "blurting out": "the goddam thing wouldn't work." Dickerman, *Dada*, 284–85.

149. Interview, Bandung, July 13, 1992.

POSTSCRIPT: SOMETIMES VOICES

1. William Shakespeare's *Tempest*, quoted in Charles van der Plas, "Opmerkingen over *The Tempest*," 391.

2. Plutarch, quoted in Dolar, *A Voice and Nothing More*, 3.

3. It sounded, to give a provocative but expressive example, like a well-behaved New England radio station: "People with their snot impacted voices that they paid for in college: their rumbling snot." Jack Smith, quoted in "Uncle Fishhook and the Sacred Baby Poo Poo of Art," in Kraus and Lotringer (eds.), *Hatred of Capitalism*, 247.

4. Carmichael, White, and Wessink, "Developing a Corpus of Spoken Language Variability," 2395.

5. Besides teaching Javanese at the Law College, Dr. Kats wrote books, among them the most often quoted book (until the 1960s certainly) on Javanese *wajang*, the shadow-puppet theater; see Kats, *Het Javaansche tooneel*.

6. This is also close to what Roman Jakobson and some others called *Kindersprache*, or "nursery speech." Jakobson, *Child Language*, 16.

7. The *Larousse* dictionary, quoted in Dolar, *A Voice and Nothing More*, 61. "The acousmatic voice is so powerful because it cannot be neutralized with the framework of the visible." Ibid., 79.

8. Adorno, *Jargon of Authenticity*, 13.

9. Interview, Jakarta, July 24, 1997. I believe that this is akin to "crying" as it was described for instance by Hildred Geertz in her studies of *latah*, or in other cases by James Siegel and Benedict Anderson. Geertz, "Latah in Java"; Siegel, *Solo in the New Order*, 28–32. According to an Indonesian dictionary, *latah* is "a nervous condition characterized by erratic involuntary imitative behavior," most stikingly, "uttering absurd statements." See Echols, Shadily, and Wolff, *Kamus Indonesia Inggris*, 331. Elsewhere, Siegel wrote about a young woman, the victim of recent communal brutality in Central Java: "Her father's death and the threats against her left her speechless." Siegel, *Naming the Witch*, 152. Anderson, describing another moment of crisis, writes about "eruptions" of language. See Anderson, *Under Three Flags*, 21. This may be also not far away from what Marcel Proust defined as "stuttering efforts at silence." Proust, *In Search of Lost*

Time, 302. Traces of defiance are often observed in that kind of speech: "The young speaker frequently perseveres obstinately in these deviations and resists every attempt at correction." Jakobson, *Child Language*, 15.

10. Nancy, *Inoperative Community*, 62. Here is my disappointment with Jakobson. He got so close, and this is especially relevant to this book, to appreciating the cries of the hawkers, to babbling and to aphasia, the speech of the aging and the old. But he remained a structuralist, and "babbling" was kept out of his arena of what one should study in language, perhaps not just because of "lack of time." To him the dialogue of the young, old, sick (or subjugated), whose drama he seemed well to realize, remained a "dummy dialogue." See especially Jakobson, *Child Language*, 24–25; also Jakobson, *Six Lectures on Sound and Meaning*, 60, 111.

11. Nancy, *Inoperative Community*, 62.

12. Wittgenstein, *Remarks on Colour*, sec. III, § 165.

13. Dolar, *A Voice and Nothing More*, 69.

14. Ibid., 60. As for the unemitted words, see Nietzsche: "Silence is an objection; swallowing things leads of necessity to a bad character—it even upsets the stomach." "Ecce Homo," in *Basic Writings of Nietzsche*, 685. Similar to Nietzsche, but more profound, I think, is what we find in that epic from Sumatra: "[Some] words were not expressed, they just died in her heart." Collins, *Guritan of Radin Suane*, first night, canto 75, 125.

15. Nancy, *Inoperative Community*, 70. And also, a "passage of the Politics situates the proper place of the polis in the transition from voice to language . . . in the relation between *phonè* and *logos*. . . . the community of these things makes dwelling and the city." Aristotle's *Politics*, quoted in Agamben, *Homo Sacer*, 7–8.

16. Nancy, *Being Singular Plural*, 7.

17. Nancy, *Inoperative Community*, 67–68.

18. "The Storyteller," in Benjamin, *Selected Writings*, 3:153–55.

19. *Hikayat Hang Tuah*, translated by Hendrik M. J. Maier, quoted in Day, *Fluid Iron*, 258.

20. Notebook, summer 1997, no. 4.

21. Epistle of James, quoted in Cornish, *Reading Dante's Stars*, 57.

22. "Pidato 17 Augustus 1958," in Sukarno, *Dari Proklamasi sampai Takari*, 365. See (hear) also Sukarno's Independence Day speech of 1960: "My voice carries on, over the whole nation between Sabang [in the west], Merauke [in the east] and beyond. . . . not just the voice. It is courage. It is soul" (ibid., 435); or his Independence Day speech of August 17, 1963: "THUS THE VOICE OF THE REVOLUTION RINGS. . . . The Indonesian people gather at the CENTRAL STADIUM OF SUKARNO. . . . Here and now, I am not just SUKARNO—the private person, but SUKARNO—THE EXTENSION OF THE TONGUE OF THE INDONESIAN PEOPLE, THE EXTENSION OF THE TONGUE OF THE INDONESIAN REVOLUTION. . . . All that has been hidden inside my body thus overflows!" Ibid., 563–64, 567–68.

23. "Pidato 17 Augustus 1962," ibid., 554, 557, 558.

24. Ibid., 650. A few years after Sukarno's death, in 1978, the "main pillars" of Sukarno's contributions to Indonesian history had been inscribed onto his tomb in Blitar. The first of these pillars was the "Extension of the Tongue of the People," only as the second one came, "The Proclaimer of the Indonesian Republic." Labrousse, "Le deuxième vie de Bung Karno," 189. One may say that modern Indonesia, through its center, the capital, the city of Jakarta, is as if it were built by Sukarno's voice. In the view of many Indonesians, including some prominent architects and urban planners, the core of Jakarta, and of Indonesia, the burden of the urban, modern, and national axis, is Gelora Bung Karno, "The Tempestuousness of Sukarno," a stadium and a complex of sports fields, parks, parking lots, paths, and overpasses. Here there is a companion to Jakarta's crucial traffic junction, the Semanggi Flyover nearby. See "Ulang Tahun," in Marco Kusumawijaya, *Jakarta*, 51. One may compare this also, in the frame of the same twentieth century (without judging the ethics of it), with the "Schmittian thesis" and "the principle of Führung": "The word of the Führer is not a factual situation that is then transformed into a rule, but is rather itself rule insofar as it is living voice." Agamben, *Homo Sacer*, 172–73.

25. "For it is doubling that produces the formal rhythm of spacing . . . an experience of fission . . . sense of deferral of opening reality to the 'interval of breath.'" Krauss, *Originality of the Avant-Garde*, 109. Rosalind Krauss is here referring to Jacques Derrida's "spacing."

26. See Cornish, *Reading Dante's Stars*, 135, on Aristotle's and an "angelic" notion of time.

27. "Story [in contrast to music] . . . can only present itself in successive events, as movement toward an end, and not as something suddenly brilliantly present." Mann, *Magic Mountain*, 531–32.

28. Aristotle's *Politics* and Plato's *Republic*, quoted in Dolar, *A Voice and Nothing More*, 46.

29. Plato's *Republic*, quoted ibid., 47.

30. Foucault, *Archeology of Knowledge*, 6. Similarly, Walter Benjamin thought, "the mistake of all interpretation lies in presenting the residue of the poetic reduction as meaning." Paraphrased in Fenves, *Arresting Language*, 223.

31. Blanchot, "Absence of the Book," 327.

32. Interview, Jakarta, May 16, 2000.

33. Notebook, summer 2000, no. 6.

34. Kundera, "Hledání přítomného času," 29–30.

35. Adorno, *Jargon of Authenticity*, 76–77.

36. Interview with Jusuf Ronodipuro, Jakarta, November 25, 1998.

37. Lapian, "Catatan permulaan," 3, 6. For a scholar, sure, it is a part of his or her urge and pleasure to "bring something home," a sort of sublimated desire, in the sense G. W. F. Hegel liked to call *Aufheben*, something "canceled, preserved, and lifted up." See Nietzsche, "Ecce Homo," in *Basic Writings of Nietzsche*, 727n4. In a more specific, postcolonial context, Clifford Geertz described this as "the appropriation of the voice

of the weak by those of the strong . . . ventriloquizing others, making off with their words." Geertz, *After the Fact*, 129.

38. Adorno, *Jargon of Authenticity*, 9–10.

39. "February 1943," in Chairil Anwar, *Voice of the Night*, 17; I have modified the translation.

40. The "voice underground" is from Dickens, *Tale of Two Cities*, 47.

41. Nancy, *Inoperative Community*, 77. My emphasis. "The Western philosopher [and she might say scholar] wonders very little about the relation of speaking between subjects." "The Sharing of Speech," in Irigaray, *Way of Love*, 15.

42. "Kisah yang ditulis Waktu Batu," in Latif et al., *Waktu Batu*, xviii.

43. Ibid., xix–xx.

44. Echols, Shadily, and Wolff. *Kamus Indonesia Inggris*.

45. "Kisah yang ditulis Waktu Batu," in Latif et al., *Waktu Batu*, xx–xxi.

46. Heidegger's *Being and Time*, 1927, quoted in Adorno, *Jargon of Authenticity*, 110–11.

47. Heidegger's *Being and Time*, quoted ibid., 131.

48. Says Wittgenstein, "In every serious philosophical question uncertainty extends to the very roots of the problem. We must always be prepared to learn something totally new." Wittgenstein, *Remarks on Colour*, sec. I § 15, 4; also ibid., sec. III, §§ 44–45, 23. Ronell may be referring to the same thing when she speaks about the "newly acknowledged openness to failure." Ronell, *Test Drive*, 98. Another mode of the zone may be Barthes's *neuter* (or "the Neutral"), especially in its capacity to "baffle paradigm" and to "sidestep assertion." See Barthes, *Neutral*, 6, 11, 44.

49. Latif et al., *Waktu Batu*, 70.

50. Ibid., 72, 75.

51. On a letter by St. Augustine on the Crucifixion as "not opposed to" annual celebrations of Easter, see Cornish, *Reading Dante's Stars*, 41.

BIBLIOGRAPHY

INTERVIEWS

Names in capital letters are those used in the text when quoting from interviews. The list is arranged alphabetically according to these names. It should be noted that many Indonesians have only one name.

ALI Algadri, Surabaya, July 23, 1992; ALWIN, Jakarta, August 30, 1999; ASRUL Sani, Jakarta, July 25, 1997; Carolus BANGGA, Ende, May 24, 2000; BEBSI Soenarjo, Jakarta, August 27, 1999; Gusti Raden Ayu BROTODININGRAT, Surakarta, August 9, 1995; DAINO, Jakarta, August 22, 1999; Soejatoen Poespokoesoemo DAMAIS, Jakarta, August 20, 1995; DAPIN, Yogyakarta, August 4, 1995; DES ALWIS, Jakarta, June 20, 1992; Omar DHANI, Jakarta, August 20, 1999; EFENDI Saleh, Bandung, August 21, 1993; GESANG Martohartono, Surakarta, August 8, 1996; HAMID Algadri, Jakarta, July 30, 1996; Claudius HARDJO, Blitar, August 13, 1997; HARDJONEGORO (Go Tik Swan), Surakarta, August 6, 1995; HARDOYO, Jakarta, August 16, 1995; HARTINI Sukarno, Jakarta, August 23, 1997; HASYIM DARIF, Surabaya, July 23, 1992; Louise Christiana Lobu HOUTEIRO, Ende, May 24, 2000; Imrad IDRIS, Jakarta, November 25, 1998; ISLAM Salim, Jakarta, August 21, 1999; JUSUF Ronodipuro, Jakarta, November 25, 1998; KARKONO Kamajaya Partokusumo, Yogyakarta, August 5, 1997; KEMAL Idris, Jakarta, July 15, 1997; KOENTJARANINGRAT, Jakarta, November 23, 1998; LASMIDJAH Hardi, Jakarta, August 22, 1995; Yusuf Bilyarta MANGUNWIJAYA, Yogyakarta, August 3, 1997; MARDI SUWITO, Surakarta, July 20, 1992; Djoehaeni MASKUN, Jakarta, July 26, 1994; Jusuf MAWENGKANG, Jakarta, July 7, 1992, and November 16, 1997; MINARSIH (Mien) Wiranatakoesoemah Soedarpo, Jakarta, July 19, 1995; MINGGU, Ende, May 24, 2000; MIRIAM Saleh Boediardjo, Jakarta, July 14, 1997; MOEDJONO, Blitar, August 13, 1997; MULYONO, Surakarta, July 20, 1992; Ida MUNARDJO, Jakarta, November 20, 1998; Anak Agung Istri MUTER, Jakarta, July 28, 1996; NARYO Carito, Kartasura, August 14, 1997; Gusti Raden Ayu NOEROEL Kusumawardhani, Bandung, August 26, 1999; OEI Tjoe Tjat, Jakarta, August 8, 1999; OEY Hay Djoen, Jakarta, August 18, 1999; ONG Hok Ham, Jakarta, August 24, 1999; Edmundus PAREIRA, Sikka, May 22, 2000; POLITON,

Menado, July 27, 2000; Poncke PRINSEN, Jakarta, May 16, 2000; Kangjeng Gusti Pangèran Haryo PUGER, Yogyakarta, August 5, 1997; PURBO Suwondo, Jakarta, August 30, 1999; RAHMIATI Hatta, Jakarta, August 18, 1997; Gertrudes Johan RESINK, Jakarta, July 17, 1997, and July 25, 1997; ROESLAN Abdulgani, Jakarta, July 24, 1997; ROOSSENO Soerjohadikoesoemo, Jakarta, August 25, 1995; ROSIHAN Anwar, Jakarta, July 19, 1995; RUSLI, Yogyakarta, August 2, 1996; SARLI, Jakarta, November 14, 1998; Frans SEDA, Jakarta, June 3, 2000; Politon Wartu SEKA, Menado, July 27, 2000; Maludin SIMBOLON, Jakarta, December 3, 1998; SOEDARMONO, Jakarta, December 3, 1998; SOEDARPO Sastrosatomo, Jakarta, July 21, 1995; SOELISTINA Soetomo, Jakarta, August 18, 1993; Selo SOEMARDJAN, Jakarta, July 23, 1997; SOEMARTONO, Jakarta, July 16, 1992; SOEMITRO Djojohadikoesoemo, Jakarta, August 19, 1997; SOERONO Hendronoto, Yogyakarta, July 17, 1992; Siti Larang Djojopanatas-SOSRO Kardono, Jakarta, July 28, 1992; SRIHADI Sudarsono, Bandung, July 13, 1992; SUKARSIH Moerwoto, Jakarta, July 20, 1992, and December 1, 1998; Pram SUTIKNO, Utrecht, July 6, 1998; Edi SUWARDI, Bandung, July 14, 1995; THEODORUS, Maumere, May 22, 2000; Martinus TIMU, Nita, May 10, 2000; Suzana TIMU, Nita, May 10, 2000; TOETI HERATY Roosseno, December 28, 2000; Dina TOLANG, Menado, May 29, 2000; TORAR, Surabaya, July 24, 1992; Surastri Karma TRIMURTI, Jakarta, July 6, 1997; USMAN Gunadi, Bandung, July 14, 1995; VIOLETTE Salim Sjahroezah, Yogyakarta, July 18, 1992; WAHDI Sumanta, Bandung, July 13, 1992; Arini Djojohadiprawiro WAWOROENTOE, Menado, May 28, 2000; Willem Johan WAWOROENTOE, Menado, May 28, 2000; Wim WERTHEIM, Wageningen, July 4, 1998; Ben WOWOR, Menado, May 28, 2000.

WRITTEN WORKS

Abeyasekere, Susan. *Jakarta: A History*. Singapore: Oxford University Press, 1987.

Abidin Kusno. "From City to City: Tan Malaka, Shanghai, and the Politics of Geographical Imagining." *Singapore Journal of Tropical Geography* 24, no. 3 (2003): 327–39.

———. "The Significance of Appearance in the 'Zaman Normal,' 1927–1942." Unpublished manuscript, 2005.

Abrioux, Yves. *Ian Hamilton Finlay: A Visual Primer*. Edinburgh: Reaktion Books, 1985.

Adorno, Theodor W. *The Jargon of Authenticity*. Trans. Knut Tarnowski and Frederic Will. Evanston, Ill.: Northwestern University Press, 1973.

———. *Minima Moralia: Reflections from Damaged Life*. 1951. Trans. E. F. N. Jephcott. London: Verso, 1999.

Agamben, Giorgio. *Homo Sacer: Sovereign Power and Bare Life*. Trans. Daniel Heller-Roazen. Stanford, Calif.: Stanford University Press, 1998.

Akihary, Huib. *Architectuur en stedebouw in Indonesië 1870–1970*. Zeist: Rijksdienst voor de Monumentenzorg, 1988.

Anderson, Benedict. "The Language of Indonesian Politics." *Indonesia*, no. 1 (1966): 89–116.

———. *Under Three Flags: Anarchism and the Anti-colonial Imagination*. London: Verso, 2005.

Aragon, Louis. *Paris Peasant*. 1926. Trans. Simon Watson Taylor. Boston: Exact Change, 1994.

Arendt, Hannah. *Eichmann and the Holocaust*. 1963. New York: Penguin, 2006.

Augé, Marc. *In the Metro*. Trans. Tom Conley. Minneapolis: University of Minnesota Press, 2002.

———. *Non-places: Introduction to an Anthropology of Supermodernity*. Trans. John Howe. London: Verso, 1995.

Ballegoijen, Michiel de Jong van. *Spoorwegstations op Java*. Amsterdam: De Bataafsche Leeuw, 1993.

Barthes, Roland. *Camera Lucida: Reflections on Photography*. Trans. Richard Howard. New York: The Noonday Press, 1989.

———. *The Neutral: Lecture Course at the Collège de France (1977–1978)*. Trans. Rosalind E. Krauss and Denis Hollier. New York: Columbia University Press, 2005.

———. *Writing Degree Zero*. Trans. Annette Lavers and Colin Smith. New York: Farrar, Straus and Giroux, 1988.

Baudelaire, Charles. "The Philosophy of Toys." 1853. *Essays on Dolls*, by Heinrich von Kleist, Charles Baudelaire, and Rainer Maria Rilke, trans. Idris Perry and Paul Keegan, 15–30. London: Syrens, 1994.

Baudrillard, Jean. *Simulacra and Simulation*. Trans. Sheila Faria Glaser. Ann Arbor: University of Michigan Press, 1994.

Benezra, Neal, et al. *Juan Muñoz*. Washington: Hirshhorn Museum and Sculpture Garden, Smithsonian Institution, 2001.

Benjamin, Walter. *The Arcades Project*. Ed. Rolf Tiedemann. Trans. Howard Eiland and Karin McLaughlin. Cambridge, Mass.: Harvard University Press, 1999.

———. *Selected Writings*. Vol. 1, *1913–1926*. Ed. Marcus Bullock and Michael W. Jennings. Cambridge, Mass.: Harvard University Press, 1996.

———. *Selected Writings*. Vol. 2, *1927–1934*. Ed. Michael W. Jennings, Howard Eiland, and Gary Smith. Trans. Rodney Livingstone et al. Cambridge, Mass.: Harvard University Press, 1999.

———. *Selected Writings*. Vol. 3, *1935–1938*. Ed. Michael W. Jennings, Marcus Bullock, Howard Eiland, and Gary Smith. Trans. Edmund Jephcott et al. Cambridge, Mass.: Harvard University Press, 2002.

———. *Selected Writings*. Vol. 4, *1938–1940*. Ed. Howard Eiland and Michael W. Jennings. Trans. Edmund Jephcott et al. Cambridge, Mass.: Harvard University Press, 2003.

Blackburn, Simon. *The Oxford Dictionary of Philosophy*. Oxford: Oxford University Press, 1994.

Blanchot, Maurice. "The Absence of the Book." *The Infinite Conversation*. Trans. Susan Hanson. Minneapolis: University of Minnesota Press, 1993.

——— . *The Writing of the Disaster*. Trans. Ann Smock. Lincoln: University of Nebraska Press, 1995.

Brakel, Koos van, et al. *Indië omlijst: Vier eeuwen schilderkunst in Nederlands-Indië*. Amsterdam: Koninklijk Instituut voor de Tropen, 1998.

Brecht, Bertolt. *Poems, 1913–1956*. Ed. John Willett and Ralph Mannheim. New York: Routledge, 1987.

Breton, André. *Manifestoes of Surrealism*. Trans. Richard Searer and Helen R. Lande. Ann Arbor: University of Michigan Press, 1969.

Carmichael, Lesley, with Richard White and Alicia Wessink. "Developing a Corpus of Spoken Language Variability." *Journal of the Acoustical Society of America* 114, no. 4 (2003): 2395.

Certeau, Michel de. *The Writing of History*. Trans. Tom Conley. New York: Columbia University Press, 1988.

Cervantes, Miguel de. "Ingenious Gentleman Don Quixote de La Mancha." 1605. *The Portable Cervantes*. Trans. Samuel Putnam. New York: Penguin, 1978.

Chairil Anwar. *The Voice of the Night: Complete Poetry and Prose of Chairil Anwar*. Trans. Burton Raffel. Athens: Ohio University Center of International Studies, 1993.

Cixous, Hélène. *Three Steps on the Ladder of Writing* Trans. Sarah Cornell and Susan Sellers. New York: Columbia University Press, 1993.

Collins, William A. *The Guritan of Radin Suane: A Study of the Besemah Oral Epic from South Sumatra*. Leiden: KITLV Press, 1998.

Cornish, Alison. *Reading Dante's Stars*. New Haven, Conn.: Yale University Press, 2000.

Dagognet, François. *Étienne-Jules Marey: A Passion for the Trace*. Trans. Robert Galeta with Jeanine Herman. New York: Urzone, 1992.

Darsono, Alam. *Kinderogen*. Amsterdam: Thomas Rap, 2001.

Day, Tony. *Fluid Iron: State Formation in Southeast Asia*. Honolulu: University of Hawai'i Press, 2002.

Dickens, Charles. *A Tale of Two Cities*. 1859. London: Penguin, 1994.

Dickerman, Leah, ed. *Dada*. Washington: National Gallery of Art, 2006.

Dolar, Mladen. *A Voice and Nothing More*. Cambridge, Mass.: MIT Press, 2006.

Düchting, Hajo. *Paul Klee: Painting Music*. Trans. Penelope Crowe. Munich: Prestel, 1997.

Duras, Marguerite. *The Sea Wall*. 1950. Trans. Herman Briffault. New York: Pellegrini and Cudahy, 1952.

Echols, John M., Hassan Shadily, and John U. Wolff. *Kamus Indonesia Inggris: An Indonesian-English Dictionary*. Jakarta: Gramedia, 1982.

Fenves, Peter D. *Arresting Language: From Leibniz to Benjamin*. Stanford, Calif.: Stanford University Press, 2001.

Foucault, Michel. *The Archeology of Knowledge and the Discourse on Language*. Trans. A. M. Sherdian Smith. New York: Pantheon, 1972.

——— . *Discipline and Punish: The Birth of the Prison*. Trans. Alan Sheridan. New York: Vintage, 1979.

———. "Nietzsche, Genealogy, History." *Language, Counter-memory, Practice: Selected Essays and Interviews*, ed. Donald F. Bouchard, trans. Bouchard and Sherry Simon, 139–64. Ithaca, N.Y.: Cornell University Press, 1980.

Frampton, Kenneth. *Le Corbusier*. New York: Thames and Hudson, 2001.

Fryberger, Betsy G., ed. *The Changing Garden: Four Centuries of European and American Art*. Berkeley: University of California Press, 2003.

Geertz, Clifford. *After the Fact: Two Countries, Four Decades, One Anthropologist*. Cambridge, Mass.: Harvard University Press, 1995.

Geertz, Hildred. "Latah in Java: A Theoretical Paradox." *Indonesia*, no. 5 (1968): 93–104.

Grijns, Kees, and Peter J. M. Nas, eds. *Jakarta-Batavia: Socio-cultural Essays*. Leiden: KITLV Press, 2000.

Hatta, Mohammad. *Verspreide geschriften*. Vol. 1. Jakarta: Balai Buku Indonesia, 1952.

Heidegger, Martin. *Poetry, Language, Thought*. Trans. Albert Hofstadter. New York: Harper, 1971.

———. *The Question Concerning Technology and Other Essays*. Trans. William Lovitt. New York: Harper, and Row, 1977.

Heilbut, Anthony. *Exiled in Paradise: German Refugee Artists and Intellectuals in America, from the 1930s to the Present*. Berkeley: University of California Press, 1997.

Holt, Nancy, ed. *The Writing of Robert Smithson*. New York: New York University Press, 1979.

Irigaray, Luce. *The Way of Love*. Trans. Heidi Bostic and Stephan Pluháček. London: Continuum, 2002.

Jakobson, Roman. *Child Language Aphasia and Phonological Universals*. 1941. Trans. Allan R. Keiler. The Hague: Mouton, 1968.

———. *My Futurist Years*. Ed. Bengt Jangfeldt and Stephen Rudy. Trans. Rudy. New York: Marsilio, 1992.

———. *Six Lectures on Sound and Meaning*. 1942. Trans. John Mepham. Cambridge, Mass.: MIT Press, 1978.

Jay, Martin. *Downcast Eyes: The Denigration of Vision in Twentieth-Century French Thought*. Berkeley: University of California Press, 1994.

Jembatan Antar-Generasi: Pengalaman murid SMT Djakarta 1942–1945. Jakarta: Sinar Harapan, 1998.

Jordan, David P. *Transforming Paris: The Life and Labors of Baron Haussmann*. Chicago: University of Chicago Press, 1995.

Kafka, Franz. *The Trial*. 1925. Trans. Willa and Edwin Muir. New York: Schocken, 1983.

Kahin, George McTurnan. *Nationalism and Revolution in Indonesia*. Ithaca, N.Y.: Cornell University Press, 1952.

Kandinsky, Nina. *Kandinsky und ich*. Munich: Kindler Verlag, 1976.

Kats, Jacob. *Het Javaansche tooneel: Wajang poerwa.* Weltevreden: Commissie voor de volkslectuur, 1923.

Koolhaas, Rem. *Conversations with Students.* 2nd ed. New York: Princeton Architectural Press, 1996.

———. *Delirious New York: A Retroactive Manifesto for Manhattan.* New York: Monacelli Press, 1994.

Kracauer, Siegfried. *The Mass Ornament: Weimar Essays.* Trans. Thomas Y. Levin. Cambridge, Mass.: Harvard University Press, 1995.

———. *The Salaried Masses: Duty and Distraction in Weimar Germany.* 1930. Trans. Quintin Hoare. London: Verso, 1998.

Kraus, Chris, and Sylvère Lotringer, eds. *Hatred of Capitalism: A Semiotext(e) Reader.* Los Angeles: Semiotext(e), 2001.

Krauss, Rosalind E. *The Originality of the Avant-Garde and Other Modernist Myths.* Cambridge, Mass.: MIT Press, 1985.

Kundera, Milan. "A la recherche du présent perdu." *L'infini,* no. 36 (1991): 19–42.

———. "Hledání přítomného času." *Můj Janáček,* 9–40. Brno: Atlantis, 2004.

Labrousse, Pierre. "Le deuxième vie de Bung Karno, analyse du mythe (1978–1981)." *Archipel,* no. 25 (1983): 187–214.

Ladd, Brian. *The Ghosts of Berlin: Confronting German History in the Urban Landscape.* Chicago: University of Chicago Press, 1998.

Lapian, Adri. "Catatan permulaan bagi pewawancara." *Lembaran Berita Sejarah Lisan,* no. 11 (1985): 3, 6.

Latif, et al. *Waktu Batu: Teater garasi; Laboratorium penciptaan teater, 2001–2004.* Magelang: Indonesiatera, 2004.

Le Corbusier. *Aircraft.* New York: Universe, 1935.

———. *Towards a New Architecture.* 1923. Trans. Frederick Etchells. New York: Dover, 1986.

Lefebvre, Henri. *The Production of Space.* Trans. Donald Nicholson-Smith. Cambridge: Blackwell, 1991.

Le Goff, Jacques. *History and Memory.* Trans. Steven Rendall and Elizabeth Claman. New York: Columbia University Press, 1992.

Mann, Thomas. *The Magic Mountain.* 1924. Trans. John E. Woods. New York: Vintage, 1996.

Manusama, Ir. Johannes Alvarez. *Eigenlijk moest ik niet veel hebben van de politiek: Herinneringen aan mijn leven in de Oost 1919–1953.* Utrecht: Moluks Historisch Instituut, 1999.

Marco Kartodikromo. *Pergaulan orang buangan di Boven-Digoel.* 1931. Jakarta: Gramedia, 2002.

Marco Kusumawijaya. *Jakarta: Metropolis tunggang-langgang.* Jakarta: GagasMedia, 2004.

Masak, Tanete A. Pong. "Le cinéma indonésien (1926–1967)." PhD dissertation, École des Hautes Études en Sciences Sociales, Paris, 1989.

Masheck, Joseph, ed. *Marcel Duchamp in Perspective*. Cambridge, Mass.: Da Capo, 2002.

Matu Mona. *Sedjarah penghidupan komponis W. R. Supratman*. 1941. Medan: Tagore, 1952.

McIntyre, Angus. "Sukarno as Artist-Politician." *Indonesian Political Biography: In Search of Cross-cultural Understanding*, ed. McIntyre, 175–97. Clayton, Victoria: Monash Papers on Southeast Asia, 1993.

Mertins, Detlef, ed. *The Presence of Mies*. New York: Princeton Architectural Press, 1994.

Mihardja, Achdiat Karta. *Atheis*. 1949. Trans. R. J. Maguire. St. Lucia: University of Queensland Press, 1972.

Moenzir, IzHarry Agusjaya, ed. *Gesang: Mengalir meluap sampai jauh*. Jakarta: Balai Pustaka, 1999.

Moos, Stanislaus von. *Fernand Léger: La ville: Zeitdruck, Großstadt, Wahrnehmung*. Frankfurt am Main: Fischer Verlag, 1999.

Mrázek, Rudolf. *Engineers of Happy Land: Technology and Nationalism in a Colony*. Princeton, N.J.: Princeton University Press, 2002.

———. *Sjahrir: Politics and Exile in Indonesia*. Ithaca, N.Y.: Southeast Asia Program Publications, Cornell University, 1994.

Nancy, Jean-Luc. *Being Singular Plural*. Trans. Robert D. Richardson and Anne E. O'Byrne. Stanford, Calif.: Stanford University Press, 2000.

———. *The Inoperative Community*. Trans. Peter Connor et al. Minneapolis: University of Minnesota Press, 1991.

———. *The Sense of the World*. Trans. Jeffrey S. Librett. Minneapolis: University of Minnesota Press, 1997.

Nietzsche, Friedrich Wilhelm. *Basic Writings of Nietzsche*. Ed and trans. Walter Kaufmann. New York: Modern Library, 1968.

Overy, Paul. *De Stijl*. London: Thames and Hudson, 1991.

Pascal, Blaise. *Selections*. Ed. and trans. Richard H. Popkin. New York: Macmillan, 1989.

Pelt, Robert Jan van, and Caroll William Westfall. *Architectural Principles in the Age of Historicism*. New Haven, Conn.: Yale University Press, 1991.

Plas, Charles van der. "Opmerkingen over *The Tempest*," *Fakkel* 1, no. 5 (1941): 391–401.

Pramoedya Ananta Toer. *Larasati (Ara): Roman revolusi*. 1960. Jakarta: Hasta Mitra, 2000.

———. *Tales from Djakarta: Caricatures of Circumstances and Their Human Beings*. Ithaca, N.Y.: Southeast Asia Program Publications, Cornell University, 1999.

Proust, Marcel. *In Search of Lost Time*. Vol. 3, *The Guermantes Way*, 1920–21. Trans. C. K. Scott Moncrieff and Terrence Kilmartin. New York, Modern Library, 1993.

Reid, Anthony. *Southeast Asia in the Age of Commerce*. Vol. 1. New Haven, Conn.: Yale University Press, 1988.

Rhodius, Hans, and John Darling. *Walter Spies and Balinese Art*. Zutphen: Terra, 1980.

Rilke, Rainer Maria. *The Lay of the Love and Death of Cornet Christopher Rilke*. 1906. Trans. M. D. Herter Norton. New York: W. W. Norton, 1963.

———. *The Notebooks of Malte Laurids Brigge*. 1910. Trans. M. D. Herter Norton. New York: W. W. Norton, 1992.

Rimbaud, J. N. Arthur. *Complete Works, Selected Letters*. Trans. Wallace Fowlie. Chicago: University of Chicago Press, 1966.

Rivera, Diego. *My Art, My Life: An Autobiography (with Gladys March)*. New York: Dover, 1991.

Ronell, Avital. *Stupidity*. Urbana: University of Illinois Press, 2002.

———. *The Test Drive*. Urbana: University of Illinois Press, 2005.

Roosseno: Pakar dan perintis teknologi sipil Indonesia. Jakarta: Pembimbing Masa, 1989.

Roth, Joseph. *Right and Left / The Legend of the Holy Drinker*. 1929, 1939. Trans. Michael Hofmann. Woodstock, N.Y.: Overlook Press, 1992.

Rush, James R. *Opium to Java: Revenue Farming and Chinese Enterprise in Colonial Indonesia, 1860–1910*. Ithaca, N.Y.: Cornell University Press, 1990.

Salmon, Claudine. "The Batavian Eastern Railway Co. and the Making of a New 'Daerah' as Reflected in a Commemorative Syair Written by Tan Teng Kie (1900)." *Indonesia*, no. 45 (1988): 49–62.

———. *Literature in Malay by the Chinese of Indonesia: A Provisional Annotated Bibliography*. Paris: Archipel, 1981.

Sartre, Jean-Paul. *Baudelaire*. Trans. Martin Turnell. New York: New Directions Books, 1967.

Scott, James C. *Seeing Like a State: How Certain Schemes to Improve the Human Condition Have Failed*. New Haven, Conn.: Yale University Press, 1998.

Segalen, Victor. *Essay on Exoticism: An Aesthetics of Diversity*. Ed. and trans. Yaël Rachel Schlick. Durham, N.C.: Duke University Press, 2002.

Shiraishi, Takashi. *An Age in Motion: Popular Radicalism in Java, 1912–1926*. Ithaca, N.Y.: Cornell University Press 1990.

Siegel, James T. *Naming the Witch*. Stanford, Calif.: Stanford University Press, 2006.

———. *A New Criminal Type in Jakarta: Counter-revolution Today*. Durham, N.C.: Duke University Press, 1998.

———. *Solo in the New Order: Language and Hierarchy in an Indonesian City*. Princeton, N.J.: Princeton University Press, 1993.

Simmel, Georg. *Simmel on Culture: Selected Writings*. Ed. David Frisby and Mike Featherstone. London: Sage, 1997.

Soemardjan, Selo. *Biografi, komat-kamit*. Ed. Abrar Yusra. Jakarta: Gramedia, 1995.

Soesilo, H. Moh. *Perjalanan hidup*. Bandung: n.p., n.d.

Srihadi dan paradigma seni rupa Indonesia. Jakarta: Kalam, 1999.

Stassen, K. J., et al. *Kun je nog zingen, zing dan mee!*. Batavia: Noordhoff-Kolff, 1939.

Sukarno. *Dari Proklamasi sampai Takari: Terbitan berisi Pidato Proklamasi diutjapkan oleh P. J. M. Presiden Republik Indonesia pada tiap tanggal 17 Augustus sedjak tahun 1945 sampai 1965*. Jakarta: Prapantja, 1965.

Sumitro Djojohadikusumo. *Jejak perlawanan begawan pejuang*. Jakarta: Sinar Harapan, 2000.

Suryadinata, Leo. *Prominent Indonesian Chinese*. 2nd ed. Singapore: Institute of Southeast Asian Studies, 1995.

Sutton, John. *Philosophy and Memory Traces: Descartes to Connectionism*. Cambridge: Cambridge University Press, 1998.

Tarkovsky, Andrey. *Sculpting in Time: Reflections on the Cinema*. Trans. Kitty Hunter-Blair. Austin: University of Texas Press, 2003.

Tsuchiya Kenji. *Democracy and Leadership: The Rise of the Taman Siswa Movement in Indonesia*. Trans. Peter Hawkes. Honolulu: University of Hawai'i Press, 1987.

Virilio, Paul. *A Landscape of Events*. Trans. Julie Rose. Cambridge, Mass.: MIT Press, 2000.

———. *Speed and Politics: An Essay on Dromology*. Trans. Mark Polizzotti. New York: Semiotext(e), 1986.

Vollenhoven, Cornelis van. *Het adatrecht van Nederlandsch Indië*. Vols. 1–3. Leiden: Brill, 1918–33.

Vuyk, Beb. *Kampdagboeken: Drie verhalen, dagboeken en aantekeningen*. Utrecht: Veen, 1989.

Walraven, Willem. "De Clan." *Fakkel* 1, no. 9 (1941): 702–3.

Wertheim, Wim, and Hetty Wertheim-Gijse Weenink. *Vier wendingen in ons bestaan: Indië verloren-Indonesië geboren*. Breda: De Geus, 1991.

Winter, Jay. *Sites of Memory, Sites of Mourning: The Great War in European Cultural History*. Cambridge: Cambridge University Press, 1995.

Wittgenstein, Ludwig. *Last Writings on the Philosophy of Psychology*. Vol. 1–2. Ed. G. H. von Wright and Heikki Nyman. Trans. C. G. Luckhardt and Maxmilian A. E. Aue. Chicago: University of Chicago Press, 1982.

———. *Philosophical Investigations*. Vols. 1–2. Trans. G. E. M. Anscombe. Oxford: Blackwell, 2003.

———. *Remarks on Colour*. Trans. Linda L. McAlister and Margarete Schättle. Berkeley: University of California Press, 1978.

———. *Tractatus Logico-Philosophicus*. 1921. Trans. D. F. Pears and B. F. McGuinness. London: Routledge, 1974.

Wolff, John U., ed. *The Role of Modern Indonesian Chinese in Shaping Modern Indonesian Life*. Ithaca, N.Y.: Southeast Asia Program Publications, Cornell University, 1991.

Wrede, Stuart, and William Howard Adams, eds. *Denatured Visions: Landscape and Culture in the Twentieth Century*. New York: Museum of Modern Art, 1991.

Yampolsky, Philip. "Forces for Change in the Regional Performing Arts of Indonesia." *Bijdragen tot de Taal-, Land- en Volkenkunde* 151, no. 4 (1995): 700–725.

INDEX

Adorno, Theodor, 98, 109, 238, 248
Affandi (painter), 219
Alexander the Great, 163
Altars, 40
Amusement parks, 116–17, 122–23
Anderson, Benedict, 204
Anti-Chinese pogroms, 79, 104
Anticolonialism, 65–66, 178, 237
Antiquities Service, 47
Anwar Chairil, 248
Arab community, 98, 99, 171
Arahmaiani, Ms., 242–43, 248
Archimedes, 13
Architecture: building materials, 33–34; dwelling and, 25; of horizon, 3; of internment camps, 282 n. 229; Javanese house styles, 26; of mass housing, 210–11; of Sukarno, 9, 13; use of concrete, 12, 13–14, 259 n. 41; vernacular, 25
Arendt, Hannah, 196
Aristophanes, 239
Art Circles, 192, 215, 225
Auctions, 50, 59–60, 64, 97
Augé, Marc, 8–9, 43

Balzac, Honoré de, 69
Bambang, Dr., 201
Bandung Technical Institute. *See* Technische Hoogeschool (Bandung)

Banknotes, design of, 217, 220
Barricades, 9, 910
Barthes, Roland, 21
Batik, 82–85, 230
Baudelaire, Charles, 45, 46
Beds, Javanese, 39
Benjamin, Walter, 45, 46, 55–56, 141, 187, 241; on Berlin Childhood, 187; Critical theory and, 218; on looking, 202; the spectacular and, 192
Bernoulli, Daniel, 13
Bernoulli, Johann, 13
Bildung, 138
Blackburn, Simon, 15
Blanchot, Maurice, 8
Blueprints and Patterns Building, 17, 22
Bodies of water, 88–90
Boedi Oetomo, 134
Books and textbooks, 161, 162–64, 199–200, 205
Bourdieu, Pierre, 283 n. 19
Boven Digoel camp, 179–86; entertainment in, 184; housing, 182; learning in, 182–83, 185; servants in, 182, 184
Brecht, Bertolt, 9, 125
Breslau, Muller, 14
Breton, André, 12–13, 98, 202
Bridges: concrete and, 14; destruction/rebuilding, 13
Broz, Jovanka, 18

Camp Makassar, 65
Cars, 93–98
Cawang-Sudirman Interchange, 14
Central Heroes' Cemetery (Jakarta), 22, 23
Childhood: batik and, 82; crying and, 133–34; feasts and, 115–17; gardens and, 76; gates and, 74; houses and, 26, 29, 32–34, 41–43, 56, 60, 77–78; roads and streets and, 90–93; wheeled vehicles and, 91–92
Chinese community, 79, 98–100, 104, 214; schools, 143–44
Cinema. *See* Movies and movie houses
Cities: abstraction and, 122–23; post-colonial, 2, 12, 16, 33; varied cultures in, 101
Civil engineering, 13–14
Cleanliness, 1
Clothing, Javanese, 151
Clubs and sound, 111–12
Communication and rhythm, 13
Concrete in building, 12, 13–14, 259 n. 41
Connectedness and distance, 25
Conscious Woman Movement. *See* Sadar Istri

Dancing, *126*, 146–49
Dancing, Javanese, 48
Darlang, F., 21
Da Vinci, Leonardo, 13
Death and spirits, 43
Debate clubs, 170–72
Delacroix, Eugène, 69
Department of Railways, 19
Descartes, René, 31
Dewi Sri (rice goddess), 40
Diponegoro, 106
Discipline: Javanese culture and, 167–68; school, 166–68
Distance and connectedness, 25
Dix, Otto, 112

Documentation, 244–45
Dolar, Mladen, 235
Dutch community, 99, 101–3; language, 156–57; not touching and, 105; schools, 130, 137, 143–44, 157, 158
Dwelling, 25, 29, 55, 69, 121–22, 133, 195. *See also* Houses

Eating etiquette, 55
Edison, Thomas, 206
Education. *See* Schools
Eland, Leo, 204
Electricity, 1, 41–43, 48, 58, 100, 226, 261 n. 82
Enframing, 203–4, 213
Engels, Friedrich, 269 n. 107
Engineer in Neth. Indies, The (journal), 12
Erres Radios, 50
Euler, Leonhard, 13, 14
Eurasian community, 99, 237; as buffer, 105–6; music/*krontjong* and, 107; schools, 130, 143–46

Feasts and childhood, 115–17
Fences: childhood and, 74; Eurasians as, 105–6; as passage, 75–76; peddling and, 82
Films. *See* Movies and movie houses
Foucault, Michel, 244
Franck, César, 112
Fraternité, 124
Freedom: death of, 22; expropriation and, 141; houses and, 69; movement, 5; school and, 144, 170, 177; vehicles and, 95
Freud, Sigmund, 43, 248
Freyssinet, Eugène, 14
Fulton, Robert, 204

Galileo, 13
Gamelan, 48, 49, 85, 111, 114, 120, 183
Games, 44

Index

Gardens and childhood, 76
Gates: childhood and, 74; as passage, 75–76
Gedung Pola. *See* Blueprints and Patterns Building
Geertz, Clifford, 209
Genealogies, 108–9
Geometrical order, 9
German Revolution (1918–19), 11–12
Goethe, Johann Wolfgang von, 46, 200
Golden Pen award, 4
Gramophones, 50, 115
Guerillas, 66–67

Hába, Alois, 112
Hals, Frans, 215
Happy Hubbub, Miss, 21
Hatta, Mohammad, 14; burial place, 22; death of, 6; as freedom fighter, 19; internment of, 180, 182, 183; library of, 20, 184; statue of, 17; writing of, 178
Hatta, Rahmiati, 18–20
Haussmann, Georges-Eugène, 14, 210, 270 n. 122
Heidegger, Martin, 25, 166, 196; on enframing, 203
Heraty, Toeti, 15
Herb drinks, 3–4, 74
Heroes of the Revolution Day, 23
Hindemith, Paul, 112
History: classes in, 164; eras in, 13–14; passing on, 8
Hoedoyo, Sapto, 220
Holmes, Sherlock, 5–6
Holt, Claire, 21
Holtorf, Gunther, 108
Hooke, Robert, 13, 14
Hoostraaten, Samuel van, 223
Hospitality, 58
Hotel des Indes, *24*
Hotel Indonesia, 14, 77
Houses: altars, 40; attachment and, 59; bathrooms, 27, 29–30; bedrooms, 38–41; childhood and, 26, 29, 32–34, 41–43, 56, 60, 77–78; color and, 55–56; freedom and, 69; intimacy and, 84; itinerants and, 81–82; as leftovers, 57–58; memories and, 28–32, 34–38, 68–69, 77–78; modernity and, 32, 33–34, 57, 59, 60, 75, 81, 103, 195–96; moving and staying, 28–29, 38, 42; roofs, 31–32; salons as core of, 58, 59–60; sameness of, 26; servants and, 35–38; service, 60; shops in, 79–81; as space, 195; state widows', 18–20; styles of, 26–30, 100–101; walls and, 56. *See also* Dwelling
Hugo, Victor, 25
Human suffering, reduction of, 195
Hurgronje, Snouck, 260 n. 52
Hussein, Achmad, 243

IDS. *See* Infant deficiency speech (IDS)
Indonesia Moeda, 179
Indonesian National Archives, 247
Indonesian National Library, 18
Indonesian National Party. *See* Partai Nasional Indonesia (PNI)
Indonesian National Revolution (1945–49), 2, 13, 107
Indonesian Youth Oath (1928), 172
Indos. See Eurasian community
Infant deficiency speech (IDS), 238
Ingenieur in Ned.-Indië, De. See Engineer in Neth. Indies, The (journal)
Inlanders, 99, 153
International Institute for Social History (Amsterdam), 246
Internment camps, 63–65, 75, 179–86, 282 n. 229. See also *specific camps*
Intimacy: through house, 84; memory and, 34; road to school and, 131–32; servants and, 35, 38; voice and, 242
Islamic Union. *See* Sarékat Islam

Index

305

Jakarta: colonial cityscape of, 101; floods in, 88–89; flyovers, 1, 11, 14; lights in, 2; as postcolonial city, 2, 12, 16; riots of 1997/1998, 9–10, 247; road network, 1–3, 9–11
Jakarta Cengkareng Toll Road and Overpass, 14
Jakobson, Roman, 74
Japanese internment camps. *See* Internment camps
Japanese occupation of Indonesia (1942–45), 6, 7, 13, 61–65, 75, 230
Japanese surrender to Allies, 65
Jargon of authenticity, 247, 248
Jargon of identity, 238
Javanese culture, 47; batik and, 82–85; beds and, 39; clothing and, 151; dancing and, 48; discipline and, 167–68; eating etiquette in, 55; gamelan and, 48, 85, 111, 120, 183; games in, 44; house styles in, 26–30, 100–101; Kartini schools, 173–75; krontjong and, 114; language and, 156–64, 166, 237–38; painting and, 187–90, 215–33; philosophy/*kedjawèn*, 153; puppets in, 42, 85–87, 115, 120, 167–68, 174, 214, 229; racial integration and, 99–102, 106, 117, 145, 149, 236–37; shadow-puppets in, 42, 85–87, 120, 174
Jawa Baroe (magazine), 231
Jazziness, 12
Jebat, Hang, 241, 243

Kafka, Franz, 39–40, 193
Kaja-Kaja, 182–86
Kala (god of time), 90, 251–52
Kandinsky, Nina, 12
Kartini schools, 82, 151, 173–75
Kartodirjo, Sartono, 4, 8
Kats, Jacob, 237–38
Kautsky, Karl, 246
Kedjawèn, 153

Kessler, Harry, 11
Killing of nomads, 109
Klee, Paul, 230
Knight of the Oranje-Nassau Order, 27
KNIL. *See* Royal Netherlands Indies Army (KNIL)
Kokoschka, Oskar, 112
Koninklijk Bataviaasch Genootschap Voor Kunsten en Wetenschappen, 188
Koran, 250
Kracauer, Siegfried, 2, 141, 166, 197, 272 n. 162
Krontjong/kroncong, 49, 74, 107, 113–14, 175
Kundera, Milan, 246

Language: architecture and, 25; Dutch, 156–59; as house of Being, 166; Javanese, 156–64, 166, 237–38; Malay, 159–62; motherese, 238; noise between, 237; service, 278 n. 140
Latif (author), 249
League of Nations. *See* Volkenbond
Le Corbusier: on air flight, 285 n. 58; exterior walls and, 33; on home as machine, 55, 196; houses of, 12, 16, 25, 29, 196, 203; Maison Citrohan and, 25, 123, 124; metropolitan fourfold and, 15; on nomadic inhabitants, 82; Notre Dame de la Rochelle and, 270–71 n. 126; on straight line, 257 n. 75; utopia and, 32; on visual acoustics, 110; walls of light and, 203
Lefebvre, Henri, 151
Legrange, Joseph Louis, 13
Liberation and lights, 2
Libraries, 161
Light/lights: glass and, 34; in graveyard, 22–23; liberation and, 2; memory and, 2; modernity and, 195; privacy and, 42; of publicity, 196; walls of, 203. *See also* Electricity

Listening, 246, 248–49
Lombard effect, 236
Looting, 10–11, 66
Louis XVI, 220
Lubis, Zulkifli, 243

MADILOG (Malaka), 5
Maison Citrohan, 25, 123, 124
Malaka, Tan, 5, 7
Malay language, 159–62
Mangkunegaran Palace, 28
Maruanto, Gunawan, 249
Marx, Karl, 124, 210, 218, 228, 246
May, Karl, 268 n. 148
Meer Uitgebreid Lager Onderwijs (MULO), 147, 148, 150, 168, 214
Memories/memory: houses and, 28–32, 34–38, 68–69, 77–78; intimacy and, 35; lights and, 2; noise and, 73–74; paintings and, 189; past and, 8–9; perspective and, 120–21; servants and, 35–36; stopover, 135. *See also* Remembrance
Mesjid Istiqlal, 14
Misunderstanding, 12–13
Modernity: amusement and, 118; clothing and, 150–51; *corso* and, 271 n. 143; draft of, 59; feasts and, 116; houses and, 32, 33–34, 57, 59, 60, 75, 81, 103, 195–96; liberation and, 194; lightness and, 195; *mooi Indië* and, 211–12; movement and, 100, 103, 106, 111–12; multiculturalism and, 143; naming and, 157–58; past and, 41; schools and, 155–57; signaled by colonial, 197
Moerwoto, Mr., 181, 183
Mohammed (Prophet), 108
Mooi Indië, 211–12
Movies and movie houses, 118–20, 205–8
Multiculturalism and modernity, 143
Munch, Edward, 240

Museum of Ancient Inscriptions (Jakarta), 21–23
Museum Prasasti (Jakarta). *See* Museum of Ancient Inscriptions (Jakarta)
Music: clubs and, 111–12; feasts and, 116; salons and, 48–53; in school, 165–66; street, 113–14

Nancy, Jean-Luc, 239, 241, 248
Nassau, Wilhelmus van, 164
National Monument (Jakarta), 14
National Museum (Jakarta), 82
Neighborhood: togetherness, 115–16; watch, 77
Newspapers: cuttings, 190–92, 195; houses as, 195–96; reading, 196–99. *See also specific newspapers*
Ngantung, Henk, 16–17
Nietzsche, Friedrich, 54, 213
Niewenkamp, W. O. J., 216
Noise: interruption and, 239; between language, 237; memories and, 73–74; postcolonial, 236; space and, 74, 77, 235–36; tropical, 235–36; voice and, 236, 240–44, 245, 249, 251. *See also* Sound
Nostalgia, 32, 87, 93, 104
Notre Dame de la Rochelle, 270–71 n. 126
Not touching skill, 103, 105, 109
Nur, Andri, 249

Old Dutch Graveyard (Jakarta). *See* Museum of Ancient Inscriptions (Jakarta)
Orczy, Emmuska. *See Scarlet Pimpernel* (Orczy)
Orderliness, 1
Orient, De (magazine), 229, 230, 231
Oshikawa, Noriaki. *See Patjar Merah Indonesia and Tan Malaka* (Oshikawa)
Ouborg, Piet, 215

Index
307

Oudheidkundige Dienst. *See* Antiquities Service

Painting: colors, 230; Japanese influence on, 230–31; Javanese, 187–90, *188*, 215–33; memories and, 189; modern, 215–16; noise and, 240; panoramas, 204; perspective and, 213–15, 223; *sungging*, 229. *See also* Pictures; *specific artists*
Palaces, 26–27
Papuans. *See* Kaja-Kaja
Parindra (Partai Indonesia Raja), 179, 190
Partai Nasional Indonesia (PNI), 178
Party of Great Indonesia. *See* Parindra (Partai Indonesia Raja)
Passersby, 2–3, 15, 35, 59, 79–80
Past: memory and, 8–9; modernity and, 41. *See also* Memories/memory
Patjar Merah Indonesia and Tan Malaka (Oshikawa), 5
Payen, Antoine, 189
Peddling, 73–74, 80–82, 84, 123
People's Thought. *See Pikiran Rakjat* (newspaper)
Pergerakan Banteng, 181–82
Philips Broadcasting, 111
Philips Radio, 48, 67, 111
Philosophy, Javanese, 153
Photographs, 192–95. *See also* Pictures
Pictures: for oneself, 213; as proposition, 201–5; school as, 205; text as, 197; as theater, 200; walls as, 205; as windows, 202–5. *See also* Painting; Photographs
Pikiran Rakjat (newspaper), 197
PNI. *See* Partai Nasional Indonesia (PNI)
Politics and school, 178–79
Politon, Arnold Elias, 193
Polygamy, 181

Poverty: begging and, 15–16; as commonplace, 7
Prasad, Ugoran, 249
Prinsen, Poncke, papers, 246
Proclamation of Indonesian Independence, 5, 16–17, 23, 66
Proklamasi Kemerdekaan Indonesia. *See* Proclamation of Indonesian Independence
Promenades, 186, 224
Proust, Marcel, 25, 204–5, 246
Publicity and perspective, 196
Public Voice, The. *See Soeara Oemoem* (newspaper)
Puppets, 42, 85–87, 115, 120, 167–68, 174, 214, 229

Racial integration, 99–102, 106, 117, 145, 149, 236–37
Radio, 49–50, 64, 67–68, 110–11, 114, 247
Regents, 115
Reksosamoedro, Pranoto, 7
Rembrandt, 215
Remembrance: social, 283 n. 19; space and, 3. *See also* Memories/memory
Revolution, 186, 200. *See also* Indonesian National Revolution (1945–49)
Riboet, Miss. *See* Happy Hubbub, Miss
Ridder in de Orde van Oranje Nassau. *See* Knight of the Oranje-Nassau Order
Rijn, Cornelia van, 215
Rilke, Christopher, 1, 6
Rilke, Rainer Maria, 1, 276 n. 105
Rimbaud, Arthur, 201
Riots. *See under* Jakarta
Roads and streets: childhood and, 90–93; as dangerous, 127; instrumentality and, 134; of Jakarta, 1–3, 9–11; nostalgia and, 93, 96–97; to school, 125–38; travel and, 93–98

RON. *See* Knight of the Oranje-Nassau Order
Ronell, Avital, 141
Royal Batavian Society for Arts and Science. *See* Koninklijk Bataviaasch Genootschap Voor Kunsten en Wetenschappen
Royal Netherlands Indies Army (KNIL), 90
Rudolf Boscha Observatory, 201

Sadar Istri, 181–82
Salons, 45–57; as core of house, 58, 59–60; defined, 46–47, 51; during Japanese occupation, 63–64; locations of, 50–51; music and, 48–53; objects of, 67; plasticity of, 48; as toyshop, 45–46
Santa Claus, 45
Santoso, Rahman, 82
Sarékat Islam, 177
Sayers, Charles, 204
Scarlet Pimpernel (Orczy), 5
Schinkel, Karl Friedrich, 25
Schools: books and textbooks, 161, 162–64; buildings, 138–39; clothing and, 149–52; clubs, 170–72; coeducational, 146; dances, 126, 146–49; discipline, 166–68; distance and, 125–27, 136–37; freedom and, 144, 170, 177; humiliation and, 152–54; Kartini, 82, 151, 173–75; kindergarten, 154–55; modernity and, 155–57; music in, 165–66; as picture, 205; punishment, 153–54, 167; religious, 135, 144; road to, 125–38, 154; as safe, 138; space of, 139–42, 205; sports, 140–43; testing, 169
Schwitters, Kurt, 218
Semanggi interchange, 11
Semar (god), 189
Separation: linkages and, 123; as normal, 105; windows and, 203

Servants: house and, 35–38; intimacy and, 35, 38; Japanese occupation and, 64–65; living quarters, 26, 27, 36; memory and, 35–36; status of, 37
Service cars, 93–94
Shadow-puppet theater. *See Wajang/wayang*
Shaw, G. B., 195
Shelters, 61
Shops in houses, 79–81
Siem, Tjan Tjoe, 135
Silahan, F., 17, 22
Simbolon, Maludin, 243
Simmel, Georg, 122, 124
Situmorang, Sitor, 242, 243
Sjahrir, Soetan, 20, 23, 180, 183, 239
Sociophonetics, 236, 238
Soeara Oemoem (newspaper), 190
Soetomo, Dr., 179, 190, 198
Soewandi, 111
Solo Radio Vereniging (SRV), 114
Sonora radio station, 10
Sound: gates and fences and, 75–76; memories and, 73; neighborhoods and, 85; space-producing, 111; of telephone, 109–10. *See also* Noise
Spies, Walter, 112, 117
Sports, school, 140–43
SRV. *See* Solo Radio Vereniging (SRV)
Stoffels, Hendrikje, 215
Stone Age, The: Garage Theater. *See Waktu Batu: Teater garasi*
Stopovers, 135
Street hawkers. *See* Peddling
Stutterheim, Willem Frederik, 21, 47
Suhadi, Captain, 23
Suharto, 171, 214; communists and, 77; as Harto family, 116; prisons of, 4; student protests and, 11
Sukamiskin prison, 227
Sukarno, 1, 14; as architect, 9, 13; art collection, 192; Bandung Technical

Index

309

Sukarno (*continued*)
    Institute and, 173, 201, 229; coffin of, 22; currency design and, 220–21; daughter of, 70; as engineer, 2; headwear and, 150; house of, 16, 17; Indonesian National Party and, 178; main pillars of, 291 n. 24; newspaper of, 197; overthrow of, 239; second wife, 84; on sublime places, 16; third wife, 178; trial of, 170–71; voice of, 243–44; widow of, 18
Sukarno, Fatmawati, 190
Sukarno, Hartini, 18, 19
Sultan of Yogyakarta, 28, 153
Supratman, Rudolf, 212–13
Sutyoso, 61
Suythof, Cornelis, 215

Tafsir, 250
Tagore, Rabindranath, 48
Taman Siswa, 175–77
Tarkovsky, Andrey, 231, 248
Taubert, Wilhelm, 73
Technical Institute. *See* Technische Hoogeschool (Bandung)
Technische Hoogeschool (Bandung), 173, 201, 228–29
Telephone, 50, 109–10
Television, 247
Textbooks. *See* Books and textbooks
Tirtoprodjo, Soesanto, 6
Tito, Josip Broz, 18
Tjipto, Dr., 191
Togetherness: neighborhood, 115–16; road to school and, 131–32
Toys, 43–45
Trains, 96, 98, 137

Travel, 208–9
Tugendhat House, 202–3
Twee aan twee. *See* Dancing

Union of Eastern Listeners, 12
Union of Indonesian Journalists, 4
United Nations, 171

Vendutjes. *See* Auctions
Violence: anticolonial, 65; Enlightenment and, 277 n. 112; and movement, 93; touching and, 121
Virilio, Paul, 93, 186, 190, 269–70 n. 107
Voice, 236, 240–44, 245, 249, 251
Volkenbond, 213

Wagner, Richard, 48
Wajang/Wayang, 42, 85–87, 120, 174
Waktu Batu: Teater garasi, 249, 251, 252
Walls: exterior construction, 33; of light, 203; materials of, 31; as pictures, 205
Walraven, Willem, 117, 118
Wertheim, Wim, 269 n. 106
Wild Buffalo Movement. *See* Pergerakan Banteng
Wilhelmina, Queen, 117
Windows: colonial, 204; pictures as, 202–5; as proposition, 202–4; separation and, 203
Winter, Jay, 195
Wittgenstein, Ludwig, 31, 201
World Trade Center, 26
Writing, 244, 245–46

Young Indonesia. *See* Indonesia Moeda
Youth of 1945 Museum, 20

RUDOLF MRÁZEK is Professor of History at the
University of Michigan. He is the author of *Engineers
of Happy Land: Technology and Nationalism in a
Colony* (2002); *Semesta Tan Malaka* (1994); *Sjahrir:
Politics and Exile in Indonesia, 1906–1966* (1994);
Bali: The Split Gate to Heaven (1983); and *United
States and the Indonesian Military, 1945–1965* (1978).

✦ ✦ ✦

Library of Congress Cataloging-in-Publication Data
Mrázek, Rudolf.
A certain age : colonial Jakarta through the
memories of its intellectuals / Rudolf Mrázek.
p. cm.
Includes bibliographical references and index.
ISBN 978-0-8223-4685-2 (cloth : alk. paper)
ISBN 978-0-8223-4697-5 (pbk. : alk. paper)
1. Intellectuals — Indonesia — Jakarta — Interviews.
2. Jakarta (Indonesia) — History — 20th century.
I. Title.
DS646.29.D5M73 2010
959.8'22022 — dc22   2009041449

www.ingramcontent.com/pod-product-compliance
Lightning Source LLC
Chambersburg PA
CBHW070341240426
43665CB00046B/2323